# African Archaeology

Research in Africa is now accepted as an integral part of global archaeological studies. As well as providing archaeologists with their oldest material, Africa is also widely recognised as the birthplace of modern humans and their characteristic cultural patterns. Archaeological study of later periods provides unique and valuable evidence for the development of African culture and society, while ongoing research in Africa provides insights relevant to the interpretation of the archaeological record in other parts of the world. In this fully revised and expanded edition of his seminal archaeological survey, David Phillipson presents a lucid and fully illustrated account of African archaeology from prehistory and the origins of humanity to the age of European colonisation. The work spans the entire continent from the Mediterranean to the Cape of Good Hope and demonstrates the relevance of archaeological research to the understanding of Africa today.

DAVID W. PHILLIPSON FBA is Professor of African Archaeology and Director of the Museum of Archaeology & Anthropology at the University of Cambridge. He is a Fellow of Gonville & Caius College, Cambridge.

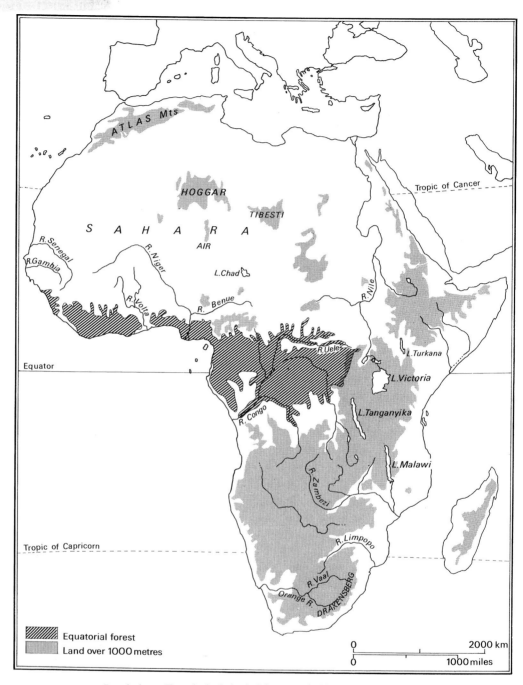

Frontispiece   The principal physical features of Africa

# African Archaeology

## Third edition

DAVID W. PHILLIPSON

*University of Cambridge*

CAMBRIDGE
UNIVERSITY PRESS

CAMBRIDGE UNIVERSITY PRESS
Cambridge, New York, Melbourne, Madrid, Cape Town, Singapore, São Paulo

Cambridge University Press
The Edinburgh Building, Cambridge CB2 2RU, UK

Published in the United States of America by Cambridge University Press, New York

www.cambridge.org
Information on this title: www.cambridge.org/9780521832366

First published 1985
Second edition 1993
Reprinted 1993, 1994, 1995, 1998, 1999, 2002
Third edition 2005

Printed in the United Kingdom at the University Press, Cambridge

*A catalogue record for this book is available from the British Library*

ISBN-13 978-0-521-83236-6 hardback
ISBN-10 0-521-83236-5 hardback
ISBN-13 978-0-521-54002-5 paperback
ISBN-10 0-521-54002-X paperback
ISBN-13 978-0-521-67310-5 African Edition
ISBN-10 0-521-67310-0 African Edition

on a seasonal basis, perhaps in separate areas and environments: contrasting archaeological assemblages may thus represent different activities of a single community or of sub-groups within that community. On the other hand, it has also been shown that certain items or styles of material culture may fulfil a symbolic function through their association with a particular society or section of a society, as is the case, for example, with some iron-smelting furnaces (Childs 1991). Although material culture distinctions do not necessarily coincide with socio-political ones, it is equally incorrect to assume that such correlations may not, in certain circumstances, exist.

For reasons such as these, African prehistory is here presented with emphasis on economic development and general life-style (including, where practicable, socio-political systems and ideology), correspondingly less attention being paid to the definition, succession and inter-relationship of named cultures and industries. However, in the present state of African archaeological studies, the old framework needs to be partially retained. In many parts of the continent, as will be made apparent in the following chapters, concerted programmes of archaeological research have never been undertaken. There are several regions, even whole countries, where chance discoveries or isolated excavations, often poorly documented, provide the only data on which a synthesis may be based. Here, the archaeologist may only be able to propose an outline succession of industrial stages, such being an essential pre-requisite for the detailed study of ancient life-styles and resource-exploitation patterns.

An ever-increasing contribution to our understanding of the past is now being made by genetic studies, not only of past and present human populations, but also of the plants and animals on which people's livelihood has depended. The potential of such studies, and the methodologies involved, are described by M. K. Jones (2001).

In writing a concise overview of African archaeology such as that contained in this book, it has been necessary to select and, on occasion, to simplify. While some geographic areas have yielded a wide range of archaeological data, in others very little is yet available. Thus it is that in certain sections of the book almost every site that has been investigated receives mention, while elsewhere a more general picture emerges from a series of comparable investigations. As a result, major changes of emphasis and interpretation may be expected to occur as research and discovery progress. Topics which have been the subject of recent in-depth research receive comparatively detailed treatment.

In the building up of an overview of African prehistory, particular attention must be paid to erecting a sound chronological framework. Several methods are available; for details of the methodologies the reader is referred to the comprehensive survey presented by Klein (1999). Age estimates based on radiocarbon analyses are particularly problematic, since it is only for the more recent periods that the relationship between radiocarbon and true ages is known. In this book ages are cited in the following manners in order to minimise confusion and to aid comparison between dates derived from different sources and methods.

(a) In chapters 2–5 ages are given in the form 'about . . . years ago'. These ages apply to periods beyond the last 7000 years and should all be regarded as approximations. They are derived from a variety of sources, mostly – for the last 50,000 years or so – radiocarbon, and no attempt has been made to calibrate or correct them unless otherwise stated.

(b) In chapters 6–8 dates since about 5000 BC are given in years BC or AD, these conventional designations being retained as those most widely and most readily understood. Here, radiocarbon dates have been calibrated and are expressed in calendar years according to the calculations presented by Stuiver and Kra (1986; Stuiver et al. 1998). At certain periods this calibration permits only approximate ages to be proposed because of variation in the radiocarbon content of the atmosphere. Precise dates such as 146 BC are derived from historical sources. All ages noted in these three chapters are thus intended to be comparable with one another, but they are not necessarily compatible with those cited in chapters 2–5.

Since more plentiful data relating to absolute chronology are now available than could be employed by the writers of previous syntheses, and in view of the evidence for disparate rates of development in different parts of the continent, this book does not employ the conventional terminology based upon broad chrono-technological subdivisions such as 'Late Stone Age', 'Neolithic' or 'Iron Age'. It has long been recognised that such terms cannot be precisely defined, but their informal use has continued, often at the expense of clarity; they are avoided in this book.

## Linguistics

Language provides an important means of classification for African populations. It has a major bearing on an individual's sense of identity and membership of a group. It also has historical validity, since people usually learn their first language from the other members of that group to which they belong by birth and/or upbringing.

There is good but by no means unanimous agreement among linguists concerning the major language families of Africa (Greenberg 1963; Heine and Nurse 2000; Fig. 1), whose present distribution is shown in outline form in Fig. 2. In the northern and northeastern regions of the continent, the languages which are spoken today belong to the super-family generally known as Afroasiatic. This includes the Berber languages of North Africa

| Family | Main divisions | Examples |
| --- | --- | --- |
| Afroasiatic | Semitic | Arabic, Amharic, Gurage, Tigrinya |
| | Berber | Berber, Tuareg |
| | Cushitic | Somali, Oromo, Afar, Sidamo, Beja |
| | Chadic | Fali, Hausa |
| Nilo-Saharan | Sudanic | Acholi, Shilluk, Mangbetu, Jie |
| | Saharan | Kanuri, Teda, Zaghawa |
| | Songhai | Songhai |
| Niger–Congo | West Atlantic | Dyola, Fulani, Temne |
| | Mande | Mwa, Mende |
| | Voltaic | Dogon, Mossi, Talensi |
| | Kwa | Akan, Bini, Ibo, Igala, Yoruba |
| | Bantu | Gikuyu, Bemba, Shona, Xhosa, Kongo |
| | Adamawa-Eastern | Mbaka, Zande |
| KhoiSan | South African KhoiSan | !Kung, ‡Khomani, Nama |
| | ?Sandawe | Sandawe |
| | ?Hadza | Hadza |

**Fig. 1:** The classification of recent African languages (after Greenberg 1963)

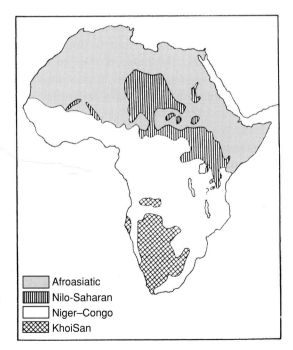

**Fig. 2:** The distribution of Africa's major language families in recent times (simplified from Greenberg 1963)

Afroasiatic
Nilo-Saharan
Niger–Congo
KhoiSan

and the Cushitic tongues centred on Ethiopia and Somalia, as well as the widespread Semitic family, the modern members of which include Arabic, Amharic and Hebrew.

To the south is a very irregularly shaped area covering much of the central and southern Sahara, the southern Sudan and parts of the adjacent savanna with an extension into parts of East Africa, where most of the modern languages are classed as Nilo-Saharan, with Nilotic and Sudanic as the principal subdivisions. Songhai, spoken around the Niger bend, may also have Nilo-Saharan affinity. It may be that the present fragmented distribution of the Nilo-Saharan languages indicates that they were formerly spoken over a more extensive area.

Most of the modern languages of West Africa belong to the Niger-Congo family, which may be extended to include Kordofanian, spoken in the western Sudan. Within West Africa these languages have developed considerable diversity. On the other hand, the distribution of one sub-group of Niger-Congo extends over the greater part of central and southern Africa, excluding the extreme southwest. These are the Bantu languages which, despite the enormous area of their distribution, show a relatively strong degree of similarity with one another. The northern limit of the Bantu languages approximates to the northern edge of the equatorial forest. In the savanna woodland to the north, the Adamawa and Ubangian languages also belong to the Niger-Congo family. Niger-Congo is sometimes linked with Nilo-Saharan to form a Niger-Saharan macrophylum (Blench 1999).

As will be shown in chapter 7, there is good evidence that the Bantu-speaking peoples have expanded from a northwestern area into sub-equatorial latitudes during the course of the last few thousand years. In significant parts of this region, these new populations replaced or absorbed people who spoke languages of the KhoiSan family, such as still survive in the southwesternmost parts of the continent. These are the languages of the Khoi (formerly sometimes called by the derogatory term Hottentots) and San (or Bushmen), who have retained into recent times their traditional herding or hunting life-styles beyond the country of the Bantu-speakers. There are indications that in earlier times KhoiSan-related languages may have been spoken as far to the north as the modern Kenya/Tanzania border area, but in regions further to the west their northerly extent is less certain.

In the absence of writing it is on modern languages that historical linguists must, of necessity, base their conclusions (Nurse 1997; D. W. Phillipson 2003a). Through studying the distribution of recent linguistic forms it is often possible to reconstruct certain features of the past languages from which the modern ones are derived, and to suggest the areas in which these ancestral languages may have been spoken. The vocabulary that is attested for these ancestral languages can tell us something about the life-styles of the people who spoke them, and about the things with which they were familiar. As different peoples came into contact with one another words were borrowed from one language into neighbouring ones; these 'loanwords' too can often be traced. It is through studies such as these that the linguistic prehistory of Africa may tentatively be reconstructed.

We have of course no precise information about the varying speeds at which particular linguistic changes proceeded. It is only in the case of languages which have a long written history that such speeds can be calculated at all precisely. Linguistics alone can provide only a relative ordering of processes and events, together with a rough estimate of the lengths of time that may have been involved. Use of glottochronological formulae to calculate the dates at which linguistic developments took place should be regarded with great suspicion, particularly when applied in non-literate contexts, since these formulae assume that language change occurs at a uniform rate. However, when links can be demonstrated between independent sequences, based respectively on archaeology and on linguistics, the chronology of the latter is placed on firmer ground. Historical reconstructions based on linguistic studies may be of particular value in supplementing the testimony of archaeology in areas where little excavation can be undertaken, and for those aspects of inter-group relationships illustrated by linguistic studies but which are difficult to demonstrate on the basis of archaeological evidence. Such linguistic reconstructions mostly relate to the past 5000 or 6000 years, although tentative attempts have been made to apply these methods to still earlier periods.

## Oral traditions

In order properly to interpret the oral historical traditions which are preserved in many African societies, we must understand the rôle that they play in those societies and the reasons for their recollection (Henige 1974; Vansina 1985). It is generally found that oral traditions are most carefully preserved and re-told among peoples who have a strong centralised political system. In such cases the function of the historical traditions is often to support the established authority, for example by explaining the origin of the ruling clan or family and the manner by which its members claim their right to rule. Several societies recognise this aspect of oral tradition and have official historians, whose task it is to preserve and transmit orthodox versions of their state histories.

Traditions which purport to relate to events of more than four or five centuries ago must generally be interpreted with particular caution. Absolute chronology (in the western sense) is not often a major interest of the

custodians of oral tradition; events may sometimes have taken place at significantly earlier periods than a literal interpretation of the traditions would
suggest (e.g. J. C. Miller 1972). As with written histories, oral historical traditions tend to concentrate their attention on political events and on the
activities of important individuals. They are not, therefore, a substitute for
archaeology as a source of historical information, and a comprehensive picture of the African past can only be built up through the use of all available
data.

## Ethnoarchaeology

Increased attention has been given in recent years to the application of
archaeological perspectives to the study of recent societies and their material culture (David and Kramer 2001). To some practitioners, the principal
aim of ethnoarchaeology is to gain insights to aid the interpretation of
archaeological data relating to earlier periods. This is an exercise which must
be approached with great caution. It cannot be emphasised too strongly that
observations of recent societies are of value only in suggesting *possible* interpretations of archaeological data; they can never themselves provide conclusive proof. Secondly, use of ethnoarchaeologically based interpretations may
carry the hidden implication that the recent peoples studied are in some
way backward or primitive. Those who practise or make use of ethnoarchaeology must beware of thus unintentionally insulting those who have
provided their inspiration. This is not to belittle the value of such studies,
provided that the models which they help to generate are applied with care
and sensitivity. Two examples may be cited: particularly valuable insights
have been obtained into the uses and significance of stone tools (e.g. Brandt
1996) and into non-western views of the past and of time (e.g. Schmidt 1995;
Stahl 2001).

## Africa in world prehistory

The archaeological picture of the African past now discernible is one of
paramount importance for the study of human prehistory. As will be shown
below, evidence for the life-style and physical characteristics of the earliest
hominids comes at present only from African sites. While it cannot be conclusively demonstrated that human beings first evolved in Africa, there is a
very strong probability that this was indeed the case. Virtually every major
subsequent stage in humankind's development may be illustrated from the
African record.

   The succession of African hunter-gatherer societies is the longest and one
of the most varied known. It extends from the origins of humanity to the

present day and, potentially, provides an evolutionary link between the studies of the social anthropologist and those of the specialist in the behaviour of non-human primates. This does not, of course, imply that modern hunter-gatherers are 'primitive' survivors from earlier times, somehow less developed than their farming neighbours. Hunter-gatherers have adapted to environments of great diversity, ranging from deserts and high-altitude glacial margins on the one hand to rain-forests and coastal swamps on the other. Major environmental changes have, of course, taken place during the period of some 2 to 3 million years with which we are here concerned, but these have not generally been so drastic as those in more northerly latitudes and, although their distribution has undergone great shifts, the range of situations exploited by prehistoric hunter-gatherers has been preserved in Africa to an extent not paralleled in other continents that were settled in Middle Pleistocene or earlier times. This continuity, both in environment and in the hunter-gatherer life-style itself, offers in Africa an unrivalled series of opportunities for interpreting major trends and processes in human development.

It has been noted by J. G. D. Clark (1969) that developments in stone-tool technology followed broadly similar stages over much of the world (Fig. 3 on p. 12). Backed-blade industries of the type represented in the European and West Asian 'Upper Palaeolithic' were thought prerequisite for the development of food-production and, ultimately, of literate civilisation. This premise, at least so far as Africa is concerned, has been seriously questioned (Shaw 1971), and the point made that, although blade industries of this type are uncommon in Africa south of the Sahara, microlithic industries such as were made by the earliest European and Levantine food-producers were produced in Africa at a remarkably early date. More recent research, summarised below, has confirmed this observation, and microlithic technology is now attested in sub-equatorial Africa at dates far earlier than in any other part of the world; not only is it significantly older than the European or Asian blade industries, but it is apparently associated with the oldest fossils so far known which may confidently be attributed to fully modern people, *Homo sapiens* or *H. s. sapiens*. These discoveries become even more important as a result of recent genetic research which suggests that all modern human populations may be descended from an African ancestor (Stringer and McKie 1996). Far from being a backwater, as has sometimes been suggested, Upper-Pleistocene Africa may have been a world leader both in the evolution of our species and in its development of technology.

Current research has also involved a major re-evaluation of the evidence for early African settled life, herding and cultivation. At least south of the Sahara, these developments are now seen to have taken place very gradually and essentially independently of comparable processes in other parts of the

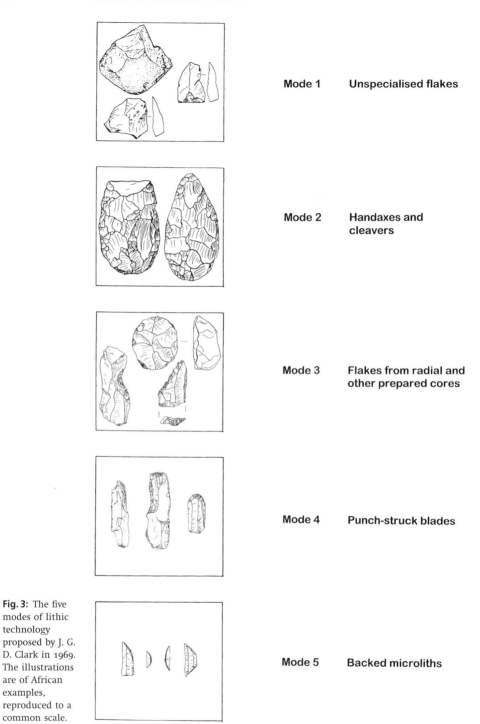

Mode 1          Unspecialised flakes

Mode 2          Handaxes and
                cleavers

Mode 3          Flakes from radial and
                other prepared cores

Mode 4          Punch-struck blades

Mode 5          Backed microliths

**Fig. 3:** The five modes of lithic technology proposed by J. G. D. Clark in 1969. The illustrations are of African examples, reproduced to a common scale.

world. Settled life appears to have come about in what is now the southern Sahara and sahel in the context of the rich and well-watered environments which prevailed there some 10,000 years ago. This same general area is now recognised as the homeland of many plant species which were subsequently brought under cultivation and dispersed to become important food crops there and in other parts of sub-Saharan Africa. Additional important crops were developed in Ethiopia, and others on the fringe of the equatorial forest. Cattle were probably locally domesticated in the eastern Sahara. Although the domestic animals herded south of the Sahara appear all to have been introduced from elsewhere, it is now clear that Africa was a major area for the initial cultivation of vegetable foods as diverse as yams, enset, rice and other cereals.

With the possible exception of the Egyptian Nile Valley, no part of Africa saw the rise of a wholly indigenous literate civilisation, for strong external influences made significant contributions to such developments along the Mediterranean littoral, in the Sudanese Nile Valley, in the Ethiopian highlands and on the East African coast. What were the main factors contributing to the rise of literate civilisation in Egypt and elsewhere which were absent in other parts of Africa? The Egyptian Nile Valley was given great fertility by the annual inundations of the Nile. Its surrounding desert constrained the physical expansion of the dense population which the fertile valley could support. Comparable situations prevailed in other centres of early civilisation: the Indus Valley, Mesopotamia, the Hwang Ho Valley and Mexico (Trigger 2003). The social stress engendered by a dense population required for its control the development of elaborate socio-political systems, an established and sanctioned order of a complexity which would have been out of keeping with the smaller, less constrained societies of most other parts of the continent. It may be argued, at least in part, that it was the richness of the African environment and its lack of physical barriers which permitted many African societies to develop their own forms and orders without the constraints imposed by literate civilisation.

Research in Africa can provide archaeologists of other regions with important insights which aid their interpretations (D. W. Phillipson 2003b). Particularly important examples relate to socio-political evolution and people's views of history (S. K. McIntosh 1999a; Stahl 2001).

It is far more relevant to consider what Africa did achieve, than what it did not (cf. Shaw 1971). It is also pertinent to view the development of African societies, as revealed by archaeology and other disciplines, from an essentially internal viewpoint before comparison is made with their counterparts in other parts of the world. Thus we are able to evaluate African achievements in terms of their African context and to appreciate the range of economic practices, technologies, socio-political systems and beliefs which was developed in the context of varied population densities, physical bound-aries, communications and available resources. Then we can see the com-prehensive manner in which varied environments were exploited. We can begin to understand why some aspects of indigenous technology reached the high level of expertise evidenced, for example, in West African casting of copper alloys, while other aspects – such as methods of transport – saw little change over prolonged periods. We can appreciate oral tradition as a counterpart of written literature, and wonder at the possible antiquity of art-forms in wood and other perishable materials which are at present only known from the most recent periods. African archaeology provides a unique view of cultural development leading to recent societies that are now appre-ciated, not as failures that have fallen by the wayside in the rise of industrial civilisation, but as examples of different – perhaps (as in several other parts of the world) more viable in the long term – expressions of human cultures fully adapted to their practitioners' circumstances.

# The emergence of humankind in Africa

## Definition and process

Before attempting an account of the African evidence for human origins, it is fitting to make some general observations about the nature of that evidence and of the research on which it is based; it is necessary also to offer some definitions of the terms that are employed both here and in the writings of others. The first point that needs to be emphasised is that the evidence, although still very incomplete, is accumulating rapidly. New discoveries or analyses can frequently necessitate radical revision of our interpretations. However, there is often a long lapse of time between the initial announcement of a discovery (whether it be made in the field or in the laboratory) and its definitive publication. There are often strong political and financial pressures on researchers to make prompt – even premature – announcements. Indeed, a disconcertingly high proportion of the evidence on which the present synthesis is based comes from such preliminary accounts. Furthermore, very rarely is a truly continuous record available for study: we have a number of brief and incomplete glimpses separated by long intervals for which no information is available. Any attempt to reconstruct a continuous sequence must take account of this limitation.

Much of the ongoing research here described is being undertaken by collaborative teams of specialists. This chapter attempts to synthesise four main interlocking strands of evidence which are often the work of distinct experts: geology and faunal studies can yield information about habitat and chronology, examination of the hominid fossils has the potential to illustrate human physical evolution, genetic studies of both fossil and modern populations are beginning to make major contributions to knowledge of their inter-relationships, while associated artefacts and their associations elucidate some aspects of cultural development.

Clearly, location of field research is determined both by the anticipated availability of evidence and by whether practical and political conditions are conducive to large-scale investigations. For example, the Rift Valley in eastern Africa offers unparalleled conditions for the preservation and subsequent discovery of materials relevant to this research, together with volcanic associations which can be dated fairly precisely; yet even here fieldwork was impracticable in Ethiopia during the 1980s because of that country's political and economic conditions. Relatively little field research relating to early hominid evolution has been undertaken in more westerly parts of Africa because the relevant remains are there more rarely preserved and less readily discovered. It follows that apparently limited geographical distributions must be interpreted carefully, and that ancient phenomena may have been far more widespread than their present physical attestation might suggest. Evidence for environmental change must be sought and its impact on past developments assessed.

Next, it is necessary to offer some observations about the terminology that is employed to classify fossils, whether of human ancestors or other creatures. This classificatory system is still based on the *Systema Naturae* devised by Carolus Linnaeus in 1735, which attributes each animal or plant to a genus (e.g. *Homo*) and, within the genus, to a species (e.g. *sapiens*). Linnaeus (who wrote more than 120 years before the publication of Charles Darwin's *On the Origin of Species* in 1859) was concerned with the classification of contemporary living things and, so far as animals were concerned, his principal criterion for defining a species was that its members should be capable of interbreeding to produce fertile offspring. This, clearly, is something which can never be demonstrated for individuals known solely from their fossil remains. Linnaeus recognised that differences in outward appearance could be misleading: for example, some birds showing only minor differences are assigned to different species, while recent breeding has produced very diverse dogs which all belong to the same species. The amount of physical variation that can be accommodated within a single species thus varies greatly. In some instances, much of this variation may be accounted for by sexual dimorphism: males and females of certain birds, for example, are indistinguishable to ornithologists without close anatomical examination, whereas female gorillas are half the size of males from which they may also be differentiated on the basis of dentition, musculature and osteology. Adoption of the Linnaean system by those who study the fossil evidence for human (and non-human) evolution thus gives rise to great difficulties, both practical and philosophical. The defining characteristic of a Linnaean species cannot be established from a fossil. Many fossils cannot be attributed with certainty to a male or a female individual; we may thus be unable to determine the degree of sexual dimorphism in a fossil population. In fact, we can obtain little if any idea from the fossil record of the amount of physical variation that can be accommodated within a fossil species. Linnaeus had no concept of evolution, so it is hardly surprising that his classificatory system cannot logically be applied to a diachronic situation of species-change. If we do make such an attempt, we must accept either the former existence of individuals intermediate between recognised species or that at some stage in the evolutionary process a female of one species gave birth to offspring of another species or even genus. Both are such manifest absurdities that they call into question our whole system of classifying fossils. The problem has often been recognised (e.g. H. J. and J. Deacon 1999), but no adequate remedy has been proposed.

As explained, we have only very hazy ideas about the amount of physical variation that should be accommodated within a Linnaean species recognised in the fossil record. Some attempts have been made (e.g. Foley 1991) to consider the extent to which an ideal classification of this material should reflect perceived similarities rather than differences. It is, of course, recognised that geographical isolation can accelerate differentiation, and this has led to the questionable practice of defining species as much by the geography of their occurrence as by their morphology. Examples (considered further below) are the division of the robust australopithecine *Paranthropus* into East African and South African species respectively designated *boisei* and *robustus*, and the division of the species formerly recognised as *Homo erectus* between African *H. ergaster* and *H. erectus* in Asia (cf. Klein 1999).

It is not only in the case of fossils that conventional classificatory terminology actually hinders our understanding of diachronic processes. Compartmentalisation is a very useful preliminary stage in developing an understanding of many variable phenomena; later, however, it can mask the nature of variation. This will be a recurring theme in many chapters of this book (cf. Panchen 1992). Colonial administrators (and some others) have sought to group their subjects into tribes which have then been regarded as watertight compartments whose validity may even extend through time (M. Hall 1983). Classification of languages has encountered similar problems. This book is concerned with the past lives of people, especially but not exclusively as illustrated by their artefacts: when archaeological study of a particular period or region is beginning, classification of artefacts into named industries is a useful approach. Such industries need to be described in terms of the technology employed and the morphology of the end-products as well, ideally, as the uses to which individual items were put and thus, in conjunction with other evidence, the activities that they could support. Eventually, reference can also be made to the geographical area where they occur and to the span of time during which they were made and/or used. Degrees of similarity may then be assessed, leading to the proposal of a classification. Here we run into difficulties which are remarkably analogous to those encountered by biologists: how can processes of change be understood and accommodated within a classificatory system which implies the existence of rigidly defined boundaries? There may, of course, have been times when a sudden change did take place, or situations where the practitioners of one industry were separated by a sharply defined frontier from those of another. Far more often, however, the transition will have been more gradual, sometimes extending through hundreds of generations or over great distances. The past, notably but not exclusively the human past, has seen a multi-dimensional reticulation of variation and change which in some circumstances and at some times has been more marked and/or more rapid than otherwise. There seem to have been, and continue to be, situations of virtual stasis and others of pronounced change – cultural and/or biological. Conventional labelling of categories cannot adequately reflect this situation. It may be possible to recognise certain overarching trends which cut across the conventional terminology. I do not argue for abandonment of classification, but for the adoption of methodologies and terminologies which reflect processes of variation as these are now understood.

A modest step in this direction, which the present writer has long advocated, is the application to studies of stone-tool industries of the categorisation into five successive modes, as proposed by J. G. D. Clark in 1969. This taxis, summarised in Figure 3, avoids the tendency to correlate stages of technological development with finite periods of time; and it also helps to minimise the artificial compartmentalisation of what were frequently continuous processes of development (D. W. Phillipson 1977a: 23; Foley 2002). The modes appear to form a homotaxial sequence of world-wide applicability; they do not represent watertight compartments, it being recognised that elements of the technologies of earlier times often continued alongside more recent innovations. This last point has frequently been overlooked (e.g. J. D. Clark and Schick in de Heinzelin et al. 2000: 51–181; J. D. Clark 2001b), which may account for prehistorians' limited adoption of J. G. D. Clark's categorisation. Although its value is restricted to discussion of very broad trends, it provides a useful means of technological comparison while avoiding potentially misleading terms such as 'Early Stone Age' which can too easily be assumed to correlate with finite periods of time.

The synthesis offered in this book takes account of these factors. It generally retains at least some aspects of conventional terminology, if only to facilitate use of other literature, but it seeks to note circumstances where, in the author's opinion, such terminology has a tendency to distort or to hinder understanding. In particular, since more plentiful data relating to absolute chronology are now available than could be employed by the writers of previous syntheses, and in view of the evidence for disparate rates of development in different areas, this book does not employ the conventional terminology based upon broad chrono-technological subdivisions such as 'Late Stone Age', 'Neolithic' or 'Iron Age'. It has long been recognised that such terms cannot be precisely defined, but their informal use has continued, often at the expense of clarity; they are avoided here.

A further source of misunderstanding is the conventional application to types of stone artefact of names such as 'scraper' or 'arrowhead' which carry an implication as to function, when there is in fact little if any definite information as to how the tools were actually used. In this book, the attempt has been made to restrict use of such functional terms to cases where there is good evidence as to the use to which artefacts were originally put, although it is recognised that some element of subjectivity necessarily remains.

Next, it is necessary to define some parameters. This is particularly important in the present chapter which attempts to discuss the initial processes of both physical and cultural evolution by which humans came to be differentiated from other animals. It has long been conventional to apply the informal terms 'hominoid' to humans and the closely related great or anthropoid apes, and 'hominid' to humans and their ancestors after the separation from the apes. We shall turn below to the problem of defining the term 'human'; first it is necessary to record that recent genetic studies demonstrate a remarkably close affinity between apes and humans (Goodman *et al.* 1990; Gagneux *et al.* 1999), to the extent that it has been suggested that a distinction at this level cannot be substantiated and that apes should be regarded as hominids, the term 'hominin' being proposed in its place to exclude the apes. Certain recent writers (e.g. Mitchell 2002) have adopted this change but the present book does not follow them: the proposed terminology does not improve understanding and is not accompanied by more precise definition of the categories to which it relates.

The once-conventional wisdom that 'man is a tool-making animal' (Oakley 1952) has been called into question by studies of chimpanzees. For years the question was fudged by invoking contrasts between tool-using, tool-modifying and tool-making, but the old definition has finally been rendered untenable by the demonstration that a *Bonobo* chimpanzee can learn to make stone tools, admittedly under laboratory conditions (C. and H. Boesch 1990; Toth *et al.* 1993). It must also be stressed that the earliest tools are not easily recognisable in the archaeological record: only stone artefacts are generally preserved and, in most circumstances, readily recognised. Modern apes use, by preference, a range of more perishable but more easily worked materials, and there is no reason to believe that early hominids were different in this regard. (The distinction must be made between an artefact, which is simply any artificially produced thing, and a tool or implement which is an artefact made, modified or selected to facilitate the accomplishment of a task.) There is no reason to suppose that early tools were made from stone before or in preference to those of other materials. Thus it is likely that the first tools, by whatsoever creature they were made, will not have been preserved.

For reasons that will be set out later in this chapter, the view has been expressed that *Homo ergaster*, first recognised in the African fossil record around 1.75 million years ago, represents both physically and culturally a major advance from the preceding hominids, whether australopithecine or *Homo habilis*. In recognition of this, use of the terms 'person' and 'people' is here restricted to *H. ergaster* and later humans.

A recent development has been the adoption of the phrase 'anatomically modern people' in place of the Linnaean designation *Homo sapiens* or *H. s. sapiens*. While, in view of the problems outlined above, this abandonment of Linnaean classification might be welcomed, it must be questioned whether the new term has actually improved understanding. It has the welcome advantage of emphasising the virtual identity of all modern people (but see A. W. F. Edwards 2003), avoiding implications that some 'races' might be more or less 'primitive' than others. On the other hand, it has had two particular effects which give rise to concern. Because it has not been accompanied by a corresponding revision of terminology relating to earlier representatives of the genus *Homo*, it has imposed a conceptual barrier between modern people and their ancestors. Secondly, and arising from this barrier, it has strengthened the view that modern people may also be distinguished on cultural and behavioural grounds, leading (as will be argued in chapter 4) to unjustified emphasis on certain aspects of the archaeological record and to a tendency to underestimate the cultural achievements of earlier hominids. It has even given rise to the suggestion (Klein 2000a) that these behavioural developments may have been brought about by genetic mutation as little as 60,000 or 50,000 years ago – a Eurocentric argument which approaches circularity.

The term 'human' is retained in this book as a purely informal noun or adjective referring to any australopithecine or member of the genus *Homo*, whatever his or her tool-making capabilities may have been, in contexts where the more precise designation 'hominid' seems inappropriate. The growing tendency to apply the word 'human' exclusively to anatomically modern *Homo sapiens* is to be deplored.

## World-wide precursors of the hominids

The story of the emergence of humankind extends far back into geological time (Fig. 4). The modern species of Old World and New World monkeys, apes and hominids are all classed as members of the Anthropoidea sub-order of the order Primates (Fig. 5). Other members of this order, with which we are not here concerned, include such animals as tarsiers and tree-shrews. Fossil remains of early primates (Klein 1999) have been recovered at many sites in the Americas, Europe and Asia as well as in Africa, extending back in time as far as the end of the Cretaceous period about 70 million years ago. The modern Old World Anthropoidea are believed to be descended from small but ape-like primates, notably that named *Catopithecus*, whose remains are

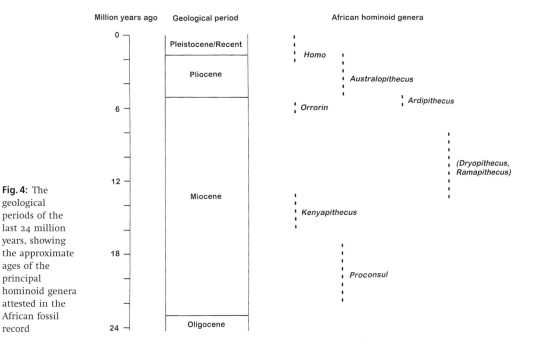

**Fig. 4:** The geological periods of the last 24 million years, showing the approximate ages of the principal hominoid genera attested in the African fossil record

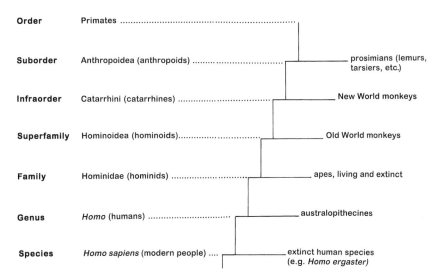

**Fig. 5:** The classification of the hominids within the order Primates

best known from deposits in the Fayum Depression of Egypt, dating from the late Eocene/early Oligocene period about 36 million years ago (Simons 1990; Simons and Rasmussen 1994).

By the beginning of the subsequent Miocene around 24 million years ago, it appears that primate evolution had proceeded sufficiently far to permit the differentiation of lines of descent that have led, on the one hand, to the modern Old World monkeys, and on the other to the great apes and modern people. The best-known fossil primate of this time is the forest-dwelling *Proconsul* from Rusinga Island in Lake Victoria (A. C. Walker *et al.* 1993). Subsequently, the hominoid line is represented around 15 million years ago in western Kenya by *Kenyapithecus*, which shows important developments in skull, teeth and wrist. It probably lived in the open woodland that became widespread in East Africa in mid-Miocene times, before the completion of the great earth movements which resulted in the formation of the Rift Valley (Pickford 1983, 1986).

In later Miocene times, between about 12 and 5 million years ago, further evolutionary development must have taken place which eventually led to the emergence of the family to which all human types, past and present, belong. With the colonisation of new environments, resulting in greater geographical spread and subsequent isolation, several distinct varieties of early hominoid developed. Fossil-bearing deposits of this time are relatively rare in Africa, and in those that have been investigated primate remains are extremely uncommon. At present the fossils of greatest relevance to the study of human origins are those from Europe and southern Asia attributed to the genera *Dryopithecus* and *Sivapithecus* respectively (Benefit and McCrossin 1995). The faces of these creatures were less snout-like than those of their ancestors, their jaws were more massive and their teeth were further adapted to use as grinders. Associated fossils of other species from the same sites indicate that these creatures favoured open savanna wood-land environments. This continued adaptation to a less restrictive habitat, doubtless linked (as the teeth indicate) with the adoption of a more omniv-orous diet, may have been a major step in the evolutionary processes which led to the emergence of humankind.

When the African fossil hominoid record resumes around 5 million years ago, it is almost exclusively in eastern and southern Africa that true hominids are represented; they occur with an abundance that contrasts markedly with the earlier periods. Despite the wide Old World distribution of the mid-Miocene hominoids, the evidence currently available suggests that it was probably in Africa that hominids first evolved.

## The earliest hominids

This section attempts an overview of the principal fossil evidence from Africa, individual sites and their archaeological materials being discussed subsequently. The picture now offered is radically different from that pro-posed in the second edition of this book (D. W. Phillipson 1993b), which serves to emphasise how rapidly knowledge is developing and how new

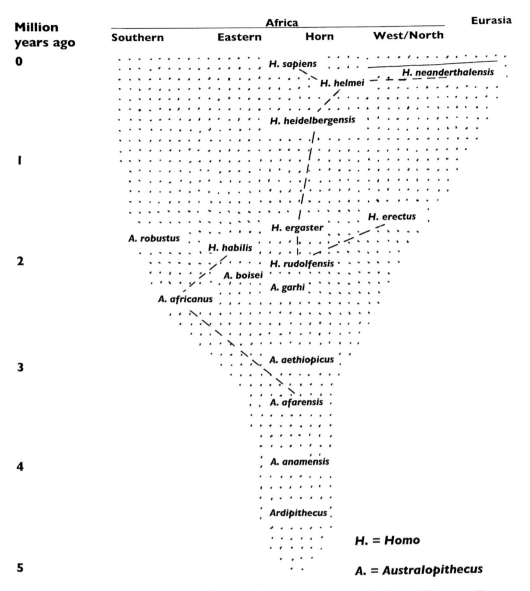

**Fig. 6:** A tentative 'family tree' of African hominids during the last 5 million years. The most widely accepted evolutionary relationships are indicated by hatched lines; discontinuities by continuous lines. (*Australopithecus robustus* and *A. boisei* are regarded as regional races in southern and eastern Africa respectively.)

discoveries may necessitate substantial revisions of current interpretations. Figure 6 attempts a summary representation of the system now proposed. It is important to realise that in both southern and eastern Africa the majority of the fossil discoveries have been made within recent years. Study of many is as yet at a preliminary stage, and there is often considerable controversy about their attribution to named species and, on occasion, their dating. Likewise, new finds are steadily being announced; these may require the modification or abandonment of existing theories. Any account of the current state of research must, therefore, be both tentative and provisional. A number of different systems are used to order the chronology of this time; these are summarised and explained in Figure 7.

It is clear from the results of recent research that it was during the period between about 8 million and 5 million years ago that the first individuals generally acknowledged as hominids must have developed. The very sparse fossil evidence is supported by genetic studies which independently suggest that the most recent common ancestor of humans and chimpanzees lived at this time (Miyamoto and Goodman 1990). So far, however, fieldwork in Africa has revealed only two relevant fossils which date from this crucial interval. These are the fragments attributed to *Orrorin tugenensis* from Lukeino in the Tugen Hills of Kenya (Senut *et al.* 2001; see also Kingston *et al.* 2002) and, less certainly, a skull from the Djourab Desert in Chad (Brunet *et al.* 2002), concerning which elaborate claims but little factual detail have been published. Estimates for the age of the Lukeino deposits range between 6.1 and 5.7 million years. Slightly more recent are fossils from the Middle Awash area of the Ethiopian Rift Valley which have been attributed to *Ardipithecus ramidus kadabba* and dated 5.8–5.2 million years ago (Yohannes Haile-Selassie *et al.* 2001). None of these recent discoveries, from Kenya, Chad and Ethiopia, has yet been published in detail or fully evaluated. Controversy (not to mention rivalry) continues, particularly with regard to the possible bipedalism of these creatures and their relationships to later hominids. Likewise, it has not yet been ascertained how these new discoveries relate to earlier reports of very fragmentary hominid fossils from late Miocene and early Pliocene sites west and south of Lake Turkana in northern Kenya, such as a piece of a jaw from Lothagam, dated to some 5.5 million years ago, and a skull fragment from a somewhat more recent context in the Chemeron Formation near Lake Baringo (Howell 1982).

It is noteworthy that the period just prior to 5.5 million years ago, which saw the acceleration of evolution resulting in the appearance of the first hominids, was one of global cooling and aridity (Williams *et al.* 1993). Further instances will be cited below when major evolutionary developments occurred under relatively arid conditions. It is only from the period beginning about 4.5 million years ago that a rather more comprehensive picture becomes available (Fig. 8). Virtually all the important fossils which illustrate this process have been recovered from sites in eastern Africa and, subsequently, from southern Africa also. It is now convenient to describe the different types of hominid that have been recognised in this crucial time-span, and the theories that have been put forward concerning their

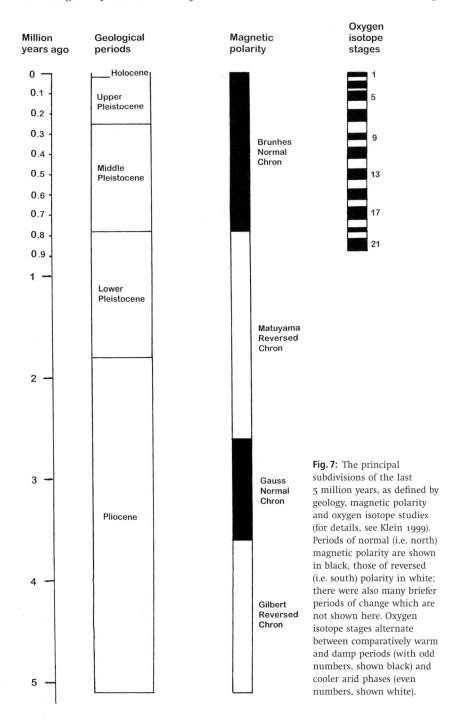

**Million years ago** | **Geological periods** | **Magnetic polarity** | **Oxygen isotope stages**

Geological periods: Holocene, Upper Pleistocene, Middle Pleistocene, Lower Pleistocene, Pliocene

Magnetic polarity: Brunhes Normal Chron, Matuyama Reversed Chron, Gauss Normal Chron, Gilbert Reversed Chron

Oxygen isotope stages: 1, 5, 9, 13, 17, 21

**Fig. 7:** The principal subdivisions of the last 5 million years, as defined by geology, magnetic polarity and oxygen isotope studies (for details, see Klein 1999). Periods of normal (i.e. north) magnetic polarity are shown in black, those of reversed (i.e. south) polarity in white; there were also many briefer periods of change which are not shown here. Oxygen isotope stages alternate between comparatively warm and damp periods (with odd numbers, shown black) and cooler arid phases (even numbers, shown white).

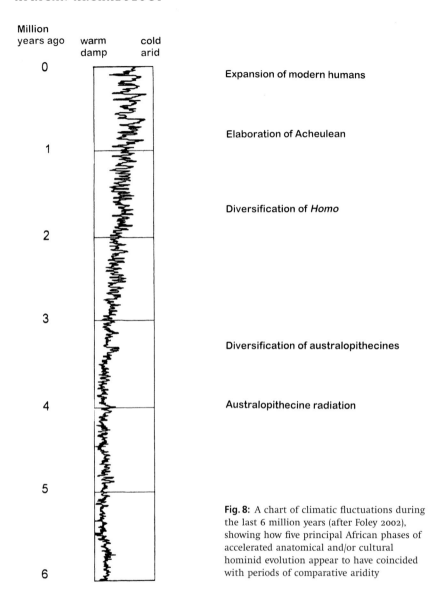

**Fig. 8:** A chart of climatic fluctuations during the last 6 million years (after Foley 2002), showing how five principal African phases of accelerated anatomical and/or cultural hominid evolution appear to have coincided with periods of comparative aridity

inter-relationships. Details of individual sites with their archaeological components and interpretations will follow in later sections.

A site beside the Aramis tributary of the Middle Awash River in Ethiopia has yielded a partial hominid skeleton plus fragments of several other individuals, all now attributed to *Ardipithecus ramidus* and dated to about 4.4 million years ago (White *et al.* 1994). Originally attributed to the genus *Australopithecus*, this creature had teeth rather like those of a chimpanzee, although it was probably largely bipedal; it evidently inhabited a moist woodland environment. Somewhat later, around 4.2–3.9 million years old, are remains of *Australopithecus anamensis* from two sites in the Lake Turkana basin of northern Kenya (M. G. Leakey *et al.* 1995). Both in dentition and in gait this creature shows development away from the features of *Ardipithecus* (than which it seems to have been significantly larger) towards those of later and better-known australopithecines.

A later species, *Australopithecus afarensis*, is much more comprehensively represented by fossils from at least five localities in Ethiopia, Kenya and Tanzania, all dating between 3.9 and 3.0 million years ago. Details of the principal occurrences are given below. Here, it is appropriate to note that *A. afarensis* was a relatively lightly built or gracile species showing several features, principally in the teeth and face, which distinguish it from later australopithecines (Johanson and White 1979; Day *et al.* 1980). Its bipedal gait is indicated both by its anatomical features and by two series of well-preserved hominid footprints at Laetoli in Tanzania (Fig. 12, below; M. D. Leakey and Harris 1987) which are demonstrably contemporary with fossils attributed to *A. afarensis*. Its forelimbs, however, suggest a continued ability to climb trees. Several features of the skull, both braincase and dentition, continue to display ape-like characteristics. Cranial capacity was in the order of 400 cubic centimetres (as compared with at least 1350 cubic centimetres for a modern person) and adult individuals were generally 1.3–1.5 metres tall. The more comprehensive fossil record means that *A. afarensis* is the earliest hominid for which the extent of sexual dimorphism may be estimated: it was significantly greater than in later hominids and closer to that seen among apes (Richmond and Jungers 1995). It has been suggested that this may indicate ongoing male competition for mates, rather than long-term pairing.

The general trend between 6 and 3 million years ago emphasised bipedal development, while retaining powerful arms which suggest frequent climbing of trees. Indeed, there are indications that all hominids known from this time inhabited well-wooded environments, effectively disproving the former belief that development of bipedalism accompanied a shift in preferred habitat from forest to savanna. Dentition only gradually evolved away from the small, thin-enamelled teeth still seen in chimpanzees towards the heavier forms characteristic of many later hominids. It is noteworthy that both these developments are attested before there is evidence for any significant increase in brain-size. In no deposits of this period has any trace of artefacts been found.

There is broad agreement that *Australopithecus afarensis* occupied an evolutionary position that was ancestral to all later hominids. By 3.0 million years ago australopithecines were present also in South Africa, as *A. africanus*, while their East African counterparts are generally designated *A. aethiopicus* or *Paranthropus aethiopicus* (see Klein 1999). Both these South and East African australopithecines, especially the latter, had more massive teeth than *A. afarensis*; some individuals (perhaps the males) had particularly powerful jaw muscles extending up the sides of the face to a 'sagittal crest' of bone running along the top of the skull from front to back. Even more robust forms subsequently appeared; opinion is again divided as to whether these are sufficiently distinct to merit placement in a separate genus, *Paranthropus*, rather than being subsumed within *Australopithecus*. Of these robust hominids, *Paranthropus (Australopithecus) boisei* appeared in East Africa around 2.5 million years ago, possibly related to or descended from *P. (A.) aethiopicus*, while *P. (A.) robustus* appeared in South Africa about 0.5 million years later, by which time the earliest representatives of the genus *Homo* are attested in both areas.

There can now be little reasonable doubt that, by about 2.5 million years ago if not before, several distinct types of hominid co-existed in broadly similar environments. The exact number of parallel hominid lineages and their relationship to each other are subjects of controversy. Until recently, the most widely accepted classification of these early hominids placed them in two distinct groups (Tobias 1980). This broad dichotomy is still accepted, although some authorities now feel that one of these categories, the australopithecines, may comprise more than one genus, being represented by the so-called gracile species *A. africanus* in South Africa and by a somewhat more robust counterpart further to the north. Although all types of australopithecine displayed the characteristics noted above, there are none the less significant differences (Klein 1999). The front teeth (incisors and canines) of *A. africanus* were appreciably larger than those of its robust counterparts; this contrasts to the generally more substantial build of the latter species. (It should be emphasised that the distinction between gracile and robust in an australopithecine context refers primarily to the dentition and associated musculature of the skull: in overall body size the two categories were very similar.)

While *A. africanus* was essentially omnivorous, *Paranthropus (Australopithecus) robustus* may have evolved a specialised predominantly vegetarian diet, to which large grinding molar teeth were well suited (Grine 1988; see also Lee-Thorp *et al.* 1994). To this feature may be linked also the massive musculature, especially that of the jaw, which in turn gave rise to the large ridges of bone to which the muscles were attached. This was probably the sole function of the sagittal crest noted above, a feature which both *P. (A.) robustus* and *P. (A.) boisei* shared with the modern male gorilla. There was also significant postcranial variation, as yet imperfectly understood, between skeletons of the different australopithecine species.

The Bouri area of the Middle Awash Basin has yielded remains of an australopithecine, designated *A. garhi* and dated around 2.5 million years ago, which, it has been suggested, shows features transitional to those of *Homo* (Asfaw *et al.* 1999; de Heinzelin *et al.* 1999). Subsequently, further fossils have been recovered and attributed to *H. erectus/ergaster* (Asfaw *et al.* 2002). This period, again one when arid conditions prevailed (de Menocal 1995), is of particular significance because of the archaeological evidence, to be discussed below, for the earliest use of tools.

The first representatives of the genus *Homo*, to a single species of which all types of modern humans belong, may now be dated as early as 2.5–2.4 million years ago, although most specimens older than 2.0 million years are very fragmentary. *Homo* may have evolved from an australopithecine such as *A. afarensis* (Tobias 1980; A. C. Walker and Leakey 1993; Klein 1999). The earliest specimens are of the type designated *Homo habilis*, known from several sites in eastern Africa and possibly from South Africa also. It was similar in overall body size to the australopithecines, but had a significantly larger brain averaging about 640 cubic centimetres, which is 45 per cent greater than the equivalent figure for *A. africanus* (Fig. 9). The teeth were smaller and more closely resemble those of modern people, as do the bones of the hand. The posture of *H. habilis* seems to have been completely upright and there is no evidence for such massive muscles, with bony ridges for their attachment, as were characteristic of the contemporary *Paranthropus (A.) boisei* and the earlier individuals now classed as *P. (A.) aethiopicus*. *H. habilis* none the less shows substantial variability and some authorities consider that its more massive representatives (such as the famous '1470' skull from Koobi Fora, Kenya) should be regarded as a distinct species, for which the name *H. rudolfensis* has been proposed (Lieberman *et al.* 1996). Virtually complete, the 1470 skull (Wood 1991) comes from a context which is securely dated to about 2.0 million years ago. The rounded skull-vault with a well-developed forehead housed a brain which, at about 800 cubic centimetres, was some 70 per cent larger than those of the contemporary *P. (A.) boisei*. The sagittal crest and massive muscle attachments of the latter species were not present in 1470.

By 1.75 million years ago, if not before, a second species of *Homo* may be recognised in East Africa. It was at one time given the designation *H. erectus* to emphasise its perceived similarity to certain East and Southeast Asian fossils, but some authorities now consider that the single designation is inappropriate and prefer to class the East African material as *H. ergaster* (Klein 1999: 287–95). As more fossils are discovered, it is becoming apparent that the *Homo* population at this time was extremely diverse (Wood 1985); its later development is described in more detail in chapter 3. One way in which these early hominid types may have been related to one another is

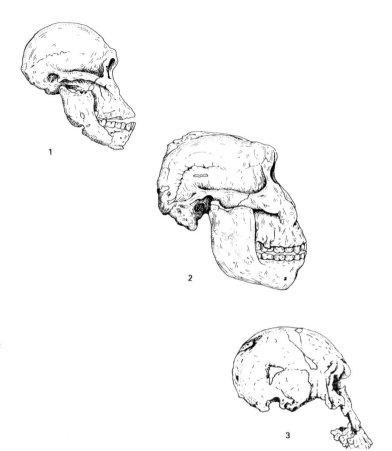

**Fig. 9:** Skulls of
1, *Australopithecus
africanus* from
Sterkfontein;
2, *A. boisei* from
Olduvai;
3, large-brained
*Homo*, cf. *H.
rudolfensis* (1470)
from Koobi Fora

shown above in Figure 6. It should be stressed that there is particular controversy concerning the relationship between *Australopithecus* and the earliest
members of the genus *Homo*; some authorities (Wood and Collard 1999) deny
that two genera are represented, regarding *H. habilis* as a gracile australopithecine. The dispute serves to emphasise the difficulty, noted above, of
describing evolutionary processes in Linnaean terms.

To conclude this survey of early hominid evolution, it may be instructive briefly to compare the physical features of *Australopithecus africanus* both
with a modern person and with a modern great ape, in this instance a
gorilla (Fig. 10). The first point that one notices is the small size of the
australopithecine: adults of both sexes stood less than 1.5 metres high and
weighed between 33 and 67 kilogrammes (McHenry 1988). Comparison of
the skulls shows that the jaws and teeth of the australopithecine, despite
the creature's small overall size, were actually larger than those of a modern
person. The brain, on the other hand, was only about one-third as large, at

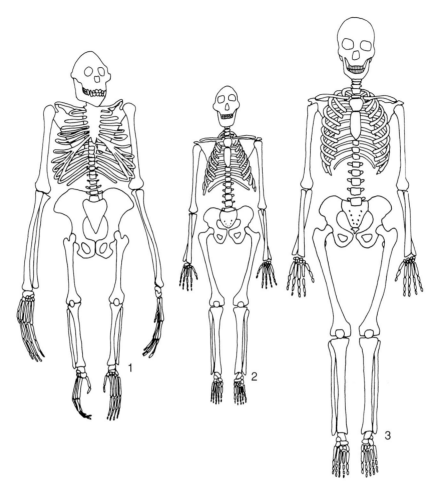

**Fig. 10:**
Skeletons, to the
same scale, of 1,
gorilla;
2, *Australopithecus
africanus*; 3, *Homo
sapiens*

about 450 cubic centimetres, which is approximately the same size as the modern gorilla's brain. In the gorilla the brain is placed behind the face, and the neck-muscle attachment is at the back of the skull. In modern people, the brain extends above the face, with the development of a true forehead, and the muscle is attached to the base of the skull. In both respects, australopithecines occupy a position intermediate between the gorilla and modern humans. In two important ways, *Australopithecus africanus* was much closer to a person than to a gorilla: the posture was completely upright, and the canine teeth were much reduced in size. A gorilla's molar teeth serve essentially a crushing function: in people and the australopithecines they are primarily grinders. Postcranially, the differences in all cases are less marked: arms became shorter and legs longer, and there are also changes to the pelvis accompanying more upright posture. The ribcage is progressively reduced in australopithecines and in modern people, presumably marking a reduction in gut-size which may have accompanied dietary emphasis on concentrated foodstuffs including meat (Aiello and Wheeler 1995; Foley 2002).

## The oldest discoveries in eastern Africa

It must be emphasised that the distribution of fossil discoveries is controlled not only by the former geographical extent of the relevant species, but also by the presence or absence of conditions suitable for their preservation, survival and eventual recovery. These conditions have occurred in both East and South Africa, but in very different situations (Fig. 11). In East Africa the lake basins of the Rift Valley provided habitats favourable for the early hominids and their associated faunas. Rapid sedimentation rates ensured the preservation of bones and their artefactual associations in comparatively undisturbed contexts and the volcanic activity of the area provided geological materials that can be dated, notably by potassium/argon analysis. Lastly, more recent developments have often led to the erosion of the deposits, thus exposing their fossil and artefact contents for collection or excavation and subsequent study. These factors have combined to stimulate very intensive field research on Plio-Pleistocene sites in eastern Africa from the 1960s onwards. In South Africa, on the other hand, bones accumulated – often through non-hominid agency – in dolomite or limestone caves, in deposits that were consolidated by minerals carried down by water seepage. They have subsequently been exposed, for the most part, in the course of mining operations. Research has been intermittent and, until recently, on a small scale. In the absence of volcanic material suitable for potassium/argon analysis, direct dating of these cave deposits has rarely proved possible, although study of the faunal remains has enabled them to be set in sequence and tentatively correlated with the dated East African succession (Howell 1982; Klein 1999).

Australopithecine remains dated between 5.8 and 3.0 million years ago (Walter and Aronson 1982) come mainly from three parts of the Rift Valley in eastern Africa: Hadar and the Middle Awash areas of Ethiopia some 500 kilometres northnortheast of Addis Ababa, the Lake Turkana Basin astride the Ethiopia/Kenya border (discussed in a separate section below), and Laetoli in northern Tanzania. The sparse specimens dated before 4.0 million years ago have been described above. More comprehensive and informative material comes from Hadar and the Middle Awash where lacustrine and river-delta deposits are separated by a series of volcanic tuffs. The arid conditions currently prevailing at these now low-lying sites have been brought about by subsequent Rift Valley earth movements. At one Hadar locality the remains

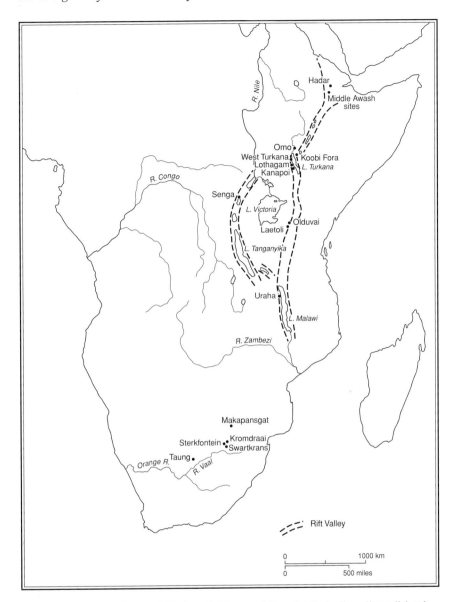

**Fig. 11:** The principal sites at which *Australopithecus* and *Homo habilis* fossils and/or well-dated Oldowan artefacts have been discovered

of thirteen early hominids, including four juveniles, were found together. The most informative discovery, however, is a 40 per cent complete skeleton of a female, popularly known as Lucy. Her pelvis and leg bones indicate a well-developed upright posture. Her original height was probably about 1.2 metres (Johanson and Edey 1981). At Laetoli, aeolian tuffs have yielded remains which consist mainly of jaws and teeth (M. D. Leakey and Harris 1987), allowing detailed comparisons to be made. Because of their physical similarity and near contemporaneity, the Laetoli and Hadar hominid fossils are generally regarded as representatives of the same species, *Australopithecus afarensis*. The Hadar discoveries are additionally important as providing the best sample of postcranial remains belonging to any eastern African australopithecine population. The same deposits at Laetoli included layers of hardened ash-covered mud in which were preserved a remarkable series of footprints of hominids and other creatures (Fig. 12), supplementing the evidence of the fossil bones that *A. afarensis* had a fully bipedal gait.

No artefacts have been recovered from the Laetoli deposits, but at Hadar and in the Middle Awash Basin small numbers of apparently artificially flaked cobbles (Fig. 13) have been reported in contexts provisionally dated to some 2.6 million years ago (H. Roche and Tiercelin 1980; J. W. K. Harris 1983; Kimbel *et al.* 1996; Semaw 2000). Not far to the south, the Bouri area of the Middle Awash has yielded stone flakes and worked bone fragments from the same locality as remains attributed to *A. garhi* and dated around 2.5 million years ago (Asfaw *et al.* 1999; de Heinzelin *et al.* 1999). These specimens and their associations await full investigation; should preliminary accounts be confirmed, these occurrences are by a substantial margin the earliest known incidence of hominid-made artefacts. They are generally attributed to the mode-1 Oldowan industry, discussed below, although they are significantly older than the occurrence after which that industry is named (Ludwig and Harris 1998).

## The Lake Turkana Basin and Olduvai Gorge

Discoveries of great richness and importance come from parts of the Lake Turkana Basin in both Ethiopia and Kenya (Coppens *et al.* 1976; F. H. Brown 1994). The area around the lower Omo River, north of the lake in southern Ethiopia, was the first to be investigated (Howell 1976), followed by intensive research in the Koobi Fora area on the northeast shore (M. G. and R. E. Leakey 1978; Wood 1991; Isaac 1997). The focus of research then shifted to the exceptionally significant sites in the western part of the basin (J. M. Harris *et al.* 1988). At times between 4 and 2 million years ago the area drained to the Indian Ocean, but both before and afterwards it has comprised a closed basin with no outlet except an overflow channel to the Nile which functions only when the Lake Turkana waters reach a very high level (Butzer 1980; Harvey and Grove 1982). The height and size of the lake have thus fluctuated considerably; it and its feeder rivers have laid down complex series of sediments, up to 1000 metres thick in places, in which hominid and other fossils are exceptionally well preserved. The principal

**Fig. 12:** The trail of hominid footprints discovered at Laetoli and dated to about 3.8 million years ago. The footprints are interpreted as those of two or three upright-walking hominids, one smaller than the others.

sediments with which we are here concerned are designated the Shungura and Usno Formations in the north, the Koobi Fora Formation in the east and the Nachukui Formation in the west; they are each separated into various members by horizons of consolidated volcanic debris known as tuffs, from which numerous potassium/argon age-determinations have been obtained,

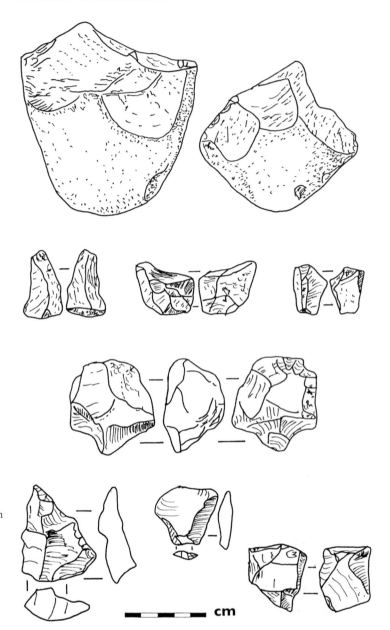

**Fig. 13:** Mode-1 artefacts: top row, from Hadar (after Roche and Tiercelin 1980); bottom row, from the KBS site at Koobi Fora (after Isaac *et al.* 1976); remainder, from the Omo Valley (after Merrick and Merrick 1976)

permitting the establishment of a remarkably detailed chronology (Fig. 14; see Klein 1999).

The long sequence of fossil-bearing deposits in the Omo Valley began about 4.0 million years ago (Howell 1976; Howell *et al.* 1987). The Omo River, flowing into the northern end of Lake Turkana, has exposed a complex series of deposits that were laid down in a variety of lakeside and riverine

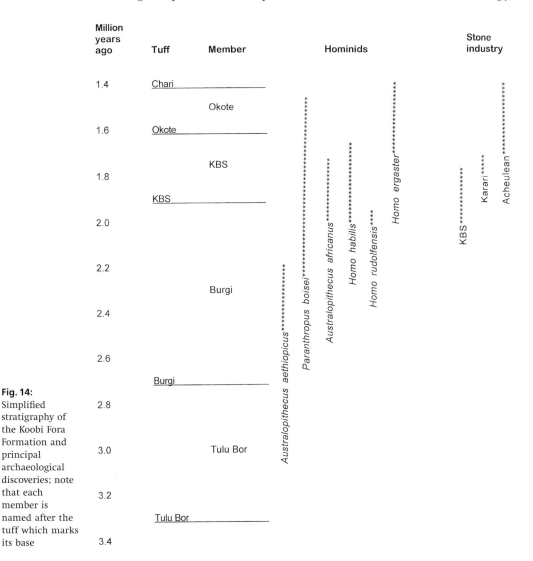

**Fig. 14:** Simplified stratigraphy of the Koobi Fora Formation and principal archaeological discoveries; note that each member is named after the tuff which marks its base

environments. These deposits have yielded abundant fossil material, mostly very fragmentary. The hominid remains consist for the most part of isolated teeth. The oldest specimens are probably almost as ancient as those from Laetoli, but they are of relatively little value in illustrating the evolution of the various hominid species.

Although the fragmentary hominid fossils from the Omo are in themselves less spectacular and informative than those from elsewhere in the basin, their associations and the stratigraphy are exceptionally informative; most belong to the period between 3.0 and 2.0 million years ago. The earlier hominid fossils are attributed to *Australopithecus afarensis*, the later ones to

*A. aethiopicus* and *Paranthropus (A.) boisei*. Stone artefacts began to be made about 2.4 or 2.3 million years ago (Howell *et al.* 1987), by which time *Homo* cf. *habilis* was present. These specimens, with those from the Nachukui Formation the earliest artefacts known from the Lake Turkana Basin, are simple flakes struck from small nodules of quartz, which was the only suitable material available in the area (Fig. 13). They are attributed to the mode-1 Oldowan industry; their characteristics and significance are discussed below.

The fossil-bearing deposits at Koobi Fora appear to span the period from rather more than 2.0 million until about 1.2 million years ago. Detailed studies have demonstrated the local circumstances in which the deposits were laid down, and thus the immediate environments in which the various species represented in the fossil assemblages lived and died. At least two, and almost certainly three, hominid lines are represented at Koobi Fora (M. G. and R. E. Leakey 1978; Wood 1991); some interpretations yield numbers as high as six. There is a robust australopithecine and possibly a more gracile variety resembling *A. africanus*. The genus *Homo* also occurs throughout the sequence. The early form, which some would attribute to a large-brained form of *H. habilis* or to *H. rudolfensis*, is best represented by the '1470' skull discussed above. There may have been a tendency at Koobi Fora for remains of *Homo* to occur predominantly in former lakeside environments, and those of *Paranthropus (A.) boisei* in riverine situations (Behrensmeyer 1976).

Concentrations of artefacts have been excavated at Koobi Fora, but unfortunately they are rarely in direct association with the hominid fossils. Although artefacts have occasionally been found in earlier contexts, the most informative occurrence, attributed to the Oldowan industry, is at the 'KBS site', dated to about 1.8 million years ago (Isaac *et al.* 1976; Isaac and Harris 1978; Isaac 1997). The KBS site appears to have been originally located in the sandy bed of a seasonal stream and its area was perhaps restricted by the availability of shade. Shortly after the site's apparently brief occupation, volcanic activity covered the area with a thick deposit of fine ash, thus ensuring its preservation in a virtually unmodified state. The traces of hominid activity cover an area 12–15 metres across. It has been calculated that 400–500 stone artefacts were originally abandoned on the site. The presence of very tiny chips and splinters shows that the tools were made on the spot rather than brought to the site from elsewhere, although the lava from which they were made must have been carried from about 5 kilometres away. Broken animal bones, including those of porcupine, pig, waterbuck, gazelle, hippopotamus and crocodile, were also preserved. Only 1 kilometre to the south, in a similar ash-filled stream channel, were found many bones representing the remains of a single hippopotamus. These were mixed with over a hundred stone artefacts, mostly flakes, essentially similar to, but less varied than, those from the KBS site. Whether or not the hippopotamus was killed by hominids, there can be little doubt that it was butchered, and that stone tools were manufactured on the site for this purpose. The significance of these Oldowan artefacts and of the sites from which they have been recovered is discussed in greater detail below (pp. 49–50). Somewhat later contexts at Koobi Fora have yielded a distinct series of artefacts for which the name 'Karari industry' has been proposed; this material is discussed in chapter 3.

The succession provided by the Nachukui Formation is the longest in the Lake Turkana Basin, extending from about 4.3 until 0.7 million years ago, the members from between 3.0 and 2.0 million years ago being particularly informative. Hominid fossils, although not particularly numerous, are sometimes exceptionally complete. The relatively robust *Paranthropus (Australopithecus) aethiopicus* (pp. 27–8 above) was present as long ago as 2.5 million years (A. C. Walker *et al.* 1986), subsequently becoming significantly more common and representing about half of the total hominid sample. Specimens of *P. (A.) boisei* and one of *Homo habilis* occur in poorly dated contexts within the period 2.3–1.6 million years ago; from the beginning of this time-span, Oldowan artefacts are also attested (H. Roche *et al.* 1999). By about 1.6 million years ago, a more advanced hominid is attested in the fossil record by a partial male skeleton from Nariokotome which may confidently be attributed to *H. ergaster* (A. C. Walker and Leakey 1993). This juvenile individual, further discussed in chapter 3, had an even larger cranial capacity than his predecessors, and presented a striking contrast with *P. (A.) boisei*, which may have been his only hominid contemporary. Oldowan artefacts derive from Nachukui contexts some 2.35 million years old, almost exactly contemporary with their Omo counterparts (Kibunjia 1994), while Acheulean-type artefacts (see chapter 3) were in use around 1.6 million years ago (Klein 1999, citing H. Roche), when *H. ergaster* was also present in the area.

Further confirmation of the co-existence of early *Homo* and a robust australopithecine comes from Olduvai Gorge in northern Tanzania (Fig. 15). Here, natural erosion has exposed a deep series of superimposed beds which contain abundant artefact and fossil assemblages covering the greater part of the last 1.8 million years (L. S. B. Leakey 1965; M. D. Leakey 1971; Hay 1976; Johanson *et al.* 1987; Blumenschine and Masao 1991). In the lowest horizons, Bed I and the lower part of Bed II, laid down in lakeside conditions between 1.86 and 1.75 million years ago, remains of both hominids are found in association with concentrations of Oldowan stone artefacts. It is considered unlikely that members of two hominid genera would have occupied the same environmental niche at the same time and been engaged

**Fig. 15:** Olduvai Gorge

in the manufacture and use of apparently identical artefacts; although this argument is not conclusive, it is probably safe to assume that the Oldowan artefacts were the work of *H. habilis*, who was physically, and presumably also intellectually, the more advanced of the two.

As at Koobi Fora, concentrations of the earliest stone artefacts have been investigated *in situ* at Olduvai. Although there is some doubt as to the extent to which non-human forces may have contributed to their disposition, several sites in Bed I and the lower part of Bed II provide possible evidence for the former existence of some simple type of shelter, notably a setting of stones which may have served as the foundation of some kind of windbreak and which enclosed the densest part of the artefact scatter on one particular site (Fig. 16). There is, however, controversy over the extent to which these sites are truly unaffected by post-depositional disturbance. Faunal material from these Olduvai sites includes numerous remains of small creatures and fish, the collecting of which may have been a major subsistence activity. However, the previously held belief that such small

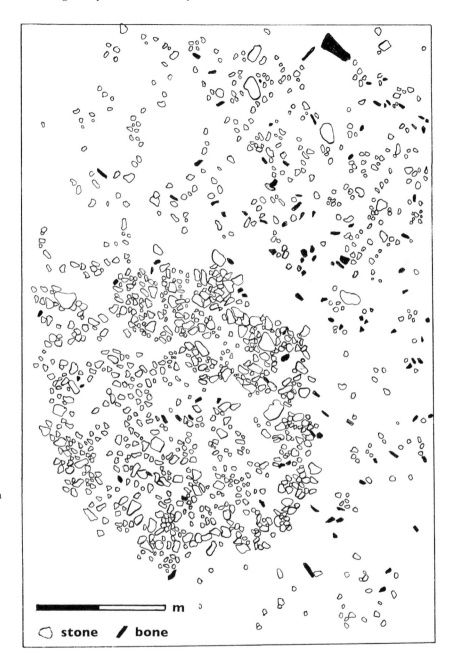

**Fig. 16:** Plan of a stone circle on an occupation horizon at site DK in Bed I at Olduvai Gorge (after M. D. Leakey 1971). This may represent the base of a shelter constructed of branches.

creatures were more abundantly represented in the oldest sites at Olduvai, being then gradually supplanted by larger species, is not supported by recent investigations.

## Central and south-central Africa

Although early hominid fossils have mainly been recovered at sites in eastern and (as will be shown below) South Africa, artefacts of demonstrably Plio-Pleistocene age are also known from two places in the intervening regions. These are at Senga on the Semliki River of easternmost D. R. Congo (J. W. K. Harris *et al.* 1987) and in the Chiwondo Beds south of Karonga on the northwestern shore of Lake Malawi (Kaufulu and Stern 1987; J. D. Clark *et al.* 1995). An age as great as 2.3 million years has been suggested for the Senga artefacts, but the evidence is not compelling (Boaz *et al.* 1992). The Plio-Pleistocene Chiwondo Beds have yielded abundant faunal material; hominid remains are scarce although, at Uraha, they have yielded a mandible best attributed to *Homo rudolfensis*, the heavily built variety of *H. habilis* (Bromage *et al.* 1995). If the age of this occurrence, apparently in the order of 2.5-2.4 million years, is confirmed, the Uraha hominid may be one of the oldest known representatives of the genus *Homo*. Far to the west, in Chad, tooth and jaw fragments resembling those of *Australopithecus afarensis* have been published as *A. bahrelghazali* (Brunet *et al.* 1996), although doubts have sub-sequently been expressed about both the identification as a separate species and the dating (cf. Klein 1999). These discoveries in Chad, D. R. Congo and Malawi serve to emphasise the large part played by chance in securing the preservation of the earliest archaeological remains, and also the extent to which future research may radically alter our present knowledge. However, the absence of hominids in very large fossil assemblages both in the extreme south and in the far north of Africa (Hendey 1981; Raynal *et al.* 1990) strongly suggests that, prior to 2.0 million years ago, these creatures may have been restricted to the equatorial latitudes of the continent.

## South Africa

Remains of *Australopithecus* have been found at sites in three parts of South Africa; in one of these regions remains of *Paranthropus* and, less certainly, early *Homo* also occur. As noted above, the sites comprise dolomite or lime-stone caves where fossil bones became incorporated in earthy deposits which have since hardened to produce the rock-like material known as breccia. The first discovery was made during quarrying operations at Taung, near the Harts River 130 kilometres north of Kimberley, in 1924 (Fig. 17). It consisted

**Fig. 17:** Calcified breccia and travertine deposits at Taung. The cairn in the foreground commemorates the discovery of *Australopithecus africanus* in 1924.

of a magnificently preserved complete skull of a juvenile hominid who had probably been about three years old at the time of death. Publication of the specimen (Dart 1925) stressed the view that it belonged to a previously unknown creature intermediate between apes and modern humans. It was on the basis of this single, immature specimen that *Australopithecus africanus* was named. Its discovery made surprisingly little impact upon archaeological thinking at that time, because Southeast Asia and Europe were then believed to have been the main areas where the early stages of human evolution had taken place. A further problem was, and remains, that of establishing the absolute age of the Taung hominid which seems, like the other animal bones with which it was associated, to have been brought to the site by a leopard, eagle or other predator (Berger and Clarke 1995). The site has yielded no artefacts. Estimates of its age have varied between 2.8 and 1.0 million years, with the consensus now favouring the earlier part of this range. Doubt has even been expressed whether this juvenile specimen is best attributed to *A. africanus* at all (Peabody 1954; Butzer 1974; Tobias 1978a; McKee 1993).

From 1936 onwards further discoveries began to be made in South Africa, first at the sites of Sterkfontein, Swartkrans and Kromdraai in the Blaaubank Valley near Krugersdorp, and then at Makapansgat some 300 kilometres to the northeast near Mokopane (formerly Potgietersrus) (Brain 1993; Klein 1999 and references; H. J. and J. Deacon 1999; Kuman and Clarke 2000). More recently, further sites have been discovered in the Sterkfontein vicinity (Mitchell 2002 and references). Between them these sites have yielded the remains of several hundred australopithecines. Although over the years these specimens have been attributed to a bewildering variety of species and genera, it is now widely believed that most of them belong to two species: *A. africanus* and *Paranthropus (A.) robustus*. What may be the oldest specimen, a remarkably complete skeleton from Member 2 at Sterkfontein for which an age around 3.3 million years has been proposed (Partridge *et al.* 1999), shows features which suggest that it may be morphologically as close to *A. afarensis* as to later *A. africanus* (Clarke 1998, 1999).

There has been considerable controversy over the precise nature of these sites and how the bone concentrations amongst which the hominid remains occurred came to be accumulated. It was at one time thought that many of the animal bones at Makapansgat had been selected by hominids and taken to the site for use as tools (Dart 1957), an hypothesis based upon the uneven representation of different body parts and upon the seemingly standardised fractures on many of the bones. This view, which involved acceptance of a tool-making status for *Australopithecus*, is not generally held today; the breakage patterns are paralleled at other sites where there is no possibility of hominid agency (Brain 1967). The differential representation of body parts

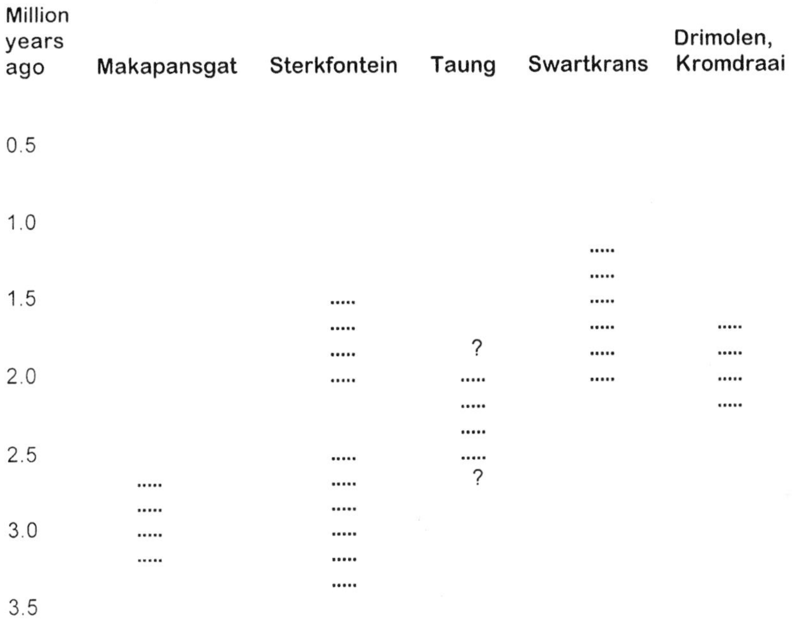

| Million years ago | Makapansgat | Sterkfontein | Taung | Swartkrans | Drimolen, Kromdraai |
|---|---|---|---|---|---|
| 0.5 | | | | | |
| 1.0 | | | | | |
| | | | | ..... | |
| | | | | ..... | |
| 1.5 | | ..... | | ..... | |
| | | ..... | | ..... | ..... |
| | | ..... | ? | ..... | ..... |
| 2.0 | | ..... | ..... | ..... | ..... |
| | | | ..... | | ..... |
| | | | ..... | | |
| 2.5 | | ..... | | ..... | |
| | ..... | ..... | ? | | |
| | ..... | ..... | | | |
| 3.0 | ..... | ..... | | | |
| | ..... | ..... | | | |
| | | ..... | | | |
| 3.5 | | | | | |

**Fig. 18:** Chronological chart showing the probable ages of the South African australopithecine sites

is also like that which occurs at leopard lairs where carcasses are often deposited in trees, out of reach of scavengers, for consumption at leisure. It is now believed that, over prolonged periods, hominid carcasses were brought to such trees by leopards and that their bones thus gradually accumulated in the caves and rock crevices below (Brain 1981). The Makapansgat hominid-bearing deposits are best dated around 3.0 million years ago, when the area enjoyed a high-rainfall sub-tropical environment (Rayner *et al.* 1993). All the hominid fossils from this site are now attributed to *Australopithecus africanus*. Objects generally accepted as artefacts do not occur at Makapansgat until significantly later.

Despite various attempts, no wholly satisfactory method has yet been devised for directly dating the South African australopithecine sites, which lack volcanic deposits such as have yielded potassium/argon dates for the early hominid sites in East Africa. On the basis of comparisons of the faunal assemblages with those of the relatively well-dated East African sequences, supplemented by measurements of palaeomagnetism and the provisional results of other newly developed techniques, it has however proved possible to show that the South African sites probably fall within the period between 3.4 and 1.4 million years ago (Fig. 18). The earliest occurrences are those at Makapansgat and the earliest part of the Sterkfontein sequence. Significantly, in both these deposits *Australopithecus africanus* is the only hominid represented, and there are no stone tools. After what may have

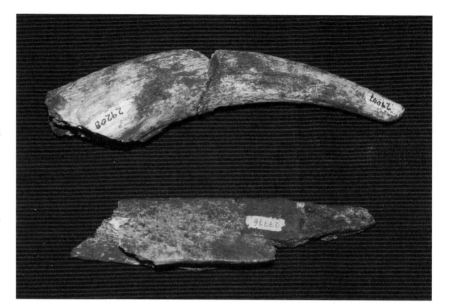

**Fig. 19:** Horn and bone tools from Swartkrans, 1.0–1.5 million years old, believed to have been used for digging up edible roots and tubers, or for opening termite mounds. The larger (horn) tool is 14 cm long.

been a substantial gap in the local sequence, there are further occurrences at Sterkfontein and in the Older Breccia at Swartkrans. Here, *Paranthropus (A.) robustus* is the only australopithecine species present. There are also fragments of burnt bone which may represent an early use of fire, whether or not this was fully controlled. Stone tools attributed to a mode-1 Oldowan industry are present only in the Sterkfontein area, in contexts for which faunal associations suggest a maximum age of around 2.0 million years (Kuman 1994, 1998). Heavily utilised bone fragments (Fig. 19) also occur but it is not yet clear whether their use was contemporary with the Oldowan; their polish suggests possible use to obtain underground plant foods, grubs or termites (Backwell and d'Errico 2000). Remains of a creature attributed to the genus *Homo*, possibly *H. habilis*, have also been recorded in somewhat later horizons at Sterkfontein and at Swartkrans, associated with stone artefacts (Clarke 1988; J. D. Clark in Brain 1993; Kuman and Clarke 2000) which, as noted below in chapter 3, are accepted by most archaeologists as akin to those from upper Bed II at Olduvai. The finds from Kromdraai also probably belong to this same general period – perhaps about 2.0 million years ago or shortly thereafter, by which time *A. africanus* was probably no longer present in South Africa (Kuman *et al.* 1997); it should be noted that the Kromdraai artefacts were not found in direct association with fossil hominids, but came from an adjacent cave, the link being demonstrated by faunal association. As will be further discussed in chapter 3, fossil fragments from

Swartkrans, Sterkfontein and the recently discovered nearby site of Drimolen have been attributed to *H. ergaster*, with ages subsequent to 1.8 million years ago.

## The earliest tool-makers

As has been shown, incontrovertible archaeological evidence for the earliest recognisable stages of human material culture comes almost exclusively from Ethiopia and from Kenya, and dates from between 2.5 and 2.0 million years ago. This particular time-span is not well represented at South African sites where, although earlier contexts have yielded hominid fossils, there is as yet no conclusive evidence for tool-making older than 2.0 million years. In both regions, the earliest recognised artefacts are of stone and belong to J. G. D. Clark's 'mode 1' of stone-tool technology (p. 18, above). They are attributed to the Oldowan industry named after Olduvai Gorge where Bed I and the lower part of Bed II have yielded what is now seen to be a rather late occurrence of this industry. Despite the very long period of time over which these artefacts were produced, little development has been discerned (Ludwig and Harris 1998); occurrences from the Ethiopian Rift Valley, the Lake Turkana Basin and Sterkfontein are all sufficiently similar to justify their inclusion in the Oldowan taxon.

The most important characteristic of the Oldowan, in contrast with all later stone industries, is the absence of standardisation (Toth 1985a; Toth and Schick 1986; Kuman 1996; Isaac 1997). It appears that the basic process employed was banging together two stones or pounding one with another so as to detach sharp flakes from which could be selected artefacts suited for a particular need; on occasion a flake might receive simple retouch, or the core itself might be employed. Most of the artefacts are flakes, up to 6–7 centimetres long, very few of which show any signs of deliberate shaping or trimming. The artefacts from the lower part of the Olduvai sequence clearly bear a close technological resemblance to those from the KBS and contemporary sites at Koobi Fora. There are, however, some significant differences. Whereas unretouched flakes predominate at Koobi Fora, at Olduvai there is a higher proportion of cores or core-tools, including cobbles from which a few flakes have been removed as if to produce a cutting or chopping edge. Flake tools, some of remarkably small size, are also a feature of assemblages from Olduvai (Fig. 20). The variations in artefact size and morphology need not necessarily reflect cultural traditions, but may be explained at least in part by reference to the nodules and flaking qualities of the different raw materials from which the artefacts were made (Ludwig and Harris 1998; Stiles 1998).

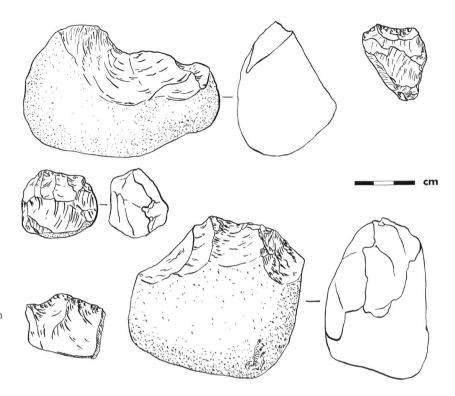

**Fig. 20:** Oldowan artefacts from site DK at Olduvai Gorge (after M. D. Leakey 1971)

Isaac (1997: 296) has described the Oldowan as involving 'little more than least-effort solutions for needs for sharp edges' and noted that 'this classification need not imply participation in a common culture tradition system. However, it is entirely credible that across East Africa there existed a loose network of stone-tool-making social groups of early hominids, which over time were subject to the diffusion of cultural information.' Since there is no widely accepted evidence that particular artefact types were reserved for special purposes, it is only through experiment and the study of traces of wear on the flakes that we can discover the uses to which they were put. Such studies on Oldowan stone flakes from Koobi Fora (Keeley and Toth 1981; Toth in Isaac 1997) have yielded evidence for the probable cutting of wood, meat and bone. The last of these uses is also demonstrated by cut-marks on bones recovered at several sites (Bunn and Kroll 1986). Among many other uses which may be surmised are the grubbing up of roots and tubers, opening nuts and seed pods, and extracting grubs from the bark of trees. It is also perfectly possible that a major function of the Oldowan artefacts may have been the production of wooden tools which have not survived in the archaeological record but which could also have served some of the above purposes.

Several early hominid sites have yielded traces of burning (J. D. Clark and Harris 1985), but there is much uncertainty whether this was purposefully controlled. Fire does, of course, occur naturally, and may have contributed significantly to changes in vegetation at various times in the past, as well as to hominid dietary practices, security and ability to survive in hostile environments. It may be supposed that human control over fire came about in at least two stages: transfer and maintenance of naturally occurring fire, followed by ability to make it. So far, archaeologists have made little agreed progress with resolving the chronology of these developments.

It is clearly important to ascertain, if possible, which hominid or hominids were the makers of the Oldowan artefacts. The picture is made more complex by the presence in both eastern and southern Africa at this time of hominids which most authorities believe to represent more than one genus: *Australopithecus* and *Homo*. It should be noted that the earliest lithic artefacts occur only in areas where the presence of early *Homo* is also indicated; *Australopithecus*, on the other hand, is frequently found without such associations. The earliest artefacts at Hadar, Middle Awash and in the Omo Valley are all contemporary with the first local attestation of *Homo*. The same is true in South Africa. It is noteworthy that, on osteological grounds, the hand of *Homo habilis* is believed to have been better adapted to precise manipulation of tools than that of at least some australopithecines (Susman 1998). It may thus be argued that *Australopithecus* is unlikely to have been the maker of Oldowan stone artefacts.

It must be stressed that those recognisable artefacts attributed to the Oldowan probably represent a late stage of what is likely to have been a prolonged process of development. We have noted the absence of standardised tool-types and suggested that sharp flakes were selected for immediate purposes. Such selection may previously have been applied to stones which had not been purposefully fractured and which it would be virtually impossible for the archaeologist to recognise as artefacts. Others, long-since perished, may have been made of wood. The development from tool-use to tool-making may have been long and hesitant. We know that tool-use today is not a prerogative of the hominids, so this development may be one which stretched far back into Pliocene or even earlier times where no archaeological record has yet been recovered. The initial stages may have involved the use of random hammerstones, then the use of chance-struck flakes, both processes preceding the intentional bashing of stones in order to produce sharp edges. The earliest artefacts will only be properly understood when we can suggest the uses to which they were put, and research to this end is only just beginning.

Although our knowledge is still very incomplete, it is possible from the evidence so far available to draw some tentative conclusions about the life of early *Homo* at sites where Oldowan artefacts have been recovered. The KBS site at Koobi Fora has been noted above; an interesting feature of the faunal remains is that animals are represented from several different environments: hippopotamus from the lake and gazelle from the drier inland plains, for example. The different source-areas of the species represented suggest that the early hominids may have used the site as a home-base and brought back to it carcasses or joints of meat that they obtained elsewhere from more than one source, whether as prey or as carrion. This observation suggested to Isaac (1978) that one of the most basic features of human behaviour, the transport of food in order to share it, had already been developed. This interpretation has been the subject of much controversy; some prehistorians consider that the site may represent a succession of brief activities rather than a single episode, that the bone accumulations owe little to hominid agency, and that their association with stone tools merely indicates that several species, including hominids, frequented the same place for some purpose such as getting water (Binford 1981; Potts 1984, 1986; but see also Blumenschine and Masao 1991; Rose and Marshall 1996). A second type of site, known both at Koobi Fora and at Olduvai, shows less controversially that the early hominids on occasion made use of temporary butchery sites for the dismemberment or consumption of single carcasses too large to be transported entire, such as elephant and hippopotamus.

Some prehistorians have tended to assume that the bones recovered on Oldowan (or later) sites are necessarily those of animals that were hunted for food. It must be stressed that this may be an unjustified assumption. Several studies of the various possible mechanics of bone accumulation have shown that hominid activities need not always have been responsible. Furthermore, animal food was not necessarily obtained by hunting. There is an increasing body of evidence that the early hominids frequently obtained their meat by scavenging (Shipman and Rose 1983; Shipman 1986; Bunn and Kroll 1986). Animals killed by other carnivores seem to have been obtained by the early hominids and either butchered on the spot or removed for consumption elsewhere. The range of species eaten is thus more indicative of wild carnivores' predation abilities than of hominid hunting skills. Other potential sources of animal protein include capturing small animals, reptiles or insects. It is also important not to underestimate the significance of vegetable foods in early hominid diets, as often indicated by fossil dentition: unfortunately traces of foods in these categories are hardly ever preserved in the very early archaeological record. However, as Foley (2002) has pointed out, there is biological evidence that Plio-Pleistocene hominids may have become progressively more dependent than their predecessors on concentrated foodstuffs such as meat.

It has for long been believed that, for the period considered in this chapter, hominids were restricted to the African continent. The date at which they first expanded into Eurasia remains a matter of controversy (Turner 1999). Some stone-artefact assemblages from southern Spain have been compared with those of the African Oldowan (Gibert *et al.* 1998) and an age in excess of 1.0 million years has been proposed. The argument is not wholly convincing, however, and the presence of similar assemblages apparently preceding the Acheulean in more recent contexts on the Atlantic coast of Morocco (Biberson 1961; Raynal *et al.* 1995) provides no support for attributing such an early date to the Spanish material. Intensive research in Israel (Bar Yosef 1987; Goren-Inbar and Saragusti 1996; Guérin *et al.* 1996) has provided a clearer indication that the earliest hominid presence in this key area linking Africa with Eurasia belonged to Acheulean times, perhaps slightly before 1.0 million years ago. This conclusion is not so far convincingly contradicted by ongoing research at Dmanisi in Georgia (Gabunia *et al.* 2000) or by recent age determinations in Indonesia (Swisher *et al.* 1994). Lowered sea levels in the Late Pliocene may have left a land-bridge between the Horn of Africa and southern Arabia at Bab el Mandeb (Milliken 2002). The age and nature of the earliest hominid occupation of Eurasia remains very poorly understood, but there is little reason to suppose that it is of any relevance to the early periods of hominid development discussed in this chapter.

Our knowledge of the early hominids is, and will presumably always remain, very incomplete. We can learn something of these creatures' appearance and physical abilities from their fossil remains. We can learn about some of the places they frequented and some of the foods that they ate. Their artefacts, when made of imperishable materials, can tell us something about their technological abilities. Taken together, these factors allow us to reconstruct a very incomplete view of their life. The list of what we do not know is far longer. What was the social basis for the groups of hominids that left remains such as those at the KBS site? Was there any socio-political unit larger than such a group? Were such associations permanent? How did they exploit the seasonally shifting and changing resources of their African homeland? All these questions, like the all-important ones of intellect and communication, are ones that research is only now beginning to address. A consensus is none the less emerging that the levels of group size and co-operative behaviour indicated at this period need not imply abilities in vocal communication very much more advanced than those exhibited by modern great apes.

# 3 The consolidation of basic human culture

## Acheulean and Sangoan in Africa

This chapter deals primarily with one of the most remarkable and least understood phenomena of world prehistory: the enormously wide distribution, both in time and space, of people who made stone artefacts of the type conventionally known to archaeologists as 'Acheulean'. (Problems of definition are considered below.) These artefacts first appeared in the archaeological record, in eastern Africa, about 1.6 million years ago; and they seem to have survived in most areas until the period between 350,000 and 250,000 years ago: a time-span of at least 1.25 million years. In addition to Africa, Acheulean-type artefacts are found in Europe and Asia, from Spain and Britain in the west and north, to India and perhaps China in the east. In some parts of the Old World they are the oldest known manifestation of human settlement (but see Carbonell *et al.* 1999). The name is taken from Saint Acheul in the Somme Valley of northern France, one of the places where these characteristic stone artefacts were first recognised during the mid-nineteenth century. Also discussed here, because they are seen as a final manifestation of the Acheulean tradition, are the African stone-artefact assemblages designated Sangoan after Sango Bay on the western shore of Lake Victoria (cf. G. H. Cole 1967).

Although the Acheulean has often been regarded as an entity, there are good reasons to believe that this long period was one during which important human behavioural developments occurred in the conceptual, social and organisational fields, as well as in the more readily discernible technology (J. D. Clark 1996). There are some indications, as will be shown below, for group activities that may have required linguistic communication for their organisation. The evidence for these processes is essentially circumstantial and difficult to interpret (Gibson and Ingold 1993; Mellars and Gibson 1996; Noble and Davidson 1996; McPherron 2000). Significant physical and biological evolution of hominids also took place at this time (Klein 1999), and the geographical distribution of tool-makers was greatly expanded. This, together with the larger numbers of known later sites, must indicate a substantial increase in human population. Adaptation to varied environmental conditions is also attested, with the ability to obtain food and safety in circumstances markedly different from those of the restricted areas known to have been occupied by the earliest hominids. As environments fluctuated,

52

so did the areas subject to hominid settlement. Stone-knapping techniques were adapted with notable skill to utilise different raw materials, which now had rather less effect on the form of the finished product than had been the case in earlier times. The picture remains incomplete and open to differing interpretations, but there can be little doubt that, by the time of the latest Acheulean, humankind had developed many abilities and characteristics that earlier hominids had lacked.

The hominids responsible for the Acheulean and Sangoan were all members of the genus *Homo*. For much of the relevant period, until about 700,000 years ago, robust australopithecines – *Paranthropus (Australopithecus) boisei* and *P. (A.) robustus* – were also sometimes present in the same general areas, but it seems unlikely that they shared responsibility for the Acheulean with the hominid here termed *H. ergaster*. (As noted in chapter 2, some scholars prefer to retain the designation 'African *H. erectus*' in place of '*H. ergaster*'.) By late Acheulean times, it appears that *Homo* had evolved considerably in the general direction of modern people; while some authorities informally designate fossils of this type as archaic *H. sapiens*, others (e.g. Rightmire 1996, 1998) prefer to attribute them to *H. heidelbergensis*. Although no hominid fossils are known which are incontrovertibly associated with the Sangoan, it may be reasonable to assume that those responsible were of archaic *H. sapiens* type. Further discussion of these hominids is placed at the end of this chapter.

The Acheulean has conventionally been defined by the presence, with variable frequency, of the stone implements known as handaxes. These are characteristically pear-shaped, pointed or ovate in outline and biconvex in cross-section, usually 12 to 20 centimetres in length and often flaked over at least part of both surfaces (Fig. 21). A fairly sharp edge may be restricted to the area of the more pointed end or may extend around all or the greater part of the implement's periphery. The earliest handaxes tend to be crudely shaped, fewer than a dozen flakes having been removed from them: the scars which mark the position of these flakes are deep, suggesting the use of a simple stone hammer. These handaxes are usually fairly thick in relation to their breadth. In later assemblages, although crude examples may continue, there are also much more finely flaked specimens with shallow scars such as may have been produced by use of a softer (wood or bone) hammer or by indirect percussion; these implements are generally thinner and more symmetrical in cross-section. In many Acheulean assemblages, particularly in Africa, there are also found implements known as cleavers (Ranov 2001). Similar in size and manner of production to the handaxes, these were often made on large flakes and have a straight or transverse cutting edge in place of the point. Acheulean stone-knapping corresponds to J. G. D. Clark's 'mode 2' lithic technology (cf. p. 18, above). Despite uncertainties as to the uses to

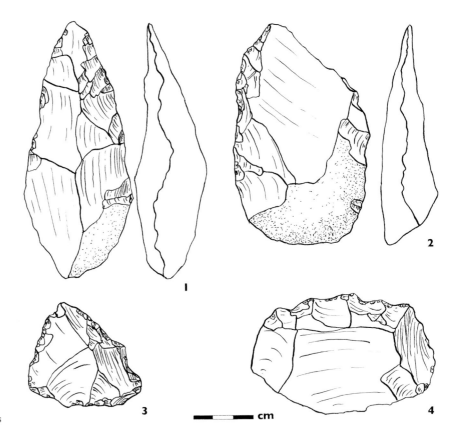

**Fig. 21:**
Acheulean-type
artefacts from
Montagu Cave,
South Africa
(after Keller
1973): 1,
handaxe;
2, cleaver; 3–4,
retouched flakes

which these artefacts were originally put, the terms 'handaxe' and 'cleaver' are so widely used and understood that they have been retained in this book.

So ubiquitous and numerous are these handaxes and cleavers in some Acheulean assemblages that it seems they were used for several different purposes. Despite the implication of the conventional designations, these implements were probably used for purposes different from those that these names suggest. Patterns of damage of the type caused by heavy digging are rarely discernible, but generally we have little definite knowledge of the uses to which these artefacts were put (cf. L. Phillipson 1997), although microscopic studies of edge-wear (e.g. Keeley 1980; Beyries and Roche 1982; Binneman and Beaumont 1992) and plant residues (Dominguez-Rodrigo *et al.* 2001) are beginning to produce significant results. Experiments have shown that the cleaver in particular is remarkably effective as a butchering instrument (P. R. Jones 1980) and for skinning large game. Handaxes were probably particularly versatile, and may have been used for butchery, as weapons, and for numerous other purposes (Kohn and Mithen 1999; Gamble and Marshall

2001). In some instances tools have been found in association with other evidence for a particular activity, such as butchering a carcass, and cut-marks on the bones may provide additional evidence for the use of these artefacts.

Although handaxes and cleavers are generally regarded as the most characteristic features of Acheulean assemblages and, indeed, are often seen as their defining feature, they are not the only types of implement which occur. Numerous flakes – both those removed in the course of handaxe-production and others – were used untrimmed as cutting and scraping tools, or were retouched into a variety of relatively unstandardised forms. Some artefacts are indistinguishable from individual specimens seen in mode-1 industries. Cores, which sometimes include types resembling Oldowan ones, may have been discarded as waste or used as choppers.

Stone-artefact assemblages that have been designated Acheulean occur in most parts of Africa (Fig. 22). That they have not been recorded from the densely forested regions of West Africa and the Congo Basin probably reflects a genuine discontinuity in their distribution rather than lack of research. It thus seems probable that it was the makers of these artefacts who were responsible for the first human settlement of much of the continent away from the eastern savanna, to which the earliest such phenomena had apparently been restricted (J. D. Clark 1967, 2001b). Just when this major expansion took place cannot yet be ascertained, but such evidence as is available suggests a date of about a million years ago. This was probably also the time when some tool-makers moved from Africa into adjacent parts of Southwest Asia; their extension into Europe may have been significantly later (Milliken 2002).

Throughout Africa and, indeed, in many other regions of the Old World, Acheulean-type stone tools are remarkably standardised. Detailed investigation is hindered by the scarcity of demonstrably primary-context, single-event assemblages. Comparative studies suggest, however, that much of the variation that does occur is due to the flaking qualities and nodule sizes of the available raw materials (Gamble and Marshall 2001). At first sight, the artefacts also show relatively little consistent change through time although, as noted above, the Acheulean remained the dominant tool-making tradition for some 1.3 million years. Despite this apparent standardisation, it would not be prudent to propose that there was a single Acheulean industry, using the term 'industry' in the same sense as has been applied for more recent periods. The artefact assemblages so designated are chronologically and geographically very widely distributed; and they sometimes vary considerably in composition (as will be shown below), with their main diagnostic components (the handaxes and cleavers) differing so much in frequency, and presumably in function, that they are best regarded merely as belonging to the same mode-2 technological taxon. In other words, the Acheulean

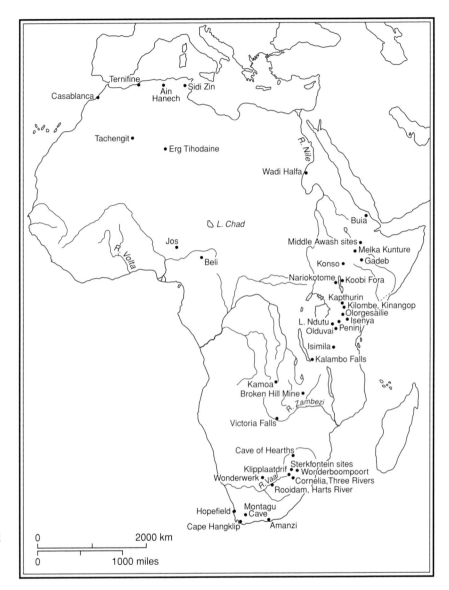

**Fig. 22:** Principal Acheulean and related sites in Africa

should not be regarded as an industrial or cultural entity on grounds other than the very general technological and/or morphological similarity of its stone artefacts. It would be premature, in the present state of knowledge, to assume any stronger affinity among the life-styles of its makers.

In most areas there is a marked variation in the proportions in which handaxes and other tool types are represented even in the few assemblages which can be dated and which have been preserved for study in their

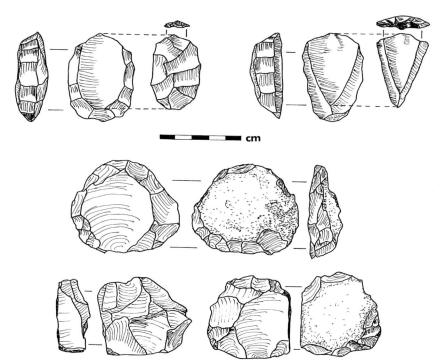

**Fig. 23:** Core preparation. The illustrations in the top row are of idealised Levallois examples (after Schick and Toth 1995); the other specimens are from Nubia (after Wendorf 1968).

entirety. There are also contemporaneous assemblages from which handaxes and cleavers are largely or completely absent, and there has been considerable controversy as to whether or not these should be regarded as belonging to the Acheulean. The causes for this variation are not yet properly understood. Most likely a number of cultural and economic factors were all partly responsible, such as style, personal or group preference, raw material availability, and the range of activities that were undertaken at the different sites. These activities may in some cases have been linked with season, environment or subdivision within the social group. It is therefore not surprising that archaeologists have not been able to recognise significant patterning in this variation, either between different geographical areas or through time.

In some areas, the later phases also saw the adoption of techniques whereby core-preparation could be used to pre-determine the form of a flake; this may be regarded as a development linked to increased expertise in biface production. While not ubiquitous, locally distinct techniques of this type have been recognised in southern, eastern and northern Africa, as well as in Europe (Dibble and Bar Yosef 1995; Schlanger 1996; see also Fig. 23). The designation 'Levallois', established in the latter area, has also sometimes been applied to some local African equivalents. Such loose usage is not followed in this book, where the general term 'prepared-core' is preferred, and particular local manifestations are discussed individually. These varied techniques had a common purpose: to ensure that standardised flake tools could be produced without extensive marginal trimming. Although closely linked with handaxe-production, they became particularly common in later Acheulean industries of certain areas and survived, often in modified form or highly developed, into subsequent periods, as discussed in chapter 4.

Artefacts of Acheulean type are extremely common in certain areas of Africa, but sites where they have been found undisturbed in their original contexts are relatively few (e.g. Sampson 2001). As with the earlier periods, a high proportion of our evidence of this time comes from eastern Africa. Proximity to water appears to have been an important factor in determining areas suitable for settlement; and some of Africa's great river valleys are thus particularly rich in Acheulean-type remains. Noteworthy in this respect are the Vaal (Sohnge *et al.* 1937; H. J. and J. Deacon 1999: 81–3), the Zambezi (J. D. Clark 1950, 1990), and the Nile valleys (Sandford and Arkell 1933; Sandford 1934). As these rivers have developed and their rates of flow fluctuated, most of the early sites on their banks have been disturbed or destroyed, and the artefacts which they contained have been moved, sorted and selectively incorporated in fluviatile deposits (Fig. 24). Such movement may not only alter the configuration of larger artefacts, it may destroy or remove smaller ones altogether, leaving a greatly distorted picture of the original assemblage. Although in certain circumstances the artefact contents of successive river deposits may give us some information about the local archaeological sequence, this disturbed material is now recognised as having very limited value; research emphasis has therefore shifted away from the great river valleys to the location and excavation of undisturbed sites.

In much of central Africa (and indeed over a much wider area extending from Botswana to Ethiopia and Sudan), the stone-tool assemblages immediately following those designated Acheulean are of the type known as Sangoan (see p. 52 above). In many parts of the Congo Basin, Sangoan-type assemblages are the earliest trace of human settlement yet found (Mortelmans 1962; Van Noten 1982). They comprise massive pointed core-tools, but also a significant proportion of lighter-duty retouched flakes (Fig. 41, below). Unfortunately, as with their earlier counterparts, virtually no research has yet been undertaken to try and establish the uses to which these Sangoan artefacts were put. Much of the regional variation that has been recognised may be attributed to the varying quality of the raw materials that were available for stone-knapping. Many Sangoan sites appear to belong to a time when semi-arid conditions prevailed and when the equatorial forest was significantly less widespread and dense than it had been previously (McBrearty 1987). The suggestion previously made (e.g. J. D. Clark 1970) that the

**Fig. 24:** Air view of the Victoria Falls on the Zambezi River. The Falls are 2 kilometres wide and almost 100 metres high. Downstream of the present Falls a series of zig-zag gorges marks the positions of former waterfalls. Gravel deposits now preserved near the edges of the gorges were laid down on the bed of the river and have been exposed by its subsequent down-cutting. Study of stone artefacts preserved in these gravels (J. D. Clark 1950, 1990) enabled a sequence of industries to be proposed and correlated with the back-cutting processes of the Victoria Falls.

Sangoan represents an adaptation to heavily forested conditions and that some of its characteristic artefacts were used for woodworking is thus no longer tenable.

These general points having been made, it is now appropriate to survey the archaeological evidence for the Acheulean and Sangoan in the various regions of Africa, before returning to a more detailed consideration of overall issues. Organisation of the regional evidence is not easy in view of the enormously long time-span involved; a basically geographical arrangement has been adopted.

## Acheulean in eastern Africa

The earliest appearance of Acheulean-type industries in eastern Africa is difficult to pinpoint. The archaeological record at this time, about 1.7–1.5 million years ago, presents a confusing complexity of artefact assemblages; the situation is further obscured by the terminology that is conventionally applied. It is helpful first to discuss the archaeological evidence from the sites of Koobi Fora and Olduvai Gorge which, although probably not the earliest, are most comprehensively known.

In the Koobi Fora area east of Lake Turkana, several sites have yielded the distinctive Karari industry (J. W. K. Harris and Isaac 1976; Isaac 1997). So far known only from Koobi Fora, the Karari industry occurs on a number of sites stratified between the Okote Tuff of 1.65 million years ago and the 1.39 million-year-old Chari Tuff (F. H. Brown 1994). By contrast, all artefact assemblages from below the Okote Tuff are attributed to the simpler Oldowan KBS industry (p. 38 and Fig. 13, above). Like the KBS ones, Karari sites are mostly located near ancient stream-courses. Karari artefacts include numerous cores which have often been regarded as heavy-duty tools, some of them bifacially worked. Edge-trimmed flakes are also represented. A good level of stone-working skill is evidenced and some types closely resemble artefacts once regarded as characteristic of much later periods (Fig. 25). At other broadly contemporary sites, such as that code-named FxJj 50 (Bunn *et al.* 1980), the simpler artefacts of KBS type continued to be made.

The Karari industry appears largely, but perhaps not completely, to have replaced the KBS industry of the Oldowan tradition at Koobi Fora by about 1.5 million years ago. These advances were broadly contemporary with the appearance in the Lake Turkana Basin of a new hominid, *Homo ergaster* (Fig. 26), both at Koobi Fora around 1.8–1.7 million years ago and, somewhat later, at Nariokotome on the west side of the lake.

The Nariokotome hominid remains (A. C. Walker and Leakey 1993), dated to about 1.6 million years ago, comprise the near-complete skeleton of an immature male whose physical appearance would have been far closer to that of modern people than that of *Homo habilis* or the australopithecines had been. He was probably about 10 years old at death. He had an elongated physique, with narrow hips and a barrel-shaped chest which contrasted with those of his predecessors. His cranial capacity was approximately 880 cubic centimetres, representing a 40 per cent increase over the average for *H. habilis*. Had he reached maturity, it is estimated that he would have been about 1.8 metres tall and 68 kilogrammes in weight – comfortably within the ranges displayed by modern human populations. It should be emphasised that, although Acheulean-type artefacts have been recovered from deposits

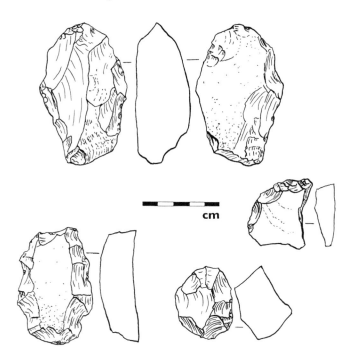

**Fig. 25:** Artefacts of the Karari industry from Koobi Fora (after Isaac and Harris 1978)

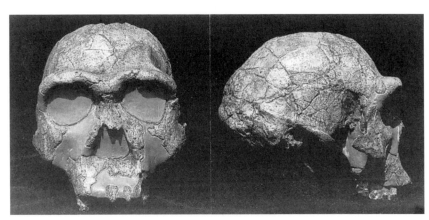

**Fig. 26:** Skull of *Homo ergaster*, Lake Turkana Basin

of the Nachukui Formation west of Lake Turkana which are contemporary with – or slightly older than – the Nariokotome skeleton (H. Roche, cited by Klein 1999), none was found in direct association with these hominid remains.

At Olduvai Gorge, various artefact assemblages of this age, first occurring in the middle part of Bed II, have been divided between 'Developed Oldowan' and 'Acheulean' categories (M. D. Leakey 1971, 1975, 1976). They show both a greater variety of tool types and more standardisation than do the Bed-I industries (pp. 40–2 above). Developed Oldowan assemblages contain a few simply flaked bifacial tools which recall the more numerous, and generally more competently flaked, handaxes and cleavers of the assemblages described as Acheulean (Fig. 27). However, both are here regarded as part of the overall range of variation within a loosely defined Acheulean (pp. 84–6 below).

In the middle and upper parts of Bed II at Olduvai, stone tools are more numerous relative to the faunal remains than was the case in the lower levels. The same is true for Beds III and IV (M. D. Leakey and Roe 1994), although in no case can one be certain that the site is undisturbed and that no non-human agencies have contributed to its disposition. It is also noteworthy that large animals, such as rhinoceros and giraffe, are more commonly represented on the later sites: the two observations may well be interconnected. By this time the Bed-I lake had largely dried up and an open grassland environment is indicated. It has been argued that the majority of the hominid sites at Olduvai represent dry-season encampments (Speth and Davis 1976; see also Blumenschine and Masao 1991). The Olduvai sequence is summarised in Figure 28.

The earliest hominid fossils from Olduvai have been noted in chapter 2. Specimens attributed to *Paranthropus (Australopithecus) boisei* continue into the upper part of Bed II, but *Homo habilis* appears to have been replaced by *H. ergaster* in upper Bed II and in Beds III and IV (Rightmire 1979b, 1990; M. D. Leakey and Hay 1982). Later forms of *Homo* are poorly represented at Olduvai, but a fragmentary skull from Lake Ndutu, some 20 kilometres to the west (Mturi 1976; Clarke 1976, 1990), is attributed to *H. heidelbergensis* and may be broadly contemporary with the latest occurrences of Acheulean-type artefacts at Olduvai.

Artefacts of Acheulean type are well documented by 1.5–1.4 million years ago in deep water-lain deposits with interbedded volcanic tuffs at Konso (formerly known as Konso-Gardula) in southern Ethiopia (Asfaw *et al.* 1992; Yonas Beyene *et al.* 1996, 1997), but have not yet been published in detail. Hominid fossils include several that are attributed to a robust australopithecine and two *Homo ergaster* specimens (Suwa *et al.* 1997; Klein 1999).

In the Middle Awash area of the Ethiopian Rift Valley, establishment of an absolute chronology for the Acheulean-type artefact assemblages has proved problematic (Renne in de Heinzelin *et al.* 2000); mode-2 industries were almost certainly present there by 1.0 million years ago and continued until well after 400,000 years ago. In some instances, *in-situ* occurrences were associated with the remains of a single large animal, usually a hippopotamus or elephant; these are interpreted as butchery sites. An age determination of about 640,000 years, relating to volcanic deposits in the Bodo and Dawaitoli

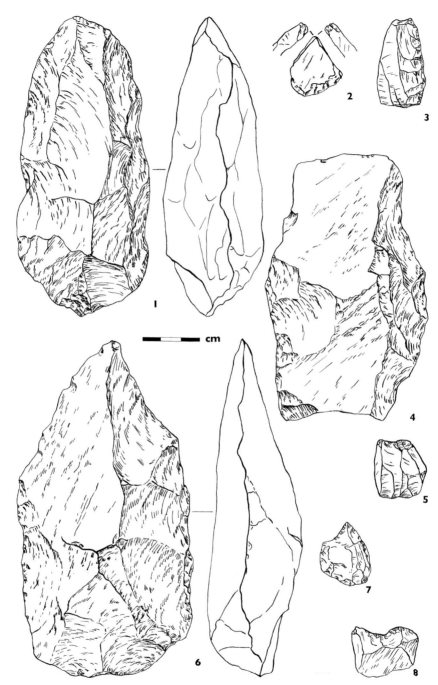

**Fig. 27:** Stone artefacts from Bed II at Olduvai Gorge (after M. D. Leakey 1971): 1, 6, handaxes; 2, burin or graver; 3, 8, edge-retouched flakes; 4, cleaver; 5, scaled piece; 7, flake retouched to a point, perhaps for use as an awl

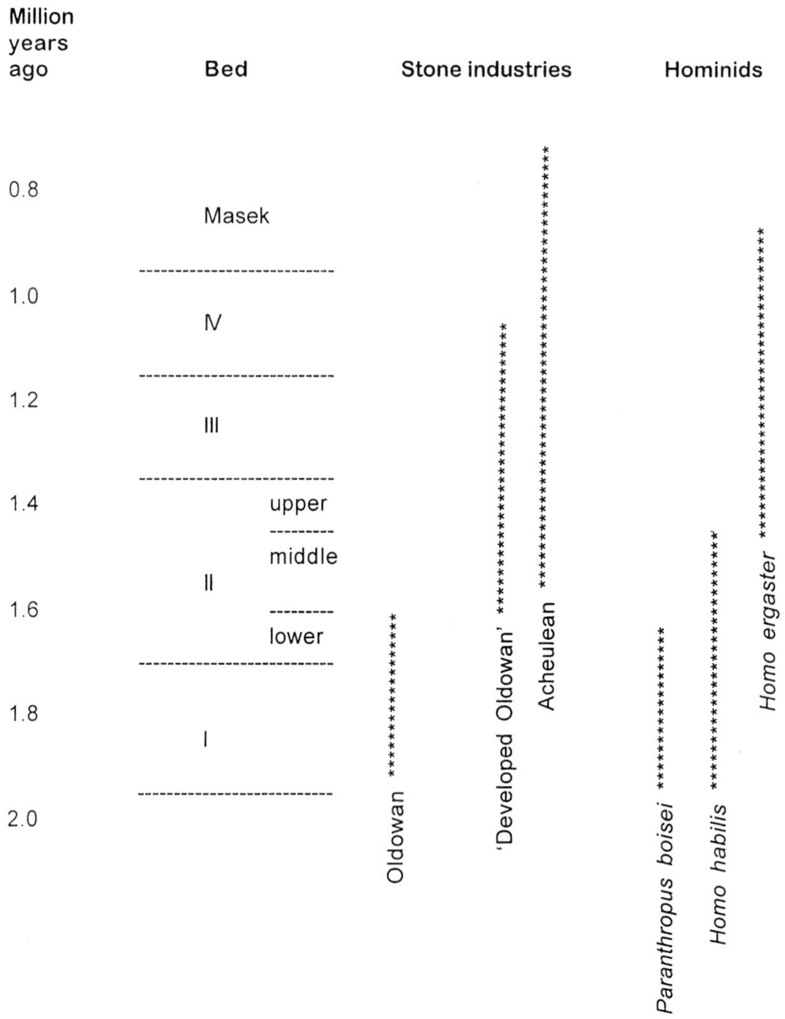

| Million years ago | Bed | Stone industries | Hominids |
|---|---|---|---|

**Fig. 28:** Summary of the archaeological sequence at Olduvai Gorge. The Acheulean and 'Developed Oldowan' are believed by many to be facies of the same tradition.

0.8  Masek

1.0  IV

1.2  III

1.4  upper

middle

1.6  II

lower

1.8  I

2.0

Oldowan

'Developed Oldowan'

Acheulean

*Paranthropus boisei*

*Homo habilis*

*Homo ergaster*

areas where a hominid skull (discussed below) and artefacts of types designated 'Middle Acheulean' and 'Oldowan' have been recovered (J. D. Clark *et al.* 1994), is more problematic. If the age of the 'Oldowan' assemblages, including one that was found in probable association with hippopotamus bones, is confirmed, it will be tempting to compare it with those lacking bifaces in Bed III at Olduvai, noted above. Sites with very small handaxes and prepared radially flaked cores (cf. p. 92 below) are also present in the Middle Awash area: their position in the sequence cannot yet be demonstrated, but they may belong to a very late phase.

In the Middle Awash Valley, numerous hominid fossils have been recovered from contexts associated with Acheulean-type artefacts (White in

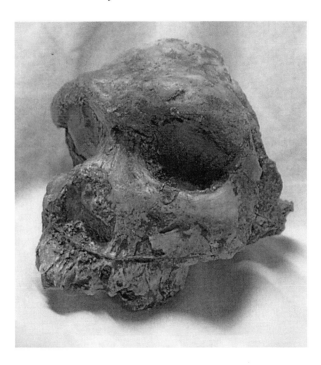

**Fig. 29:** The Bodo skull

de Heinzelin *et al.* 2000), but only in one case are significant details yet available. The Bodo skull (Fig. 29), found in 1976 in deposits subsequently dated to 600,000 years ago, displays features generally regarded as intermediate between those of *Homo ergaster* and those of *H. sapiens* (Conroy *et al.* 1978; Rightmire 1996). It is strikingly similar to the skull from Broken Hill mine at Kabwe in Zambia, discussed below, designated 'archaic *H. sapiens*' or '*H. heidelbergensis*'. White (1986) describes cut-marks which suggest that the Bodo skull may have been purposefully defleshed. A skull from Buia, across the border in what is now Eritrea, is probably somewhat earlier in date (Abbate *et al.* 1998).

A further early East African occurrence of Acheulean-type artefacts is at Peninj, beside Lake Natron, near the Kenya/Tanzania border northeast of Olduvai (Isaac 1967; see also Dominguez-Rodrigo *et al.* 2001). Two *in-situ* Acheulean horizons have been located in deep deposits that indicate a lake-shore environment similar to that of the present time. The finely preserved lower jaw of a robust australopithecine was found in a context somewhat earlier than the Acheulean-associated horizons, which are dated by potassium/argon analysis to about 1.4 million years ago (Isaac and Curtis 1974).

Probably somewhat later, but at least one million years old, is the first evidence for Acheulean-related occupation of the Ethiopian plateau (Cachel

**Fig. 30:** Handaxes and other Acheulean-type artefacts preserved as discovered at Olorgesailie

and Harris 1998). This evidence, indicating settlement of terrain more than 2300 metres above sea level now frequently subject to night frost, comes from several areas. At Melka Kunture near Addis Ababa (Chavaillon 1979), a long series of occurrences, including some which have been described as 'Oldowan', has been investigated but remains incompletely published. One of these Acheulean-type occurrences has yielded a jaw fragment attributed to *Homo ergaster*. On the Gadeb Plain to the southeast, early Acheulean-like material is of particular interest as it provides evidence that raw material for tool-making was carried over a substantial distance (J. D. Clark and Williams 1978; J. D. Clark 1987).

Some of the most informative occurrences of Acheulean-type artefacts in Africa are at Olorgesailie in the Kenyan Rift Valley, some 50 kilometres southwest of Nairobi (Isaac 1977; Potts 1989). Here, several major concentrations of handaxes, cleavers and other stone artefacts were deposited over a long period in a succession of lake-shore environments (Fig. 30). It is evident that the places most favoured for settlement were either on a low rocky promontory, or on patches of sand which generally occurred in the channels of seasonal streams draining into the lake. Acheulean people seem to have preferred to camp in these dry watercourses rather than on the shore of the lake itself. Comparison with modern Rift Valley lake basins suggests reasons for these preferences: the stream beds provided open sandy ground in an area that was elsewhere covered with hummocks of coarse grass, and the trees lining the channel supplied welcome shade that was absent on the lake shore. Water from holes dug in the bed of the channel was likely to be less saline than that of the lake. The rocky promontory might have been used in the wet season, when the streams were flowing, and when the extra height provided relief from mosquitoes.

Most of the Olorgesailie Acheulean-type occurrences are thought to have suffered some degree of sorting or movement as a result of water action since the sites were abandoned. However, even if the artefacts were not recovered absolutely in their original positions, it was possible to estimate from the extent of the artefact scatters that the camp areas were generally between 5 and 20 metres across. The larger scatters may represent areas of successive shifting use, or the presence of groups larger than a single nuclear family.

Bone was not always well preserved at Olorgesailie, and no hominid fossils have been found there. At one locality remains of many giant baboons were discovered, and these may represent a troop that was attacked whilst sleeping in the trees overgrowing the site. The presence of many stones, which must have been carried to the site from elsewhere and which were of a suitable size and shape for use as missiles, lends support to this suggestion. This may be an early instance where hunting, as opposed to scavenging, is indicated.

Many of the Olorgesailie artefacts are made of types of stone which must have been brought there from some distance away. The scale of this transport makes it seem highly likely that, by this stage in their development, people had invented some sort of bag for carrying their possessions from one place to another. While it seems highly probable that the makers of Acheulean-type artefacts at Olorgesailie, like their counterparts elsewhere, collected and made much use of vegetable foods, no firm evidence for this has been preserved.

A particularly noteworthy feature of these lithic assemblages is the range of their variation, both in composition and in artefact style. In some, handaxes and cleavers were the most frequent tool-types; in others, they were virtually absent. While in some instances size-sorting of the artefacts by water action may have contributed to this variation, it is very unlikely to have been the prime cause. Also, in the same area and at the same time there is a great range in quality of workmanship and other stylistic features within the same artefact categories. It seems reasonable to suppose that this variation was primarily due to differences in the skill and preferences of individual tool-makers or social groups, as well as to the intended uses of the artefacts. If this were the case, it might imply that tool-making was essentially a taught skill (I am indebted to Dr L. Phillipson for this suggestion). Further examples of this variation may be seen at the Kenyan sites of Kilombe and Isenya (Gowlett 1978; H. Roche *et al.* 1988).

The various occurrences of Acheulean-type artefacts at Olorgesailie are all contained within a single geological formation, although they are scattered through about 40 metres of its vertical thickness. It is therefore probable that they were deposited at intervals over a substantial period of time, perhaps extending over thousands of generations. Unfortunately, it has not proved possible to date the site very precisely. The best interpretation of potassium/argon dates for pumice contained in the Olorgesailie Formation suggests an age between 1.0 and 0.5 million years ago (Bye *et al.* 1987; Potts 1989). This is not contradicted by other lines of investigation, such as faunal comparisons with dated sites elsewhere in East Africa.

A later, perhaps near-final, stage of the East African Acheulean may be represented by a poorly understood site on the Kinangop Plateau of central Kenya which has yielded a potassium/argon date in the order of 400,000 years for an industry of small handaxes, flake points and side-scrapers (Evernden and Curtis 1965). Similar developments may be discerned elsewhere in East Africa, as at Kapthurin near Lake Baringo, Kenya, where a hominid mandible is claimed to be associated with an Acheulean-type lithic assemblage showing use of a well-developed prepared-core technique (D. M. Leakey *et al.* 1969; Cornelissen *et al.* 1990). An age of about 200,000 years has been suggested, but comparison with evidence from other regions indicates that this may be too young.


## Acheulean in south-central Africa

Some relatively late occurrences of Acheulean-type artefacts occur at a site at Kalambo Falls near the southern end of Lake Tanganyika (Fig. 31); they are particularly important because of the preservation of wood and other plant remains. The Kalambo River, which here forms the border between Tanzania and Zambia, flows over the edge of the Rift escarpment as a spectacular 220-metre single-drop waterfall. Immediately above the waterfall, the Kalambo Valley is very narrow; successive blocking and unblocking of this stretch has on several occasions caused the formation of a small lake in the wider section of the valley further upstream. In the silts and shore deposits of these ancient lakes abundant traces of prehistoric occupation have been preserved, both in near-primary and in secondary contexts (J. D. Clark 1969, 1974, 2001a). The earliest such traces so far recovered represent two phases associated with late Acheulean-type handaxes and cleavers, but it is not impossible that even older material may lie beneath the modern water level.

**Fig. 31:** The 220-metre-high Kalambo Falls. The Acheulean and later archaeological sites are in the small lake basin through which the Kalambo River flows above the Falls.

At an early stage in the research at Kalambo Falls, radiocarbon dates were obtained which indicated for these Acheulean-type artefacts an age of about 55,000 to 50,000 years. These results were at the very furthest end of the radiocarbon dating method's time-range; and more recent work has shown that they should be regarded as representing minimum, rather than finite, ages. New uranium-series analyses and comparison with dated successions in other regions suggest that the true age of this material may be between 400,000 and 300,000 years (J. D. Clark 2001a: 25–8, 665–74). Broadly similar artefacts preserved in a riverside situation at Isimila in southern Tanzania, about 300 kilometres east of Kalambo, are probably of comparable antiquity (Howell *et al.* 1962; Hansen and Keller 1971), and the same may be true of the Kamoa site in D. R. Congo some 500 kilometres to the southwest (Cahen 1975).

The artefact-bearing horizons at Kalambo cover substantial areas which probably represent shifting foci of small-scale activity. On several horizons at the bottom of the investigated sequence, abundant Acheulean-type artefacts were recovered, apparently only minimally disturbed since they were originally abandoned by their makers on banks of sand and gravel beside the river, presumably during the dry season. The handaxes and cleavers are exceptionally large and uniformly finely worked, owing probably in large part to the excellent fine-grained silicified sandstone that was plentifully available in the immediate vicinity. They show little if any evidence for the development of a prepared-core technique. Bone was not preserved, but wood did survive; several pieces show signs of having been cut or shaped deliberately (Fig. 32). Traces of burning on some of the wood indicate the presence of fire, but there is no way of knowing whether this fire was used and controlled by the site's inhabitants, or merely derived from naturally generated 'bush' fires. In this context it may be significant that none of the areas investigated presented features which could plausibly be interpreted as hearths. Particularly interesting is an arc of stones enclosing an area of about two square metres which, it has been suggested, may represent the base of a simple shelter or windbreak. Two hollows filled with compressed grass may have been sleeping places. Seed pods and the remains of fruit show that a range of vegetable foods was exploited.

The silts which incorporated the Acheulean materials at Kalambo Falls contained pollen grains which have been identified to provide a reconstruction of the local vegetation. Conditions warmer and drier than those of today are initially attested, with swamps and riverine gallery forest in the valley, but dry woodland beyond. The final Acheulean-type artefacts at Kalambo appear to have been deposited during a time with a cooler, damper climate, associated with a type of forest which today only survives in this part of central Africa at considerably higher altitudes; these assemblages show trends towards some of the typological features characteristic of later periods (J. D. Clark 1964). Further climatic change may also provide the background for subsequent developments in the Kalambo Falls sequence; those designated Sangoan are described below (pp. 81–2) and the later ones in chapter 4.

Although long-since destroyed, a cave at the Broken Hill mine near the town of Kabwe on the central plateau of Zambia is of great significance because of the discovery there, during mining operations in 1921, of human

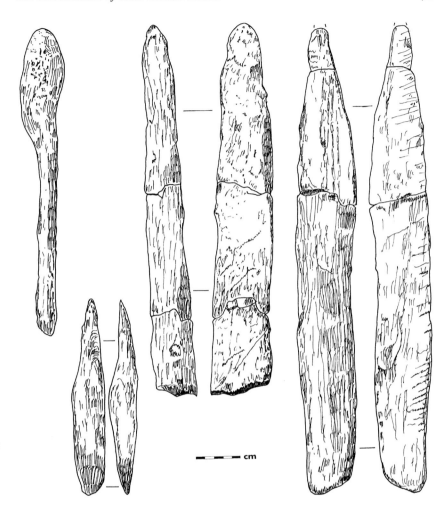

**Fig. 32:** Wooden objects, with probable traces of working, from Acheulean levels at Kalambo Falls (after J. D. Clark 2001a)

remains representing at least four individuals, including a superbly pre-served cranium originally attributed to *Homo rhodesiensis* (Pycraft *et al.* 1928). Unfortunately little was recorded concerning the precise circumstances of the discovery, and its true archaeological associations are consequently uncertain (J. D. Clark *et al.* 1950; J. D. Clark 1959). However, as will be shown below, there is some evidence that the Broken Hill cranium may belong to the same time-span as the late Acheulean-type assemblages of about 400,000 years ago; the site is therefore discussed here.

Most of the artefacts recovered from the Broken Hill cave, although not necessarily in direct association with the cranium, are flakes and retouched flakes, some of which were struck from prepared cores. In the absence of

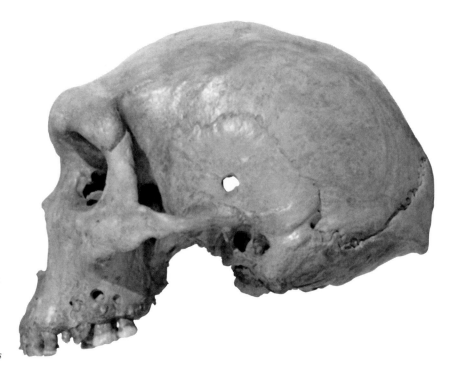

**Fig. 33:** Skull from Broken Hill Mine, Kabwe, attributed to *Homo heidelbergensis* or to an archaic form of *H. sapiens*

handaxes, cleavers or other core-tools, they were originally attributed to the post-Acheulean industry known as Charaman and now regarded as a facies of the Sangoan (p. 81). An occurrence with handaxes of Acheulean type has subsequently been located in the vicinity, and other assemblages lacking handaxes are now known from the same time-span. Of the large animal species represented in the abundant faunal collection from the cave, a quarter are now extinct, suggesting a Middle-Pleistocene age (Klein 1973).

The Broken Hill cranium (Fig. 33), with its pronounced brow ridges and receding forehead, has a capacity of 1280 cubic centimetres, which is well within the range shown by modern populations. Its closest parallel is the skull from Bodo in the Middle Awash Basin of Ethiopia, noted above. The evolutionary position of these hominids is discussed below; here it needs merely to be noted that some authorities attribute them to *Homo heidelbergensis*, others to an archaic sub-species of *H. sapiens* intermediate between *H. ergaster* and *H. s. sapiens*. Despite the uncertainties about its age and archaeological associations, the specimen is of major significance as one of the few hominid fossils from sub-Saharan Africa which may represent the makers of the later Acheulean-type artefacts (Klein 1999).

## Acheulean in southern Africa

Despite the large mass of Acheulean-type artefacts that has been recovered from south of the Zambezi, the amount of reliable information which it yields is disappointingly meagre (Klein 2000b). Although hundreds of occurrences are known, less than a score come from sealed contexts and even fewer relate to single events (cf. Shackley 1985). The absence of volcanic activity during the Pliocene and Pleistocene epochs in southern Africa means that none of this material has been dated by the potassium/argon method; estimates of its age depend very largely on correlations of faunal assemblages, climatic fluctuations and geomagnetic reversals with those known and dated in East Africa. The general picture that emerges is that the oldest artefacts of Acheulean type so far recognised in southern Africa are from Sterkfontein near Krugersdorp, dated less than 1.7 million years ago, probably between 1.5 and 1.0 million years ago. Occurrences of artefacts and/or *Homo ergaster* fossils here and at the nearby sites of Swartkrans, Kromdraai A and Drimolen (Kuman *et al.* 1997; Kuman and Clarke 2000) may be broadly contemporary.

Hominids may not have been present in cooler (southerly) and drier (westerly) parts of South Africa until after 1.0 million years ago, when Acheulean-type artefacts are first attested there. On faunal grounds it may be suggested that one of the oldest such occurrences in these regions is that at Cornelia in northern Free State Province (H. B. S. Cooke 1974), and one of the most recent at Duinefontein 2, near the Atlantic coast not far to the north of Cape Town (Klein *et al.* 1999).

Among other South African sites yielding artefacts of Acheulean type, the few which are thought on geological or technological grounds to be early are all in river gravels or other disturbed contexts: these include Klipplaatdrif and Three Rivers near Pretoria (Mason 1962). At the nearby suburb of Wonderboompoort, large quantities of Acheulean-type artefacts accumulated in a natural defile which could have been used for trapping game. Unusually, some of the most informative occurrences of such materials in South Africa, all probably late, have been found in caves: the Cave of Hearths (Mason 1962) near Mokopane, Wonderwerk near Kuruman (Beaumont 1990; Fig. 34), and Montagu Cave (Keller 1973) in Western Cape Province.

Further sites of note are those in spring deposits at Amanzi near Uitenhage (H. J. Deacon 1970), where vegetable remains including worked wood fragments are also preserved, on an 18-metre raised beach at Cape Hangklip (Sampson 1974), and in eroding sands at Hopefield (also known as Elandsfontein) north of Cape Town. The Hopefield deposits (Singer and Wymer 1968) have also yielded a hominid skull-vault with pronounced brow

**Fig. 34:**
Wonderwerk
Cave

ridges, variously attributed by earlier writers to *Homo erectus* or to an early
form of *H. sapiens*, but now generally regarded as a further example of
*H. heidelbergensis* which is, on the evidence of the associated fauna, somewhat earlier in date than the specimen from Broken Hill mine. There is no
reason to believe that any of these Cape occurrences, or others in the arid
western parts of southern Africa, are significantly older than about 600,000
years. A partial skull from Florisbad in Free State Province (Clarke 1985) is
probably even more recent, as is discussed below in chapter 4.

It has long been recognised that use of a prepared-core technique has a
high antiquity in South Africa, where it has been conventionally designated
the 'Victoria West technique', used to produce large flakes as blanks for
handaxes and cleavers (Fig. 35; McNabb 2001). Recent investigation of a site
on the Harts River near Taung (Kuman 2001) has clearly demonstrated that
this technique arose in a local Acheulean context.

In parts of the South African interior, the final Acheulean assemblages
contain small well-finished handaxes with rounded butts and concave sides,
formerly regarded as representing a distinct 'Fauresmith industry'. It is now
realised that these artefacts are almost always found in those areas where
lydianite (hornfels) was the preferred raw material for tool manufacture
(Humphreys 1970); their technological distinctiveness, however, remains
incompletely understood. One of the most informative assemblages is that
from Rooidam near Kimberley (Fock 1968). Sampson (2001) has argued that
southern Africa at this time supported a denser human population than
other parts of the continent or, indeed, of the world.

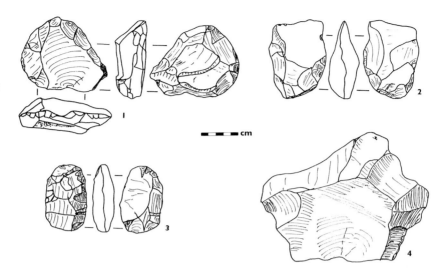

**Fig. 35:** Artefacts from a site on the Harts River near Taung, showing the 'Victoria West technique' of core-preparation (after Kuman 2001): 1, 4, prepared cores; 2, 3, cleaver and handaxe produced from such flakes

## Acheulean in West Africa and the Sahara

The archaeological evidence for the first human settlement in West Africa is still poorly known. It seems probable that this area was not inhabited by the very earliest hominids, such as are known from the eastern part of the continent; it is nevertheless possible that such populations were originally present but that their remains have not been preserved or are yet to be discovered. For example, archaeological traces of this period may perhaps be preserved in the Chad area, where lake deposits are known to extend to great depths (Tillet 1985).

There can be no doubt that true handaxes of Acheulean type were sometimes made in West Africa, although there is as yet no convincing demonstration of their age. The most notable occurrences are along the Volta River in Ghana, and on the Jos Plateau in Nigeria (Fig. 36). In the latter area (Soper 1965), river gravels mined for tin extraction have been found to contain numerous handaxes, cleavers and other Acheulean-type artefacts, as well as material which is clearly of much more recent date. None, however, has been recovered from primary or datable contexts.

Surveys of other West African occurrences of early artefacts, mostly in disturbed or poorly documented contexts, have been reported by several archaeologists (Davies 1964, 1967; Shaw 1985; Allsworth-Jones 1987, 2001). A number of places in West Africa, notably Beli in northeastern Nigeria, have yielded artefacts which would not be out of place in either an Oldowan or an Acheulean assemblage. However, since these discoveries all come from disturbed and undated contexts, there is no convincing evidence for an Oldowan presence in West Africa.

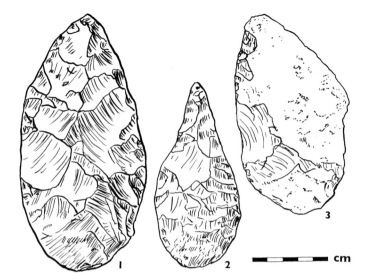

**Fig. 36:** West African Acheulean-type artefacts from the Jos Plateau, Nigeria (after Shaw 1978): 1, 2, handaxes; 3, cleaver

Similarly, in the Sahara, although artefacts of Acheulean type have been found in many places, there are very few assemblages that have been carefully excavated from undisturbed situations (J. D. Clark 1980, 1992). The occasional collections that appear on typological grounds to be early are all from secondary contexts, most notably in southern Morocco and central Mauritania. Later Acheulean material seems to be more widely distributed. Where its original geological associations can be ascertained, these indicate conditions wetter than those of the present, and this is confirmed both by study of the faunal remains and by pollen analysis. It appears that there were major fluctuations in the Saharan climate during the time when Acheulean-type artefacts were produced. Only local studies of these have so far been undertaken and no overall picture has yet emerged. As in other areas, water-side locations were clearly preferred, and it may be that human habitation was far more extensive during wetter phases. A typical Saharan site is at Erg Tihodaïne, in southern Algeria between the Tassili and Hoggar massifs, where presumably late artefacts of Acheulean type occur in the clays of a former swamp, together with bones of extinct types of elephant and buffalo, as well as other creatures which cannot survive in the area today (Reygasse 1935; Arambourg and Balout 1955; H. Thomas 1979).

Several regional technological and stylistic variants may be recognised in the Saharan Acheulean. For instance, there is an incidence of developed prepared-core technique in the Wadi Saoura of central Algeria, as at Tachengit: cores were prepared to yield large flakes requiring only minimal trimming to produce effective cleavers (Balout 1967; Alimen 1978; Dauvois

1981). There is, however, little chronological information, so we cannot ascertain whether these variants were in fact contemporary with one another.

## Acheulean in North Africa

Parts of North Africa have yielded evidence for a long sequence of Acheulean-type industries; it has also been suggested that there may be indications of earlier human occupation akin to the Oldowan. Unfortunately, direct dating of these North African sites has not proved possible. The tentative chronology originally proposed was based upon faunal correlations with the European sequence and upon connexions with high sea levels which, it was believed, could be attributed to phases of the northern-hemisphere glacial succession. Both methods, especially the latter, have been shown to be tenuous and now merit little reliance; comparisons with the dated material from eastern Africa are thus difficult to establish. The current consensus is that hominid penetration of large areas of the Sahara and of northwestern Africa did not take place until, at the earliest, 1.0 million years ago, perhaps as late as the beginning of the Middle Pleistocene (J. D. Clark 1992).

The most complete picture comes from the Casablanca area on the Atlantic coast of Morocco (McBurney 1960; Biberson 1961, 1967, 1971; Debénath 2000). The detailed subdivision of this sequence into technological phases, as originally proposed, is now felt to lack adequate support since in relatively few instances were assemblages recovered from primary contexts. The earliest traces of human activity in this region are associated with beach deposits about 100 metres above the modern sea level. It is generally believed that this beach was formed during a period of warm climate at a relatively early phase of the Middle Pleistocene. Two series of stone artefacts have been recognised in these deposits, distinguished mainly on the basis of their physical condition. The rolled series, evidently derived from still earlier deposits, consists of pebbles from which flakes had been removed in one direction only. The second series, which is in fresher condition, has had flakes removed in two directions so as to produce a jagged cutting or chopping edge. Unfortunately, there are very few artefacts in either of these series, and it must be emphasised that they have not been recovered from their original positions, being disturbed by wave action, soil slip and other natural agencies.

The first appearance of handaxes in the Casablanca sequence is in deposits which, being between 60 and 70 metres above the present sea level, must be significantly later than those described in the preceding paragraph. The most generally accepted dating for this episode is approximately 500,000 years ago. If this order of magnitude is supported by future research (and it must be admitted that the chronology at present remains extremely tentative), then the development of the Acheulean in Morocco must have lagged far behind the corresponding events in eastern Africa. On the basis of the same correlation, even the earliest occurrence of humanly chipped stone at Casablanca may be less than 1.0 million years old. It is clear that human occupation of North Africa and Europe covers a significantly shorter timespan than the corresponding sequence in eastern Africa (Isaac 1972; Klein 1999; Rolland 2001). The relationship with analogous occupation of the Iberian peninsula remains to be satisfactorily demonstrated.

Some degree of confirmation for the presence in northwestern Africa of early stone industries lacking handaxes comes from the site of Ain Hanech near El Eulma in Algeria, where the faunal remains, including many species now extinct, suggest an age at the beginning of the Middle Pleistocene, about 700,000 years ago, if not earlier (Arambourg and Balout 1952; McBurney 1960; Sahnouni 1998). The Ain Hanech artefacts (Fig. 37) are flaked to a roughly spherical shape, with jagged edges; they resemble in some respects objects which are frequent in the East African assemblages designated 'Developed Oldowan'. A few handaxe-like objects from Ain Hanech may be attributable to a subsequent phase represented in a higher layer. The Ternifine site (now Tighenif), not far from Oran in northwestern Algeria, lies beside a spring whose deposits contained abundant faunal remains of early Middle Pleistocene types, demonstrably later in date than those from Ain Hanech. The Ternifine artefacts appear to belong to a fairly early stage of the North African Acheulean (Balout *et al.* 1967; Geraads *et al.* 1986). Three human mandibles and a skull fragment, all exceptionally well preserved, are of *Homo ergaster* type (Fig. 38).

The Casablanca sequence of Acheulean-type industries is best exposed at the Sidi Abderrahman and Thomas quarries (Fig. 39; see also Raynal and Texier 1989). While the sea was retreating from a level of undetermined maximum height, handaxes, cleavers and other artefacts were laid down upon the beach and subsequently buried beneath a massive sand dune which, as the sea level dropped still lower, accumulated on the old shoreline. This beach, consolidated into sandstone, is exploited by quarrymen whose activities have been responsible for unearthing much of the Casablanca sequence. Later, the sea rose again, cutting back the dune to form a cliff, in which several caves came into being. Beach deposits in these caves are between 27 and 30 metres above modern sea level, which enables their formation to be correlated provisionally with some part of a prolonged interglacial period around 300,000 years ago, to which many important European Acheulean occurrences also belong. Two of these caves exposed at Sidi Abderrahman, the Grotte de l'Ours and the Grotte des Littorines, are of particular significance because they were occupied by people soon after the formation of

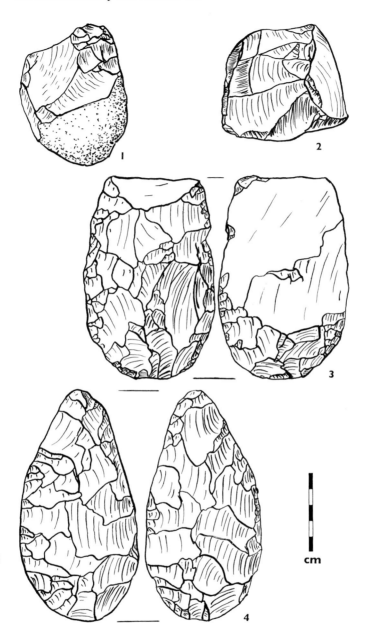

**Fig. 37:** North African artefacts (after McBurney 1960): 1, 2, flaked spheroids from Ain Hanech; 3, 4, cleaver and handaxe from Sidi Zin

the 30 metre beach. Abundant well-made handaxes, cleavers, flake tools and other artefacts were recovered; many of both the handaxes and the cleavers were made on flakes struck from remarkably massive cores. Several successive handaxe-bearing horizons occur in these caves and, in one of the upper ones at the Grotte des Littorines, part of a human lower jaw was recovered,

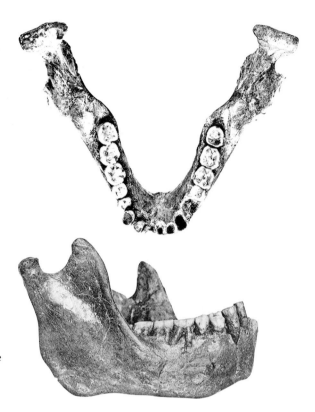

**Fig. 38:** Mandible of *Homo ergaster* from Ternifine (now Tighenif)

**Fig. 39:** Schematic section of deposits exposed in the walls of the Sidi Abderrahman quarry near Casablanca (after McBurney 1960). The figures on the left indicate approximate heights above mean sea level.

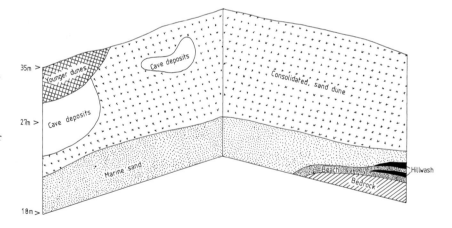

closely similar to somewhat earlier examples from Ternifine in Algeria. Originally attributed to *Homo erectus/ergaster*, these fossils are not now considered to be more than 300,000 years old and are widely regarded as an early modern form retaining some *H. erectus* features (Hublin 1985). Probably somewhat more ancient is a similar mandible from the nearby Thomas quarry

(Sausse 1975), also associated with artefacts of Acheulean type, albeit a sparse occurrence. The final Acheulean assemblages at the Sidi Abderrahman caves include superbly finished handaxes with a twisted, S-shaped profile and also flakes struck from carefully prepared cores. Although none of these coastal sites has yielded any evidence for the exploitation of marine foodstuffs, this does not necessarily mean that such were not used.

To the east, the Libyan coastland has yielded no informative occurrences of Acheulean-type materials; such information as we possess about the Acheulean of Northeast Africa comes from the Nile Valley and its immediate environs. Here there are numerous occurrences in the Wadi Halfa area which may pre-date the Nile's capture of its southern tributaries. Where this material is in an undisturbed context, it appears to represent quarry or tool-making sites rather than settlements (Chmielewski 1968). There is no evidence for the absolute age of this material, nor of that recovered from the alluvial terraces of the Egyptian Nile Valley (J. D. Clark 1980, 1992; Hassan 1980).

## Sangoan assemblages

As noted above, the stone-tool assemblages immediately following the Acheulean over a huge area extending from Botswana to Ethiopia, including also Sudan and West Africa (Fig. 40), are of the type generally designated Sangoan. They are characterised by the crude, pointed, triangular-sectioned core-tools often referred to as picks, thick handaxes or core-axes and a variety of small retouched or utilised flakes (Fig. 41). These components occur in very variable frequencies. The heavy core-tool element is generally dominant at sites which occupy river-valley situations or thickly wooded environments; it is assemblages of this type that have conventionally been designated Sangoan. In more open-plateau situations, notably between the Zambezi and the Limpopo, the light-duty flake-tool element dominates the assemblages, which have been regarded as belonging to a Charaman industry taking its name from an open site in northwestern Zimbabwe. The Sangoan and Charaman are here regarded together as linked facies in a continuum of variation which began in the Acheulean (J. D. Clark 1982a).

Some of the most informative Sangoan occurrences overlie the Acheulean at Kalambo Falls (Sheppard and Kleindienst 1996; J. D. Clark 2001a). Particularly abundant remains of this period also occur in the valley of the Kagera River, west of Lake Victoria, on the modern border between Uganda and Tanzania. All the Kagera material, however, occurs in disturbed river-gravels; East Africa has so far yielded very few undisturbed Sangoan horizons comparable with those at Kalambo Falls. The principal exception is at Muguruk, near the Winam Gulf of southwestern Kenya, where a near-pristine industry

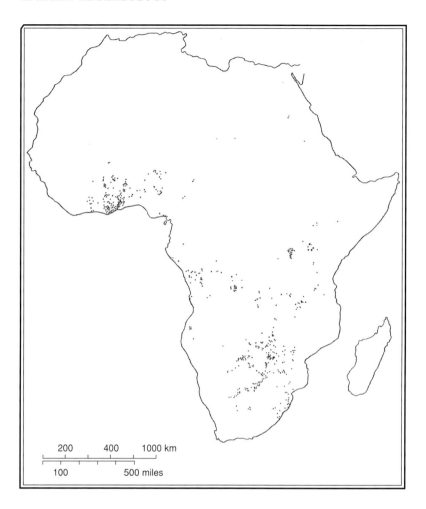

**Fig. 40:** The distribution of principal Sangoan sites

investigated by McBrearty (1988) includes Sangoan-type artefacts in an undated context without associated fauna.

Detailed study of this Sangoan/Charaman material has been hampered by the fact that the only unmixed unsorted assemblages from stratified contexts are either extremely small, like those designated Charaman from the basal horizons of Bambata and Pomongwe caves in the Matopo Hills of Zimbabwe (C. K. Cooke 1963, 1969), or lacking in associated fauna, like the Sangoan from Kalambo Falls (J. D. Clark 1964, 1969, 2001a). Much of this material has an antiquity in excess of 250,000 years, although the possibility that the Zimbabwe occurrences may be more recent cannot be ruled out.

At least the more southerly parts of West Africa appear to fall within the distribution of Sangoan-type artefacts (see p. 81, above) similar to those

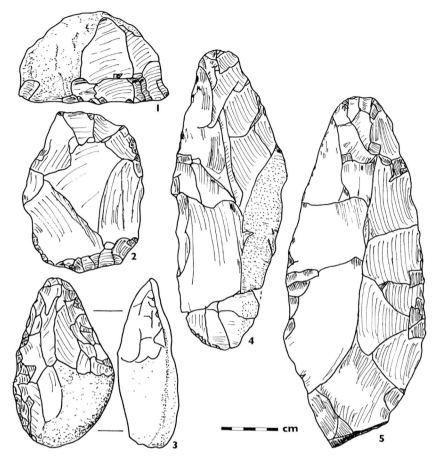

**Fig. 41:** Sangoan artefacts from the Luangwa Valley, Zambia (1–3, after J. D. Clark 1950) and from Kalambo Falls (after J. D. Clark 2001a): 1, core or 'push-plane'; 2, edge-retouched flake; 3, pick; 4, 5, core-axes

found further to the south and east, although certain features serve to differentiate the West African finds from their neighbours. Sangoan artefacts occur at numerous localities in the gravels and terraces of the major rivers of Nigeria and Ghana (especially the Volta) and in the coastal regions of Ghana, where drier conditions would have caused contraction of the forest. With the exception of a few finds near the headwaters of the Gambia River in southern Senegal and Guinea, artefacts of Sangoan type have not been convincingly reported from west of the Ivory Coast; this absence may to some extent reflect the vagaries of research emphasis (Davies 1964, 1967; Wai-Ogusu 1973; Paradis 1980; Chenorkian 1983; Allsworth-Jones 1986, 2001).

It has been argued that some of the typical Sangoan-style tools were used for woodworking, and that the development of the Sangoan was a response to a wetter climate and a resultant spread of forest cover (J. D. Clark 1970).

Although plausible, such an argument rests upon very slender foundations, for we have no direct information about the uses to which individual artefacts were put, and the evidence for a shift to wetter conditions at this time is less convincing than was once believed. The scarcity of single-episode, well-studied assemblages precludes a more detailed consideration of this problem, although related phenomena in several regions of Africa will be discussed below. Unfortunately no comprehensive faunal assemblages come from demonstrably Sangoan or Charaman contexts in this part of Africa, nor are there any associated hominid fossils.

## Acheulean/Sangoan artefacts and their makers

The initial appearance of Acheulean-type artefacts in eastern Africa is, at first sight, puzzling. The former view, based on the sequence at Olduvai Gorge, that there was a demonstrable linear development from Oldowan, into Developed Oldowan, into Early Acheulean, is now disproved stratigraphically and has few adherents. In contrast, some archaeologists have suggested that the first appearance of Acheulean materials at Olduvai may represent an intrusion into the sequence of a different stone-tool-making tradition whose earlier stages had taken place elsewhere. This hypothesis is now supported by the discovery of Acheulean-type artefacts in earlier contexts further to the north, at Konso and West Turkana. Perhaps the most reasonable interpretation of the currently available facts is that the Acheulean, beginning about 1.7 million years ago in what is now Ethiopia, represents the dominant surviving technological tradition which prevailed after a long period which saw accelerated diversification in the physical and cultural evolution of hominids.

In eastern Africa, hominid fossils of this period include at least three species and, according to some classifications, as many as six; the artefacts are similarly varied and include the types which have been named Karari, Developed Oldowan and Early Acheulean (see Fig. 42). It is relevant to consider the extent to which these assemblages represent distinct cultural developments, perhaps being the work of different groups of hominids, rather than variations of a common tradition. Archaeologists are far from agreement concerning the significance of this diversity, but there is increasing support for the view that it may represent diverse facies of a single tradition. The point may be understood by considering the status of the Karari industry (p. 60 above). Isaac (1997) regarded the Karari industry as a variant of the Oldowan; here, by contrast, it is viewed as part of the diverse development which ultimately gave rise to the Acheulean (see also Cachel and Harris 1998). The Karari industry represented a major advance

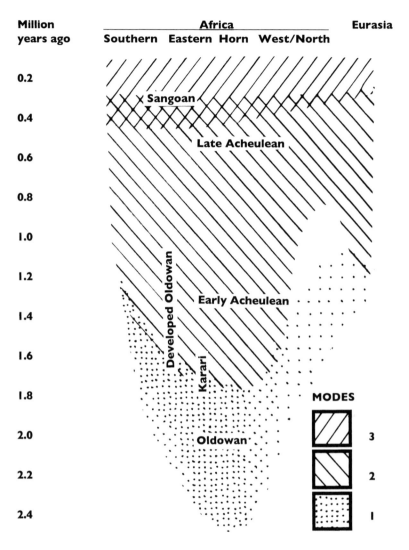

**Fig. 42:** Early traditions of lithic technology in Africa

in tool-making ability as illustrated both by the manual dexterity and control of stone-flaking technique which the artefacts demonstrate, and by its makers' ability to visualise and then to produce a standardised artefact type whose final shape bore little or no resemblance to that of the initial piece of raw material. The Karari industry was but one of several parallel developments which appear in the archaeological record at approximately this time, reflecting a probable period of experimentation and the development of tools specifically intended for particular purposes. This in turn led to the teaching and learning of technological tradition and to the beginnings of standardisation in place of the more random tool-making of earlier times. Such periods of accelerated evolution separated by consolidation and continuity have been recognised as recurrent features of hominid development (cf. Isaac 1972) and, indeed, of most forms of animal evolution. Not infrequently, they may be linked with periods of environmental stress (cf. Vrba *et al.* 1992; Foley 1994; Reed 1997). So far in this book, we have recognised such periods approximately 5.5, 2.8 and 1.7 million years ago (cf. pp. 24 and 27–8, above); it is noteworthy that all appear to have been periods when comparatively cool, dry conditions prevailed (Williams *et al.* 1993; de Menocal 1995). Such conditions seem to have been particularly conducive to accelerated evolution and diversification.

From the middle of Bed II onwards, the Olduvai sequence contains varied assemblages which some archaeologists (e.g. M. D. Leakey 1971) have interpreted as representing two parallel traditions – Developed Oldowan and Acheulean. It is, however, hard to envisage how they could have maintained their separate identities for the enormously long period – about 500,000 years – which this view requires, even if (as some have suggested) they were the work of different hominid species existing at the same time and in the same place. A more economical hypothesis, therefore, is that these assemblages represent different aspects of a single tradition, such as continued also into far more recent times when it was characterised more exclusively by artefacts of Acheulean type (Gowlett 1986). The influence of raw-material availability on this early diversity has not yet been evaluated conclusively. While it has been demonstrated that different types and sizes of rock were used as raw materials for the various Olduvai assemblages, further research is needed to ascertain whether these were deliberately selected or imposed by availability at a particular time and place (cf. Stiles 1991, 1998). A similar situation has been observed in the broadly contemporary Middle Awash sequence, where it has been suggested that mode-1 technology may have been employed for activities undertaken in stable floodplain environments, mode-2 assemblages corresponding to situations beside shifting streams (J. D. Clark *et al.* 1994; J. D. Clark and Schick in de Heinzelin *et al.* 2000). It is only very rarely that the archaeological record yields convincing evidence for the complete replacement of an established technology by an innovation.

In due course, the African Acheulean provided the context for major cultural developments. It is useful to view these against the background of the considerable physical evolution which took place among the hominids that were responsible for the Acheulean artefacts. There can be little reasonable doubt that the earlier African Acheulean, in the wide sense of that term here proposed, was the work of hominids varyingly attributed to African *Homo erectus* or to *H. ergaster* (cf. Wood 1992). As we saw, fossil remains of this type which have been recovered from eastern and South Africa illustrate a relatively large-brained (average around 900 cubic centimetres) hominid with heavy brow ridges and a low cranial vault (Rightmire 1990, 1996; Klein 1999). At Olduvai, it appears that both *H. ergaster* and a robust australopithecine were present at this time, represented by the middle and upper levels of Bed II. If only one hominid type was responsible for the stone industries, this was probably *H. ergaster*. This would accord with evidence for the hominids responsible for the earlier Acheulean in other parts of Africa.

The partial skeleton of *Homo ergaster* from Nariokotome in Kenya suggests that this taxon had developed considerably in build and stature from the presumably ancestral *H. habilis*; only comparatively minor differences in the postcranial skeleton are apparent between *H. ergaster* and modern humans. Few anthropologists would now disagree that *H. sapiens* evolved from *H. ergaster/erectus* during the long Middle Pleistocene time-span represented in the archaeological record by the later Acheulean industries. Prior to about 700,000 years ago, no hominid more advanced than *H. ergaster/erectus* is attested anywhere in the world. Later Acheulean industries in several parts of Africa and Europe are associated with a distinct grade of hominid which some specialists have designated *H. heidelbergensis*, while others prefer the less formal 'archaic *H. sapiens*'. Particularly informative African examples of this taxon come from Bodo in Ethiopia, Lake Ndutu in Tanzania, Broken Hill mine in Zambia, and Hopefield in South Africa; specimens from Morocco should probably also be included.

It is tempting to see this division in hominid associations reflected in the artefact typology. Early attempts to recognise numerous successive stages of increasing refinement of handaxe production, as at Olduvai (L. S. B. Leakey 1951) and in the Vaal River gravels (van Riet Lowe 1952), are not supported by recent evidence; in fact, it is becoming increasingly apparent that only two basic stages may be recognised: an earlier Acheulean with thick, minimally trimmed bifaces, and a later Acheulean with more varied, thin, elaborately flaked examples (Roe in J. D. Clark 2001a). Much of the typological variation observed between Acheulean assemblages is perhaps better attributed to differences in raw-material availability than to cultural tradition. These considerations lead to the proposition that, in addition to the burst of accelerated evolution 1.7–1.5 million years ago which resulted in the emergence and subsequent expansion of *Homo ergaster* and the Acheulean, there may have been an analogous if less visible event around 0.8 million years ago which saw the relatively rapid transition to *H. heidelbergensis* and the later Acheulean.

The extent of such few undisturbed sites as have been preserved and fully investigated suggests that population groups may have numbered between twenty and fifty individuals. As in earlier times, these sites, which seem often to have had more intensive or long-lasting use than had those of their Oldowan counterparts, were supplemented by sites used for specific activities such as butchery or tool manufacture. It is noteworthy that remains of the not-readily-transportable elephant are more frequently encountered on butchery sites than at base-camps, including those in caves (Shackley 1985). The preservation of evidence for hunting and/or scavenging almost certainly tends to overemphasise the importance of meat in the Acheulean diet at the expense of grubs, insects or vegetable foods, traces of which have rarely survived. (It is necessary once again to emphasise that animal bones from archaeological sites do not necessarily represent the remains of food.) When meat was demonstrably eaten, it is often impossible to distinguish between kills and carrion although, where many carcasses of a single species occur together, as at Olorgesailie and at Olduvai, several individuals may have hunted together in a group. Such a level of organisation implies that the hominids responsible had developed some capacity for planning and communication, as is further discussed below (pp. 89–90). Thereafter, the individuals who were most successful, in the evolutionary sense, were those with the greater communicative and co-operative skills. It is in these cultural and cognitive fields, rather than in the basic stone-tool-making technology, that we can most readily appreciate the progress which took place during the Acheulean time-span.

Indications of the way handaxes were made, held and used show a level of dexterity analogous to that of modern people (L. Phillipson 1997). The hominids' slim, elongated build was adapted to an upright, fully bipedal life-style. The comparatively narrow hips suggest that the trend towards difficult childbirth and long post-natal maturation had already begun; this may have resulted in greater male involvement in caring for mother and child. Taken as a group, fossils attributed to *H. ergaster* show a much smaller degree of sexual dimorphism than do those of any earlier hominid taxon; this has been interpreted as indicating that males' ongoing competition for mates was being replaced by long-term pairing. Prolonged infantile dependence would have been accompanied by increased educational and intergenerational socialising and teaching opportunities, resulting in strengthened cultural and behavioural tradition. If these interpretations are correct, then the arrival of *H. ergaster* and the Acheulean represents a major advance in human physical and cultural evolution. It has been argued above that these events in North Africa took place very much later than they did in the east and south.

The progressive standardisation and elaboration of tool types and processes of manufacture observed in later Acheulean assemblages may also be interpreted as a further indication that their makers were becoming increasingly able to talk to one another. This development may be linked neurologically to preferential right-handedness (Isaac 1976; Ludwig and Harris 1998), which is demonstrable by this time (Toth 1985b; L. Phillipson 1997). Cranial asymmetry, also discernible in *Homo heidelbergensis* but only controversially in earlier hominids, is an osteological manifestation of these developments (Tobias 1991). Much discussion of this topic has been marred by the tendency to regard language development as a single event rather than a prolonged multi-stage process (but see Aiello 1996; Jablonski and Aiello 1998). The extraordinary and, in functional terms, probably unnecessarily fine finish of some handaxes suggests the existence of basically aesthetic standards, in turn implying that cultural values now extended into non-utilitarian spheres (L. Phillipson pers. comm.; Kohn and Mithen 1999). Later Acheulean people may thus be seen as having taken substantial steps towards modern human culture (Butzer and Isaac 1975; Gowlett 1986; Mellars and Gibson 1996).

By later Acheulean times, people eventually spread to most parts of Africa except those most densely forested and the highest mountain ranges; their sites were almost invariably located beside or within easy reach of water; there is now evidence that caves were occasionally occupied. Although the evidence is inconclusive, controlled use of fire may have been achieved by late Acheulean tool-makers (Gowlett *et al.* 1981; J. D. Clark and Harris 1985).

As noted above, Acheulean sites seem generally to have been located in places with easy access to open water; this correlation is probably not due solely to factors of preservation. Studies of the few South African sites where faunal remains have been preserved in association with Acheulean artefacts and which are, by implication, comparatively late suggest that the climate was generally wetter than that which has prevailed in more recent times (Klein 1988) or indeed that indicated at the time the tradition initially appeared. Taken together, these observations raise the possibility of fluctuating population dispersal, with more restricted settlement during drier periods. In areas such as the Sahara and southwesternmost Africa, this could have had a major effect on the extent of Acheulean penetration at certain times.

Despite this restriction, it is clear that, in comparison with their predecessors, Acheulean hominids possessed a progressively improved capacity for planning as they learned, perhaps from waterside bases, to exploit their environment over a wider area and in a more comprehensive fashion (Gowlett 1996). Hominid settlement extended to higher altitudes, some 2300 metres above sea level, as in the Ethiopian and Lesotho highlands; this may be an indication that clothing was coming into use. The probable concomitant invention of receptacles for carrying, for which independent evidence has been cited above, would have had far-reaching implications for hominids' mobility, adaptiveness, range of material culture and, most important, forward-planning ability so as to keep things for use at some future time.

Although much change may still remain undetected by archaeologists, there is enough to suggest that the conservative nature and apparent uniformity suggested by initial impressions of Acheulean-type artefacts may be misleading. None the less, in purely technological terms, the artefacts provide testimony for the strength of a cultural tradition which developed about 1.6 million years ago and was maintained for about 1.25 million years, even if we may question the conclusion that their makers were 'not only extremely conservative . . . but they appear to have been relatively rare and inconspicuous members of the ancient large mammal community' (Klein 2000b: 107).

# 4

# Regional diversification and specialisation

## The 'Middle Stone Age' and the 'Late Stone Age'

Developments throughout Africa from rather more than 250,000 until about 10,000 years ago show an accelerated shift away from broad cultural uniformities towards the establishment of increasingly distinct regional traditions. These trends may most readily be traced in the archaeological record by study of stone-artefact typology; but it is sometimes possible to go beyond such investigations in an attempt to illuminate the nature of the ancient societies which, to an increasing extent, may be seen as ancestral to recent African populations. Despite this growing diversity, developments seem to have followed roughly parallel courses with inherent continuity in different parts of Africa and, indeed, in other regions of the Old World (J. G. D. Clark 1977). The reasons for this are not yet fully understood, and the various stages were not necessarily reached at the same time in different areas. In recent years, the study of the earlier part of this period has received increased international attention because of the realisation that it may have been particularly important in the physical and cultural development of modern people.

The period with which this chapter is concerned has conventionally been divided by archaeologists of sub-Saharan Africa into the 'Middle Stone Age' and the 'Late Stone Age'. As research has progressed, it has become apparent that there was no sharp divide between these, any more than there was between industries of the so-called Middle Stone Age and their predecessors; the distinctions have become increasingly hard to define on other than arbitrary grounds. It is now recognised that there was a much stronger degree of continuity between them than was previously believed. It should be emphasised that, as with the Acheulean and the Sangoan, the named stone-tool industries described here are not always clearly defined. Prehistorians have often attempted to recognise compartments in what were really continuous ranges of variation through both time and space, as has been emphasised above (pp. 15–20). A related problem has arisen from the tendency of some archaeologists, particularly those working in northern parts of Africa, to present their discoveries in terms of concepts previously adopted beyond the Mediterranean.

Recent research has also demonstrated that this period of African prehistory, like many others, covered a far longer time-span than was formerly believed. Much of it lies beyond the range of radiocarbon dating and it is now recognised that many such age determinations of 40,000 years or more are in fact minimum rather than absolute dates. Several absolute dating methods are becoming available for earlier times; most remain experimental and their preliminary results should be regarded as tentative (Klein 1999; Schwarcz 2001).

Broadly speaking, the industries formerly designated 'Middle Stone Age' display a stone-tool-making technology derived from that illustrated by final Acheulean and/or Sangoan artefacts, being often based upon elaborations (eventually with reduced size) of a prepared-core technique (pp. 57–8 above). The division between chapters 3 and 4 of this book is thus to some extent arbitrary. In due course, small radially flaked plano-convex cores became the norm, providing more economical use of raw material but losing some benefits of intentional preparation: these artefacts are here referred to as radial cores. This is the mode-3 technology of J. G. D. Clark (1969), and was marked in several regions of Africa by the production of parallel-sided flakes, or blades, some of which were subsequently trimmed into a variety of standardised forms. So-called 'Late Stone Age' industries generally show a further reduction in artefact size, and the resultant tiny tools (microliths) were often fitted into handles, several sometimes being used together to form a composite tool. This innovation, which characterises Clark's mode-5 technology, arose in sub-Saharan Africa in a mode-3 context; it involved devising a new way of steeply trimming the edges of flakes or blades in order to blunt them, so that they did not split their hafts or cut their users' fingers. This blunting retouch, known as backing, also served to provide a key for the mastic that was used to hold the stone inserts in place in their hafts. Studies of edge-wear and mastic remains have provided some indications of the various ways in which such artefacts may have been used (L. and D. W. Phillipson 1970; D. W. Phillipson 1976; Wadley and Binneman 1995); and in rare instances complete hafted specimens have survived, as in certain South African caves (J. D. Clark 1958; H. J. Deacon 1966) and at Columnata in Algeria (Cadénat and Tixier 1960). It is highly probable that some backed microliths were used as tips and/or barbs for arrows which are first indicated in the archaeological record around this time. Ancient Egyptian specimens (J. D. Clark *et al.* 1974) are also informative in this connexion (Fig. 43). Use of the bow and arrow, especially with poison applied to the latter, would have revolutionised hunting.

In North Africa, including the Sahara and the Nile Valley, archaeologists have conventionally referred to lithic industries using terminology akin to those used in Europe or the Levant (see Kleindienst 2001). Mode-3 industries have here been frequently designated 'Middle Palaeolithic', and mode-5 ones 'Epipalaeolithic' or 'Mesolithic'. In some of these areas there also occur

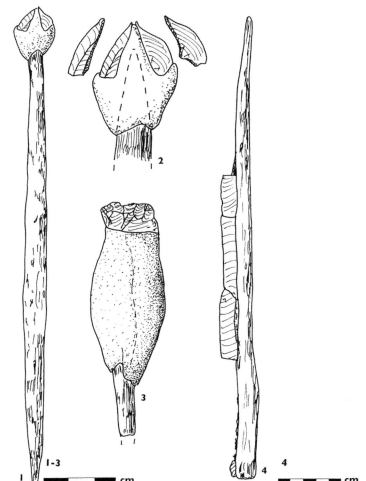

**Fig. 43:** Mounted microliths: 1, 2, composite arrow-point of microliths set in mastic; 3, retouched flake set in mastic, from Plettenberg Bay, South Africa (nos. 1–3 after Sampson 1974); 4, wooden handle with mounted backed bladelets, from Fayum, Egypt (after Caton-Thompson and Gardner 1934)

industries which belong to J. G. D. Clark's mode 4, based upon the production of long parallel-sided blades struck from prismatic cores by means of punches; the term 'Upper Palaeolithic' has sometimes been applied to these North African industries, as it usually is to their European counterparts. The apparent idiosyncrasy of these industries in an African context may be due largely to the fine isotropic materials from which they were made, stone with similar qualities being comparatively rare in more southerly parts of the continent.

Throughout the period covered by this chapter, people in Africa remained hunters and gatherers, obtaining their food from wild sources. Their material culture became more elaborate, with regional specialisations increasingly apparent – tendencies which may be attributed, at least in part, to their progressive mastery of the natural environment and to their development of more efficient methods of exploiting the wild sources of food which it supplied. Different situations offered varying potential, and distinct technologies were developed to utilise these, with parallel trends in conceptualisation and communication abilities. Despite increasing inter-regional diversification, it will be seen that technological development followed broadly parallel (but not necessarily contemporaneous) courses in different parts of Africa. Chapters 5 and 6 will discuss how, in regions north of the equator, the later makers of mode-5 microlithic industries eventually adopted the food-producing economies which formed the basis for future developments throughout the continent.

Changing environments at this time are being increasingly studied both on a long-term, continental scale (Hamilton and Taylor 1991) and in greater local detail (cf. Gamble and Soffer 1990; Hassan 2002). Useful summaries are available for North Africa and the Sahara (Vernet 1995), West Africa (Dupont *et al.* 2000), eastern and equatorial regions (Elenga *et al.* 1994; Bonnefille *et al.* 1995; de Busk 1998), and southern Africa (J. Deacon and Lancaster 1988; Stokes *et al.* 1998; Tyson 1999; D. S. G. Thomas *et al.* 2000). The general picture that emerges is one of numerous minor fluctuations around a general trend of reduced temperature and increased aridity corresponding to the last glacial period, beginning around 60,000 years ago and reaching its maximum about 18,000 years ago, with comparatively rapid amelioration thereafter. Such periods of cool aridity were marked by increased severity and extent of desertification in both northern and southern Africa, and by marked reductions in the areas covered by equatorial forest, with corresponding shifts in the disposition of intervening isohyets and vegetational zones (Bonnefille 1999). It is probable, although detailed evidence remains incomplete, that broadly comparable changes took place in earlier times also. Coastal regions saw major changes in sea level, which dropped during glacial periods, exposing extensive coastal plains in some areas, notably the southernmost coast of South Africa.

The precise identity of the hominids responsible for the first post-Acheulean industries remains obscure. It is clear, in general terms, that they belonged to archaic representatives of *Homo sapiens* more advanced than those designated *H. heidelbergensis* discussed in chapter 3. It has been estimated that this differentiation may have occurred within the period between 350,000 and 250,000 years ago (Bräuer *et al.* 1997). There are, perhaps surprisingly, far fewer well-preserved and adequately documented human fossils from African contexts of this period than there are from late Pliocene and early Pleistocene times. Particular interest thus attaches to specimens (discussed below) from the Middle Awash, Omo-Kibish in southern Ethiopia, Singa in eastern Sudan, and Florisbad in the Free State Province of South Africa, despite uncertainties concerning their archaeological associations and, in some cases, their dating. Sites in southernmost Africa are more comprehensively understood but their hominid fossils are mostly fragmentary. For more recent periods the picture is somewhat clearer: mode-5 industries throughout Africa appear to have been the work of people who were fully modern anatomically. Far more human skeletons have been recovered from sites of the last 20,000 years than are available for earlier periods; it is sometimes possible to make very tentative attempts at recognising the ancestors of some of Africa's recent populations, as is explained in chapter 5.

This general period has become one of major interest and controversy because studies of both mitochondrial and nuclear DNA in modern human populations world-wide seem to indicate that all of them are descended from a single ancestor or a small ancestral population that may have lived in Africa about 500,000–100,000 years ago (Cann *et al.* 1987; Mountain *et al.* 1993; Stringer and McKie 1996). This genetic research is still at a relatively early stage; the data are, however, increasing rapidly. Much controversy has arisen from uncertainty over the speed of change in mitochondrial DNA and, in particular, whether this takes place at a more-or-less constant rate. It is, however, indisputable that all modern human populations, despite their geographical and cultural diversity, are extremely similar genetically – far more so, indeed, than other primates whose distributions are in every case far more restricted (Ruvulo *et al.* 1993). It was originally suggested by Cann and her colleagues (1987) that the African common ancestor of modern humans had lived in the general period 280,000–140,000 years ago which, according to current interpretations, would correspond with immediately post-Acheulean developments. This estimate was later expanded to 500,000–50,000 years ago (Stoneking and Cann 1989), while others (e.g. Wolpoff 1989) argued for an age closer to 1.0 million years, which would imply that the common ancestor was *Homo ergaster* or *H. erectus*, not *H. sapiens* at all.

More recently, the controversy has focussed particularly on its implications in the prehistory of Europe for the relationship between Neanderthals and the modern people who replaced them there rather less than 50,000 years ago (Mellars 1993). This has led to the assumption that modern behaviour originated world-wide at about that time (e.g. Klein 1999, 2000a). This proposal, of breathtaking Eurocentricity, effectively ignores the African evidence which it is one of the aims of this chapter to evaluate. Some degree of support for the original hypothesis, that modern people originated in Africa some 280,000–140,000 years ago, is provided by skeletal material discovered at several African sites, notably but not exclusively in South Africa, which – as will be shown below – suggests that such persons were indeed living in that part of the continent more than 100,000 years ago, as was first pointed out by Beaumont *et al.* in 1978 (see pp. 98–102 below).

With increasing emphasis on the anatomical and genetic homogeneity of modern human populations, many authorities have abandoned their attempts to retain the Linnaean classificatory system, and refer simply to 'anatomically modern people'. This has given rise to the search for elements of behaviour and culture which may be deemed equally 'modern' or, at least, may be correlated exclusively with 'anatomically modern people' (Klein 1995). If, as most now agree, anatomical modernity first arose in Africa (albeit at a date significantly earlier than that for which many have recently argued), it is reasonable to seek the beginnings of cultural modernity in that continent also. The regional evidence for these long, gradual and complex processes will be evaluated below, with an attempted synthesis at the end of the chapter (pp. 141–6).

With the passage of time, human culture became more complex, and its archaeological remains are consequently more varied as well as more abundant. Furthermore, as people developed life-styles closer in many ways to our own, the surviving traces of their activities are easier for us to interpret. The thought-processes and beliefs that lie behind these activities may, for these more recent periods, occasionally be illustrated in the archaeological record through the investigation of such cultural manifestations as graves, settlement layout or rock art. Such clues will be touched upon at appropriate places in the regional survey which follows.

## Southern Africa

It is convenient to begin this survey in southern Africa where there has been a greater amount of recent high-quality archaeological research on this general period than in most other parts of the continent. Not only is the prehistoric sequence there relatively well known (although many striking gaps in our knowledge remain), but there are indications that the major cultural developments of this period seem to have taken place there at least as early as did their counterparts elsewhere in the continent or, indeed, in other parts of the world. Much of the research that will be described has been undertaken very recently, and most has been published only in a series of preliminary reports. Environmental circumstances have been summarised by J. Deacon and Lancaster (1988).

Most of southern Africa lies outside the area where Sangoan industries are generally recognised, and the end of the local Acheulean is particularly ill-defined. There is, regrettably, no site which provides evidence for the change from the Acheulean to its immediate successors, such as is available further to the north at Kalambo Falls (p. 120 below). At those rare places, such as the Cave of Hearths near Mokopane (Mason 1962), Wonderwerk near Kuruman (Beaumont 1990) or Montagu Cave in Western Cape Province (Keller 1973), where Acheulean deposits are overlain by later material, a long gap is apparent between the two phases. The date of the first post-Acheulean assemblages is also uncertain, although it is now clear that such material has a far greater antiquity in South Africa than was, until the 1980s, considered likely.

Some of the earliest relevant material comes from springs at Florisbad, 40 kilometres northwest of Bloemfontein in Free State Province, which were frequented over a long period, resulting in a succession of open-air occupation horizons on some of which distinct activity-areas can be recognised (Kuman and Clarke 1986; Kuman *et al.* 1999; Bamford and Henderson 2003). A human skull discovered in the early 1930s cannot, unfortunately, be located precisely within this sequence but direct dating of the specimen suggests that it may be about 250,000 years old (Clarke 1985; Grün *et al.* 1996). Although its brow ridges are significantly less pronounced than those of the Broken Hill specimen (see p. 72), it retains a number of archaic features and is best regarded as intermediate between *Homo heidelbergensis* and *H. sapiens* (Foley and Lahr 1997), perhaps following the trend claimed for the Hopefield/Elandsfontein hominid noted above (pp. 73–4). If this intermediate form requires attribution to a separate species, the designation *H. helmei* has priority (Dreyer 1935; cf. Lahr and Foley 2001). Faunal remains suggest that the Florisbad sequence may have continued, presumably intermittently, for more than 100,000 years, but it has not proved possible to demonstrate significant change in the associated stone industries, which are of mode-3 type throughout. Worked wood is also preserved.

At Border Cave in northernmost KwaZulu-Natal, on the frontier with Swaziland, the post-Acheulean sequence extends back more than 200,000 years (Beaumont 1973; Butzer *et al.* 1978; Grün and Beaumont 2001). No comprehensive account of the Border Cave investigations has yet been published, but preliminary accounts imply that the oldest industry at this site was based on the production of parallel-sided flake-blades from prepared cores. It was succeeded by an occupation represented by artefacts, originally described as 'Epi-Pietersburg', which appear to be analogous to those of the broadly contemporary Howieson's Poort industry, discussed below (p. 100). A later mode-3 industry is tentatively dated between 60,000 and 40,000 years ago. Published accounts indicate that, by about 38,000 years ago, an industry originally designated 'Early Late Stone Age' was being produced at Border Cave. It is characterised by the frequent use of small bipolar cores and by the rarity of formally retouched tools; backed microliths are absent. Particular interest attaches to the fossil human remains (Beaumont *et al.* 1978; Rightmire 1979a; Beaumont 1980; Grün and Beaumont 2001), which attest

**Fig. 44:** The Klasies River Mouth sites, seen from the east prior to excavation in 1967–68

the presence of 'anatomically modern people' since pre-Howieson's Poort times.

At Klasies River Mouth on the south coast, 40 kilometres west of Cape St Francis, several dating methods combine to indicate that the earliest occupation took place at least 120,000 years ago (Singer and Wymer 1982; H. J. Deacon and Geleijnse 1988; Thackeray 1989; H. J. Deacon 1989, 1995), during the Last Interglacial period when the sea stood approximately 6–8 metres above its present level. The remarkable sequence of industries at this site, supplemented, where necessary, with evidence from other sites on the south Cape coast, may be used as a framework for an account of the stone-tool industries of southernmost Africa during the past 120,000 or more years.

Investigation of the cave complex at Klasies River Mouth (Fig. 44) has revealed archaeological deposits more than 18 metres in total depth, ranging in age from about 120,000 years to 1000 years ago. The earliest industry, retaining no trace of Acheulean technology, was of mode-3 type; this tradition continued through the greater part of the sequence, parallel-sided and pointed flake-blades being produced from the local quartzite beach-cobbles (Thackeray and Kelly 1988). A small proportion of these pointed flake-blades was retouched unifacially and may, along with unretouched specimens, have been hafted for use as spearpoints. On a number of examples the bulb of percussion was flaked away, as if to make hafting easier; other retouched

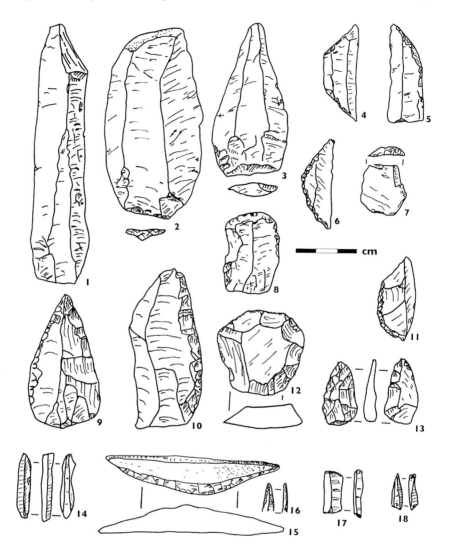

**Fig. 45:** Artefacts from Klasies River Mouth (after Singer and Wymer 1982): 1–4, from the lowest horizon; 5–8, from the Howieson's Poort industry. Artefacts of the Bambata and Tshangula industries (after Sampson 1974): 9, 10, Bambata-type industry from the Cave of Hearths; 11–13, Tshangula industry from Pomongwe; 14–18, artefacts of the Robberg industry from Sehonghong (after Mitchell 2002)

tools included the edge-retouched pieces conventionally known as 'scrapers' (Fig. 45). This stone industry continued, with one notable interruption which will be described below, for perhaps as much as 80,000 years. Throughout this period, both terrestrial and marine creatures were exploited for food, although there is little if any evidence for fishing as opposed to shellfish-collecting. Initially, large land animals such as eland and buffalo dominate the associated faunal remains, suggesting a mixed forest–grassland environment. There has been controversy over the extent to which these remains represent the prey of hunters rather than scavengers (Binford 1984; Milo 1998); opinion now favours the former, supported by the discovery of the tip of a stone point embedded in the vertebra of a giant buffalo. Later, somewhat colder conditions are attested both by the changed representation of shellfish species and by the increased numbers of bones from the smaller antelope. Eventually, the sea fell below its present level, so that the caves overlooked broad coastal plains, now again inundated. Subsequently there was a prolonged period when the Klasies River Mouth sites were only rarely visited, lasting until they were re-occupied about 3000 years ago.

One archaeological phase at Klasies River Mouth which marks a pronounced discontinuity in the development of the mode-3 industry has been the focus of much research, speculation and controversy. A markedly distinct stone industry was then produced, of a type known at several other southern African localities – including Border Cave – and named after the site of Howieson's Poort near Grahamstown (J. Deacon 1995). Its age has been disputed, but most scholars now place it around 70,000 years ago (H. J. Deacon 1995, 1998). This corresponds with a period of falling sea level at the end of the Last Interglacial, when the exposure of extensive coastal plains may have brought significantly different environmental conditions and food resources within the range of the site's inhabitants. The Howieson's Poort industry has large numbers of small blades, mostly 2–4 centimetres long and often trimmed by steep backing into crescentic or trapezoidal forms anticipating, by tens of thousands of years, the significantly smaller mode-5 implements of more recent millennia. Small edge-retouched and notched pieces are also represented. The local quartzite was mostly unsuitable for making such small delicate tools, and finer-grained materials were carefully sought and collected. Not surprisingly, the makers of the Howieson's Poort industry appear to have hunted more of the smaller antelope, such as the steenbok, than had their heavily armed predecessors. Seafood was still collected, although the shoreline was probably some distance away. H. J. Deacon (1989) regarded the Howieson's Poort as 'a distinct substage of the Middle Stone Age . . . confined to areas south of the Zambezi', although a similar phenomenon has subsequently been indicated at Mumba in northern Tanzania (p. 127 below) and may be present elsewhere in the intervening regions. This interlude was clearly an integral element in the economic and technological diversification of the period, but much controversy surrounds its detailed interpretation (e.g. Wurz 1999); many of the proposed interpretations fail to address the clear similarity in technology if not in size with much later mode-5 industries. The available dating evidence is as yet insufficient to support the widespread assumption (e.g. H. J. and J. Deacon 1999) that all Howieson's Poort occurrences are contemporaneous. After the Howieson's Poort interlude, Klasies River Mouth was re-occupied, albeit less intensively, by people whose mode-3 stone industry was remarkably similar to that of the initial occupation.

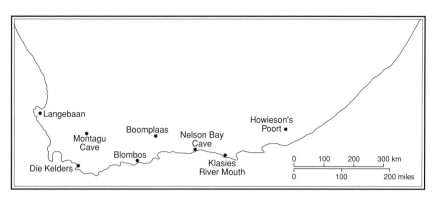

**Fig. 46:** The principal archaeological sites in southern-most Africa which have yielded mode-3 and related materials

The South African Howieson's Poort is probably the earliest industry yet known anywhere in the world to be dominated by mode-5 technology. Parallel technological developments took place in several regions of Africa in later times when, in most cases, the artefacts were significantly smaller. Possible explanations for these phenomena are discussed in a later section of this chapter (pp. 141–6).

Fragmentary human fossils recovered from Klasies River Mouth in association with the mode-3 industries (Rightmire 1978; Rightmire and Deacon 1991; H. J. Deacon and Schuurman 1992) are attributed to 'anatomically modern people'. All the specimens are small fragments, and it has been suggested that this may be due to the practice of cannibalism (White 1987). Unfortunately, a few isolated teeth are the only human remains that have been recovered from the Howieson's Poort horizon. The excavations at Klasies River Mouth have provided important information on hunting strategy, with its emphasis on the young of certain species, notably buffalo (Klein 1978). The extent to which vegetable foods were exploited at this time remains to be demonstrated.

Further sites in southernmost Africa (Fig. 46) add to the data provided by the Klasies River Mouth research (Thackeray 1992; H. J. and J. Deacon 1999; Mitchell 2002). One of the most informative is Die Kelders (Thackeray 2000; Grine 2000; Feathers and Bush 2000). Human footprints at Langebaan, on the west coast north of Cape Town, are broadly contemporary with the initial occupation of Klasies River Mouth (Roberts and Berger 1997). At Mossel Bay in Western Cape Province (Keller 1969), the evidence of early excavations demonstrates a sequence parallel to that at Klasies River Mouth some 200 kilometres to the east. Between them, Nelson Bay Cave at Plettenberg Bay (Klein 1974; J. Deacon 1978) preserves a mode-3 industry overlain, after a gap in occupation, by successive occurrences of the industries designated Robberg and Albany (dated respectively 19,000–12,000 and 12,000–8000 years ago) which are further described below. More recently, excavations in

**Fig. 47:** Ochre with engraved lines, from Blombos Cave

a coastal cave at Blombos near Mossel Bay have attracted much attention (Henshilwood *et al.* 2001a): a sequence of mode-3 industries extends back before 100,000 years ago, associated with fragmentary human remains which are described as anatomically modern (Grine *et al.* 2000; Grine and Henshilwood 2002). The significance of simple bone tools and of worked ochre fragments from this site (Fig. 47), dated before 70,000 years ago (Henshilwood and Sealy 1997; Henshilwood *et al.* 2001b, 2002; d'Errico *et al.* 2001), has been exaggerated, as will be discussed below (pp. 143–5). Inland, at Boomplaas Cave in the Cape Folded Mountains, a similar sequence shows Robberg and Albany industries overlying a long succession of blade-based occurrences which have not yet been described in detail but which include a Howieson's Poort horizon towards the base of the finely stratified deposits (H. J. Deacon 1979, 1989, 1995).

It seems that mode-3 technology based upon the production of flake-blades, such as is present in the earliest levels at Klasies River Mouth, was a fairly early post-Acheulean development in several parts of South Africa (Volman 1984). In the north, such industries, known as Pietersburg after the town now renamed Polokwane, are best seen in the long sequence at the Cave of Hearths (Fig. 45). Here, Pietersburg material overlies that attributed to the final Acheulean but, as noted above, the two assemblages are separated by a thick sterile deposit representing a period of unknown duration when the site was unoccupied (Mason 1962). The Pietersburg industry is typified by large numbers of long, parallel-sided flake-blades, often with trimming or use-wear along their edges. Disc-cores and triangular points are both relatively rare. Similar assemblages come from a number of sites in the Free State and Northern Cape Provinces, where the artefacts' morphology was influenced by the preferred raw material – lydianite – that was obtained in large quantities at several outcrops in the middle Gariep Basin and transported over a wide area. It is noteworthy that the latest

**Fig. 48:** Sibudu
Cave

Acheulean assemblages from the Cave of Hearths show a tendency towards
the production of elongated flake-blades; and the Pietersburg may thus represent a local development from an Acheulean ancestor between the Vaal
and Limpopo rivers. Industries of Pietersburg type seem to have continued
in use for tens of thousands of years; the greater part of this material lies
beyond the range of radiocarbon dating (Thackeray 1992).

Rose Cottage Cave near Ladybrand in Free State Province provides the best
view of later developments in this part of the South African interior (Wadley
1996, 1997, 2001a; Harper 1997; Ouzman and Wadley 1997; A. M. B. Clark
1997, 1999). Stratified deposits, containing abundant organic materials, are
preserved to a depth of 6 metres and are thought to have accumulated over a
period in excess of 100,000 years. The Rose Cottage sequence may, in general
terms, be seen as a continuation of that at Florisbad. A definitive account is
awaited, but it is clear that Rose Cottage Cave contains a long succession of
mode-3 industries ending about 28,000 years ago, with a Howieson's Poort
interlude not sharply defined and as yet undated. Stylistic change in the
lithic artefacts seems to have accelerated markedly after about 30,000 years
ago.

In KwaZulu-Natal, Sibudu Cave (Fig. 48) on the Tongati River has revealed a
sequence contemporary with the mode-3 succession at Rose Cottage (Wadley

2001b). There was no later occupation characterised by mode-5 artefacts, and human use of the site seems to have ceased around 35,000 years ago. Radiocarbon dates extend through the last 10,000 years of occupation, but the lower levels are as yet undated. Unifacial and bifacial points, some with concave bases, are characteristic. Although there are occasional backed-blade forms akin to those of the Howieson's Poort, no horizon with concentrations of such artefacts has yet been recognised at Sibudu.

The archaeology of this period in the now-arid Kalahari regions of the southern African interior remains poorly known (Lane *et al.* 1998; but see Helgren and Brooks 1983). Little is known about the archaeology of Namibia between the final Acheulean and the appearance of mode-5 industries, other than in the southwest (Vogelsang 1996, 1998). Surface occurrences suggest the presence of industries of Pietersburg and Lupemban (pp. 117–20) types (MacCalman 1963; MacCalman and Viereck 1967). The only long excavated succession is in the extreme south of the country at the 'Apollo 11 Cave', where a mode-3 sequence underlies an industry of about 12,000 years ago with many large edge-trimmed flakes (Wendt 1972, 1976). As will be shown below, this site is of particular importance because it has evidence for rock art at a very early date.

In several areas of South Africa it appears that industries based on flake-blades were followed by assemblages with sub-triangular points and other edge-retouched pieces made on flakes removed from radial cores, bearing some resemblance to the Bambata material from Zimbabwe, discussed below. The sequence in the north is well seen at two sites near Mokopane: the Cave of Hearths (Sampson 1974) and Mwulu's Cave (Tobias 1949). Broadly similar industries are recorded in the Western Cape, but they are from poorly documented contexts and their position in the general sequence of mode-3 industries is unclear; possibly they belong to the period between about 40,000 and 20,000 years ago, when sites such as Nelson Bay Cave and Klasies River Mouth were unoccupied.

It is in the context of these late blade-based mode-3 industries that the local origins of the mode-5 backed-microlith technological tradition must be sought. As in other parts of Africa, recent research has shown that the process involved was generally one of gradual transition without a clearly defined interface, except in the case of the Howieson's Poort industry, discussed above. Blade-based occurrences are reported from rockshelters in the mountains of Lesotho, at Ha Soloja, Sehonghong and Moshebi's, dating from more than 43,000 until about 30,000 years ago (Carter and Vogel 1974; Carter *et al.* 1988; Mitchell 1988, 1994, 1996). The blades show a progressive diminution in size, and backed retouch is clearly attested. Clearly, the role played by this cold high-altitude region in the development of southern African mode-5 industries requires further investigation. To the south, Strathalan Cave near Maclear has preserved what is described as a transitional (mode 3–mode 5) industry dating to about 22,000 years ago, associated with well-preserved plant materials (Opperman and Heydenrych 1990).

There are indications from Botswana that mode-5 technology may have begun there considerably more than 25,000 years ago. Many areas may have been uninhabited during the hyper-arid interlude around 18,000 years ago, except around the Tsodilo Hills and the Okavango Delta. Surface water remained at Tsodilo long afterwards (Brook *et al.* 1992), where it sustained a local fishing adaptation based on the use of barbed bone points (Robbins *et al.* 1994, 2000; see also p. 145 below).

Broadly contemporary is the Robberg industry of southernmost South Africa, dated between 19,000 and 12,000 years ago at sites such as Nelson Bay Cave (Klein 1974; J. Deacon 1978) and Boomplaas (H. J. Deacon 1979), and comprising many tiny bladelets with few standardised retouched tools (Wadley 1993; Binneman and Mitchell 1997). Its makers, like their predecessors, hunted the grassland fauna of the coastal plains. Similar microlithic industries are now known from more northerly areas, as in Lesotho (Mitchell 1988) and at Bushman Rock in Mpumalanga (Beaumont and Vogel 1972).

Between about 12,000 and 8000 years ago several sites widely dispersed across southern Africa show occupation by makers of poorly understood industries with many large edge-retouched flakes but virtually no microliths or backed pieces (Fig. 45). Although regional variants may be recognised, these industries are conveniently grouped together as the Oakhurst Complex (Sampson 1974; Mitchell 2002). At Nelson Bay Cave the abrupt change from the Robberg to the Oakhurst Complex (here represented by the Albany industry) appears to have coincided with the rise of sea level to its maximum post-glacial height, with a corresponding change in faunal availability (J. Deacon 1984).

The early appearance and development of southern African mode-5 industries is particularly problematic. Their oldest attestation is in the Howieson's Poort horizons at Klasies River Mouth and, probably, Border Cave, now dated about 70,000 years ago. In the southeastern highland areas there is evidence for continuous occupation by makers of industries comprising small blades with backed retouch for most of the last 45,000 years and perhaps longer. By 30,000 years ago these industries show features recognised as ancestral to the later mode-5 traditions. This technology is not firmly attested in post-Howieson's Poort contexts in the Western Cape until some ten millennia later, around 20,000 years ago, but this period remains poorly known as several major sites were not then occupied. Inter-regional comparisons are

**Fig. 49:** Kalemba rockshelter during excavation

hampered by inconsistent use of terminology, by the still imprecise dating of some occurrences, and by uncertainties surrounding the effects of raw material on lithic technology and typology.

From about 8000 years ago, microlithic industries became virtually ubiquitous in southern Africa (Mitchell 1997, 2002), conceivably linked with widespread adoption of the bow and arrow (cf. Binneman 1994). Many of them have been designated Wilton after a site near Alicedale in Eastern Cape Province (J. Deacon 1972; H. J. Deacon 1976). However, when a number of these assemblages are compared, a great range in the form and frequencies of tool types is observed (J. Deacon 1984; Inskeep 1987; Opperman 1996). At coastal sites this development correlates with the final rise of the sea to approximately its present level, and there is evidence that marine food resources were once again intensively exploited. Exceptional areas included the greater part of the Kalahari, which seems to have been largely uninhabited from about 9500 until about 4500 years ago (J. Deacon 1974), and the upper Zambezi Valley, where the river margins may have seen a late persistence of mode-3 stone-working techniques (L. Phillipson 1978).

A substantial number of graves throw light on the burial customs of this time. Generally, the dead appear to have been buried within the settlement area, whether this was a cave or rockshelter (Fig. 49) or in the open air. Grave goods in the form of tools, items of adornment or other personal belongings are often present and may indicate a belief that the dead would have some use for such objects. Antelope horns or warthog tusks were also sometimes buried with the deceased. Items of personal adornment are frequently encountered in graves as well as on settlement sites. Beads and pendants of bone or shell are widespread. Rock paintings suggest that such beads were sometimes sewn onto clothing or worn in the hair, as well as being threaded in strings. Ochre and other colouring matter were probably used for cosmetic and other purposes as well as for mural decoration. Much variation is apparent in the goods placed with different interments (S. Hall and Binneman 1987; S. Hall 2000). As will be shown below, painted gravestones were in vogue in the south coastal area.

Many of the dated archaeological occurrences of the period between 10,000 and 2000 years ago in southern Africa are from sites where little has been preserved apart from the stone artefacts and occasional associated faunal remains. Only rarely has vegetable matter survived, leading to an unbalanced representation of the tool-kits and diet of the people. The dry cave deposits of southernmost Africa (H. J. Deacon 1976) are therefore particularly significant. From these sites we can see that, at least in some areas, wood was used for bows, arrows, digging sticks, pegs and wedges. Bark was used for trays. Bags and clothing were made of sewn leather. Leaves were used as a wrapping material for valuables; while grass and soft undergrowth were collected for bedding. Vegetable foods were varied and often assumed considerable importance in the total diet, as they do among most modern tropical hunter-gatherer groups. Remains of plant foods provide vital information about the seasonality of settlements, confirming the often less detailed evidence of the faunal remains. In the southwestern Cape, for example, it has been argued that some hunter-gatherer groups may have moved regularly between their coastal winter settlements and summer haunts further inland (Parkington 1986, 2001; Parkington and Hall 1987; but see H. J. and J. Deacon 1999). Seasonal movement is also indicated in the uKhahlamba/Drakensberg region (Carter 1970).

As archaeological survey becomes more comprehensive, and the emphasis of research extends beyond technology and subsistence economy, it has become possible in several areas of southern Africa to recognise the social implications of group mobility. Certain large sites, often prominent rockshelters, have been interpreted as places of regular social aggregation, generally at a particular season of the year (e.g. Wadley 1987). A similar phenomenon has been recorded among certain recent San populations, the aggregations serving an important function in commodity exchange (*hxaro*), the making of matrimonial and other alliances, and suchlike activities. At other seasons the populations appear to have dispersed to smaller, more temporary encampments such as are also now recognised in the archaeological record.

## South-central Africa

North of the Limpopo, the post-Acheulean archaeology of the region centred on Zimbabwe and southwestern Zambia differs in important respects from that in South Africa. As noted in chapter 3, this region fell within the distribution of Sangoan industries into which, it has been suggested, should be subsumed those sometimes designated Charaman. These eventually gave way to lithic industries which display a well-developed mode-3 technology. The immediately post-Sangoan stone industries are now seen to have depended to a far larger extent on the production of flake-blades than was previously recognised. In central Zambia, Barham (2000, 2001, 2002b; see also J. D. Clark and Brown 2001) has shown how re-investigation of key sites and the application of recently developed dating methods can provide a wholly new understanding of this period. At Mumbwa and at Twin Rivers, artefact assemblages of Lupemban affinity (see pp. 117–20 below) have been recognised, probably dating to the general period 250,000–170,000 years ago; they include a few small and unmistakably backed pieces such as would previously have been regarded as restricted to very much later periods. Extensive use of pigment is also indicated at this time (Barham 2002a); the significance of this is evaluated below.

In Zimbabwe and some adjacent areas, on the other hand, the mode-3 industries are generally known as Bambatan after a cave in the Matopo Hills near Bulawayo. Informative occurrences have been investigated also at Pomongwe (C. K. Cooke 1963), at Redcliff in central Zimbabwe (C. K. Cooke 1978) and at Kalemba in eastern Zambia (D. W. Phillipson 1976). Unifacially trimmed sub-triangular points were produced, with occasional bifacial forms, together with a variety of edge-retouched flakes. These tools may well have served functions similar to those of their counterparts in the more southerly, and probably earlier, Pietersburg industries, but they clearly belong to a different technological and stylistic tradition. Radiocarbon dates for the Bambatan occurrences at these sites between 45,000 and 30,000 years ago probably indicate the minimum age of the industry. The faunal remains suggest that the makers of these artefacts exploited a wide range of animal species for their food. At several sites there is evidence that the climate was becoming progressively wetter during this occupation (Brain 1969). Particularly interesting is the discovery, within the Bambata industry, at three widely separated sites in Zimbabwe, of horizons marked by a proliferation of small blades (C. K. Cooke 1971, 1973). These occurrences, which are probably significantly older than 40,000 years, are possible counterparts of the more southerly Howieson's Poort. Little research has been undertaken on this material since the 1970s; Larsson (1996) has drawn attention to the need for new fieldwork and synthesis.

**Fig. 50:** Early mode-5 artefacts from Kalemba (after D. W. Phillipson 1976)

Some isolated but significantly earlier occurrences notwithstanding, it is in the context of the Bambata-related industries that we see widespread local evidence for the adoption of mode-5 techniques of backed-microlith manufacture. In most areas these industries show, with the passage of time, a significant reduction in mean artefact size. Flakes and blades with partial backing occur in most Bambata-related assemblages, becoming progressively more numerous, and the backing more extensive; crescent-shaped segments of blade with continuous backing along the curved edge frequently occur. In Zimbabwe these later ill-defined industries have sometimes been named Tshangula after a cave site in the Matopo Hills. Broadly similar occurrences are known in several areas of south-central Africa; they have been dated within the time-span 25,000 to 14,000 years ago (e.g. C. K. Cooke 1963; D. W. Phillipson 1976), although some may be significantly earlier.

North of the Zambezi the earliest true backed-microlith industry yet discovered had developed by about 19,000 years ago, as seen, for example, at Leopard's Hill near Lusaka and at several sites in northern and eastern Zambia. Tiny pointed backed bladelets and varied scrapers are the characteristic tool types of these so-called Nachikufan I industries (Fig. 50), together with bored stones, the larger examples of which resemble objects which are known to have been used in later periods as weights for digging sticks, although the functions of the smaller ones remain unknown (S. F. Miller 1971, 1972; D. W. Phillipson 1976; Musonda 1984). It seems that the development of microlithic technology proceeded at differing speeds in the various regions.

Later microlithic industries were characterised by geometrical backed forms, chiefly crescents, which replaced the single-pointed types of Nachikufan I and its counterparts. As in South Africa, these industries show considerable regional variation, the significance of which is not yet apparent. In some areas, such as southern Zambia, small convex scrapers far outnumber the backed microliths. Despite this variability, there has been a tendency among archaeologists to label most of these industries with the generic name Wilton (cf. p. 106 above). This has served to obscure the

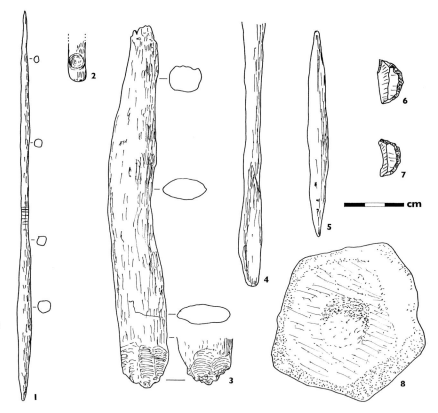

**Fig. 51:** Artefacts from Gwisho (after Fagan and Van Noten 1971): 1, 5, wooden arrow-points or link-shafts; 2, fire drill; 3, digging stick; 4, wooden spatula; 6, 7, backed microliths; 8, grinding stone

very real differences between most of the assemblages so designated, while exaggerating the idiosyncrasy of those, such as the later Nachikufan phases of northern Zambia (S. F. Miller 1972) and the Kaposwa from Kalambo Falls (J. D. Clark 1974), which have been given different names. The waterlogged sites at Gwisho hotsprings in southern Zambia (Fagan and Van Noten 1971) are of particular importance, organic materials having been exceptionally well preserved (Fig. 51), including wooden pieces interpreted as digging-sticks, heads or link-shafts from arrows, and possibly part of a bow. Some sequences in Zimbabwe, notably Pomongwe in the Matopo Hills, include occurrences attributed to the Oakhurst Complex (N. J. Walker 1995), better known from sites further to the south (p. 105 above). It now appears that economic, cultural, social and geological factors all influenced the types of tools that were used. At sites with a stratified sequence of microlithic industries, there has been noted a general decrease in artefact size with the passage of time (D. W. Phillipson 1977a).

## Rock art in southern and south-central Africa

No account of the later prehistory of this part of Africa would be complete without reference to the remarkable rock art – both paintings and engravings – that is so abundantly preserved there and which has generated a profuse and varied literature (see Summers 1959; Willcox 1963; Vinnicombe 1976; Lewis-Williams 1983; Lewis-Williams and Dowson 1989; Dowson 1992; Dowson and Lewis-Williams 1994; Garlake 1995; Solomon 1997; Russell 2000). During the past quarter-century great progress has been made in at least partially understanding the original significance of this art, but the full implications of these advances can only be appreciated with knowledge of its varied age and authorship. Without this background we cannot hope to make full use of this potentially most illuminating evidence, which relates to aspects of prehistoric life that would otherwise remain unknown.

Virtually all surviving southern African rock art occurs on the walls of shallow caves or rockshelters or on rock outcrops in the open air. It has inevitably suffered from exposure to the elements (unlike almost all European Palaeolithic paintings, which are in deep caves); it thus seems probable that most of the still-extant paintings were executed within the past few thousand years. Such arguments do not necessarily apply to the engravings which, although often fully exposed, are less susceptible to obliteration by the elements. As with many categories of archaeological evidence, much more art, executed in different circumstances or in earlier times, may not have survived, as is suggested, for example, by the frequent occurrence of ochre on settlement and burial sites.

There is an increasing body of evidence that, although much of the extant art is probably of relatively recent date, it belongs to a very ancient tradition. Painted and engraved stone slabs have been excavated from dated deposits at several southern African sites. At 'Apollo 11 Cave' in southern Namibia, detached slabs bearing naturalistic paintings of animals (Fig. 52) occur in levels dated as long ago as 28,000 years, associated with a late mode-3 industry, indicating that some southern African rock art has an antiquity comparable with that of its European and Australian counterparts (Wendt 1976). Rather later in date, but showing much greater variety, are the painted stones found in graves of the makers of microlithic industries in caves on the south coast, as at Klasies River Mouth and Coldstream Cave (Singer and Wymer 1969; Rudner 1971). Engraved stones have been excavated at Wonderwerk Cave near Kuruman in contexts of around 10,000 years ago (Thackeray *et al.* 1981), while Butzer *et al.* (1979) have argued that some of the open-air engraving sites may be more than 4000 years old. In the

**Fig. 52:**
Naturalistic
paintings
25,000–28,000
years old on
stone slabs from
'Apollo 11 Cave',
Namibia

uKhahlamba/Drakensberg, radiometric analyses suggest that some extant paintings were executed some 3000–2000 years ago (Mazel and Watchman 2003).

It is sometimes possible to distinguish older and younger works in the same site or area, either on the basis of differential weathering or through the study of superimpositions, where one image has been made over an earlier one. Confirmation of such sequences and indications of age can

**Fig. 53:**
Naturalistic rock
paintings at
Makwe near
Wedza,
Zimbabwe

sometimes be obtained when the artist has depicted phenomena such as domestic animals or European colonists, whose dates in southern Africa are known from other sources (cf. B. W. Smith and Van Schalkwyk 2002). By these means it has been demonstrated that, in several parts of southern Africa, rock art continued to be executed into the last few centuries, often maintaining stylistic traditions that had been established in far earlier times. It is to these late expressions that most of our data regarding the meaning and significance of the art relate, but it is pertinent to cite such evidence here since it may perhaps provide an indication of the original function of the more ancient art.

Most southern African rock paintings are naturalistic representations of people and animals (Fig. 53); other natural or artificial objects, other than personal accoutrements, are only rarely depicted. The wide variety of animal species shown, both identifiable and 'mythical', and the range of human activities, equipment and clothing, has attracted considerable attention. Less interest has until recently been accorded to the varied geometrical or schematic motifs, presumably because these lack the obvious aesthetic appeal of the naturalistic art. The latter paintings show a tendency to develop from simple outlines or flat silhouettes towards use of shading in monochrome or polychrome and an increased mastery of perspective: these latest features are best represented by paintings (Fig. 54) in the uKhahlamba/Drakensberg which probably represent the finest

**Fig. 54:** Rock painting at Mpongweni, KwaZulu-Natal

achievements of African rock artists. Among the engravings, animals and schematic motifs predominate, human figures being rarely shown. Here, finely engraved outlines are generally earlier than are pecked silhouettes (Figs. 55, 56).

Several writers, viewing southern African rock art from a primarily foreign viewpoint, have stressed its undoubted aesthetic qualities and suggested that the painters' main object was to create a thing of beauty. This 'art for art's sake' explanation can no longer be accepted in view of detailed comparisons that have been made between, on the one hand, the arrangement and subject matter of the paintings and, on the other, ethnographic records relating to southern San-speaking peoples in the nineteenth and twentieth centuries (Vinnicombe 1976; Lewis-Williams 1981; Lewis-Williams and Dowson 1989; cf. also Solomon 1997). The eland is the animal most frequently represented in the paintings but not, by contrast, in the faunal remains preserved at occupational sites; this species is known to have occupied an important place in the belief systems and symbolism of recent San communities. Close parallels may be drawn between certain painted scenes and rites practised by nineteenth/twentieth-century San on occasions such as puberty and marriage. Many paintings have otherwise inexplicable features that may be understood in terms of shamanistic trance, such as played an important rôle

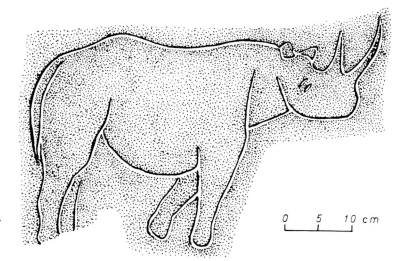

**Fig. 55:**
Line-engraving
from Doornkloof,
South Africa
(after Willcox
1963)

**Fig. 56:** Pecked
engravings,
Klipfontein,
Northern Cape

in the lives of the southern San. Only three examples need be cited. Paintings
of human figures in the Western Cape and KwaZulu-Natal provinces of South
Africa often show lines descending from the nostrils: trance among the
San is frequently accompanied by nose-bleeding. A strange, forward-leaning,
half-crouching stance, not infrequently represented in the paintings, is

**Fig. 57:** Rock paintings showing people in trance (after Lewis-Williams 1983)

identical to that adopted by dancing San when entering trance states (Fig. 57). San emerging from trance have described their experience as feeling like riding on the back of a serpent; and paintings in the Matopo Hills of Zimbabwe show an enormous snake, sometimes double-headed, with numbers of people standing on its back. These interpretations should not, of course, detract from appreciation of the paintings' aesthetic quality although such appreciation is inevitably tied to the cultural background of the individual beholder.

The lines and dots which comprise most of the schematic or non-representational designs are interpreted by Lewis-Williams and Dowson (1988) as 'entoptics' – visual patterns or hallucinations experienced under certain circumstances by people of many cultural backgrounds. More recently, it has been persuasively demonstrated that much schematic art (Fig. 58) may be attributed to herding peoples rather than to hunter-gatherers (S. Hall and Smith 2000; B. W. Smith and Ouzman 2004). Independent studies attribute an analogous significance to much of the rock art further to the north, as will be described in chapter 7. It seems appropriate to conclude that rock art can only be interpreted adequately with reference to the belief systems of the artists. It is fortunate that some of the southern African art was executed by societies sufficiently recent for these systems to be at least partially understood, but untested assumptions that superficially similar rock art in other parts of the world necessarily has similar shamanistic connotations should be regarded with grave suspicion (Clottes 2002).

## Central Africa

Environmental change in central Africa resulted in major fluctuations in the extent of the equatorial forest (cf. Brooks and Robertshaw 1990). Such processes are as yet well documented only for the last 20,000 years, for which

**Fig. 58:**
Schematic rock
paintings in
South Africa's
Northern Cape
Province of the
type now
attributed to
herding peoples

a series of maps has been published by Bonnefille (1999). There is no reason to believe that similar changes did not take place in earlier times also. Since stone is extremely rare in many parts of this region, it is likely that some groups depended largely on artefacts made of perishable materials which have not yet been recovered by archaeologists. It appears that even the areas of densest forest were at least occasionally subject to human habitation during this general period (Fiedler and Preuss 1985; Lanfranchi 1996; cf. also Fig. 59).

By about 250,000 years ago, if not earlier, Sangoan industries (pp. 81–4) gradually gave way to those known as Lupemban. Classic Lupemban artefacts are characterised by refined bifacial stone-working techniques, seen especially on core-axes and on long double-ended points which may have been mounted for use as spearheads. They are found abundantly in the area of the Plain of Kinshasa beside the Malebo (Stanley) Pool (Van Moorsel 1968), and also in the river gravels of the Dundo area in northern Angola which have been mined extensively for diamonds (J. D. Clark 1963). It is now recognised that these classic forms may owe much to geological factors exemplified by the availability of fine-grained isotropic raw material in large pieces. As noted above, industries of Lupemban affinity have recently been recognised in central Zambia, provisionally dated between 250,000 and 170,000 years ago; occasional small backed tools have been recognised in a Lupemban context at Twin Rivers, Lusaka (Barham 2000, 2001, 2002b; J. D. Clark and Brown 2001). A similar age is probable at Kalambo Falls, where Lupemban-type artefacts overlie the Sangoan horizons. Unlike much of the

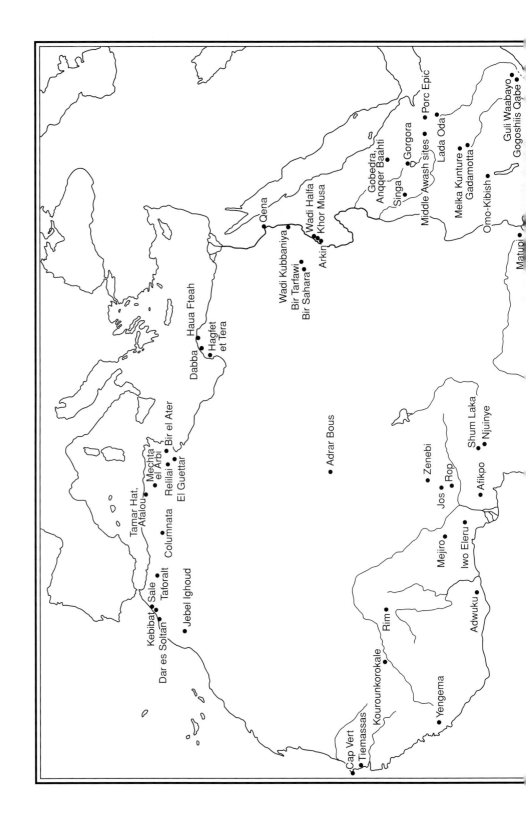

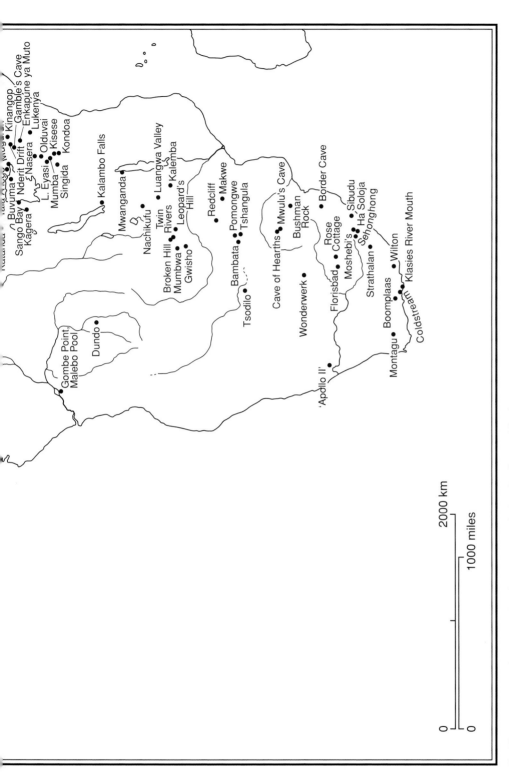

**Fig. 59:** Occurrences of post-Acheulean/Sangoan stone industries discussed in chapter 4

Kinangop,
Gamble's Cave
Enkapune ya Muto
Buvuma Lukenya
Sango Bay Nderit Drift Olduvai
Kagera Nasera Kisese
L. Eyasi Kondoa
Mumba Singida
Kalambo Falls

Mwanganda
Luangwa Valley
Nachikufu Twin Kalemba
Rivers Leopard's
Hill
Redcliff
Makwe
Bambata Pomongwe
Broken Hill Tshangula
Mumbwa Mwulu's Cave
Gwisho Cave of Hearths Border Cave
Tsodilo Bushman Sibudu
Rock
Wonderwerk Rose Mosebi's Ha' Soloja
Florisbad Cottage Sehonghong
'Apollo II' Strathalan
Montagu Boomplaas Wilton
Coldstream Klasies River Mouth

Gombe Point,
Malebo Pool
Dundo

2000 km

1000 miles

0
0

earlier material at Kalambo, the Lupemban does not occur on undisturbed floors, but is incorporated in a thick rubble layer representing scree and erosion in the valley after a period of downcutting (J. D. Clark 1964, 2001a). Here and at several north-Angolan sites pollen has been preserved which suggests that the vegetation and climate at this time did not differ significantly from those of the present. Also provisionally attributed to the Lupemban, although the characteristic bifacial points are not represented in this specialist context, is a butchery site at Mwanganda in northern Malawi (J. D. Clark and Haynes 1970), for which an age of at least 300,000 years is now considered probable. The implements, scattered among the bones of a single elephant, consist almost exclusively of edge-retouched flakes, with a few core-tools.

It is now recognised that there is no adequate basis for the multi-phase sequence of post-Acheulean industries formerly proposed for the Kinshasa area (Cahen and Moeyersons 1977; Cahen 1978). The artefacts occur in poorly stratified sands, as at Gombe Point, and it is now clear that considerable mixture has taken place, both between artefacts originally deposited at different levels, and of the materials sampled for radiocarbon dating. Consequently, neither the typological composition of the industries nor their chronology should be regarded as securely established.

At Katanda on the Semliki River north of Lake Edward/Rutanzige in easternmost D. R. Congo, a series of mode-3 industries has been recovered from contexts for which an age between 170,000 and 80,000 years is indicated (Brooks *et al.* 1995; Yellen 1996). Apparently associated with these stone industries are barbed bone harpoon-heads akin to those previously recorded from nearby Ishango and for which a much later date has been widely accepted (Brooks and Smith 1987; see also pp. 157–8 below). Controversy continues to surround the high antiquity claimed for the Katanda harpoons, which has been proposed as supporting the case for the early development of modern human behaviour in sub-Saharan Africa, discussed and evaluated below (pp. 143–5). In view of the widespread distribution of such harpoons in later times (Yellen 1996), it would be unwise to accept the great age proposed for the Katanda examples until further evidence is available.

The development of microlithic mode-5 technology in central Africa has conventionally been considered in two regional subdivisions (cf. Cornelissen 2002). In the savanna regions such as those in much of Zambia and southern Angola, on the one hand, true mode-5 industries appeared at an early date, as noted on p. 109, having their roots in the earlier industries designated Bambata. An early microlithic occurrence at Matupi in the extreme northeast of D. R. Congo (Van Noten 1977; Mercader and Brooks 2001) is often considered in this connexion. Probably extending back for some 40,000 years, it belongs to a time when, in contrast with its present situation, Matupi apparently lay a short distance outside the equatorial forest. On the southern fringes of the forest, on the other hand, a local largely microlithic industry known as the Tshitolian gradually developed from the preceding Lupemban tradition. A gradual reduction in artefact size is apparent through the Lupemban–Tshitolian sequence, together with a shift in emphasis from flakes struck off radial cores to parallel-sided blades. Backed microliths are frequent in the Tshitolian, especially the flared trapezoidal form known as *petits tranchets* that may have been hafted as transverse arrow-points (Figs. 43, 51); these became smaller and more numerous with the passage of time (Cahen and Mortelmans 1973; S. F. Miller 1988). Pointed core-tools and leaf-shaped points continued, generally smaller than previously. In southern D. R. Congo it is noteworthy that sites in the more densely forested river valleys have yielded a higher proportion of backed microliths, while assemblages from the more open plateaux contain larger bifacially worked tools. The distribution of comparable industries extends to the northwest into Congo, Gabon and Cameroon (Clist 1989a; Lanfranchi and Schwartz 1990).

It may now be suggested that the dichotomy between the Tshitolian and its more dominantly microlithic counterparts may not have been so clearly defined as was once thought. The classic Lupemban industries are now seen as a localised manifestation of a very widespread technological tradition, its apparent idiosyncrasy perhaps partly due to the raw material that was available. In the broadest sense, environmental factors will have had some effect on human activities and the types of tool that were required to perform them, but the overall picture that is now slowly emerging is a mosaic of variation on a widespread common theme, rather than two clearly defined zones.

Studies of the archaeology of central Africa are greatly hampered by the sparseness and uneven coverage of research (cf. Fig. 59), by the almost complete absence of faunal and floral remains and the total lack of hominid fossils. Such rock art as has been located in this area (where rocky outcrops are often rare) appears to be of late date; it is discussed in chapters 7 and 8. In addition, as has been shown above, doubt has been cast upon the stratigraphic integrity of many of the open-air Kalahari Sand sites which formed the basis for much of the sequence previously proposed. Despite these problems, the region is seen as having occupied a key position in continent-wide trends during the later stages of the Middle Pleistocene and the early part of the Late Pleistocene (see Fig. 7 on p. 25). Recent research has emphasised both the wide distribution and the significance of Lupemban industries. No longer recognised simply by the presence of large foliate bifacial points, these are now seen as occupying a crucial position in the development of inter-regional variation and of the transition from mode 3 to a mode-5 (microlithic) technology (Barham 2002b). Lupemban affinities are recognised as far south as Namibia and, as will be argued below, the North African Aterian may have greater affinity with the sub-Saharan Lupemban than with broadly contemporary European or Levantine technological traditions. It may be anticipated that, as research progresses, geographical and chronological subdivisions of the Lupemban tradition will be recognised, and their contribution to later developments more widely recognised.

## Eastern Africa

Some areas, notably in Kenya, have been intensively examined, but elsewhere enormous areas remain virtually unexplored by archaeologists, whose attention has tended until recently to be concentrated on the very rich sites belonging to the earliest Stone Age periods. Although in some instances they are not well documented, eastern Africa has yielded a number of fossils which may be regarded as early representatives of anatomically modern humans. Potentially the most significant is the recently announced discovery at Herto in the Middle Awash Basin of three skulls, apparently dated between 160,000 and 150,000 years ago (White *et al.* 2003). They display physical characteristics which clearly belong to *Homo sapiens*, with some archaic features, being significantly more modern, for example, than the Bodo, Broken Hill or Hopefield specimens. Unfortunately, the archaeological associations of the Herto skulls remain unclear, both Acheulean-type and mode-3 artefacts being reported from the same horizons (J. D. Clark *et al.* 2003). Particular interest also attaches to three specimens from deposits of the Kibish Formation in the lower Omo Valley of Ethiopia (Day and Stringer 1991; Day *et al.* 1991). Neither their stratigraphic positions nor their cultural associations are known with any clarity, but direct dating suggests Late Pleistocene ages analogous to those from Klasies River Mouth (p. 101; Klein 1999). An earlier and even more poorly documented discovery from Singa near the Blue Nile in east-central Sudan (Stringer 1979; Stringer *et al.* 1985; McDermott *et al.* 1996) shows comparable modern features. Previously considered recent, it is now recognised as belonging to the general period around 150,000 years ago. Probably broadly contemporary are a skull from Ngaloba at Laetoli (Magori and Day 1983; Klein 1999) and isolated teeth from Mumba rockshelter (Bräuer and Mehlman 1988), both in Tanzania.

Eastern Africa is a region of great environmental variation, from glaciated mountains, to semi-arid deserts, to mangrove-fringed ocean shores

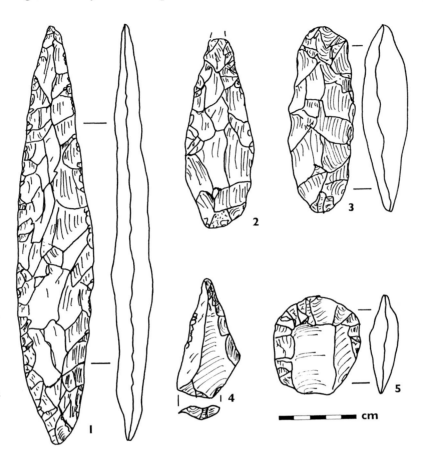

**Fig. 60:**
Lupemban
artefacts: 1, 2,
from Musolexi,
Angola (after J. D.
Clark 1963); 3–5,
from Kalambo
Falls (after J. D.
Clark 2001a)

(W. M. Adams *et al.* 1996). These features have themselves varied through time but are, throughout, reflected in the archaeology. In the area around Lake Victoria, which was for much of this time an internal drainage area with no outlet to the north, the immediately post-Acheulean industries were of Sangoan type, discussed in chapter 3. Presumably later are Lupemban-type industries (Fig. 60), best known from Muguruk (McBrearty 1988) and nearby sites such as Yala Alego (O'Brien 1939; S. Cole 1964). This sequence is paralleled by abundant discoveries in Rwanda and Burundi (Nenquin 1967; Van Noten 1982). Throughout this area the published data are unfortunately virtually restricted to typological descriptions; there are few if any undisturbed assemblages from sealed stratified contexts and no reliable age determinations. Recent research on the Kapthurin Formation near Lake Baringo in Kenya has, however, done much to clarify these matters and to provide confirmation both of the high antiquity of these developments and of their relationship with the Sangoan (Cornelissen 1992; McBrearty *et al.* 1996; McBrearty 1999, 2001; Deino and McBrearty 2002).

In addition to the Middle Awash Basin, where research is ongoing (Kalb *et al.* 1982; White *et al.* 2003), scattered localities in Ethiopia and Eritrea have yielded lithic industries which may be regarded as early manifestations of mode-3 technology; unfortunately they are at present incompletely documented. At Melka Kunture near Addis Ababa, horizons stratified above the Acheulean material noted in chapter 3 contain a series of assemblages in which bifacial tools became progressively rarer and smaller, being gradually replaced by sub-triangular points and flakes with shallow retouch along their longer sides (Hours 1973; Chavaillon 1979). Full details of these discoveries have not yet been published, nor are age determinations available. It is, however, relevant to note potassium/argon dates about 180,000–150,000 years ago for a site used for the manufacture of mode-3 artefacts on obsidian outcrops at Gadamotta near Lake Zwai, some 70 kilometres south of Melka Kunture (Wendorf and Schild 1974).

Mode-3 assemblages, characterised by the presence of sub-triangular points and edge-retouched pieces, often made on flakes struck from radial cores similar in general terms to those from south-central Africa attributed to the Bambata industry, are widely distributed in eastern Africa. As argued above, the distinction between the industries designated Bambata and those whose Lupemban affinities are now recognised is less clearly defined than the conventional nomenclature would imply. In eastern Africa, the chronology of these industries, like the activities and life-styles of their practitioners, awaits detailed investigation (but see Barut 1994; Merrick *et al.* 1994; Ambrose *et al.* 2002), although they appear to have been broadly analogous to those of their counterparts further to the south. Industries of this type have been noted in Ethiopia and Somalia (J. D. Clark 1954; Brandt 1986), where they may extend back into the relatively moist conditions of the Last Interglacial period. At Porc Epic cave near Dire Dawa such an industry is associated with a human mandible of near-modern form (J. D. Clark and Williams 1978; Bräuer 1984). At Olduvai Gorge such material occurs overlying Bed IV in the Ndutu Beds (M. D. Leakey *et al.* 1972), where its age may exceed 100,000 years. At nearby Lake Eyasi a similar industry with some Sangoan-like artefacts is associated with fragmentary human crania which show morphological features akin to those of the specimen from Broken Hill mine, Kabwe, attributed to *Homo heidelbergensis* (Mehlman 1987). Many further occurrences await detailed publication (cf. Anthony 1972; Kalb *et al.* 1982). Related mode-3 industries also occur in the early stages of several of the local sequences which have been established on the basis of cave or rockshelter excavations, notably those at Nasera (Mehlman 1977) on the eastern edge of the Serengeti Plain, at Lukenya Hill (Gramly 1976; Barut 1994) near Nairobi, and at Enkapune ya Muto west of Lake Naivasha (Ambrose 1998b).

In some parts of eastern Africa, as in certain more southerly regions, the mode-5 techniques of bladelet production and of backing retouch can now be traced back to far earlier periods than were previously considered relevant. New data are available relating to these developments in the central Rift Valley and adjacent highlands of Kenya (Kyule *et al.* 1997; Ambrose 1998b; Ambrose *et al.* 2002). Technological developments here, although idiosyncratic, are easily discerned since the majority of artefacts are made from obsidian. Deep deposits at Marmonet Drift in the Naivasha-Nakuru basin preserve a mode-3 industry interstratified with layers of volcanic ash for which absolute dates have not yet been announced. The archaeological sequence at Enkapune ya Muto rockshelter, high on the Mau escarpment, extends from at least 70,000 years ago into recent times. A mode-5 industry designated Sakutiek, with numerous small edge-retouched tools, backed flakes and bladelets, began there as much as 50,000 years ago, replacing a mode-3 manifestation.

By at least 20,000 years ago, as in northern and eastern Zambia, there is evidence that microlithic industries containing quantities of backed bladelets and some geometrical microliths were widespread in the highlands of Tanzania and southern Kenya. The best-described occurrences are still those from Kisese rockshelter in central Tanzania (Inskeep 1962) and at Lukenya Hill (Gramly 1976) where such artefacts are associated with a fragmentary human skull showing – it has been claimed – features resembling those of recent negroid populations (Gramly and Rightmire 1973). A similar but rather later industry comes from Buvuma Island in Ugandan waters of Lake Victoria (Van Noten 1971). Somewhat earlier material from the Naisiusiu Beds near the top of the Olduvai Gorge sequence (M. D. Leakey *et al.* 1972) may partly owe its distinctive appearance to the fact that many of its artefacts are made of obsidian.

In the more northerly parts of eastern Africa, there are very few dated sequences that can be compared with those noted above. At Laga Oda in the escarpment of the southeast Ethiopian plateau near Dire Dawa, a backed-microlith industry was established at least 16,000 years ago (J. D. Clark and Williams 1978). In more northerly parts of Ethiopia an industry based on the production of large blades may have intervened between the mode-3 and the backed-microlith industries, as at Gobedra and Anqqer Baahti rockshelters near Aksum in Tigray (D. W. Phillipson 1977b; Finneran 2000). J. D. Clark's (1954) proposal of a similar 'Hargeisan' stage in northern Somalia is not borne out by more recent research (Brandt 1986).

A comparable blade industry is clearly demonstrated further to the south: the Eburran industry, formerly known as the Kenya Capsian, is restricted

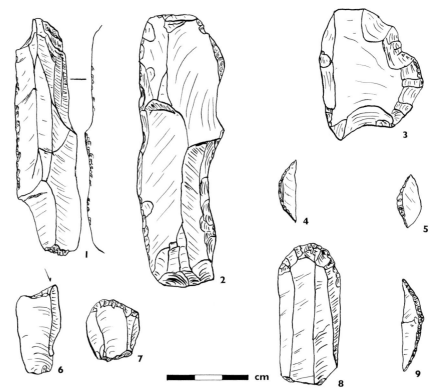

**Fig. 61:** 1–5, artefacts of modes 4 and 5 from Gobedra (after D. W. Phillipson 1977b); 6–9, Eburran artefacts from Gamble's Cave (after L. S. B. Leakey 1931)

to a small area near Lake Nakuru in the eastern Rift Valley of south-central Kenya. It is best represented at Gamble's Cave and Nderit Drift, dated between 13,000 and 9000 years ago (L. S. B. Leakey 1931; Isaac *et al.* 1972; Ambrose *et al.* 1980), although related industries continued into more recent times, as at Enkapune ya Muto (Ambrose 1998b). The fine large artefacts of the early Eburran (Fig. 61) – it is typified by large backed blades, crescent-shaped pieces, edge-retouched flakes and 'burins' with a sharp transverse edge produced by removal of a narrow spall – are almost all of fine obsidian; the similarity with more northerly blade industries may be largely fortuitous.

By 10,000 years ago backed-microlith industries were generally ubiquitous in eastern Africa. These industries, despite their general similarities, show a confusing complexity of variation; no really convincing and meaningful classification of them has yet been proposed. In the north our knowledge comes from widely scattered localities: Gobedra and Laga Oda in Ethiopia, for example, as well as from Gorgora near Lake Tana (L. S. B. Leakey 1943). In Somalia, the Doian industry has unifacial and bifacial points alongside backed microliths, notably at Gogoshiis Qabe and Guli Waabayo (J. D. Clark 1954; Brandt 1986). Further to the south were the specialised fishing settlements of this period beside Lake Turkana, discussed in chapter 5. Elsewhere, except in the parts of the Rift Valley where obsidian was plentiful and whence it was sometimes evidently traded to neighbouring areas (Merrick and Brown 1984; Merrick *et al.* 1994), the microlithic industries are generally of quartz and of rather informal character. The longest and best-documented sequences are those at the Lukenya Hill (S. B. Kusimba 2001), Kisese and Nasera sites noted above. Similar material comes from northern and western Uganda (e.g. Nelson and Posnansky 1970).

The makers of the microlithic industries of between 10,000 and 2000 years ago were probably responsible for the earliest extant East African rock paintings. Such paintings are only surely known from north-central Tanzania and show some stylistic parallels with their counterparts in southern Africa. Isolated naturalistic animal figures and stylised humans are the most frequent motifs, shown either in outline or in flat monochrome. The best-known sites are in the Kondoa and Singida areas (Fosbrooke *et al.* 1950; Masao 1979; M. D. Leakey 1983; Anati 1986). The naturalistic art tradition did not continue here into such recent times as it did in southern Africa, and its interpretation is more problematic. In general terms, however, it is possible that it fulfilled much the same functions; certain features, such as the frequency of eland representations, are common to both areas, although it would be premature to suggest that shamanistic trance experience contributed as much to rock art in East Africa as it did further to the south. It should not be assumed that the belief-systems and practices of the southern African San were ubiquitous in what is now Tanzania (Schepartz 1988; see also Morris 2003).

Although the data are from widely scattered sites in quite different environments, and although long detailed sequences are so far lacking, the succession of post-Sangoan stone industries in eastern Africa is now seen to have been broadly analogous to, and lasted for about as long as, that revealed by more intensive research further to the south. With the possible exception of Mumba in northern Tanzania (Mehlman 1991) there is, however, no evidence for any very early appearance of full-fledged mode-5 technology such as that represented by the Howieson's Poort industries south of the Limpopo. The earliest post-Acheulean industries are not based to the same extent on flake-blade production but, in contrast to the situation in the south, true mode-4 industries are attested in the more northerly parts of eastern Africa. The reasons for these distinctions will not be properly understood until comprehensive data relating to the economy and life-style of this period have been recovered from eastern African sites.

## West Africa

Like those of the Acheulean and the Sangoan, the subsequent stone industries of West Africa have not been thoroughly investigated, although abundant remains are known to exist (Fig. 62). It is clear that the region saw
extensive environmental changes involving significant shifts in vegetational
zones. Considerable confusion surrounds the sequence of West African stone
industries in post-Sangoan times because so much of our information is
based upon undated collections from disturbed contexts or surface exposures. However, there can be little doubt that in several areas, such as
Cap Vert in Senegal, southwestern Mali and central Guinea, there existed
assemblages typified by large, lance-shaped points akin to, but generally
cruder than, those of the central African Lupemban. It is difficult to be
certain about the true distribution of this material, because of the superficial similarity between some of its artefacts and those of much later times
(cf. MacDonald and Allsworth-Jones 1994). More clearly recognised are the
generalised mode-3 industries based on radial cores and flakes which were
made into points and edge-retouched flakes rather like those from more
easterly and southerly regions, and also showing superficial similarity to
artefacts from further to the north that have been designated Levalloiso-
Mousterian (see p. 131). In West Africa, such material occurs widely in river-
gravel deposits in Sierra Leone and on the Jos Plateau of Nigeria, where
they belong to a later cycle of erosion and deposition than does the local
Acheulean. A particularly rich occurrence is in the outwash gravels below
Zenebi Falls, for which a very late radiocarbon date is most unlikely to represent the true age, which remains unknown since no undisturbed assemblage
of this type has been excavated *in situ* anywhere in West Africa (Soper 1965;
Shaw 1978; Allsworth-Jones 1986, 2001).

There has been more research into later periods, at least in some areas,
and a rather fuller picture may thus be drawn. The only sequence which
illustrates the early development of mode-5 industries in West Africa is at
the rockshelter of Shum Laka in the Grassfields of northwestern Cameroon
(de Maret *et al.* 1987; Lavachery 2001; Cornelissen 2003). Here, a microlithic
industry in quartz was being produced significantly before 30,000 years ago
and continued with little discernible change through a period that was envi-
ronmentally relatively stable until less than 10,000 years ago. The date of its
first appearance is not yet known, but earlier industries of Sangoan type are
recorded in the same general region at Njuinye (Mercader and Marti 2003).
At the rockshelter of Iwo Eleru in the now forested zone of southwestern
Nigeria, a microlithic industry is known from about 12,000 years ago (Shaw
and Daniels 1984). This early horizon at Iwo Eleru also yielded a human

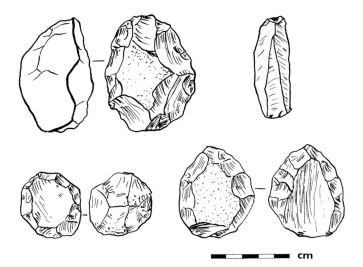

**Fig. 62:** Mode-3 artefacts from Nigeria (after Shaw 1978)

cm

burial which is stated to show negroid physical features (Brothwell and Shaw 1971). The stone assemblage, which included a very low proportion of intentionally retouched tools, was characterised by crescent-shaped, triangular and trapezoidal microliths. It continued with only minor change for some 9000 years. Around 5500 years ago, pottery and ground-stone artefacts made their appearance. These late pottery-associated industries are described and discussed in chapter 6. Comparable microlithic industries without associated pottery are known elsewhere in Nigeria, notably at Mejiro near Oyo Ile (Willett 1962), at Rop on the Jos Plateau (B. Fagg *et al.* 1972), probably in the lower levels at Afikpo rockshelter in eastern Nigeria (Andah and Anozie 1980), and also at Bingerville in Ivory Coast where its age is similar to that at Iwo Eleru (Chenorkian 1983).

Elsewhere in West Africa, the earlier microlithic industries, before the start of pottery manufacture, have only been found in a few areas, but may have been originally widespread (Shaw 1981). Such an occurrence at Rim in Burkina Faso has an age of over 5000 years. In Ghana there are numerous surface finds which may belong to this period, as at Adwuku, but none has been dated precisely. By contrast, sites in Guinea and Sierra Leone, such as Yengema (Coon 1968), have yielded crudely flaked core-tools, edge-retouched flakes and a few backed blades. Such material, like analogous finds from the Congo Basin, apparently represents an adaptation to forest life; if so, the presence of a true backed-microlith industry at Iwo Eleru remains to be explained, unless that site's surroundings have become only recently afforested. Material from Kourounkorokale near Bamako is described in chapter 5. In the far west, in Senegal, the lagoonside Tiemassas

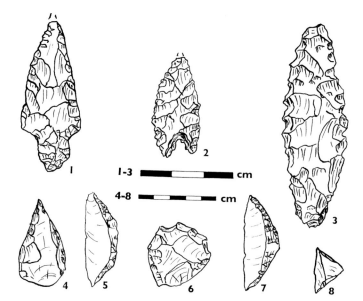

**Fig. 63:** West African mode-5 artefacts: 1–3, bifacial points from Tiemassas (after Dagan 1956); 4–8, microliths from Rop (after Shaw 1978)

site 80 kilometres south of Dakar has yielded a pre-pottery microlithic occurrence. Backed blades and crescents here are large and crude: they are associated with bifacially flaked leaf-shaped points (Fig. 63). More than one phase of occupation is probably represented in these extensive exposures for which, unfortunately, no absolute dating is currently available (Dagan 1956, 1972).

Despite the very incomplete nature of our evidence, the following tentative synthesis can be offered. It is clear that mode-5 technology in West Africa began more than 30,000 years ago, although it is not yet firmly attested west of Cameroon until about 12,000 years ago. For many millennia prior to this date the Sahara was largely uninhabited, and so the microlithic industries to the south, as in other areas of sub-Saharan Africa, were probably indigenous developments. In some densely forested regions of West Africa, such as southeastern Nigeria, Sierra Leone and Guinea, non-microlithic industries continued until the last few millennia (Shaw 1981; MacDonald and Allsworth-Jones 1994). The characteristic artefacts of these industries are crude core-tools, hoe-like or axe-like in form, perhaps used for forest clearance and for digging. Cultivation of tubers may have begun at an early date in those West African areas where yams are today the staple food. The plausibility of such a contrast, perhaps between about 6000 and 4000 years ago, between an essentially hunting life-style in the West African savanna and a vegecultural one in the forests, will be further explored in chapter 6.

## North Africa and the Sahara

The archaeology of the northern parts of Africa has for the most part been studied in an essentially Mediterranean, rather than an African, context. Both the conceptual framework and the terminology conventionally employed thus differ in some important respects from those used in other parts of the continent (cf. Kleindienst 2001). In the present work it is the African aspects and connexions that are stressed, and North Africa will be shown to have occupied a more central and innovative place in prehistory than some earlier accounts would suggest.

As the following account will make clear, North Africa and the Sahara have seen environmental changes at least as great as those in any other part of the continent, and the region's prehistory must be viewed in that context. The time of the Acheulean in the Sahara appears to have been followed by an arid phase when many previously inhabited areas were abandoned, which may explain the episodic nature of the archaeological record in many areas (e.g. Tillet 1985). Sites in Morocco which have yielded very small hand-axes and cleavers as well as flake-tools appear to belong to this arid period: similar artefacts also occur at a few places in the Sahara, notably in south-eastern Libya (Biberson 1967; Arkell 1964; J. D. Clark 1980). With the return of moister conditions more than 130,000 years ago, settlement again became widespread. Best known from the Algerian and Moroccan Maghreb, the artefacts then in use were of the mode-3 type generally known as Mousterian or Levalloiso-Mousterian, after their closely similar and broadly contemporary European and Levantine counterparts. Although small, heart-shaped handaxes occur in some of these North African Mousterian assemblages, light-duty tools are the most characteristic element, being made generally on flakes removed from prepared or radial cores (van Peer 1991). Long edge-retouched flakes and sub-triangular points, perhaps for projectiles, were the most common implement types.

The industries which subsequently became widespread have, despite their diversity, been conventionally grouped together under the name Aterian, after Bir el Ater, near Tebessa, Algeria (Camps 1974; J. D. Clark 1980; Kleindienst 2001). The Aterian is generally defined by the presence of a variety of flake tools possessing well-worked tangs, which may have facilitated hafting (Fig. 64). These include not only specimens which resemble projectile points, but also varied shapes of edge-retouched flakes and pieces which, bearing little intentional retouch other than that which forms the tang, may be broken or reworked points. There are, of course, major problems with defining a distinct cultural or even industrial entity on the basis of a single morphological feature, especially one whose function is so poorly understood. Artefacts designated Aterian are encountered through most of the

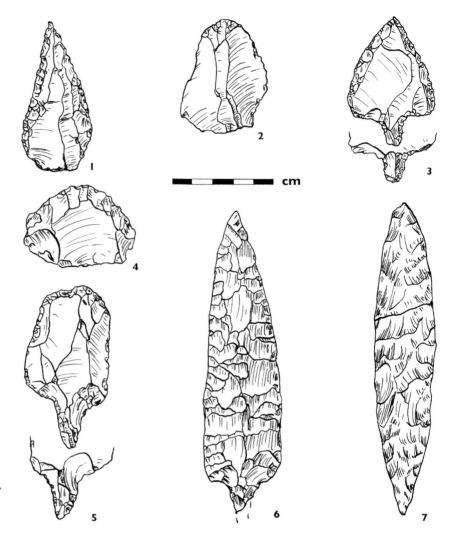

**Fig. 64:** Aterian artefacts (after Camps 1974: 1–5, from Bir el Ater; 6, 7, from Adrar Bous

Sahara, from the Atlantic coast almost as far east as the Nile. In several parts of this vast region, as at Adrar Bous in Tenere, bifacial points are another regular component of the Aterian assemblages (J. D. Clark *et al.* 1973). Assemblages from later sites in both areas include numerous parallel-sided blades in addition to flakes struck from radial cores. This marks a technological development parallel to, and perhaps connected with, the advent of mode-4 industries in Cyrenaica (see p. 134). These general observations apart, although several local versions have been recognised (e.g. Debénath *et al.* 1986), regional and temporal variation within the Aterian complex remains very poorly understood, as does its dating. Whatever its status, the Aterian seems to have been an exclusively African phenomenon, no trace of it having been found on the Iberian peninsula. South of the Sahara, analogous industries have been reported from northern Ghana (Davies 1967). In the east, confusion has arisen over the terminology applied to mode-3 industries from the oases of the Western Desert in Egypt (Wendorf *et al.* 1993; Kleindienst 2001), but it seems clear that those designated Aterian according to the generally accepted criteria did not extend so far as the Nile Valley.

Chronologically, the Aterian seems to belong to a period when reduced temperatures prevailed in northern Africa, resulting in glaciers on the High Atlas mountains and a general spread of vegetation zones to lower altitudes. In the Sahara, evergreen vegetation, primarily of Mediterranean species, grew in the highlands, and lower evaporation rates ensured that the rivers flowing from these highlands watered the adjacent parts of the otherwise relatively dry intervening plains (Van Campo 1975). In such a situation was the site of Bir Tarfawi in the Western Desert of southwestern Egypt where, probably between 130,000 and 70,000 years ago, people living beside a shallow lake were able to hunt a variety of animals, including gazelle, warthog and ostrich (Wendorf *et al.* 1993). Species included ones which are now restricted to the Mediterranean zone as well as some of more southerly affinities; rhinoceros remains have been found on Aterian sites as far to the north as El Guettar in southern Tunisia (Camps 1974). In southwestern Libya, the Aterian appears to be older than 60,000 years (Cremaschi *et al.* 1998; Cremaschi 2002), while in Morocco it may have continued until the last glacial maximum as steadily increasing aridity made much of the Sahara progressively unsuited to human settlement. Neither the Nile nor the Niger had by then attained its present course or extent: the upper reaches of the Niger flowed northeastwards into the present inland delta where its waters were lost by evaporation. Lake Chad was probably almost completely dry (Williams and Faure 1980). Such conditions, which coincided with a severe period of glaciation in northern Europe, continued in the Sahara until about 13,000 years ago.

The identity of the people responsible for the North African and Saharan mode-3 industries has recently been clarified. At Jebel Irhoud, Kebibat and Sale in Morocco and at Haua Fteah in Cyrenaica human fossils recovered in association with Levalloiso-Mousterian artefacts were formerly believed to resemble contemporaneous European neanderthalers; they are now regarded as closer to anatomically modern people (Ennouchi 1962; McBurney 1967; Hublin 1993, 2001; Klein 1999). The implication of this re-assignment is that there can have been little population transfer across the Straits of Gibraltar at this time, despite the apparent similarity of the pre-Aterian stone industries on the two sides during the final Middle Pleistocene (but see Barton *et al.* 2001). By later, Aterian, times, a fully modern population is attested in North Africa – as at Dar es Soltan, Morocco – of the heavily built type sometimes designated 'Mechta-Afalou', which continued to inhabit the Sahara until much later millennia (Hublin 1993). Continuity between these two human types seems likely but need not be assumed for, at the few sites (such as Adrar Bous in Niger and Bir Sahara in the Egyptian Western Desert) where Aterian artefacts are stratified over those of Levalloiso-Mousterian type, there was once again an arid intervening period during which much of the area may have been uninhabited.

Mention has already been made of the archaeological sequence in Cyrenaica. This part of northern Libya possesses, at the great cave of Haua Fteah, the most complete succession of Upper Pleistocene industries known from any part of North Africa (McBurney 1967; Close 1986). The oldest levels at this site have not yet been excavated, but it is known that Levalloiso-Mousterian occupation of the cave was established by at least 60,000 years ago. This industry continued through the period when its southerly Aterian counterpart flourished in the Sahara. It was preceded, in the lowest levels yet investigated at Haua Fteah, by an apparently quite distinct industry, which has been named the Libyan Pre-Aurignacian, based upon the production of parallel-sided blades struck from prismatic cores (Fig. 65). The makers of this mode-4 industry were accomplished hunters of wild cattle, gazelle and zebra; unlike their successors they also collected sea-food. This industry is not known from any other African site, although broadly comparable technology is attested in South Africa at an analogous time-depth (cf. pp. 98–102 above). Fairly close parallels have also been suggested in the Levant. Its local precursors in Cyrenaica remain unknown.

After the Libyan Pre-Aurignacian phase, Levalloiso-Mousterian occupation of Haua Fteah continued for more than 20,000 years until about 40,000 years ago when it was abruptly replaced by a more developed blade industry, called Dabban after another Cyrenaican site. The Dabban clearly belongs with the great complex of broadly contemporary mode-4 industries in Europe and western Asia conventionally known as the Upper Palaeolithic. Its most characteristic features were backed blades, edge-retouched flakes and narrow, chisel-like 'burins'. Here again, the closest connexions of this phase of the Haua Fteah sequence appear to be with the Levant, but it should be noted that it first appeared in Cyrenaica at broadly the same time as the beginning of the Saharan desiccation which led to the eclipse of the Aterian. Cooler conditions at that time are likewise indicated at Haua Fteah. With relatively little change, the Dabban occupation continued until about 14,000 years ago, when it was abruptly replaced, possibly with some overlap, by a mode-5 industry known as the Eastern Oranian, characterised by large numbers of small backed bladelets.

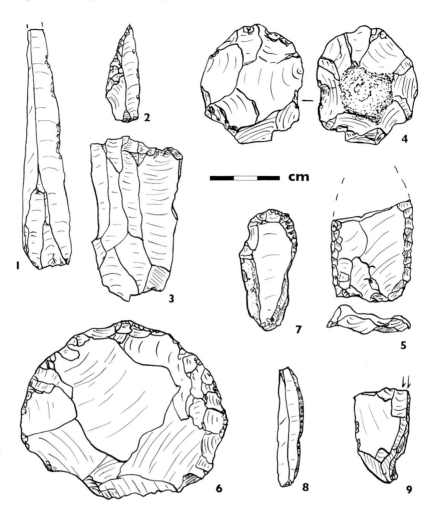

**Fig. 65:** Artefacts from Haua Fteah (after McBurney 1967): 1–3, Libyan Pre-Aurignacian; 4–6, Levalloiso-Mousterian; 7–9, Dabban

The Eastern Oranian, known also at other Libyan sites such as Hagfet et Tera, takes its name from its apparent close similarity to an industry of the Maghreb farther to the west. This Oranian industry was widespread in the North African coastland and hinterland from south of Rabat as far east as Tunis (Camps 1974, 1975). In recent years the Oranian has been more generally referred to as 'Iberomaurusian'. This term does not follow the standard practice of naming an archaeological industry after a site at which it has been recognised and described, and it carries unwarranted implications concerning connexions between Africa and the Iberian peninsula; the original name 'Oranian' is here retained. There is no evidence for continuity between the Aterian and the Oranian; probably there was a long intervening period when much of the region was uninhabited. So far, the earliest known Oranian occurrences are those located in Morocco and Algeria; at Tamar Hat on the coast of eastern Algeria an occupation dated some 20,000–16,000 years ago is attributed to this industry (Saxon *et al.* 1974; see also J. Roche 1971). The industries here designated Oranian and Eastern Oranian are restricted to zones of Mediterranean vegetation along the North African littoral in the Maghreb and Cyrenaica, being interrupted only at the Gulf of Sirte where desert conditions extend almost to the shore. At the time when these industries were made, sea levels were significantly lower than at present, and their distribution may have been continuous across the coastal plain that was then exposed.

Remains of the Oranian people have been discovered in several extensive cemeteries, notably at Taforalt, Columnata some 200 kilometres southwest of Algiers, and Afalou bou Rhummel, adjacent to Tamar Hat. They belong without exception to the anatomically modern Mechta-Afalou type, noted above, which had a long ancestry in North Africa (Chamla 1978). This is a further, albeit inconclusive, argument in support of a local origin for the Oranian industry. They were buried in extended or, at later sites, contracted positions. At Columnata, several skeletons were covered with settings of large stones, in one case capped by horns of wild cattle, *Bos primigenius*. The presence in the graves of red ochre and perforated shell indicates, apparently for the first time in the Maghreb, the practice of personal adornment (Fig. 66).

During the Oranian occupation, species of pine and oak which are now restricted to high altitudes in the Atlas Mountains were more widely distributed, indicating cooler climatic conditions during the final stages of the last glaciation. In this environment abundant animal species were available for hunting; this activity may be reflected in the survival of numerous small open-air sites, evidently briefly occupied, which contrast with the large, repeatedly re-occupied cave sites. Barbary sheep were intensively hunted and there is disputed evidence that, at Tamar Hat, the herds may have been managed by selective culling at a time when grazing on the coastal plain was curtailed by rising sea levels (Saxon *et al.* 1974; Klein and Scott 1986; di Lernia 1999). Land and water molluscs were also collected, particularly in later Oranian times, following the rise in sea level.

By about 10,000 years ago the Oranian unity had broken down and several local short-lived blade industries, such as that named Columnatan, are found in the Maghreb. Of particular interest is the so-called Typical Capsian, attested from about 8500 years ago in a restricted area of the Algeria/Tunisia border country south of Tebessa, as at Relilai. It is characterised by the large size of its artefacts, among which burin-shaped pieces and backed blades varyingly predominate. Many of its sites are middens of land-snail shells.

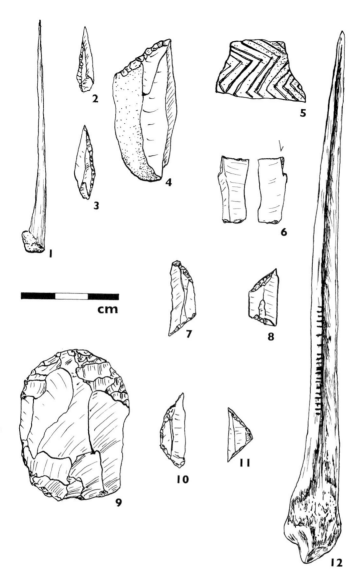

**Fig. 66:** 1–4, Oranian artefacts from Taforalt; 5–12, Capsian artefacts from Relilai and Mechta el Arbi (all after Camps 1974). 1 and 12 are bone points, 5 is a fragment of decorated ostrich-eggshell.

Far more widespread, being found as far afield as western Algeria, is the more microlithic Upper Capsian, which is somewhat earlier in date than the Typical Capsian (P. E. L. Smith 1982) and is also frequently found on shell-midden sites. At Columnata it replaced the Columnatan about 7500 years ago; at Relilai the corresponding event seems to have taken place a few centuries earlier. Crescentic, triangular and trapezoidal backed microliths, backed bladelets and notched or denticulated flakes are the most frequently encountered stone tools, together with a variety of bone artefacts. Much

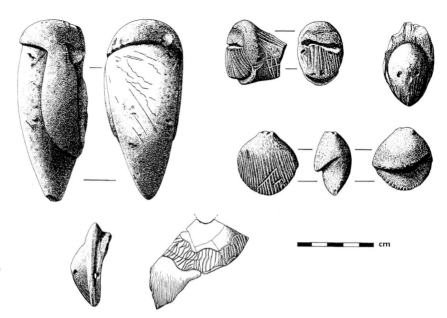

**Fig. 67:** Capsian carvings on stone and ostrich-eggshell (after Camps 1974)

artistic ingenuity was applied to the engraved decoration of ostrich-eggshells, and to the carving of small stone ornaments (Fig. 67). In addition to the collection of land-snails, hunting is well attested, in an environment which shows reduction of forest cover. Industries related to the Upper Capsian (which, like its predecessors, may have been the work of a Mechta-Afalou population, although it has been suggested that some skeletons show affinity to more recent Mediterranean peoples) are also found in the adjacent Saharan regions (Sheppard and Lubell 1990) and at Haua Fteah, where it has been called Libyco-Capsian. The greater part of the Sahara remained uninhabited until around 12,000 years ago; discussion of its resettlement after that time is best postponed until chapter 5.

The archaeological sequence of the Nile Valley, even at this early period, differs sufficiently from those of neighbouring areas that it is best considered separately. At least during the Pleistocene and Holocene phases when better-watered conditions prevailed, communication between the central Saharan highlands and the Nile would have been facilitated by the now-dry Wadi Howar, flowing eastwards from Ennedi to join the Nile near Dongola (Keding 1998). As a result of investigations which originated as rescue operations prior to the flooding of Lake Nasser, the prehistory of Nubia is more completely understood than that of neighbouring regions. Since the 1970s, however, most research in this region has concentrated on later periods.

Post-Acheulean industries named, following Levantine terminology, Levalloiso-Mousterian are best known from the area upstream of Luxor as far as Sudanese Nubia. Traces of their counterpart further downstream have presumably been destroyed by erosion or deeply buried by accumulations of silt. Several successive stages have been recognised, of which the earliest, designated Mousterian, shows considerable diversity, with at least three variants that are believed to reflect different activities (Wendorf and Schild 1976). In one of these variant Mousterian industries small handaxes occur, although never in large numbers. Wild cattle (*Bos primigenius*) was the preferred prey at these sites, which are too old to be dated by the radiocarbon method.

Later Mousterian assemblages show some Aterian affinities and may be broadly contemporary with that complex in the desert to the west. These artefacts show accomplished use of a prepared-core technique, with rare tanged pieces and bifacial leaf-shaped points similar to those of the southern Saharan Aterian. At Arkin near Wadi Halfa stone-knapping production sites are located at the raw-material outcrops, where the leaf-shaped points were roughed out (Chmielewski 1968). Nearby, at Khor Musa, is a contemporary occupation site where, for the first time in this region, most of the food debris comprises the remains of fish (Wendorf 1968). Further to the south, near Khartoum, a comparable industry has large, elongated foliate points akin to those of the Lupemban, possibly suggesting an extension of the equatorial forest environment along the valley of the White Nile at this time (J. D. Clark 1980).

Another site at Khor Musa has given its name to the final phase of this group of industries, where the earlier artefact types are accompanied by blade tools and burin-shaped pieces of the same general type as those in the Libyan Dabban industry. The Khormusan is now considered to be broadly contemporary with the Dabban, at least 35,000 years old (Fig. 68). It occurs on extensive sites where both fish and land mammals were eaten (Wendorf 1968; Wendorf and Schild 1976). Further downstream, near Qena, chert for tool-making was obtained from underground mines (Vermeersch *et al.* 1990; Vermeersch 2002); a child's burial, described as 'anatomically modern', was found nearby, associated with mode-3 artefacts dated between 80,000 and 50,000 years ago (Vermeersch *et al.* 1998).

Following the Khormusan, at least 25,000 years ago, began a period where the prehistory of the Nile Valley was characterised by even more diverse local industries of restricted temporal and spatial distribution. One of the earliest, the Halfan, is found on hunting/fishing camps in the Wadi Halfa area. Its tools, made on small blades, are in clear contrast with those of the Khormusan, which it eventually replaced (Marks 1968). Downstream, in Upper Egypt, the time-span of the Halfan was taken by non-microlithic

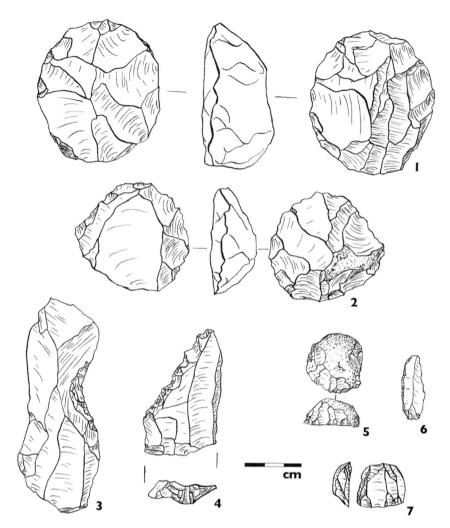

**Fig. 68:** Artefacts from Nubia (after Wendorf 1968): 1–4, Khormusan; 5–7, Halfan

industries grouped under the name Edfuan, in which blade technology accompanied a continuation of the Levallois technique. At Wadi Kubbaniya near Aswan, intensive use of vegetable foods is attested about 18,000 years ago, although the claim for the early use of barley at this site has been disproved by subsequent research (Wendorf *et al.* 1989; Barakat 2002). From about 17,000 years ago the local industries became progressively more microlithic, as with the Fakhurian which was contemporary with the later Edfuan and Halfan (Lubell 1974).

These markedly disparate industries co-existing at the same time so close together suggest that we are dealing not merely with activity variants, but with the presence of distinct population groups whose boundaries were not necessarily coterminous with those of the stone-tool industries currently recognised. Perhaps, in the closely circumscribed habitat provided by the Nile Valley, pressure of numbers was already stimulating technological innovation as part of the competition for control of, or access to, resources. Alternatively, diverse populations may have been brought together by shared environmental pressures into a circumscribed area. Such processes may have stimulated social contact and reinforced group differentiations, identity and rivalry. This situation continued into the period from about 15,000 to 11,000 years ago when water levels in the Nile, like those in the Saharan and East African lakes, rose. The important economic innovations which accompanied these developments are the subject of chapter 5.

The foregoing survey of the post-Acheulean stone-tool makers in North Africa, the Sahara and the Nile Valley has brought out two main points. First, throughout the whole of this area except the Mediterranean littoral, the distribution and nature of human settlement has been largely dependent upon changing environmental conditions. Major manifestations of this dependence are that settlement apparently ceased in much of the Sahara during the arid period following the florescence of the Aterian, and the dense concentration of occupation in parts of the Nile Valley. Secondly, and in part causally related, at a remarkably early date a widespread series of innovative practices evolved to maximise the food-yielding capacity of the natural environment. These developments were intimately connected with the presence of closely circumscribed communities which, as is reflected in their material culture, showed considerable ingenuity in adapting their life-style to varied situations. Subsequently, as will be shown in chapter 5, similar developments are found over a far wider area.

## Changing life-styles and technology

At first sight, this chapter has presented a bewildering mass of data of very varying quality, ranging from the results of modern, scientific excavations to details pieced together from observations of undated surface occurrences. The data relate to three strands of enquiry which have often been followed independently: hominid fossils, human genetics and material archaeology. It is now necessary to stand back from the details in an attempt to gain an overall picture of human development in Africa during the period between the final Acheulean/Sangoan industries around 350,000–250,000 years ago and the beginnings of permanent settlement.

Throughout the period discussed in this chapter archaeological sites in most parts of Africa are both larger and more numerous than those of earlier times. This cannot be explained solely by the fact that they have been preserved with less disturbance or obliteration than older sites. Virtually all parts of the continent were now at least sporadically occupied, some of them for the first time. There is evidence that a wider range of environments was subject to human exploitation, and that there was a progressive increase in the size of hominid populations both at a local and at a continental level (Lee 1963). This may indicate that people had become more adaptable and consciously responsive to environmental and other pressures. One result of this adaptability was the steady proliferation of local industries and the accompanying faster rate of cultural change that may be recognised in the archaeological record. Demographically, it was accompanied by increases both in the size of individual groups and in overall population levels. A corresponding acceleration in the development of non-material culture is indicated, for example, by the burial customs and artistic traditions, as well as by the personal adornment that has been preserved. By the end of the period many of the foundations for the diverse richness of later African cultures had already been laid.

The African hominid fossils of this period have been evaluated by, among others, Klein (1999) and Rightmire (2001). The picture that emerges is one of generally uniform development from *Homo heidelbergensis* to an early form of *H. sapiens*. The designation *H. helmei* is sometimes applied to an intermediate species. The model proposed above in chapter 2 demonstrates that it would be inappropriate to seek a definite point in time or place where this transition took place; it is sufficient to note that the presence of archaic *H. sapiens* is indicated in most regions of Africa by the end of the Middle Pleistocene. Subsequent further developments led to the emergence of 'anatomically modern people' in eastern and southern Africa, and probably also in North Africa and other parts of the continent, between 200,000 and 100,000 years ago.

Genetic studies have not yet been undertaken on African human fossils and are based almost exclusively on recent samples. Such studies have focussed largely on attempts to illustrate the origins of modern populations, with a particular focus on Europe. As noted above (pp. 95–6), this has led to a tendency to attribute human genetic modernity to a rapid and recent transformation (e.g. Klein 2000a) which is supported neither by other lines of enquiry nor by theoretical considerations. Since genetic mutations occur primarily in individuals rather than across populations, it has proved difficult to produce a diachronic interpretation of modern data which does not involve improbably small populations or bottlenecks. Despite uncertainty about the details and the chronology, there is broad acceptance of the view that anatomically modern people first evolved in Africa and spread from there to other parts of the world.

Turning to the archaeological record, it is clear that, despite local variations, technological developments followed broadly parallel courses throughout Africa – as, indeed, in other parts of the Old World. The general course of this development was outlined in the introductory section of this chapter and need not be repeated here. Recent research south of the Sahara has tended to blur the distinction formerly proposed between the stone-tool industries of modes 3–5 in the Congo Basin and adjacent regions on the one hand and, on the other, those in more easterly and southerly parts of the continent. Likewise, the mode-3 Aterian industry of the Sahara is now seen as having much stronger affinities with those of more southerly latitudes than was previously appreciated. As chapter 3 has shown, the origins of the prepared/radial-core tradition which is one of the defining characteristics of mode 3 can be traced far back into Acheulean times. Diversity through parallel evolution, already apparent in the final Acheulean, seems to have accelerated around 250,000–200,000 years ago and to have continued throughout the time-span to which this chapter is devoted.

More truly innovative, perhaps, was the eventually almost ubiquitous mode-5 backed-microlith technology which involved far more economical use of raw material, and the facility to repair or modify tools without resorting to their total replacement. Although direct evidence is lamentably sparse, invention of the bow and arrow may have taken place around this time, allowing much greater force and precision in the use of projectiles to which, on occasion, poison may have been applied. In parts of North and Northeast Africa, as in the Levant and elsewhere, this technology is best and conventionally seen as a development from mode-4 blade industries in which techniques for making backed retouch were frequently practised. Further to the south, however, backed microliths appear in the Howieson's Poort industries at dates which are significantly earlier than those known for comparable technology elsewhere in the world, and the roots of their development may be traced to even earlier times in south-central Africa. Archaeologists are still far from being able to explain why these parallel technological developments should have taken place; simple diffusion from a common source is not a likely explanation. In both southern and south-central Africa, recent research has demonstrated the length and complexity of the archaeological sequence of mode-3 and mode-5 industries. The very early dates proposed for Border Cave and Twin Rivers strongly suggest that the post-Acheulean/Sangoan technological traditions began at an approximate time-depth between 250,000 and 200,000 years ago. Their emergence may have taken place regionally at different times, as was demonstrably the case with the later development of mode-5 technology.

In recent years, particular emphasis has been attached to seeking archaeological evidence for trends in the development of human culture and behaviour which might parallel the evolution of anatomically modern people illustrated by current osteological and genetic studies (Crow 2002).

There is no clear agreement among archaeologists as to what might comprise a list of 'modern' behavioural elements, or how certain factors might be selected for inclusion on such a list. Elements often proposed include: technological specialisation; increased selectivity and economy in the use of raw materials; symbolism as exemplified, for example, in art, pigment use and the application of personal adornment; and, for reasons never adequately explained, the working of bone and the exploitation of aquatic resources (Stringer 2002a). The list was initially based on the comparatively well-known archaeological record of Europe, taking elements which were represented in Upper Palaeolithic contexts associated with the remains of 'anatomically modern' humans but absent from earlier contexts (Mellars 1993, 2002). Subsequent research has tended to blur this distinction, and certain criteria (notably the working of bone and the use of pigment) have been tacitly modified. Attempts to apply this schema in other parts of the world have cast further doubt on its validity (cf. Wadley 2001a). Some researchers (e.g. Willoughby 1993; Dickson and Gang 2002) have uncritically correlated the development of microlithic technology *per se* with 'modern' behaviour. There is wide acceptance that language development must have played a crucial role in the onset of cultural modernity, but little agreement as to how its stages are to be defined or how (if circular argument be eschewed) they might be recognised in the archaeological and palaeontological records. In view of the uncertain validity of the criteria employed for its recognition, it is hardly surprising that there is controversy over whether the advent of cultural modernity was a single event, perhaps linked to a genetic mutation (Klein 2000a), or whether – as here advocated – it was a more gradual process (Stringer 2002b).

The objection has been made that the list of criteria is based primarily on evidence from Europe, which is now seen as a region peripheral to the developments under investigation. It is also questionable whether the ill-defined concept of cultural modernity is appropriately tracked by the simple expedient of checking individual items on a list which has itself been subject to gradual uncritical modification. Be that as it may, the African archaeological record surveyed in this chapter provides crucial evidence both that these developments took place significantly earlier in Africa than in Europe and also that their appearances were results of gradual processes. The view that it was specifically in southern (H. J. Deacon and Wurz 2001), or southern and eastern, Africa that cultural modernity first arose is less well founded, and may be due to the fact that archaeological research in these areas has been much more intensive than has been the case elsewhere. A broader pan-African view is taken by McBrearty and Brooks (2000), who also argue convincingly that this was a long, slow development, as was in fact foreseen in the first edition of this book (D. W. Phillipson 1985b). Such a scenario is in accord with the increasing body of genetic evidence for multiple movements of anatomically modern or near-modern people from Africa over a substantial period (Lahr and Foley 1994; Quintana-Murci *et al.* 1999; Milliken 2002; Templeton 2002) which, it is now generally agreed, better fits the available fossil evidence than either the old multi-regional model (Wolpoff *et al.* 1994; cf. Lahr 1994) or the single-migration view (Stringer 2001). It also accommodates the geneticists' requirement for relatively small source-populations without resort to dramatic bottlenecks of the type hypothesised by Ambrose (1998a). This problem remains a major focus of current research.

The cultural significance of the blade-based technology which characterises the mode-4 industries of the European and Levantine Upper Palaeolithic has been evaluated by Bar Yosef and Kuhn (1999), while Ambrose (2002) has undertaken a similar exercise for mode-5 microlithic technology. The significance of bone tools is less clear: the original distinction, based on European materials, emphasised the first appearance of elaborate carving of bone in the Upper Palaeolithic, but this distinction has been lost or forgotten when the criteria have been applied to much older African materials, as at Blombos (p. 102 above). The remarkably close similarity of African barbed bone harpoons over a very wide area and, it now seems likely, through a long period of time, has been noted by Yellen (1998). Such artefacts have been subject to varied interpretations: to evaluate technological abilities, to reconstruct activities (often in conjunction with the study of non-artefactual residues), to trace typological similarities or contrasts, and as hallmarks of 'cultural modernity'.

The emphasis of much recent research has moved away from purely technological studies to a consideration of overall life-style in both the economic and socio-religious spheres. Such studies have until recently focused primarily on Holocene populations and have made greater advances in southern Africa than in other parts of the continent. As a result, complex reconstructions are now possible which view past settlement patterns as seasonally shifting foci of resource-exploitation, sometimes with alternating aggregation and dispersal of population. Similar patterns emerge from studies of the ethnography of some recent San peoples. The relevance of San ethnography for suggesting interpretations of the southern African past is further emphasised by study of the region's rock art, much of which is now seen as intimately connected with a socio-religious system based on trance and shamanism, which may have been a feature of life-styles in the region for many thousands of years.

It is now clear that Africa, and more specifically the sub-Saharan parts of that continent, occupied a key rôle in the cultural and physical development of the world's recent human populations. Archaeological, palaeontological and genetic studies all point to this conclusion. To study these processes from a Eurocentric perspective can only yield a biased, incomplete and misleading picture. Human fossils and other archaeological materials from widely distributed African regions demonstrate both the gradual evolution of anatomically modern humans and the equally gradual inception of cultural practices that are accepted as representing significant advances over those of earlier times. In Africa, these processes are now seen as having begun possibly as long ago as 250,000 years and to have continued into the period, some 50,000–35,000 years ago, when their end-results made a relatively sudden appearance in the insignificant peninsula now known as Europe. Both humanity itself and cultural/anatomical modernity were African developments. No longer can Africa be seen as peripheral to, or laggard in, the cultural innovations which distinguish modern people from their predecessors.

# 5 The beginnings of permanent settlement

This chapter describes and considers the significance of trends towards increased sedentism that occurred in final Pleistocene and early Holocene times over wide areas of northern and parts of eastern Africa. Rooted in the culture of their hunter-gatherer predecessors, some societies of this period are now seen as having provided the basis for the later adoption of herding and cultivation. The relevant literature is particularly confusing because of the various terminologies that have been applied, similar adaptations being designated Mesolithic, Epipalaeolithic, Late Stone Age or even Neolithic by different authors (cf. Vermeersch 1992). More than any other in this book, this chapter cuts across conventional time-divisions in its treatment of an important but localised process of African cultural development, but it provides a vital conceptual link between the predominantly foraging societies and those whose base in cultivation and/or herding has provided the foundation for much of the continent's more recent development.

## North Africa, the Sahara and the Nile Valley

It was noted in chapter 4 how the greater part of the Sahara had little or no human settlement during the arid period which broadly corresponded with the coldest part of the last northern-hemisphere glaciation. There are clear geomorphological traces, such as now-consolidated sand dunes (Roset 1987; Breunig and Neumann 2002), which indicate that the desert at this time extended even further to the south than it does today. However, the relatively favourable environment afforded by the Nile Valley at this time, between 20,000 and 11,000 years ago, allowed its population to increase within a tightly circumscribed area. Competition for resources and sociopolitical demarcation were the largely inevitable results of such processes. The relevant archaeological evidence may now be discussed (Fig. 69).

By this time, as shown in chapter 4, a number of communities in North Africa and the Nile Valley were engaged in the intensive and specialised exploitation of selected plants and animals. In the latter region, there is evidence for the presence of distinct localised communities. The best-documented and also one of the earliest incidences of this development is at Wadi Kubbaniya near Aswan (Wendorf et al. 1989; Barakat 2002), where tubers of wild nut-grass (Cyperus rotundus) were a major element of the diet around 18,000–17,000 years ago. It was evidently for the processing of these

147

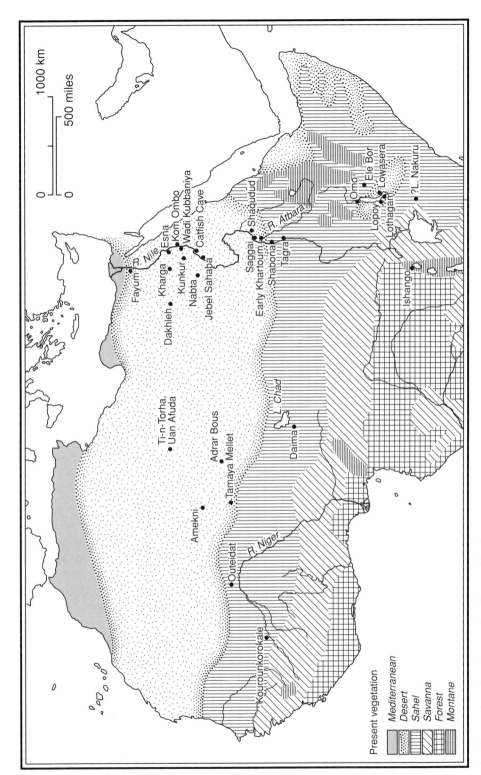

**Fig. 69:** Location of settlement sites discussed in chapter 5

Present vegetation

- Mediterranean
- Desert
- Sahel
- Savanna
- Forest
- Montane

1000 km

500 miles

R. Nile
Fayum
Kharga
Dakhleh
Kom Ombo
Esna
Kunkur
Wadi Kubbaniya
Nabta
Catfish Cave
Jebel Sahaba
Shaqudud
Saggai
Early Khartoum
Shabona
Tagra
R. Atbara
Omo
Ele Bor
Lopoy
Lowasera
Lothagam
?L. Nakuru
Ishango
L. Chad
Daima
Ti-n-Torha,
Uan Afuda
Adrar Bous
Tamaya Mellet
Amekni
Outeidat
R. Niger
Kourounkorokale

tubers, rather than cereals, that the heavily worn grindstones at the site had been used. The unusual preservation of charred tubers thus provides a salutary corrective to the tendency to emphasise ancient use of cereals at the expense of other plant foods (Hillman 1989).

During the period of high Nile levels, which lasted from about 15,000 until about 11,000 years ago linked in part to rising temperatures and the melting of glaciers in the mountains of Ethiopia, the inhabitants of the Nubian Nile Valley produced artefact assemblages whose variety demonstrates the establishment of distinct localised societies. One of these industries, the Qadan, also shows considerable inter-site variation in the comparative frequencies of the various microlithic tool types. This evidently reflects the varied activities carried out by the populations who fished, hunted wild cattle and other large ungulates, and also made considerable use of wild plant foods, including cereals. This last food source is indicated by the presence on Qadan sites of large numbers of grindstones and also by the fact that many of the microliths bear on their edges the characteristic polish known as sickle-sheen which, it has been demonstrated, may have resulted from their use to cut grasses (Unger-Hamilton 1988). The Qadan people buried their dead in cemeteries, at one of which, Jebel Sahaba, a substantial proportion of those interred could be shown to have met violent deaths (Wendorf 1968). This is perhaps a further indication of territoriality and inter-group conflict.

To the north, further downstream, other industries of this time, such as the Sebilian with its trapeziform microliths, and the Sebekian, present a similar picture of pronounced variability. On the plain of Kom Ombo, for example, at least three distinct groups are attested, and the available food resources were comprehensively exploited: those of the plain itself, the surrounding desert, the river, and its wooded fringe (P. E. L. Smith 1967). Some Kom Ombo sites seem to have been occupied on a year-round basis, and here too wild grasses were harvested. At Esna in Upper Egypt pollen analysis suggests that wild barley was, by 12,000 years ago, one of the varieties gathered on the flood plain (Wendorf and Schild 1976). Several of the animal species whose bones are represented in the food debris from sites of this period would have had narrowly circumscribed habitats and this may have enabled people to experiment with the development of management techniques over wild or semi-wild herds. These important innovations may be seen, at least in part, as responses to the concentration of population in the Nile Valley brought about by desiccation of the surrounding deserts.

Shortly after 12,000 years ago there was a remarkably rapid return to better-watered conditions in most of what is now the Sahara. Increased run-off from the highlands coupled, presumably, with higher rainfall and decreased evaporation resulted in the return of a regular flow of water to the long-dry wadis, the great enlargement of existing swamps and lakes – notably Chad – and the formation of many new ones (Petit-Maire 1988; Grove 1993). There were corresponding changes in vegetation and in the distribution of wild animals. The reasons for these large-scale trends are not fully understood. One of their most puzzling features is the rapidity with which they took place: the lakes appear to have reached their maximum heights as early as about 11,000 years ago (Hassan 1997).

Little research has yet been undertaken on archaeological sites which may confidently be attributed to the first human presence in the Sahara under the ameliorated climatic conditions of the early Holocene. Settlement more than 10,000 years ago, if it took place, must have been extremely rare. There were major short-term climatic fluctuations (Hassan 2002) and it seems likely that human settlement extended only very slowly into the newly habitable regions (Close 1992; Garcea 1993). From Mauritania to the Western Desert of Egypt, the earliest post-Aterian assemblages include characteristic pointed bladelets with basal retouch, known as Ounanian points (A. B. Smith 1993b). Assemblages of this type from the Western Desert, as at Kunkur Oasis, also contain many roughly trimmed flakes but no backed microliths, although the latter artefacts are important components of contemporary assemblages at Nabta Playa and Kharga Oasis (Schild and Wendorf 1977). At all these sites the presence of grindstones suggests that here, as at many Nile Valley sites of the same period, cereal grains – presumably wild – may have been harvested and prepared for use as food. A similar industry occurs at Adrar Bous in the Tenere Desert of Niger (A. B. Smith 1976). The degree of similarity between these Saharan industries and broadly contemporary material from southern Tunisia, such as the Upper Capsian, supports the view that part of the initial repopulation of the Sahara may have taken place from the north. Whatever the population source, it is clear that, although numerous and widespread, the Saharan sites of this time were individually of limited extent and briefly occupied, indicating a population of small mobile groups (J. D. Clark 1980). It is possible that the earliest Saharan rock art, consisting primarily of engravings of wild animals (Fig. 70), may date from this period (Mori 1974; but see also Muzzolini 1991).

By 9000 years ago significant changes had taken place, although their form varied significantly, as did local environmental conditions. Excavations in the Acacus highlands of southwestern Libya (Barich 1987) have revealed stone structures in Ti-n-Torha rockshelter (Fig. 71) which suggest some permanency of settlement. In the same area there is evidence at Uan Afuda (di Lernia 1999; see also di Lernia 1998) for intensive exploitation of large herds of wild Barbary sheep, as has been suggested for earlier times at Tamar Hat (p. 136, above). The clearest illustration of the development of sedentism at this time comes from research at Dakhleh Oasis in the Egyptian Western Desert (McDonald 1991). Between about 9000 and 8500 years ago,

**Fig. 70:** Rock engraving of long-horned *Bubalus antiquus*, Fezzan

the area's inhabitants seem to have adopted a more settled life-style, with circular stone-based huts, exploiting a significantly smaller territory than their predecessors had done. Further to the south at this time, local cattle were probably already being herded, as will be discussed below in chapter 6 (p. 175).

In well-watered situations, fishing and the exploitation of other aquatic food resources now played a large part in the economy of a vast area of the central and southern Sahara from the Nile Valley at least as far to the west as Mali. Sites were concentrated on the shores of rivers and lakes which were significantly higher and more extensive than those of today. Although at most sites hunting and grain-collecting were continued on a reduced scale, the pre-eminence of fishing now allowed larger populations to remain for longer periods of time at individual sites. Bone harpoon heads were the characteristic artefacts indicative of this new development. Pottery is also

**Fig. 71:** Stone structures at Ti-n-Torha rockshelter, Acacus

present at most sites of this type (Close 1995): it often bears the distinctive wavy-line decoration discussed in greater detail below (p. 156). In the Sahara, such pottery probably appeared at a slightly earlier date than in the Nile Valley or East Africa, being attested between 9500 and 8500 years ago in the Acacus in southern Libya, at Tamaya Mellet west of the Aïr Mountains of Niger (A. B. Smith 1980a), and at Amekni (Fig. 72) in the extreme south of Algeria (Camps 1969). Further to the west, in Mali, wavy-line pottery occurs also at Outeidat near Timbuktu (Gallay 1966), and barbed bone harpoons at Kourounkorokale near Bamako (Szumowski 1956; MacDonald 1997).

The Nile Valley industries between 12,000 and 8000 years ago are poorly illustrated by the research that has so far been undertaken. Thereafter the Nubian stone industry is of the microlithic type known as Shamarkian (Fig. 73), which includes small numbers of Ounanian points similar to those which also occur in Saharan industries of this time, as noted above. Somewhat later and far downstream, the Fayum Depression between 8000 and 7000 years ago supported lakeside camps of people who made microlithic artefacts, mounted fish jaws as points for arrows, and made their livelihood by a combination of hunting and fishing (Caton-Thompson and Gardner 1934; Wendorf and Schild 1976; Brewer 1989). This Qarunian occupation beside the extensive lake which formerly occupied the Fayum Depression provides examples of arrow-manufacturing techniques which continued in Egypt into dynastic times.

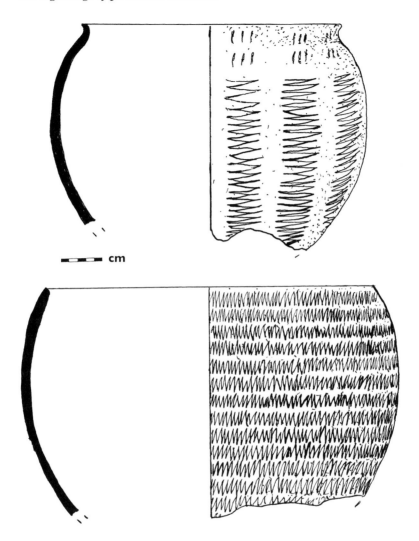

cm

**Fig. 72:** Pottery from Amekni (after Camps 1974)

It is, however, from the central Sudan that we have our most detailed knowledge of the inhabitants of the Nile Valley some 8000 years ago. The area was occupied by hunters and fishers who made use of substantial base-camps, probably occupied for much of the year, such as that which is known as Early Khartoum (Arkell 1949). (The local antecedents of its population remain unknown.) At Early Khartoum the stone industry included edge-retouched flakes, backed microliths, and larger tools for which the name 'crescent adzes' has been proposed; they are thought to have been used for the shaping of spear- or harpoon-shafts or similar wooden objects. Bone harpoon heads, barbed on one side only, were also a characteristic part of the assemblage. Stone rings and other objects, best interpreted as weights

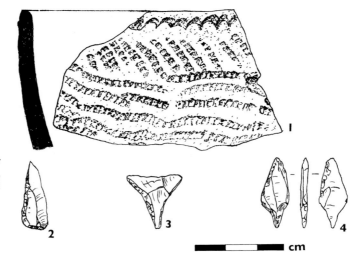

**Fig. 73:** Artefacts from Nubia (after Wendorf 1968): 1, Khartoum-related pottery; 2–4, Shamarkian microliths (4 is an Ounanian point)

for nets, suggest that harpooning was not the only method by which fish were taken. Pottery was common, generally decorated with multiple-grooved wavy lines, which may be duplicated experimentally by dragging a catfish spine over a surface of wet clay. During the later phases of the site's occupation, these designs were elaborated by jabbing the clay with a pointed object to produce a series of impressed dots (Fig. 74). Traces of sun-dried daub were recovered at Early Khartoum, suggesting that structures of some sort were erected there. Fishing and hunting were both important subsistence activities; and the presence of several swamp species in the faunal assemblage shows that the Khartoum area was significantly wetter than it is at the present time. The dead were buried, in contracted positions, in graves within the settlement. The Early Khartoum site was excavated before the development of radiocarbon dating techniques, so its age remains uncertain, although probably falling between 8000 and 7000 years ago. A related but presumably earlier site with harpoons but no pottery, at Tagra on the White Nile some 200 kilometres to the south, is dated to about 8300 years ago (Adamson *et al.* 1974).

The information derived from Early Khartoum has received significant confirmation from investigations by J. D. Clark (1989) and his colleagues at Shabona, some 140 kilometres upstream of the former site. Beside an embayment of the high-level White Nile an extensive area saw repeated settlement between about 7500 and 7000 years ago. Baked fish formed an important element in the diet of people whose material culture, including pottery, was essentially the same as that known from Early Khartoum. Wild grasses – probably *Digitaria* – were abundant, being used as temper for pottery; the excavator has suggested that the seeds may also have been collected and

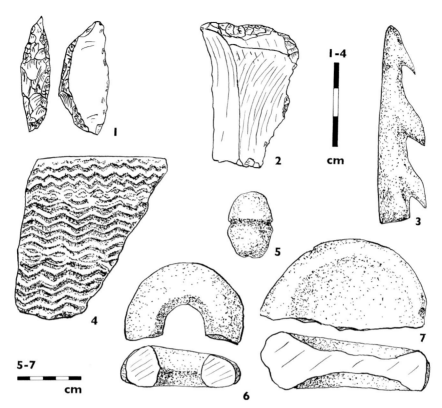

**Fig. 74:** Artefacts from Early Khartoum (after Arkell 1949): 1, backed microlith; 2, edge-retouched flake; 3, barbed bone harpoon head; 4, potsherd with wavy-line decoration; 5, grooved stone interpreted as weight for a fish net; 6, stone ring; 7, grindstone

'ground into flour to make porridge' (J. D. Clark 1989: 407). Flat depressions up to 2.5 metres in diameter may represent dwelling areas.

At Shaqadud in the Butana Plain, 150 kilometres northeast of Khartoum and 50 kilometres distant from the Nile (Marks and Mohammed-Ali 1991), a long sequence of prehistoric occupation began with settlement of Early Khartoum type which lasted from about 8000 until 6000 years ago when climatic conditions were somewhat wetter than those which prevail today. At Saggai (Caneva 1983), another site a short distance east of the Nile 30 kilometres north of Khartoum, which was more briefly occupied rather less than 7500 years ago, there is evidence for harpoon fishing, shellfish collecting and hunting, suggesting human presence at more than one season of the year.

Sites similar in general terms to Early Khartoum have been investigated in the area of the Nile/Atbara confluence (Haaland and Abdul Magid 1995); they date between 8600 and 6800 years ago with pottery in use throughout. However, in Nubia to the north, pottery seems to have remained unknown until late Shamarkian times, around 6500 years ago. There can thus be no reasonable doubt that, whatever the origin of the Early Khartoum pottery (and this will be discussed below), it does not represent a technology that spread up the Nile from Egypt. Comparable pottery does occur further to the south, despite a substantial gap in its known distribution between the Sudanese Nile Valley and Lake Turkana in northern Kenya.

By 7000 years ago, at Catfish Cave near Abu Simbel in Egyptian Nubia, a Shamarkian-like stone industry without pottery was associated with specialised fishing equipment in the form of bone harpoon heads barbed along one edge (Wendt 1966). These sites do not mark the beginning of intensive fishing in this region; at least in the Nile Valley, this had already been practised for several thousands of years (Van Neer 1989). As noted above, analogous harpoons are widely distributed in the Sahara; Nubia lay on the northeastern fringe of the area occupied by the harpoon-fishers.

'Wavy-line pottery' (Mohammed-Ali and Khabir 2003) has long been recognised as a significant and widespread innovation in Saharan Africa. First recognised in the Nile Valley, it was formerly believed to represent an expansion westwards into the desert (Hays 1974). More recent research has, however, demonstrated that some of its Saharan occurrences are significantly older than those beside the Nile (Close 1995); in fact they precede all other pottery known either in the Nile Valley or in the Mediterranean coastal regions of Africa. The available radiocarbon dates indicate a strong possibility that this early Saharan pottery was a local invention at least as early as 9500 years ago, there being no reliable evidence for any older material in adjacent areas from which the necessary technology could have been derived. Such an interpretation is fully plausible, since the accompanying relatively settled life-style, also an independent development, would have made possible the adoption of heavy fragile receptacles. These were very useful in a semi-permanent settlement but would have been ill-suited to the more mobile life-styles of earlier times.

Haaland (1992) has provided a stimulating overview of the processes leading from fishing/hunting/gathering to full mixed farming, although she concentrates on sites in the Sudanese Nile Valley and underestimates the significance of developments in more westerly areas. There can be little doubt that semi-permanent settlement preceded the practice of herding (Caneva et al. 1993) and that wild cereals were cultivated for many centuries, if not millennia, before the plants concerned display any of the morphological changes associated with domestication.

## East Africa

With one very significant exception, the East African sites relevant to this chapter are located around Lake Turkana and may be linked with its

**Fig. 75:** Old beach deposits at Lowasera, 80 metres above the present water level of Lake Turkana. The volcano, Mount Kulal, is visible in the background.

fluctuating high levels during the early Holocene (Butzer 1971). The waters of the lake rose rapidly around 10,000 years ago to a level 80 metres above its modern surface, which gave the lake nearly twice its present area and maintained an overflow channel to the northwest which eventually connected with the Nile. Deposits in the Omo Valley of southern Ethiopia, which represent a major northerly extension of Lake Turkana at this time, have yielded bone harpoons from levels dated to between 10,000 and 8000 years ago (F. H. Brown 1975). More detailed information concerning the makers of these artefacts comes from several sites located near the 80-metre beach lines on the eastern and southwestern sides of the lake in Kenya (Robbins 1974; Barthelme 1985; Stewart 1989). At Lowasera (Fig. 75) to the southeast, harpoons were probably in use by 9000 years ago; there is evidence elsewhere for a brief period of significantly lower water levels between about 7500 and 6800 years ago (D. W. Phillipson 1977c). Before this interval, pottery – where present – was rare and of wavy-line type; later sherds are much more abundant and generally undecorated. In the Lake Turkana Basin the earlier harpoons have a nick at the base for the attachment of the line; the later ones used several concentric carved grooves for this purpose (Fig. 76). The associated stone industry was, throughout, a mixture of backed microlithic elements and of large retouched flakes and core-tools, with a few grindstones. Food remains consisted almost exclusively of the bones of fish, crocodile and hippopotamus. The second harpoon-fishing phase continued until after 4500 years ago, by which time the waters of Lake Turkana were again falling; there are, indeed, indications that a similar life-style continued

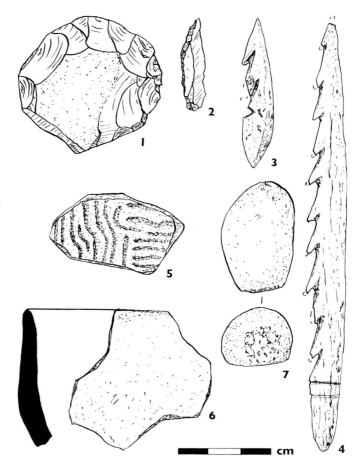

**Fig. 76:** Artefacts from Lowasera (after D. W. Phillipson 1977c): 1, edge-retouched flake; 2, backed microlith; 3, barbed bone harpoon head of early type with basal nick for attachment of the line; 4, barbed bone harpoon head of later type with basal grooves; 5, early potsherd with wavy-line decoration; 6, later undecorated potsherd; 7, hammerstone

at Lopoy, west of the lake, until less than 1000 years ago, when the lake's water-surface still stood about 18 metres above its present level (Robbins *et al.* 1980). Today, Elmolo people of the Lake Turkana littoral fish by means of barbed harpoons, now with iron heads.

Although there are inconclusive hints from the Lake Nakuru Basin in southern Kenya, the only other part of East Africa to have yielded evidence for harpoon fishermen is that around Lake Edward/Rutanzige on the border between Uganda and D. R. Congo. Here, we are concerned with a single site, Ishango on the northwestern shore, which has preserved a long sequence of occupation, although its dating remains uncertain (de Heinzelin 1957; Brooks and Smith 1987). Bone harpoon heads occurred throughout, at first barbed on both sides, latterly on one side only. The crude stone industry, of quartz, included edge-retouched flakes and some backed microliths. There was no pottery. An age of at least 7000 years is demonstrated, but there are good reasons for accepting that the site is very considerably older, perhaps as much as 18,000–16,000 years. Conditions wetter than those of the present are once again indicated by the animal bones that were preserved in the deposits; because of its outlet Lake Edward is less susceptible to changes in water level than is Lake Turkana, and its height at this time was only about 12 metres above that which prevails today. As noted in chapter 4 (p. 120 above), there are indications that fishing with bone-headed harpoons may have an even greater antiquity in this area. Be that as it may, it may be concluded that the Lake Edward Basin, which is the most southerly location of the East African harpoon-fishing adaptation, is also its oldest known manifestation. Here and around Lake Turkana, it may be shown that this adaptation developed significantly before the local beginning of pottery manufacture. When pottery did appear, its earliest East African manifestation (as represented at Lowasera) showed strong similarities with those of the Sahara and the Sudanese Nile Valley. These fishing settlements represent, of course, only one of several economic adaptations in East Africa at this time.

## Overview

These settled communities represent economic adaptations over a very wide area that parallel similar processes of environmental change (Barich and Gatto 1997; Cremaschi and di Lernia 1999). At least in North Africa and the Nile Valley, there had been for some millennia previously a tradition of intensive exploitation of various food resources, including aquatic ones, in circumstances which sometimes encouraged prolonged settlement of a particular site. Later semi-permanent settlements, beginning around 8500–8000 years ago, were characterised by the use for fishing of harpoons with barbed bone heads, and by pottery with wavy-line decoration. Contrary to previous opinion, the Nile Valley does not appear to have been the original homeland of the harpoon-fishing adaptation. On the evidence currently available the East African material of this type seems to be the oldest, a view which is strengthened by the very early date now proposed for the Ishango site, where biserially barbed harpoons were used by people who were ignorant of pottery. When pottery was developed by later hunter/fishers, it seems to have been an independent invention, perhaps originating in what is now the Sahara (di Lernia and Manzi 1998). The two characteristic elements of these settlements' archaeological remains, although often found together, thus appear to have originated separately.

The bone harpoon heads, which are widely distributed at sites in the Sudanese Nile Valley, in the southern Sahara and in parts of East Africa, at one time received undue emphasis from some archaeologists (e.g. Sutton 1974) who suggested that they may indicate a unified 'civilisation' based upon the exploitation of aquatic resources. Many of these objects were indeed used for fishing, but it cannot be assumed that this was invariably the case. At Daima, in northeastern Nigeria, a bone harpoon head was found embedded between the bones of a human skeleton (Connah 1981), demonstrating that such weapons were, at least in later times, occasionally used against human targets. Despite the basic typological similarity over a very wide area of both the bone harpoons and the pottery, these two elements can be traced to widely separated origins, and the chipped-stone assemblages with which they are associated show considerable variation, seeming generally to be rooted in distinct local traditions which may be traced back into earlier times. For these reasons it seems most satisfactory to regard the fishing settlements as representing a common adaptation (or parallel adaptations, with many shared features) to a common economic opportunity, rather than to consider them as belonging to a single uniform culture.

The fishing settlements, being concentrated in location, are the most readily recognised archaeological sites of this time. Their inhabitants were able to exploit enormously rich food resources that were obtainable with very little effort. Other means of livelihood were, however, pursued both alongside fishing and on different sites, away from permanent water. Hunting and, probably, grain collection continued in the Sahara. Elsewhere, as at Ele Bor in northern Kenya, hunters maintained their traditional life-style without pottery long after this had been adopted in the lakeside fishing settlements (D. W. Phillipson 1984; Gifford-Gonzalez 2003).

Various speculations have been expressed concerning the linguistic affinities of the early settled communities considered in this chapter. Sutton (1974) raised the question of whether their members might have spoken an ancestral Nilo-Saharan language, the recent discontinuous distribution of these languages having been brought about by subsequent movement and dispersal. Ehret's (1993) argument that early Nilo-Saharan speakers were farmers, discussed further below (pp. 211–12), is on much firmer ground, although not necessarily incompatible with Sutton's view.

The full importance of the innovations represented by the harpoon-fishing adaptation and of the settled life-style that accompanied it can only be fully appreciated when we consider the subsequent adoption of farming. This will be discussed in detail in chapter 6.

## African peoples 10,000 years ago

This is an appropriate point to view the overall distribution of African prehistoric communities at a single time, before effective farming is attested in any part of the continent. We will also examine the evidence for the distribution of human physical types at this general period and enquire to what extent it is possible to recognise populations that were ancestral to more recent ones.

The modern indigenous population of Africa comprises several varied physical types, the distinctions between which are not always readily apparent. It is appropriate in this context briefly to investigate the extent to which this diversity may be traced back in the archaeological record. Several writers (e.g. Hiernaux 1968; Weiner and Huizinga 1972) have stressed the difficulty of defining discrete recent populations even on the basis of a complete range of physical characteristics, including such features as finger prints and blood groups. In recent years, genetic research has begun to reinforce this picture of ill-defined heterogeneity (Watson *et al.* 1997; Kittles and Keita 1999), as will be explained below. Since African populations have lived in close contact with one another for many thousands of years, it is inherently highly improbable that any population will have retained in unmixed form the characteristics of any prototype which may formerly have existed. Yet it is such non-homogeneous populations that have, perforce, to form the basis for our recognition of the groupings concerned.

There are thus major problems not only of recognition but also of definition. These problems have led some authorities to ask whether it is reasonable for archaeologists to attempt to identify discrete human physical types ancestral or related to those of the present day. It is nevertheless widely recognised that there are metrical skeletal features, notably of the skull and teeth (Rightmire 1972; Irish and Turner 1990; Irish 1994), which are generally more characteristic of one population than of another. Although observed ranges of variation frequently overlap, the ranges noted in a prehistoric population may show a close degree of fit with those of a particular recent group; the affinities of isolated individuals are correspondingly difficult to determine (cf. A. W. F. Edwards 2003). Bearing these many hazards in mind, it is worthwhile to survey the views that have been proposed for the affinities of final Pleistocene/early Holocene African populations.

In the Maghreb the Oranian hunter-gatherers were replaced by the makers of the varied microlithic industries which eventually gave rise to the Capsian. It has been suggested that people of proto-Mediterranean type first appeared in North Africa at this time, joining the robust 'Mechta-Afalou' population who seem to have been the sole inhabitants of the region during Oranian times (Dutour 1989). These proto-Mediterranean people may have been at least partly responsible for the resettlement of the northern Sahara following the post-Aterian period of desiccation.

To the south, the harpoon-using fishermen of the central and southern Sahara, the Sudanese Nile Valley and parts of East Africa are represented by a few fragmentary skeletons from Ishango, Lothagam on Lake Turkana (Robbins *et al.* 1980), Lowasera (Rightmire in D. W. Phillipson 1977c), Early

Khartoum and elsewhere which are said to show negroid physical features. Similar characteristics occur in skeletons from the Qadan cemetery at Jebel Sahaba in Nubia (Wendorf 1968), where Mechta-Afalou features have also been recognised. These remains may be from a population ancestral to present-day Nilotic negroids. Other authorities, emphasising the presence of features which are also seen in KhoiSan and Northeast African 'caucasoid' populations, prefer to interpret this material as representing a more generalised 'ancestral African' physical type, which may be regarded as akin to a common ancestor of several more recent populations. This explanation also seems plausible for the varied human remains that have been recovered in association with broadly contemporary and rather later industries from southern Kenya (Rightmire 1975; see also Morris 2003).

The archaeology of this period in West Africa remains poorly understood, being covered by only two dated sequences, at Iwo Eleru in southwestern Nigeria and Shum Laka in Cameroon. In this area the hunter-gatherer people of the forest margin had adopted a backed-microlith technology akin to that of the neighbouring savanna. Elsewhere in the West African forest regions non-microlithic stone-artefact manufacture continued. A single human skeleton some 12,000 years old from the lowest level at Iwo Eleru has been described as already showing specifically negroid features (Brothwell and Shaw 1971), but the broadly contemporaneous burials at Shum Laka (Ribot *et al.* 2001) were too fragmentary to permit detailed evaluation. In other parts of West Africa, skeletal material has not been preserved. The same is unfortunately true of the whole of the Congo Basin and adjacent forested regions where the Tshitolian industries had by this time developed.

On the southern savanna many areas had seen the practice of backed-microlith production for many thousands of years. By 10,000 years ago related technology had been adopted by hunter-gatherers in most of the region except, it appears, in areas of the arid southern African interior and perhaps in parts of the upper Zambezi Valley to the north. Substantial numbers of human skeletons have been recovered in association with these industries, particularly noteworthy (although late) being the group of thirty-three individuals of about 5000–3000 years ago from Gwisho hotsprings in southern Zambia (Brothwell 1971) and a somewhat earlier series from graves in cave sites on the south Cape coast. There can be little doubt of the KhoiSan affinities of most of this material. However, some skeletons, particularly from north of the Zambezi, are also stated to show features characteristic of recent southern African negroid populations (e.g. de Villiers in D. W. Phillipson 1976). This observation serves to emphasise the difficulties in a continent where for many millennia few barriers to genetic mixing have existed. Such links do little more than reinforce the view that both

KhoiSan and negroid stocks are derived from a single generalised African ancestral population (Tobias 1978b).

By the early Holocene, it thus appears possible to make the first tentative correlations between communities represented in the African archaeological record and the ancestors of some modern populations. The principal physical types seen in recent indigenous populations may also be recognised in the archaeological material, where the distinctions between them are no more clear than they are between the modern groups. What we see in the incomplete archaeological picture so far available is the gradual process of differentiation of modern human types from ancestral populations that were genetically as mixed as those of the present day.

In recent years, considerable advances have been made over the earlier treatments of this topic, brought about by the development of genetic research and by further refinement of linguistic methodologies. In both cases, primary research is effectively restricted to modern populations, but the resultant data can yield important implications about the past. Study of the DNA in modern African populations (e.g. Passarino *et al.* 1998; Salas *et al.* 2002) permits the mapping of genetic variation independently of physical characteristics. These plots may be interpreted to generate historical hypotheses and the time-scales involved may be estimated through reference to what is known about rates of mutation (Watson *et al.* 1997; Pereira *et al.* 2001). For example, it is becoming apparent that the populations of sub-Saharan Africa are genetically far more diverse than are modern people elsewhere, and that some of these characteristics diminish in more northerly and northeasterly parts of the continent (Lalueza Fox 1997; Krings *et al.* 1999).

As noted in chapter 1, a somewhat similar methodology may be followed in the manipulation of linguistic data. It is now recognised that the several language families of Africa can probably be traced back for 7000–10,000 years or, in some cases, even longer (Blench 1999; Ehret 2003). It has been suggested that, in Africa as in other parts of the world, language change and the adoption of farming techniques may have proceeded together (Bellwood and Renfrew 2003). Some aspects of genetic continuity and variation are better understood than are processes of linguistic change: transmission of mitochondrial DNA, for example, takes place exclusively through the female line. This means that reconstruction of historical processes based on genetic evidence may sometimes have a firmer foundation than those proposed exclusively on linguistic grounds.

Attempts to correlate conclusions based on different methodologies have, in theory, considerable potential. Unfortunately, in practice, most such attempts have foundered because few scholars are adequately familiar with the methodologies and constraints of more than one discipline. For example, an attempt to use genetic divergence between groups of modern

KhoiSan-speakers to estimate the antiquity of that language family (Knight *et al.* 2003) is marred by false assumptions concerning language transmission and change. Such studies are, however, in their infancy and offer much opportunity for refinement. It is already clear that, as the nature of human variation becomes better understood and self-centred stereotypes (whatever their basis) become increasingly untenable, genetic studies – especially when used in conjunction with other approaches – offer great potential for augmenting our understanding of the history of modern human variation.

# 6

# Early farmers

## Cultivation and herding

Previous chapters of this book have discussed the stages of human development during which people relied for their livelihood on the plants and animals that were present in their natural environment, feeding on wild vegetable foods, as well as on the meat of wild animals, birds, fish and insects. In Africa, as in other parts of the world, people have been exclusively foragers for more than 99 per cent of their existence. Here, attention will be drawn to the processes by which greater control over animals and plants gradually gave rise to domestic forms (Bower 1995). In the northern half of Africa (Fig. 77), these developments were achieved by people who had not yet learned metallurgical skills; in many more southerly areas, the first use of domestic plants and animals was made by people who also worked metals, as will be discussed in chapter 7.

It has been shown in chapter 5 how, from as early as 18,000 years ago, some Nile Valley communities in Upper Egypt were making intensive use of vegetable foods in the form of tubers. It is likely that this practice has, in fact, a far greater antiquity, although its earlier manifestations have not yet been revealed by archaeology. By 15,000–11,000 years ago, people in this area had begun to utilise wild cereals in a similar way, as their successors in many Saharan regions have continued to do into recent times (Harlan 1989; Wasylikowa 1992). These practices may have been accompanied by care of wild grasses through such means as control of weeds, clearance of ground and, perhaps, occasional provision of water. Under these circumstances sowing might also have been employed to increase the density of growth in the tended places and to extend the areas colonised by the wild plants. With or without conscious selection for desired qualities, such practices may eventually have led to the development of crops morphologically distinct from their fully wild prototypes (cf. Zohary 1969; Chikwendu and Okezie 1989). By such means, some of the late Pleistocene peoples of the Nile Valley seem on occasion to have exploited wild cereals and other plants, but there is no evidence that true cultivation was developed at this time. These are among the earliest instances of intensive cereal utilisation that have yet been demonstrated anywhere in the world, and there can be no reasonable doubt that they were indigenous African achievements. But they did not lead to the widespread adoption of such practices at this early date. A later

165

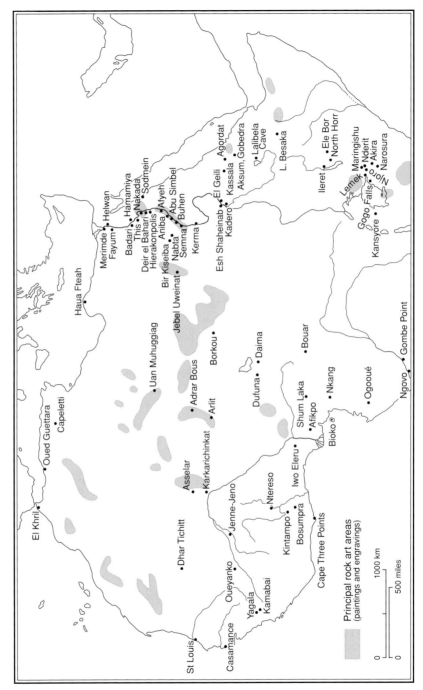

**Fig. 77:** Location of principal sites with rock art and/or evidence for early cultivation or herding

section of this chapter will offer some speculation as to why this may have been so.

Similarly, it now appears that the late Pleistocene/early Holocene peoples in several regions of northern Africa came to concentrate their exploitation of wild animal resources on single or very few species (Barich 1987). The example of the Barbary sheep (*Ammotragus lervia*) has been cited above (pp. 136, 150–1). The increased knowledge and awareness that accompanied this aspect of specialisation may have led in the direction of herding or, conversely, to conditions where animals previously herded elsewhere could readily be adopted. It will be argued below that domestic animals did not become widespread in the northern half of Africa until about the sixth millennium BC. By that time plant cultivation and animal herding had both been long established in the Levant (Bar Yosef 2003). Although it is not easy to show the extent to which some early farming practices in northern Africa may have been derived from the Levant, it is clear that many developments both here and further to the south were autochthonous (Harlan 1992). In this context it is particularly illuminating to consider where the wild forms of the various plant and animal species that were eventually domesticated may have originated. It has for long been assumed that cultivated wheat, barley and flax were all introduced into Africa from the Levant, although wild barley and, perhaps, einkorn wheat occur in several areas of Egypt where their food value was recognised from very early times (cf. p. 149, above). If we exclude crops such as maize and cassava (manioc), which are known to have been introduced from the New World within the last five hundred years, and those such as bananas brought significantly earlier across the Indian Ocean, most of the crops which are or have been cultivated in Africa belong to species that are indigenous to that continent and which must presumably have been first cultivated there. Examples are the more important types of yam, African rice, certain pulses and the cereals sorghum, finger millet (*Eleusine*), bulrush millet (*Pennisetum*) and teff (*Eragrostis tef*), together with the Ethiopian plants enset and noog (Fig. 78), all of which are derived from plants which grow wild in the sub-Saharan latitudes. It will be noted from this list that indigenous African food crops fall into three primary categories: rice, other cereals, and vegetatively propagated plants such as yams and enset. Each of these categories requires a distinct method of cultivation, and there is no reason to suppose that the development of these horticultural modes was in any way interconnected. Much discussion of early African food-crops centres on the cultivation of cereals, because of the nature of the primary evidence and its greater chances of preservation, but cereals were not necessarily the earliest such crops nor, in many areas, are they the ones that have made the greatest contribution to human nutrition.

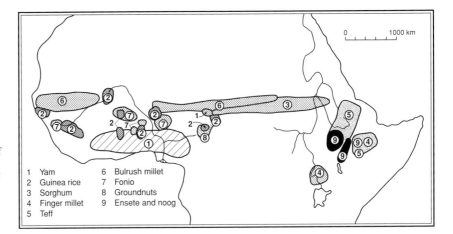

**Fig. 78:** The probable areas of the initial domestication of indigenous African crops (after Harlan 1971)

In the case of domestic animals the position is somewhat different. Sheep (*Ovis*) and goats (*Capra*) have no African wild prototypes, for it has been shown that the Barbary sheep (*Ammotragus*) is most unlikely to have given rise to any known domestic forms (Epstein 1971; Cassinello 1998). It is often difficult to differentiate between sheep and goats on the basis of the fragmentary bones that are recovered from archaeological sites, and references to 'ovicaprids' or to 'small stock' in later sections of this book will indicate remains which cannot be attributed with confidence to the correct species. Cattle present more difficulties: although it was formerly believed that domestic cattle originated in western Asia or southeastern Europe, recent genetic studies illustrating the antecedents of particular cattle breeds strongly support the view that there were in fact two centres of origin, one being in northern Africa (Marshall 1989; Grigson 1991; Blench and MacDonald 2000). Cattle of North African derivation were of paramount importance in subsequent developments throughout the continent (Grigson 2000; Marshall 2000). Although much more circumscribed in distribution, the donkey also appears to have been an indigenous African species that was domesticated in one or more of the northeastern regions (Blench 2000). Domestic fowls remain poorly understood: the earliest in Africa was probably the guinea fowl in West and North Africa. Chickens, of Asian origin, were known in Egypt from Ptolemaic times if not before, but not south of the Sahara until the first millennium AD. It is, however, abundantly clear that none of the major domestic animals of sub-Saharan Africa, other than cattle and donkeys, is derived from a species that is indigenous to that part of the continent; they must therefore have been introduced from elsewhere.

Cultivation and herding have often been considered together by archaeologists as 'food-production'. Domestic animals and cultivated plants are, however, far more than sources of food. They provide important raw materials for clothing and many other purposes, as well as stimulants and drugs. They sometimes play an important role in religious affairs and, as will be shown below, provide the basis for far-reaching social, political and economic developments. In several African societies domestic animals serve as embodiments of wealth and indicators of status. Food-production is thus just one aspect of practices which have become central to the whole lifestyles and belief-systems of many peoples. In view of this wide importance, in the following pages the term 'farming' will be employed in place of the more usual 'food-production'. Likewise, the term 'agriculture' is best avoided since it is often used ambiguously either to include or to exclude management of domestic animals. Since the cultivation of plants and the herding of animals are two quite distinct cultural activities, it is often preferable to treat them separately, without the implication that the practice of one necessarily implies the other.

A further confusion may arise from imprecise application of the term 'pastoralist' to any person or community possessing domestic animals, irrespective of the importance which these animals may have had in the overall life-style of the people concerned. Used correctly, the term applies only to societies or individuals who rely upon domestic animals for a very large component of their subsistence, and whose lives are largely controlled by the need to care for their herds. In this book, unless there is very clear evidence for true pastoralism, the more neutral term 'herder' is used to designate someone who owns or controls domestic livestock.

Here, it is appropriate briefly to evaluate the types of archaeological evidence that may be accepted as proof of ancient farming. By far the most convincing are the actual remains of cultivated plants or domestic animals, or unequivocal artistic representations of them. Pollen grains or seeds may survive under appropriate conditions, or impressions of seeds may be preserved on pottery. Some food-plants, such as yams and bananas, will by their very nature hardly ever be represented in the archaeological record, and this has led to undue emphasis on the better-preserved evidence for cereal cultivation. There are indications that study of phytoliths may fill this gap (Piperno 1988), but the relevant techniques are still under development and it is only occasionally that detailed identifications can be made (e.g. Mbida *et al.* 2000). Only recently, and still infrequently, have excavators in Africa routinely employed techniques such as flotation which are generally necessary if plant material is to be recovered comprehensively. Since, by contrast with plant remains, bones are relatively indestructible and easy to identify, archaeologists have often tended to overemphasise animals at the expense of plants. As a result, many reconstructions of ancient diets – of all periods – place excessive stress on the meat that was consumed and on other animal products, tending to minimise the vegetable component (but see van der Veen 1999). It must be admitted that this prejudice may mirror the views of some ancient African societies. Today, meat is often regarded as the most important food – a view that may be connected with the traditional division of tasks between men and women, where the provision of meat and other animal products is seen as a male task, with women obtaining most of the plant foods.

A further complication involves dating. Objects – whether artefacts, bones or plant remains – found together in a primary archaeological context may generally be assumed to be contemporaneous and, in appropriate circumstances, datable. However, in the case of small items like seeds, great care must be exercised to ascertain whether they may be intrusive from a younger or older context. Sometimes, particularly when only a few specimens are preserved, it is appropriate to pay particular attention to obtaining direct radiometric age determinations on the actual seeds or bones themselves (e.g. D. W. Phillipson 2000), as is now practicable through the Accelerator Mass Spectrometry radiocarbon method. The evidence of rock art, in which domestic animals are not infrequently depicted, may also be hard to interpret since the absolute age of such images can only rarely be determined.

Farming of both plants and animals eventually gives rise in most cases to physical differences which serve to distinguish the domestic forms from their wild prototypes. The domestication process involves deliberate selection and control of breeding. For example, preference may be given to the largest yams or to cereals which do not shed their seeds as soon as they are ripe, but retain them when harvested. Animals of docile temperament, perhaps of small size, will more readily be incorporated in controlled herds. Thus, after a number of generations, significant physical differences may be established. It follows from this that the initial stages of domestication, whether of plants or animals, are correspondingly difficult to recognise in the archaeological record (Haaland 1992). Furthermore, it now appears highly probable that the emergence of fully developed cultivating and herding economies was the result of a far longer period of intensive exploitation and experimentation than was previously realised. The distinction between gathering and hunting on the one hand and farming on the other is thus far from clear. While both plants and animals usually undergo some degree of morphological change under domestication, it can take very many generations before these become readily apparent. The absence of such changes thus cannot be taken as proof that practices leading to cultivation and herding had not begun.

Archaeological evidence for cultivation and herding, other than actual plant or animal remains, is usually less convincing. The implications of artefacts are often ambiguous: sickles and grindstones for instance provide no indication of the socio-cultural context of their use, and could have been employed for gathering and processing wild plant foods, or for other materials altogether. The nature of an ancient settlement may provide indirect evidence for its economic basis: permanence or seasonality of occupation, for example, facilities for the storage of produce or for the watering or protection of livestock may all be indicative of farming practice but often fall short of conclusive proof.

Despite the elusiveness of the evidence, the importance of the adoption of farming techniques should not be underemphasised. Practice of such techniques gave people greater control than they had generally exercised over their own supplies of food and other commodities. Although concentrated natural resources had in earlier times occasionally allowed maintenance of semi-permanent settlements, these were usually small. In several areas farming seems to have been adopted at least partly in response to environmental deterioration and population pressure, as later sections of this chapter will argue; and it in turn enabled populations to increase still further. The relatively settled life which is inherent both to cultivators and, less markedly, to herders provided a stimulus for the accumulation of material possessions beyond those which could readily be transported. A sedentary life-style could also have facilitated increased child-bearing, as pregnancy, nursing and closely spaced births are all hindrances to mobility. Communities could now more readily afford to maintain the old, the disabled, or members who specialised in activities other than herding or cultivation. The increased sizes of these communities and the frequency with which they came into contact with their neighbours must often have necessitated the development of political structures more complex than those which had existed among the simpler societies of earlier times (Ingold 1988). A far-reaching corollary may have been the replacement of communal reciprocity by forms of individual ownership.

Before detailing the archaeological evidence on a regional basis, it is useful to consider some general points relating to its interpretation. Farming depends on the availability of suitable plants to cultivate or animals to herd. Such plants and animals may be obtained in one of two ways: by exercising control over wild varieties already present in the area concerned, or by acquisition of plants or animals previously controlled elsewhere. Recent research, as this chapter demonstrates, is showing that the former trend has played a much greater part in the development of African farming than was at one time believed. The latter trend has none the less been important, not only in bringing to Africa plants and animals that had been domesticated elsewhere, but also within Africa itself. It has been subject to the constraints of numerous factors, including cultural preferences, environmental conditions and the prevalence of plant and animal diseases (Dahl and Hjort 1976; Gifford-Gonzalez 2000; Hassan 2002). Means of transmission need also to be considered, as is also true of many other cultural elements. Domestic plants and animals are, by definition, under human control; they require human intervention to move from one place to another. However, contrary to the implication of much earlier writing on the subject, this does not necessarily mean that whole human populations migrated along with their herds or crops. A comparatively small number of individuals could have been responsible for their introduction and, indeed, evidence of continuity in artefact typology often indicates that this was probably so (D. W. Phillipson 1979; Karega-Munene 1996). Against this must be set the increasing body of evidence from many parts of the world that the adoption of farming was often accompanied by language-change (Holden 2002; Bellwood and Renfrew 2003).

Such developments were not, of course, automatic. On the one hand they help to explain how such a complex civilisation as that of ancient Egypt arose apparently less than 2500 years after farming was first adopted on a significant scale in the Nile Valley. On the other hand, in many areas of Africa, peasant communities have been able to maintain themselves without centralised state systems into recent times (Bohannan et al. 1958). Nor must it be thought that farming, once adopted, necessarily led to the rapid abandonment of foraging; on the other hand, farmers seem rarely to have reverted to hunting and gathering. Both activities continued to play an important part in most precolonial African economies, while a few communities maintained an almost exclusively hunting-gathering life-style into the twentieth century. With low population densities, such as prevailed in many parts of Africa until recent times, the natural resources are such that hunting and gathering provided a level of nutrition as high as, or higher than, that achieved by farming peoples (Lee 1968; see also Brooks et al. 1984). It is nevertheless true that cultivation and/or herding have provided the economic basis for most of the major technological, artistic and socio-political achievements of African culture during the past 7000 years.

## The Sahara and North Africa

In much of northern Africa, study of early farming has been hampered by imprecise usage of the term 'Neolithic', varyingly to designate the practice of cultivation and/or herding, the presence of pottery and/or ground-stone tools, or merely attribution to an ill-defined time-period. Because of this confusion over its implications, the term is not used in this book.

The oldest plausible evidence for any form of farming in Africa comes from the Egyptian Western Desert. The first farming communities in this region appear to have been direct descendants of their late Pleistocene/early Holocene predecessors, described in chapters 4 and 5. The microlithic stone-artefact assemblages of the two phases are very similar and seem to have more in common with contemporary materials to the north than with those of the Nile Valley to the east. Indeed, the evidence currently available strongly suggests that farming began in the Western Desert at a date significantly earlier than that of the corresponding development in the Nile Valley (Hassan 1988b; Barker 2003).

The early and mid-Holocene in northeastern Africa, and almost certainly elsewhere, was a period which saw much rapid climatic fluctuation. Some episodes of major environmental change were remarkably brief (Hassan 2002). Although there is broad agreement about this general picture, the detailed sequence and the dating of some individual episodes remain controversial (Wendorf and Schild 2003); it cannot be assumed that fluctuations in neighbouring areas were necessarily contemporaneous. The scale of some of these changes was dramatic, with rainfall in certain areas up to fifteen times their modern levels, and extensive lakes in areas that are now totally arid (Petit-Maire 1991; Grove 1993). It is none the less important not to assume that lush environments were ubiquitous in the Western Desert, or elsewhere in the Sahara, during this period. There was undoubtedly more surface water than in earlier or more recent times, but this was concentrated in and around the highland areas, or in localised lakes or ponds. On the plains between these well-watered areas the vegetation remained very sparse, and the fauna consisted of such creatures as ostrich and gazelle which can survive in arid conditions. More varied faunas, like the human population, were concentrated around the ponds and other better-watered places (cf. Roset 1987; Vernet 2002).

During mid-Holocene times in the Western Desert, as in the Nile Valley, people seem to have experimented with the control of wild animals, including antelopes and giraffes. The evidence for this comes from rock art, notably that at Jebel Uweinat in southeastern Libya, which unfortunately cannot be dated (Fig. 79). Giraffes are shown tethered and being led by halters (Van Noten 1978). With the concentrations of human and animal populations which are attested, it is easy to see how such experimentation could have taken place, perhaps following the exploitation of wild Barbary sheep discussed in chapter 5. Animals thus controlled may have been taken to the Nile Valley, where they are known to have been in demand.

The first evidence for farming in the Western Desert comes from Bir Kiseiba and from nearby Nabta Playa, a pond-basin of 100 square kilometres near the Egyptian/Sudanese border (Wendorf *et al.* 2001). The sites

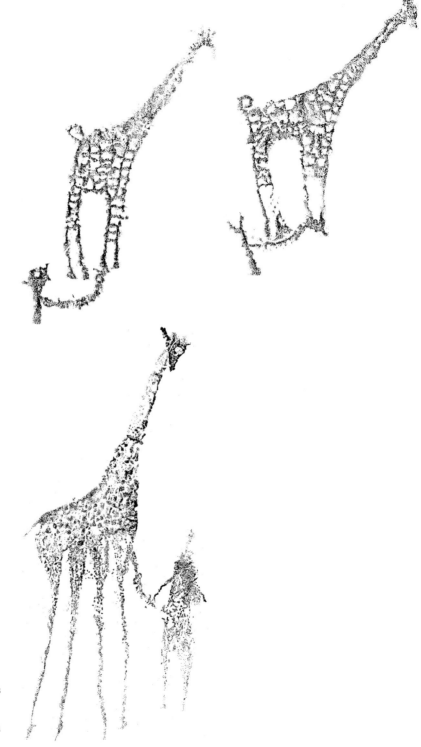

**Fig. 79:** Rock engravings at Jebel Uweinat, showing giraffes tethered or restrained by a halter (after Van Noten 1978)

that were occupied beside the pond margin around the eighth millennium BC were more extensive than their precursors, featuring house floors, hearths and rows of storage pits. It seems that the sites' inhabitants were indigenous to the area rather than new arrivals from elsewhere, and that they continued the hunting-and-gathering economy of their predecessors. The stone industry was essentially the same as it had been in earlier times, but with the addition of concave-based points which may have served as arrowheads (Wendorf and Hassan 1980; Banks 1984). Pottery bowls stamp-decorated with a rocked comb were locally made. Hunting of the wild fauna evidently continued, but cattle were increasingly represented from about 8000 BC; arguments that they were domesticated are now widely accepted although the case is not wholly conclusive, being based primarily on the size of the beasts and indications that human effort was devoted to watering them (Gautier 1987, 2002; Close and Wendorf 1992; Wendorf and Schild 2003). It has been suggested, on not wholly persuasive grounds, that the cattle may have been brought to this part of the Western Desert during a period when the local vegetation was comparatively lush, having been initially domesticated elsewhere, conceivably in what is now the northwestern Sudan. There can be little doubt that the presence of domestic bovids in the eastern Sahara significantly preceded the local appearance of sheep or goat, which are not attested at Nabta before 5800 BC. The abundant and varied plant remains at Nabta include seeds of sorghum and millet, but none was demonstrably domesticated; it is possible that incipient cultivation was practised but had not yet given rise to morphological change in the grains concerned (Wendorf *et al.* 1998; Barakat 2002). It may have been during the sixth millennium BC, when several periods of severe drought are attested, that cattle herding extended into both the Nile Valley and the central Sahara.

On the North African coast, to the west of the Nile, the beginning of farming is best illustrated at Haua Fteah in Cyrenaica (McBurney 1967). Here, by the early sixth millennium BC or shortly thereafter, the local Libyco-Capsian stone industry (p. 138, above) was followed by a period of occupation during which the economy of the site's inhabitants was based upon herds of domestic ovicaprids. There is no evidence for the presence of domestic bovids, which appear to have been restricted to more southerly regions at this time. The artefact assemblages show signs of continuity from the Libyco-Capsian, with pottery in evidence from about 5000 BC, but it is clear that the livestock must have been introduced to the area from elsewhere – presumably from the Levant. Not only does Haua Fteah provide no evidence for the gradual development of herding, but the sheep/goats that were kept there were clearly not descended from the wild Barbary sheep which had been intensively hunted by the Libyco-Capsians and their contemporaries in the

Maghreb and the Fezzan. Interestingly, ovicaprids also made their appearance at Sodmein Cave in the Egyptian Red Sea Hills at this same time – about 5800 BC – in generally similar circumstances (Vermeersch *et al.* 1996). The evidence for domestic animals in Cyrenaica and the Red Sea Hills was thus at least as early as that for the Nile Delta region (pp. 187–8 below). There is no evidence that cereal agriculture, which was practised in the Delta, was known further to the west at this time.

In the Maghreb (Sheppard and Lubell 1990), pottery appeared in the context of the Capsian-related stone industries by the sixth millennium BC. From this time onwards the somewhat diverse industries north of the Atlas Mountains and extending eastwards to Tunisia have generally been classed by archaeologists as 'Neolithic of Capsian tradition'. In fact, several distinct traditions may be recognised. In northernmost Morocco, adjacent to the Straits of Gibraltar, the earliest pottery, as at El Khril near Tangier, is decorated with impressions of cardium shells, in a manner widespread in the western Mediterranean coastland (Jodin 1959). To the east, in coastal Algeria, the pottery at Oued Guettara is impressed at the rim with sticks or plant stems (Camps 1974). Throughout this area it seems likely that the introduction of domestic ovicaprids was broadly contemporary with the beginning of pottery manufacture: bones of such animals were recovered from the lowest levels of El Khril and may represent the first type of farming to be practised in this part of North Africa. At Capeletti Cave in the Aures Mountains of eastern Algeria, transhumant herding of cattle and small stock was practised from the mid-fifth millennium BC onwards by people who do not seem to have had any knowledge of cereal cultivation (Roubet 1979). The human remains found associated with these 'neolithic' industries are described as being of predominantly Mediterranean type, and it has been suggested that some of these people were directly ancestral to the more recent Berbers (McBurney 1975; Camps 1982).

In several areas of the central Sahara there is similar evidence for cultural continuity between the earliest farmers and their predecessors – who in some instances included harpoon-using fishers. The sequence in southwestern Libya is particularly informative (Garcea 2001; Cremaschi 2002). Attention was drawn in chapter 5 to the extensive former lakes in the Fezzan; these shrank or disappeared during a brief arid interlude between 6500 and 6300 BC but then expanded again. The lakes of this second phase had camps of cattle herders along their shores, with ovicaprids in evidence from about 5700 BC. Further evidence comes from the adjacent Acacus massif where the skull of a shorthorn ox at Uan Muhuggiag appears to date from about 4900 BC. At the same site, rock paintings of cattle, buried in the archaeological deposits, are argued to be earlier than 3400 BC (Mori 1965; Shaw 1977; Barich 1998; Cremaschi and di Lernia 1999). There were numerous grindstones but no positive evidence that cereals – or any other plants – were cultivated;

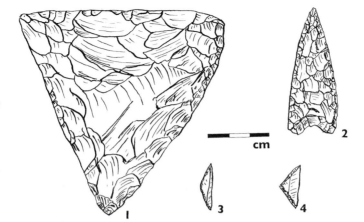

**Fig. 80:** Artefacts from Adrar Bous (after Camps 1974): 1, bifacial triangular knife; 2, bifacial projectile point; 3, 4, backed microliths

intensive use of wild cereals seems probable. The associated mode-5 stone industry and stamp-decorated pottery are characteristic of those found on sites of this time over an enormous area of the Sahara, although regional variants may readily be recognised (e.g. Barich 1987, 1992, 1998; Muzzolini 1993; Close 1995; Barker 2003).

One such variant is the Tenerean, best known from Adrar Bous and Arlit in Aïr but extending eastwards to Borkou in Chad (Bailloud 1969; J. D. Clark *et al.* 1973). The industry (Fig. 80) dates between 5000 and 3300 BC, the skeleton of a domestic shorthorn ox from Adrar Bous (Carter and Clark 1976; Van Neer 2002) being dated to the mid-fifth millennium. Domestic small stock were also herded but the sole evidence for plant exploitation, other than the ubiquitous grindstones, consists of a single impression on a potsherd of a grain that is thought to be sorghum. Hunting was also important, and the prey included warthog, antelope, hippopotamus and rhinoceros. Pottery and ground-stone axes show some resemblance to those from the broadly contemporary Nile Valley sites of Esh Shaheinab and Kadero (pp. 181–3 below). Backed microliths were abundant. Projectile points and disc-shaped knives were bifacially flaked.

Our knowledge of the early Saharan herders may be amplified by study of the rock paintings and petroglyphs which are widely distributed in the highlands (Le Quellec 1987; Caligari 1993; Muzzolini 1995). Only rarely has it proved possible to date individual paintings precisely, but several attempts have been made to distinguish stylistic sequences, notably in the Hoggar, Acacus and Tibesti highlands. These sequences may then tentatively be linked by their subject-matter with the archaeological succession to provide a provisional chronology (e.g. Muzzolini 1991, 1993). There may have been an initial phase with engravings, rather than paintings, which depict exclusively wild animals (p. 150); since, however, the same techniques were sometimes used in representations of cattle, it cannot be regarded as

**Fig. 81:**
Round-headed
painted figure,
Tassili

conclusively proven that there is a 'pre-pastoral' phase in the Saharan rock
art sequence (Mori 1974). The most numerous paintings are those portray-
ing pastoral scenes in which long-horned cattle are associated with human
figures, some of which have distinctive rounded heads (Figs. 81, 82). Later
styles, believed to date from the late second millennium BC onwards, are
marked by the successive appearance of horses and camels (P. E. L. Smith
1968; Muzzolini 1986; A. B. Smith 1993a). The art shows many details of

**Fig. 82:** Rock painting of a pastoral scene, Tassili

clothing and illustrates the domestic, social and ritual life of the Saharan herders (Dupuy 1993; Le Quellec 1993; Holl 1995). Breeds of cattle may also be recognised, as may the practice of artificial deformation of the horns (Schwabe 1984; cf. also J. Brown 1990), which has continued in the Sahara, as in parts of East Africa, into recent times. Milking and use of cattle for riding are also depicted.

To the southwest the beginning of herding seems to have taken place rather later, as shown in the Tilemsi Valley which enters the Niger from the north near Gao. In the upper part of the valley, cattle herders lived at Asselar in about 3300 BC, but they probably did not penetrate the previously uninhabited flood plains to the south until early in the third millennium, when the Karkarichinkat sites were occupied. At these sites cattle are represented both by abundant bones and by clay figurines. Fishing, hunting and fowling are also attested, but there was no evidence for the cultivation of any vegetable foods. This movement down the Tilemsi Valley may be regarded as the first stage of the southward spread of cattle-herding into West Africa (A. B. Smith 1974, 1980b; Van Neer 2002; see also p. 203).

The results of research at Dhar Tichitt, located near the southern edge of the desert in south-central Mauritania, have often been cited as suggesting that cereal cultivation in the western Sahara was a relatively late

**Fig. 83:** Dhar Tichitt stone enclosures: (top) from the air, and (below) as preserved on the ground

development. This view must now be modified, and the adoption of cultivation seen in its socio-political context (Holl 1989). The site lies within the natural distribution area of wild varieties of both sorghum and bulrush millet. Remains of extensive villages, comprising numerous stone-walled compounds (Fig. 83), occur along a limestone cliff over a distance of some 40 kilometres. Numerous radiocarbon dates indicate that the occupation of the complex extended from the mid-third to the early first millennia BC, a period which saw progressive desiccation of the local environment and shrinking of the lakes at the foot of the cliff. Bones of cattle and goats are preserved, while the pottery retains impressions both of wild grains and of cultivated bulrush millet (*Pennisetum*). Initial research by Munson (1976) appeared to indicate that the farming of millet at Dhar Tichitt began shortly before the middle of the second millennium BC and did not achieve economic importance until several centuries later. Reinterpretation by Holl (1985a, 1985b) suggests, however, that the differences in food sources do not reflect a chronological sequence so much as varying, seasonally determined economic practices. If this was indeed the case, the Dhar Tichitt sequence would fit more conformably within the general picture now emerging in several parts of the Sahara (Amblard 1996; Wetterstrom 1998).

Detailed conclusions should not be drawn from the very incomplete coverage of the research that has so far been undertaken in the Sahara. A general picture is, however, beginning to emerge. Rich concentrations of resources in often hostile environments stimulated, as was described in chapter 5, the development of a sedentary life-style at several places in the Egyptian Western Desert, leading in due course to the domestication of local cattle and the use of sorghum and millet. By the beginning of the sixth millennium BC these innovations had spread to several widely dispersed parts of the Sahara. It was probably shortly afterwards, around 5800 BC, that domestic ovicaprids were introduced from the Levant into Africa, where their remains have been discovered in Cyrenaica, in the Red Sea Hills and, some centuries later, in the Nile Delta. Further discussion is best postponed until data relating to the Nile Valley have been presented.

## The Nile Valley

Despite the evidence for early experiments, described in chapters 4 and 5, the permanent adoption of farming techniques in the Nile Valley is known only from a relatively late date. In the Khartoum area, for example, there is no indication that any form of farming was practised before the late fifth millennium BC (Hassan 1986a; Haaland 1992). Recent research has shown that the settlement pattern at this time was far more complex than had originally been anticipated. The first relevant site to be excavated was that of Esh Shaheinab, 50 kilometres north of Khartoum (Arkell 1953), where the material culture is clearly a development of that represented at Early Khartoum (pp. 153–4 above). The site had a river-bank location and fishing was evidently of major importance. Barbed bone harpoon heads were now pierced at the base for attachment of the line, and shell fish-hooks were

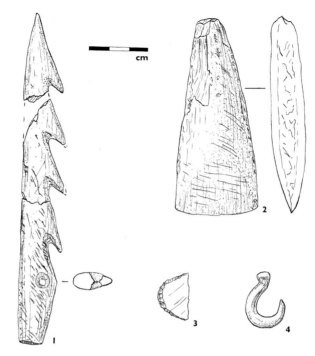

**Fig. 84:** Artefacts from Esh Shaheinab (after Arkell 1953): 1, barbed bone harpoon head with perforated base; 2, bone adze; 3, backed microlith; 4, shell fish-hook

also in use. Axes and adzes, finished by grinding, were fashioned from both bone and stone (Fig. 84). Both the microlithic stone industry and the pottery resemble those from Early Khartoum and some Saharan sites, but the pottery was now burnished and also included new types resembling contemporaneous Pre-Dynastic Egyptian wares. Beads were made from amazonite which appears to have been brought from Tibesti, over 1700 kilometres distant. The animal bones recovered were originally believed to represent wild species, with a few small goats, but it was subsequently recognised (Peters 1986) that domestic animals, including cattle, were present in larger numbers.

It now appears that farming in the central Sudanese Nile Valley during the closing centuries of the fifth millennium BC was both intensive and complex (Haaland 1987). Much of the evidence comes from Kadero, a site which covered an area of 4 hectares on the edge of the flood plain northeast of Khartoum (Krzyzaniak 1978, 1984). Here, at the same time as the occupation of Esh Shaheinab, cattle were herded in very large numbers along with sheep and goats; about 90 per cent of the animal bones recovered from Kadero were of domestic species. There were enormous numbers of heavily used grindstones. Grain-impressions on pottery showed that sorghum, finger millet and panicum were the principal cereals used.

Although not morphologically distinguishable from wild grains, they do appear to have been collected and processed on a substantial scale and may have been cultivated. Hunting and fishing were both of marginal importance. The dead were buried within a circumscribed area. The Kadero site, by its size and evidence for prolonged use, may be regarded as a base settlement. Other sites in the locality were occupied by smaller groups on a seasonal basis and used for different economic activities, including fishing. The overall picture which is emerging from current research is of a community which occupied several different sites on a seasonal cycle, using various food resources according to their availability, possessing large numbers of domestic animals and perhaps also cultivating cereals at some of their locations. Further evidence in support of this view comes from El Geili, some 30 kilometres north of Kadero, across the river from Esh Shaheinab (Caneva 1988). This complex situation provides an excellent demonstration of the dangers in drawing detailed conclusions from the investigation of single sites which may yield very incomplete pictures of ancient life-styles (Mohammed-Ali 1982).

Away from the Nile, there are indications that a similar situation prevailed along the now-dry Wadi Howar (Richter 1989), which extends eastward from the highlands of eastern Chad to join the Nile near Dongola. As research continues in this area, it may be expected more clearly to demonstrate connexions between the Sahara and the Nile Valley. During the better-watered conditions that prevailed for much of the mid-Holocene, these connexions would have been more readily made than has been possible more recently, as indicated also by settlement in more northerly areas that are now virtually inaccessible desert (Schuck 1989).

Downstream, pottery which seems to be related to that from Esh Shaheinab occurs at a number of sites in the Dongola region and extending into Nubia, where it is sometimes associated with the stone industry known as Abkan. In Lower Nubia the earliest fully farming community known to archaeologists is the so-called A-Group, which probably arose around the middle of the fourth millennium BC (Fig. 85). The Abkan affinities of the stone artefacts found on A-Group sites, together with some features of their pottery, suggest that the A-Group was of indigenous Nubian origin; it was subsequently much influenced by contact with Pre-Dynastic peoples of Egypt (pp. 189–91; O'Connor 1993a). Trade between the two areas was extensive, with Egyptian flint and a wide range of manufactured goods including stone vessels, copper tools, palettes, amulets and the like finding their way southwards. It was presumably raw materials that went to Egypt in exchange: commodities such as ivory, and ebony from further to the south. The A-Group people are known mainly from their graves, which occur in large

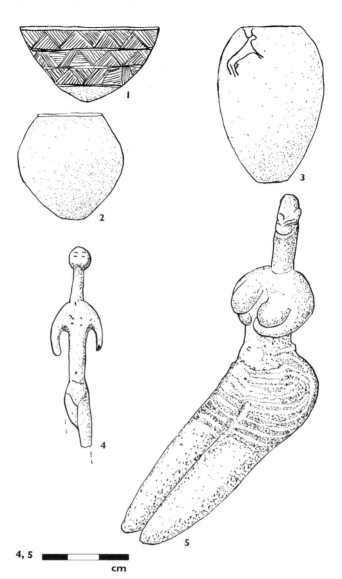

**Fig. 85:** A-Group artefacts from the Wadi Halfa area (after Nordström 1972): 1–3, types of pottery vessels (not to scale); 4, 5, human figurines

cemeteries and show burial customs similar to those which prevailed in Egypt (H. S. Smith 1991). Sheep and goats were herded, with smaller numbers of cattle. Wheat and barley were cultivated; linen cloth was in use, but may have been imported from Egypt rather than made from locally grown flax. Fishing and hunting were both practised. Although many people lived in insubstantial shelters, others – perhaps an élite – were housed on a grander scale, as at Afyeh near the First Cataract, where an A-Group settlement consisted of rectangular houses with up to six rooms, dating from about 3000 BC (W. Y. Adams 1977). The reasons for the end of the character-istic A-Group settlement at about the time of the end of the First Dynasty in Egypt (approximately 3100–2900 BC) are poorly understood, but may have been connected with growing imbalance of authority as centralised Egypt grew more belligerent and substituted raiding for trade. A Fourth-Dynasty incursion (2600–2500 BC; see pp. 189–90 below) is recorded as having resulted in the capture of 7000 people and 200,000 domestic animals (Breasted 1906).

For several centuries Egyptian contact with Nubia was at a reduced level. From Sixth Dynasty times (2300 BC) onwards Nubian archaeology is again better known, the indigenous population being known as the C-Group (Trigger 1976; J. H. Taylor 1991). Particularly in the south, there is evidence for cultural continuity between the latter and people living east of the Nile, in the Red Sea Hills. Although domestic cattle, represented in grave-goods and depicted on pottery, clearly occupied a more important place in the lives of the C-Group than in those of their predecessors, faunal remains suggest that their herds also included numerous small stock. Settlements were initially small and consisted mainly of large circular houses with the bases of their walls built of stone. More complex structures are attested in later times. Graves, as at the Aniba cemetery, were sometimes marked by stelae. Luxury goods of Egyptian origin were obtained on a moderate scale, but local crafts, notably potting, were highly developed. There is evidence that Egyptian contacts now extended further upstream than pre-viously, probably at least as far as the Dongola Reach, beyond the Third Cataract.

In Middle Kingdom times (2000–1600 BC) the Egyptians established a mil-itary occupation of northern Nubia and erected a series of massive forts, as at Semna south of the Second Cataract, to secure Egyptian control of trade and access to the area's gold deposits. This period saw the rise of a rich culture at Kerma, located in the most fertile part of Sudanese Nubia at the northern end of the Nile's Dongola Reach. The formative stages at Kerma are not fully understood; probably an essentially indigenous society gradually became subject to increasing Egyptian influence, although its specifically Nubian features remained dominant (cf. O'Connor 1993b). For reasons that are not known to us, but which may be connected with polit-ical troubles in their homeland, the Egyptians retreated from Nubia under the Thirteenth Dynasty, late in the eighteenth century BC, and this provided Kerma with a further boost. Herding of cattle and ovicaprids contributed greatly to Kerma's prosperity, as indicated both in the settlement sites and in the grave-goods placed in the extensive surrounding cemeteries. Kerma was both a political capital and a religious centre; among its most impres-sive monuments are huge brick structures known locally as defuffas, and

**Fig. 86:** The brick substructure of one of the royal burial mounds at Kerma

the graves where its powerful rulers were buried, accompanied by the bodies of numerous retainers, under large mounds up to 80 metres in diameter (Fig. 86). Great wealth was evidently accumulated through Kerma's control of wide-ranging trade, and a remarkable level of craftsmanship was attained, particularly in pottery. Egyptian stylistic influences remained strong but many local features are apparent (Reisner 1923; Dunham 1982; Bonnet *et al.* 1990; Bonnet 1991, 1992).

Early in the Eighteenth Dynasty (around 1500 BC) Nubia was re-occupied by the Egyptians, the old forts were repaired, and Kush was conquered. This time the Egyptianisation of Nubia was cultural as well as political, as is witnessed by the temple of Ramesses II at Abu Simbel, erected in the thirteenth century BC (Fig. 87). Both the C-Group culture and its Kerma manifestation withered away. From about 1000 BC, Kush ceased to be ruled by Egyptian-appointed viceroys and became an independent kingdom. In the eighth century BC the king of Kush conquered Egypt and established the Twentyfifth Dynasty.

It is now necessary to turn northwards, to the Egyptian Nile Valley, and to return to the period which saw the beginning of farming there. As will be apparent, the picture contrasts markedly with that obtained in the Sudan. It was probably owing to the abundance and reliability of wild food resources there, and despite much early experimentation, that the beginning of

**Fig. 87:** The temples at Abu Simbel, before clearing and restoration (after Gau 1822)

farming on a significant scale in the Egyptian Nile Valley seems to have been abrupt and late in comparison with its inception in the Western Desert (pp. 173–5; cf. Hassan 1986b, 1988b; Wetterstrom 1993). In the Delta and in the Fayum Depression small villages of farming people broadly resembling those from adjacent parts of southwestern Asia were established from about 5200 BC (Fig. 88). That at Merimde on the western side of the Nile Delta, dated around 4800 BC, may be cited as an example (Baumgartel 1955; Hawass *et al.* 1988). It covered an area of some 18 hectares and consisted of small oval dwellings measuring only about 2 by 3 metres, built of lumps of mud mixed with straw, sunk slightly into the ground and presumably originally roofed with reed thatch. These structures were set on either side of narrow lanes and interspersed with mud-lined storage pits, basket granaries and open shelters which appear to have been used as workshops. The dead were buried within the settlement in mat-lined graves. Bifacially flaked stone tools and undecorated pottery serve to link this settlement with its counterparts in the Fayum Depression (Caton-Thompson and Gardner 1934; Brewer 1989). The economic basis for these Lower Egyptian settlements was the cultivation of barley, emmer-wheat and flax. Cattle, sheep, goats and pigs were kept, as were dogs. The earliest Nile Valley attestation of the domestic donkey, an indigenous African species, dates from about this time. Hunting and fishing continued to be practised. Although the Fayum settlements

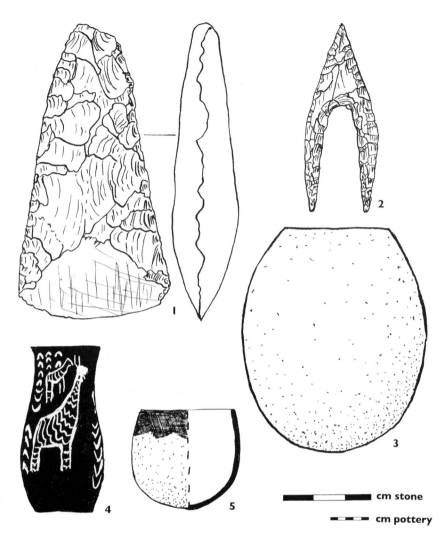

**Fig. 88:**
Pre-Dynastic
Egyptian
artefacts (after
Arkell 1975): 1–3,
ground stone
axe, arrowhead
and pot from
Fayum; 4, Nakada
I pot; 5, Badarian
bowl

may have been of short duration, that at Merimde and allied sites such as those near Helwan were clearly occupied on a permanent basis, with farming on a substantial scale supporting communities which probably numbered well over a thousand persons (Hoffman 1980). In such circumstances specialist craftsmen were able to establish themselves, and non-utilitarian products such as stone vessels and objects for personal adornment proliferated.

Subsequently there arose the Egyptian cultures conventionally known to archaeologists as 'Pre-Dynastic', because they flourished prior to the sequence of numbered dynasties that form the chronological framework for the literate civilisation of ancient Egypt. For many years the Pre-Dynastic cultures were known mainly from their graves, and their ordering and chronology were based upon detailed typological studies of their pottery. A succession of closely related industries was thus proposed, consisting of Badarian, Nakada I (Amratian), Nakada II (Gerzean) and Nakada III. The earlier phases occur in the 200-kilometre stretch of the Nile Valley south of Asyut; their descendants spread rapidly both to the north and to the south. It is only in recent years that significant settlement sites of the Pre-Dynastic period have been investigated. Of prime importance is the town at Hierakonpolis, 100 kilometres north of Aswan: estimates of its population vary greatly but it is likely to have held well over 5000 people. Other settlements include those of Badari and Hamamiya. Both round and rectangular houses are attested. The farming economy followed the pattern of the earlier sites, with the cultivation of barley and emmer-wheat and the herding of domestic cattle and ovicaprids, supplemented with hunting, fishing and the gathering of wild plant foods (Hoffman 1980; Hassan 1988a).

Technological advances at this time included the development of methods of superb pressure-flaking to impart a regular rippled finish to stone tools. Fine stone vessels were now carved from basalt, alabaster and even porphyry. Occasional small copper objects appear early in the Pre-Dynastic period, mainly pins and beads; they seem to have been produced by hammering native (unsmelted) metal. In later Pre-Dynastic times, from Nakada II (around 3600 BC) onwards, techniques of copper-smelting were introduced, presumably from western Asia where they had been known for many centuries, and flat axes, daggers and knives were cast. Fine basketry was made, linen was woven and the simple black-topped pottery was now supplemented by more elaborate wares with painted decoration (Nicholson and Shaw 2000).

The general trend through much of the fourth millennium BC was one of steady development of centres such as Hierakonpolis, Nakada and This, with increasing evidence for craft specialisation and social stratification. It appears that these centres, and many others, each became the nucleus of a small state, with its own king and patron deity (Spencer 1993). By about 3100 BC, or slightly before, a unified kingdom was established over the whole of the Egyptian Nile Valley north of Aswan, ruled by the pharaohs of the first of the thirty dynasties (Fig. 89) which provide the conventional framework for the history of ancient Egypt (James 1979). The unification of Egypt was not achieved without conflict, and the First Dynasty pharaohs are often depicted as conquerors or plunderers. Concurrently with these political developments there was a marked florescence in crafts and industries, which must have been connected with the start of extensive trade in raw

| Period | Dynasty | Date BC |
|---|---|---|
| Early Dynastic | I | c. 3100–2890 |
| | II | c. 2890–2686 |
| Old Kingdom | III | c. 2686–2613 |
| | IV | c. 2613–2494 |
| | V | c. 2494–2345 |
| | VI | c. 2345–2181 |
| First Intermediate | VII–XI | c. 2181–1991 |
| Middle Kingdom | XII | 1991–1786 |
| | XIII | 1786–1674 |
| Second Intermediate | XIV–XVII | 1674–1567 |
| New Kingdom | XVIII | 1567–1320 |
| | XIX | 1320–1200 |
| | XX | 1200–1085 |
| Late Dynastic | XXI | 1085–945 |
| | XXII–XXIII | 945–730 |
| | XXIV–XXV | 730–656 |
| | XXVI–XXXI | 664–332 |

**Fig. 89:** The chronology of ancient Egypt

materials. We now find for the first time evidence for contact with the older literate civilisations of Mesopotamia, and certain Egyptian innovations in art and technology – including methods of building with bricks – may owe much to the latter area. It was even formerly suggested that the Egyptian state system itself may have been of Mesopotamian inspiration, but it is important to emphasise its unique local character. The same is true of the Egyptian hieroglyphic script which developed under the First Dynasty (Fig. 90).

A huge amount of research has been devoted to the study of ancient Egypt, often with little if any reference to its African connexions. This has become such a specialised field that it is often designated a separate discipline: Egyptology. A detailed description of ancient Egyptian civilisation lies beyond the scope of this book, but some of its essential features may be summarised (James 1979; J. D. Clark 1982b; Kemp 1989; Nicholson and Shaw 2000), not only to redress the separatist trends of some studies but also to facilitate an evaluation of the influences which ancient Egypt and its African neighbours exerted on one another (cf. O'Connor and Reid 2003). The first point which requires emphasis is the civilisation's remarkable continuity through three thousand years. The second is its great material wealth, based both upon the annual Nile flood laying down fertile silts which supported the agriculture needed to feed the population concentrated in the narrow valley (Bowman and Rogan 1999), and upon the acquisition of raw materials through large-scale external trade.

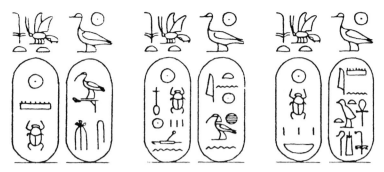

**Fig. 90:** Ancient Egyptian hieroglyphic writing. Egyptian hieroglyphic writing was developed about 3100 BC and continued in use with remarkably little change until the end of the fourth century AD. Its meaning seems to have been forgotten soon afterwards and it was not re-deciphered until the early nineteenth century.

It incorporates some seven hundred signs. Most of these are ideograms – simplified pictorial representations of the concepts to which they relate. Some of these ideograms also had a phonetic value representing one or more consonants. (Vowels were not indicated in ancient Egyptian writing, so it is often not possible to ascertain the original pronunciation.) Often ideograms and phonetic symbols were combined. For example *depet* – meaning 'boat' – could be written ⬭ (hand = d) ⬜ (stool = p) ⌓ (loaf = t) ⛵ (boat). Reading is further complicated by the fact that words were not divided and that inscriptions could be written from left to right, right to left, or vertically.

Royal names may be recognised by their inclusion in an oval shape or cartouche, as in the examples above which give, from left to right, the names of the Eighteenth Dynasty pharaohs Tuthmosis III, Akhenaten and Tutankhamun.

The head and epitome of the Egyptian state was the divine ruler, the pharaoh. The whole complex bureaucracy of the state was ultimately responsible to him and, particularly in the earlier periods, senior officials were often members of the royal family. The pharaoh was also the figurehead of the official religion, the personification of the sun-god Ra, counterpart of Osiris the god of the land of the dead. Material preparation for life after death was of immense importance to the ancient Egyptians, as is shown by the complex efforts made to protect deceased bodies by mummification and to immure them with many belongings in elaborate tombs. As a result, archaeological research for many years tended to concentrate on the tombs of the dead rather than on the settlements of the living. The royal tombs in particular reflect the great wealth and concentration of resources, both human and material, at the pharaohs' disposal, whether they were buried in the mighty pyramids of the Old Kingdom or in the hidden underground chambers of the New Kingdom (Fig. 91).

In evaluating the structural achievements and technological skill of the ancient Egyptians it is necessary to remember the limitations under which they worked. The wheel was unknown before the New Kingdom, yet the pyramids, for example, were built of stone blocks weighing over 2.5 tonnes,

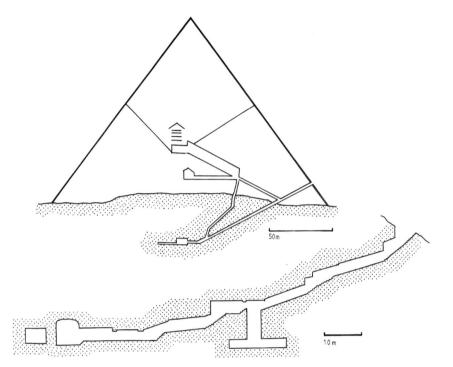

**Fig. 91:** Egyptian royal tombs (after James 1979): top, pyramid of Khufu, Fourth Dynasty; below, rock-cut tomb of Seti I, Eighteenth Dynasty

presumably moved and erected with the aid of rollers and levers. Copper, bronze and gold were effectively the only metals used, for iron did not come into regular use before the Twentysixth Dynasty in the seventh century BC.

Much of our information about ancient Egyptian history comes from the records that were carefully maintained by the Egyptians themselves, notably by the priests who were regarded as the guardians of the state's accumulated wisdom. The value of this source of information was recognised in ancient times, as by the Greek historian Herodotus in the fifth century BC. Idealised scenes of everyday life, at least for the upper classes of society, were often depicted on the walls of tombs. Here we see representations of the ships which carried Egypt's trade along the Nile and further afield. We see the huge bands of labourers – enslaved foreign captives and peasants providing work as a tax-payment – on whom the state's public works depended. It is from this source also that we obtain our sole information about another little-understood aspect of Old Kingdom culture: the capture and taming of animals such as gazelle, oryx and even perhaps giraffe (J. D. Clark 1971; see also Fig. 92). Ancient Egypt was responsible for major advances in knowledge in such fields as literature, mathematics, medicine and law (J. R. Harris 1971), discussion of which falls outside the scope of this book.

The political history of ancient Egypt may be summarised briefly. Since much of our information comes from contemporary written sources,

**Fig. 92:** Relief carving at Kalabsha, Nubia (after Gau 1822), showing the taming of wild animals including gazelle and other antelope, ostrich, monkeys and a big cat, perhaps a leopard

knowledge of this topic is of a different order of detail from that which is available for other parts of Africa at this time; the chronology is also known with far greater precision.

After the Early Dynastic period, when the Nile Valley was already largely isolated by Saharan desiccation, and during which the unification of the Egyptian state was consolidated, the accession of the Third Dynasty in about 2700 BC marks the start of the first great period of prosperity, the Old Kingdom. Through patronage and control of trade, power and wealth were effectively concentrated in the hands of the ruling dynasty. This is reflected first and foremost in the scale at which resources and manpower were devoted to state works, notably to the construction of pyramids for the burial of deceased pharaohs.

By later Old Kingdom times the pharaoh's control over the state bureaucracy seems to have weakened, and the proportion of Egypt's resources that was devoted to royal works was consequently diminished; for example, the Fifth-Dynasty pyramids were smaller than those of the Fourth Dynasty. Shortly after 2000 BC, following a period of contraction from the peak of Old-Kingdom prosperity and wide-ranging trade, Egyptian political unity broke down during the First Intermediate period of some two centuries. Famine may have added to the general impoverishment of this time. Reunification under the Eleventh Dynasty, based at a new capital near Thebes, heralded the Middle Kingdom. Egypt's authority in Nubia was further strengthened at this period, as shown by the erection of the forts which have been noted above.

The new-found stability was short-lived, however, and during the Thirteenth and Fourteenth Dynasties there was a rapid succession of pharaohs as different factions competed for supremacy. Early in the resultant Second Intermediate period a group of invaders from Palestine – the so-called Hyksos rulers – took advantage of Egypt's weakness and established themselves in Lower Egypt as the Fifteenth Dynasty in about 1670 BC. The rise

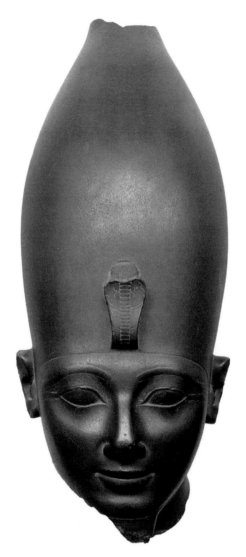

**Fig. 93:** Crowned head from a green schist statue of the Eighteenth-Dynasty pharaoh, Tuthmosis III; height: 45 cm

of independent Kerma, described above, may have been facilitated by Egyptian weakness at this time. Increased frequency of trade-goods of Palestinian origin, particularly in the Delta, indicates greater contact with western Asia during the period of Hyksos rule.

Eventually, a dynasty (the Seventeenth) from Thebes in Upper Egypt expelled the Hyksos rulers and re-established Egyptian unity and independence. The New Kingdom which followed marked the greatest florescence of ancient Egyptian power and prosperity. Egyptian control was re-established over Nubia as well as over substantial areas of the Levant, all governed by a complex imperial bureaucracy set up by the pharaoh Tuthmosis III (Fig. 93). Egyptian trade ranged far and wide, even to the Land of Punt far to the southeast (p. 205). During the Eighteenth Dynasty occurred the remark-able reign of the pharaoh Akhenaten, who attempted to impose monotheism in place of the traditional religion. Akhenaten's successor was the young Tutankhamun, the only pharaoh whose tomb has been discovered virtually undisturbed and unrobbed, to reveal the full richness and splendour which surrounded the New-Kingdom rulers.

From the Twentyfirst Dynasty onwards, Egypt's cohesion once again broke down, and from the eleventh to the seventh centuries BC Libyan, Asian and Nubian contenders vied with Egyptians for control of the state. The Twentyfifth Dynasty originated in Kush and finally, as will be described in chapter 7, lost control of Egypt to an invasion from Assyria, after which ancient Egypt was controlled by a succession of foreign rulers, with only brief interludes of independence.

At this stage in the narrative, it is appropriate to offer a brief summary of the evidence for early cultivation and herding in the Nile Valley. The first point that requires emphasis is the late date at which these innovations took place in comparison with the situation in the Sahara. The earliest farming communities so far recognised in the Egyptian Nile Valley and its immediate environs are those in the Fayum Depression and in the Delta. Their cultivated wheat and barley and their domestic ovicaprids were all of species farmed in earlier times in western Asia and it is presumably there that their ultimate origin should be sought. Even then, their first attestation in the Nile Valley, around 5200–4800 BC, is several centuries later than the presence of ovicaprids both in Cyrenaica and in the Red Sea Hills. Somewhat later, during the second half of the fifth millennium, cattle-herding was also adopted, this time from the west, in most parts of the Nile Valley as far south as the central Sudan. In the latter area it was accompanied by the use (if not the formal cultivation) of locally available cereals such as finger millet and sorghum. Subsequently, with progressive desiccation, many parts of the Sahara became unsuited for farming. In the ensuing dispersal of population, areas were settled where local cereals and other plants grew more successfully than wheat and barley; and thus millet and sorghum were eventually brought under more formal cultivation. Overall, there appears to have been a gradual expansion of farming from the north and east to the south and west. In the process domestic animals were introduced into areas where their species were previously unknown, and indigenous African plants were cultivated.

## West and Central Africa

It has been shown botanically that many of the food-crops traditionally culti-vated in the western sudanic region and the adjacent forest fringes belong to species that are indigenous to the sub-Saharan latitudes. Among the cereals

**Fig. 94:** Sorghum

the most important are bulrush millet (*Pennisetum*), fonio and various types of sorghum (Fig. 94). The homelands of these species extend in a broad belt from the Nile Valley to Senegal, as indicated above in figure 78 (p. 168). Distinct techniques are used for the cultivation of African rice in the valleys of the Niger and Benue (R. J. McIntosh 1998). The propagation of yams (Fig. 95), which is presumed to have originated near the northern fringes of the West African forests, involves distinct methods yet again. It would be unwise to assume a common source for these varied types of indigenous African agriculture. Unfortunately, conclusive primary archaeological evidence for early cereal cultivation is scarce, for rice exceedingly rare and for yams non-existent. In the last case, physical traces of the crop itself are

**Fig. 95:**
Traditional
yam-storage in
eastern Nigeria

highly unlikely to survive in the archaeological record, and the artefacts traditionally used are almost all perishable. Pending the refinement of techniques for studying phytoliths, it is therefore necessary to rely upon less certain indicators and upon inference, as will be attempted below. It will be clear to the reader that, a few major projects notwithstanding, recent archaeological research has been sparse in this region; parts of the account that follows thus depend on widely dispersed and incomplete information.

In West Africa as a whole, predominantly mode-5 stone industries, as described in chapter 4, continued in use until the beginning of iron-working. However, an important change is attested from about the late fifth millennium BC onwards, when two previously unknown cultural items made their appearance. These were pottery and ground-stone axe-like or hoe-like implements (Shaw 1977, 1981). It seems likely that these innovations were somewhat earlier in what is now Nigeria and Cameroon than they were further to the west. There is no evidence for the practice of any type of cultivation or herding before these items appeared and, in later times, they were certainly used in connexion with such activities. It would be wholly misleading, however, to assert that the presence of pottery and/or ground-stone artefacts in an archaeological assemblage necessarily indicates that its makers were farmers. This very tentative archaeological reconstruction receives some measure of support from palaeoenvironmental investigations (Sowunmi 2002) which indicate widespread reduction in forests in more westerly regions after 3000 BC. This could be due to lower rainfall and/or to clearance for agriculture; increased occurrence of pollen from oil palm, which frequently colonises newly cleared ground, strengthens the latter possibility. Archaeological evidence from Ghana provides some degree of support for these hypotheses.

At Bosumpra Cave near Abetifi in Ghana, a microlithic industry basically similar to that from earlier, pre-pottery, sites is associated with simple pottery and ground-stone hoe-like or axe-like implements (Shaw 1944; A. B. Smith 1975). This occupation had begun by the end of the fifth millennium BC and lasted intermittently for over 3500 years, with pottery and ground-stone artefacts becoming progressively commoner with the passage of time. If they were not farmers (and there is no firm archaeological evidence that they were), the inhabitants of Bosumpra were presumably able in some way to follow a reasonably settled life-style permitting the use of such a fragile, heavy type of equipment as pottery. Comparable conditions also prevailed by the mid-fifth millennium on the Ghana coast, at settlements where the economy was based on the exploitation of marine food resources (Calvocoressi and David 1979).

At Iwo Eleru rockshelter in southwestern Nigeria (the lower levels of which were described in chapter 4), pottery and ground-stone implements likewise first appear around the middle of the fifth millennium. At about the same level there is reported the earliest occurrence of implements bearing so-called sickle-sheen (see p. 149), but this does not necessarily mean that the inhabitants harvested – or cultivated – cereals (Shaw and Daniels 1984). A rockshelter at Afikpo in southeastern Nigeria probably provides a counterpart sequence (Andah and Anozie 1980).

In more westerly regions of West Africa, significant differences are apparent. In the Ivory Coast, pottery and ground-stone artefacts are found in association with microlithic industries both on inland sites and in coastal shell mounds, but cannot yet be shown to be earlier than the late third millennium BC (Mauny 1973). In Sierra Leone, however, similar associations at Kamabai and Yagala rockshelters extend back to around the end of the fourth millennium (Atherton 1972). Throughout this region discoveries of ground-stone artefacts need to be evaluated with care because these objects were extensively traded in ancient times from factory sites such as those near Cape Three Points in Ghana, on Bioko Island and in the Oueyanko Valley near Bamako in Mali. They have also been sought after and preserved until recent times in the belief that they possess magical properties, being preserved, for example, on altars at Benin (Connah [1964]). Reliable information concerning prehistoric industries in Guinea and Guinea-Bissau is almost totally lacking. In Senegal, on the other hand, extensive shell middens (Fig. 96) attest coastal settlement, with pottery, beside the Casamance estuary and near Saint Louis; in the latter area the occupation dates

back to the fourth or late fifth millennium (Linares de Sapir 1971; Ravisé 1970).

Firm indications of cultivation or herding in West Africa are surprisingly late in date. In Ghana, for example, the earliest primary evidence comes from Kintampo-industry contexts, in about the eighteenth century BC; these sites appear to be restricted to the forest margin and the southern part of the woodland savanna to the west of the Volta. The Kintampo industry (Stahl 1985, 1994; Casey 2000; d'Andrea and Casey 2002) presents a sharp discontinuity with its predecessor and may indicate influences from the north and west, apparent both in the pottery decoration and in the typology of the stone arrowheads. At one site bones of ovicaprids and, less certainly, small domestic cattle have been reported: if confirmed, the cattle could be of a type ancestral to the modern dwarf shorthorn breeds of West Africa. Wild animals were also represented. Oil-palm nuts and cowpeas were preserved in the Kintampo deposits. A highly characteristic but enigmatic artefact which is frequently encountered on Kintampo sites is a soft stone slab with deeply scored surfaces (Fig. 97). The purpose of such objects remains completely unknown. Suggestions include use in pottery manufacture, or for grating yams, or for removing hard skin from the feet. The Kintampo people lived in villages with rectangular wattle and daub structures (Dombrowski 1980); at Ntereso, overlooking the White Volta 50 kilometres west of Tamale, the settlement covered an area of at least 750 square metres. The northern

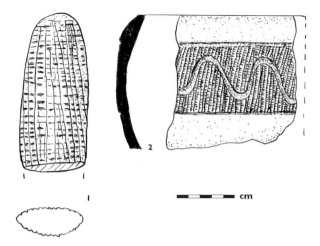

**Fig. 97:** Artefacts from Kintampo sites (after Davies 1967): 1, stone rasp; 2, decorated potsherd

affinities of the Kintampo industry seem to be particularly strong with the Tilemsi Valley area north of the Niger bend in Mali (p. 179).

Archaeological evidence from these more northerly regions does not yet allow any comprehensive assessment of early farming practices. An exception is provided by current research in Burkina Faso and adjacent regions (Breunig *et al.* 1996; Gronenborn 1998; Frank *et al.* 2001; Breunig and Neumann 2002), which has yielded evidence for encampments dating between 2200 and 1000 BC. There is no evidence for herding, but cultivation may have begun around the mid-second millennium; the earliest remains of an actual crop are of *Pennisetum*, about 1000 BC. In the Chad Basin, the early and mid-Holocene was marked by a very extensive lake, 'Mega-Chad', with which is associated a remarkable dug-out canoe 8.4 metres long found at Dufuna in northern Nigeria and dated to about 7000 BC (Breunig 1996), together with somewhat later shoreline settlements with pottery but no evidence for cultivation or herding. This lake began to shrink after 5000 BC; eventually its dry floor was settled by cattle herders of the Gajiganna Complex, probably of more northerly origin. Present from about 1800 BC, these herders made use of numerous wild grasses and began to cultivate small quantities of *Pennisetum* from about 1200 BC. Later settlement of the basin is best known from the Bornu plains in the extreme northeast of Nigeria (Connah 1976, 1981), where a composite sequence at Daima (Fig. 98) and neighbouring sites extends back to the late-second millennium BC; the settlements comprised durable wooden-walled, clay-floored houses (see also Holl 2002). In the absence of local stone, many tools were made of bone. The pottery shows little change during the sequence. Domestic cattle and goats were present throughout, although hunting and fishing were also important activities. Similar mound-sites are known from north and east of the lake in both Chad and Cameroon.

**Fig. 98:**
Excavation
through the deep
accumulation of
occupation
deposits at
Daima

Further to the east, at Shum Laka near Bamenda in Cameroon, stamp-decorated pottery seems to have been in use as early as about 5000 BC, associated with chipped hoe-like stone artefacts (de Maret *et al.* 1987; Lavachery 2001). Ground-stone implements are known from many areas of Cameroon, from Gabon and as far south as the lower reaches of the Congo. Their age in the north remains uncertain, but it has been suggested that they may be as old as 3000 BC in the Estuaire and Ogooue provinces of Gabon, where village sites have been discovered with pottery akin to contemporary wares from Cameroon, grindstones and nuts of oil palm (*Elaeis guineensis*). Particular interest attaches to the recovery of phytoliths at Nkang near Yaounde in southern Cameroon which indicate the growing of bananas during the last millennium BC (Mbida *et al.* 2000). Since the banana is thought to have been introduced to Africa from a South Asian source (De Langhe *et al.* 1994–5), this date is remarkably early and raises the likelihood that bananas may have been grown in more easterly parts of Africa in even earlier times (cf. p. 260 below). Taken together, these observations suggest that, during the last three millennia BC, the inhabitants of these coastal regions may have adopted elements of settled life based on the intensive exploitation of forest vegetable foods (Clist 1986, 1989a).

In the coastal areas north and south of the Congo River mouth it is now known that pottery, whose flat bases serve to link it with more northerly wares, together with ground-stone axe/hoes, was in use during the last centuries BC, preceding by several hundred years the beginning of iron-working in this region (Denbow 1990; de Maret 1986). Nuts of oil palm and *Canarium* have been found on several of these Ngovo-group sites, suggesting the practice of arboriculture and, possibly, other forms of non-cereal horticulture. Linguistic studies suggest that some of the inhabitants of the Cameroon/Congo region during the last millennia BC may have spoken Bantu languages.

Current research on the megalithic funerary monuments near Bouar, in the westernmost part of the Central African Republic, attributes to them a date in the last millennium BC (David 1982; Zangato 1999). Well over one hundred of these sites are now known, consisting of a rubble mound incorporating walls and cists of large, undressed stone slabs weighing up to 2 tonnes. Such monuments are widely dispersed across the sahel from Senegal to the upper Nile; in the latter region they were still in use during the twentieth century AD. No recent overview of their form, use or antiquity has been undertaken.

Despite the incomplete and widely scattered nature of the evidence, the general picture that emerges from recent research is that the forest-edge peoples in the eastern half of West Africa began to make pottery and ground-stone artefacts around the mid-fifth millennium BC, possibly somewhat earlier in Cameroon. Although both these technologies were known in the Sahara in earlier times, there is – in contrast with the later situation in more northerly and westerly regions – no reason to suppose that they were other than independent innovations. It seems probable that yam cultivation near the forest/woodland-savanna ecotone may have begun at approximately this time. Once such a plant is collected, it proliferates and provides a rich, readily available source of food (Hillman 1989; Chikwendu and Okezie 1989).

By contrast, in the more northerly savannas of West Africa, cereal cultivation and the herding of domestic animals were not begun until at least two thousand years after these traits were attested in the Sahara. Their apparent southward dispersal into West Africa seems to have occurred at about the time of the major period of Saharan desiccation, when climatic and vegetational zones would have shifted to the south. The effect which these changes may have had on the distribution of tsetse flies probably allowed the eventual entry of domestic cattle into West Africa.

In view of the foregoing, it would clearly be wrong to suggest that all farming in West Africa began as a direct result of contact with more northerly areas. It appears certain, however, that domestic animals were so derived, and probably cereal agriculture also. Yam cultivation, however, although nowhere conclusively attested in the archaeological record, may well have been an indigenous development and perhaps one which pre-dated any other form of farming in this region (cf. Coursey 1976). The antiquity of West African rice cultivation also remains totally unknown. There are good botanical and environmental reasons for regarding the Inland Niger Delta as one of the centres for early domestication of this crop and, indeed, it is there, at Jenne-Jeno, that its earliest archaeological attestation occurs: in a context dated to the first century AD (R. J. and S. K. McIntosh 1981).

## Ethiopia and the Horn

For a long time it has been recognised that the highland areas of Ethiopia must have played an important part in the development of African farming, particularly agriculture (Harlan 1969). Not only has there been considerable diversity in recent Ethiopian agricultural practices, with wheat and barley being grown, for example, alongside indigenous African crops; but there are also several food-crops which are traditionally cultivated in Ethiopia and nowhere else. The latter must presumably have been originally domesticated there: they include the tiny but highly nutritious grain teff, the banana-like plant enset, and the oil-yielding noog (Simoons 1965). Botanical studies suggest that cultivated finger millet may also have originated in the lower regions of southwestern Ethiopia. Unfortunately, very little archaeological evidence has yet been recovered to illustrate the early development of Ethiopian farming, so that many aspects, including its chronology, remain poorly understood (Brandt 1984; D. W. Phillipson 1993a; Agazi 1997a; Barnett 1999).

Only two widely separated areas of Ethiopia have yielded archaeological sequences which span the period when farming began. At Gobedra rockshelter near Aksum, in the Tigray highlands of northern Ethiopia, the earlier occupation of which was noted in chapter 4 (p. 125), pottery first appeared in association with backed microliths at a level which may date between the mid-fifth and the third millennia BC. It is possible that the camel was present at this early period, although seeds of cultivated finger millet that were excavated from the same layer are now known to be subsequent intrusions. The presence of domestic cattle is indicated at a later stage of the Gobedra sequence (D. W. Phillipson 1977b, 1993a).

Research on later sites in the neighbourhood of Aksum provides evidence, described in chapter 7, that a varied mixed-farming economy was well established by at least the middle of the last millennium BC (Anfray 1990; Bard *et al.* 2000; D. W. Phillipson 2000). Although the local antecedents of these communities remain unknown, there seems a strong probability that the origins of their cultivation and herding practices may extend back to the earlier times with which this chapter is concerned (Fattovich 1994, 1996).

The second Ethiopian sequence which is relevant to the present discussion comes from the area around Lake Besaka near the escarpment west of Harar. Here, the local backed-microlith industry was augmented early in the second millennium BC by the production of large numbers of steeply retouched tools that appear to have been used as scrapers. Domestic cattle made their appearance at the same time. Excavations also yielded a fragment of a stone bowl akin to those found on sites of the early East African herders (J. D. Clark and Williams 1978).

Away from these two areas the evidence for early Ethiopian food-production is indirect or circumstantial. The only other significant archaeological discoveries are of late date, such as those from Lalibela Cave, east of Lake Tana, which included remains of barley, chickpeas, cattle and small stock, dated to the middle of the last millennium BC (Dombrowski 1970).

It would be reasonable to propose that there were two main agricultural traditions in Ethiopia during the last 3000 or 4000 years BC, that in the north being based on cereal cultivation and that in the southwest on enset. In the latter region large numbers of ground-stone hoe-like tools were found many years ago (Bailloud 1959) in association with pottery and, only occasionally, with metal objects, but their age and significance remain completely unknown pending further research. The northern, cereal, zone is more likely to have had contact with the Nile Valley, but so far the only early sites which provide plausible evidence for such connexions are at Agordat in Eritrea and around Kassala in the Sudan. Publication of the Agordat sites (Arkell 1954) includes no absolute dates or excavation results, but the surface finds of ground-stone tools and ornaments, including an ox figurine, may possibly show some features in common with those of the Nubian C-Group in the late

**Fig. 99:** Rock paintings of domestic cattle at Genda Biftu, Ethiopia (after J. D. Clark 1954)

third millennium BC (p. 185). Fattovich's (1994; see also Sadr 1991) research in the Gash Delta near Kassala close to the Sudan/Eritrea frontier has revealed an archaeological sequence from the sixth millennium BC onwards. Cattle were herded before 3000 BC, the associated pottery resembling that from the Nile Valley; a few centuries later both cultivation and herding were firmly established, upright stone stelae were used to mark graves, and links both with Agordat and with later sites in Eritrea and northern Ethiopia may be discerned.

Rock paintings (Agazi 1997b) provide another possible source of information concerning domestic animals, notably cattle which are frequently depicted (Fig. 99). Unfortunately the paintings cannot be dated directly. Humpless longhorned cattle are shown in paintings in Eritrea and around Harar, as well as in Somalia (Brandt and Carder 1987). Ancient Egyptian records extending back to the Old Kingdom include references to the Land of Punt, now generally believed to have been in what is now northern Eritrea and adjacent regions of Sudan (Kitchen 1993; Phillips 1997). Eighteenth-Dynasty (mid-second-millennium BC) carvings at Deir el Bahari depict the presence in Punt by that time of domestic small stock, two breeds of cattle, and cultivated cereals (Naville 1898; see Fig. 100).

Linguistic research offers some supplement to the scant findings of archaeology. Vocabulary relating to the cereal–plough agriculture complex in northern Ethiopia appears to be of Cushitic origin and to pre-date the arrival of Semitic-speakers during the earlier part of the last millennium BC. Taking the story further back, intensive cereal use and the subsequent early stages of cultivation are, both in northeastern Africa and in adjacent parts of the Levant, first encountered in areas occupied by speakers of Afroasiatic languages (see chapter 1, pp. 6–8). This language family probably has a time-depth in the order of 10,000–15,000 years, which effectively covers the formative phases of incipient farming as revealed by archaeology

**Fig. 100:** Punt and its inhabitants, as represented in ancient Egypt (after Phillips 1997): 1, houses; 2, a ship and its cargo; 3, Puntites delivering their goods

(Ehret 1980, 2003). The most likely location of the homeland of the Afroasiatic languages, on the southwestern side of the Red Sea in Ethiopia and easternmost Sudan, suggests that we still have much to learn about the beginnings of Ethiopian farming.

## East Africa

The earliest evidence for herding in East Africa comes from the plains of northern Kenya. Domestic cattle and sheep/goat are represented at three sites in the Ileret area on the northeast shore of Lake Turkana, dated to the middle of the third millennium BC (Owen *et al.* 1982; Marshall *et al.* 1984;

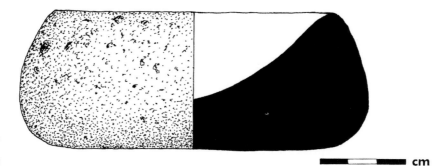

**Fig. 101:** Stone bowl from North Horr (after D. W. Phillipson 1977a)

cm

Barthelme 1985). Associated artefacts are stone bowls and pottery, including vessels with jabbed decoration and internal scoring which resemble the Nderit ware (see Fig. 103 on p. 210) of southern Kenya. Similar pottery has also been reported from sites west of Lake Turkana, which appear long to pre-date the local beginning of herding, although the age of this material cannot be regarded as certain. Fishing remained an important source of food for the early Ileret herders. These people exploited a more extensive territory than their fishing and hunting predecessors, and they brought obsidian from distant sources to use in making their microlithic artefacts.

Inland, east of Lake Turkana, an extensive and long-occupied settlement was established during the third millennium on the shores of the then shallow but extensive Chalbi Lake at North Horr (D. W. Phillipson 1977a, 1979), where the pottery, stone bowls and microliths may be compared with those from Ileret (Fig. 101). Information about the economic developments which took place at this time in more arid areas has been obtained from a rockshelter at Ele Bor, near the modern border between Kenya and Ethiopia (D. W. Phillipson 1984; Gifford-Gonzalez 2003). Here, until very recent times, meat was obtained mainly by hunting, but ovicaprids and, interestingly, camels were present in small numbers from about 3000 BC, which is also the time of the first appearance of pottery. This evidence for camels helps to substantiate their apparently early date at Gobedra in Ethiopia, noted above. Particularly important is the evidence at Ele Bor from seeds and numerous grindstones for the intensive exploitation of cereals – presumably wild – at this same period, which faunal evidence shows to have had a climate somewhat wetter than that of today. Subsequently, as the climate deteriorated, cereal use was abandoned but ovicaprids continued to be herded in small numbers.

The available archaeological evidence from northern Kenya shows that in some areas a settled life-style based at least in part on the herding of domestic stock continued until early in the present millennium. Sites of this period such as, for example, a second settlement at North Horr, contain abundant pottery. Even at this late date iron was evidently unknown or exceedingly rare and microlithic artefacts continued in use. Further climatic deterioration, leading to today's arid conditions, caused the people to adopt their present nomadic pastoral way of life within the last few centuries, involving abandonment of the use of pottery in favour of lighter and more easily transportable receptacles (D. W. Phillipson 1984).

Further to the south, the highlands of southern Kenya and northern Tanzania were the scene of one of the best-known farming complexes which pre-date the beginning of iron-working (Gifford-Gonzalez 1998). It first appears in the archaeological record late in the second millennium BC. Claims (e.g. Bower and Nelson 1978) that domestic animals were herded in this region in far earlier times are now generally discounted (Owen et al. 1982; Robertshaw and Collett 1983; Bower 1991; Marshall 2000). These industries have been named collectively 'Pastoral Neolithic' in recognition of their status as herders, but it remains an open question whether they were true pastoralists in the sense generally accepted by anthropologists or whether they practised any form of cultivation (Bower et al. 1977; Bower 1991). The term is therefore not used in the discussion which follows.

The archaeological material relating to these early East African herders seems to divide most of them into two groups. One industry, known as Elmenteitan, has a very restricted distribution in the high-rainfall area on the west side of the Kenyan Rift Valley; its flaked-stone artefacts are characterised by large double-edged obsidian blades and its pottery by plain, mostly bowl-shaped vessels. Shallow stone bowls, akin to those noted above from earlier times in northern Kenya, are also present on Elmenteitan sites. An unusual feature was the practice of cremating the dead, as at Njoro River Cave where each burial was accompanied by a stone bowl, pestle and mortar. Charred remains of a gourd and of an elaborately carved wooden vessel were also recovered from this site, as were large numbers of stone beads (M. D. and L. S. B. Leakey 1950). Dated to about the twelfth century BC, Njoro River Cave may be one of the earliest Elmenteitan sites. The industry appears to have continued well into the first millennium AD (Robertshaw 1988).

The second major grouping is less well defined, with both stone industries and pottery types showing considerable variation (Fig. 102). This may be at least partly due to inadequate consideration of the significance of such variability, particularly in the case of the pottery. Several so-called 'wares' have been recognised and named after such sites as Nderit, Narosura, Akira and Maringishu (Bower et al. 1977; Wandibba 1980). The significance of this stylistic diversity is far from clear, for none of the 'wares' has well-defined

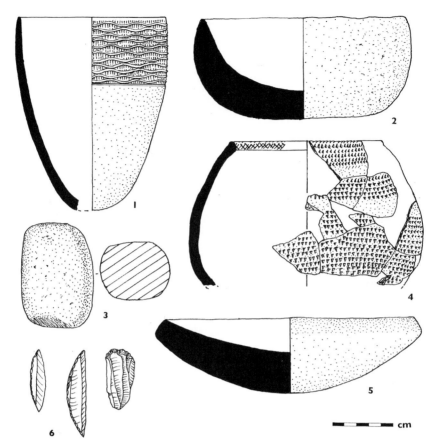

**Fig. 102:**
Artefacts from Hyrax Hill, Kenya (after M. D. Leakey 1945): 1, pottery of 'Maringishu ware'; 2, 5, stone bowls; 3, stone pestle; 4, pottery of Nderit ware; 6, backed microliths

geographical or chronological parameters and frequently more than one 'ware' seems to have been in use in the same place at the same time. The scheme was developed with exclusive reference to pottery from the Central Rift Valley, and it has not proved easy to extend it to neighbouring areas (cf. Chami 2003). Retention of this scheme has hindered improved understanding of the East African archaeological record of this period. Nderit ware (formerly known as Gumban A), characterised by decoration produced by jabbing large areas of a pot's surface with a wedge-shaped object and often by scoring of the vessel's interior surface (Fig. 103), is the only type which has clear affinities with material from other areas. As noted above, closely similar pottery occurs in association with evidence for herding in contexts of the third millennium BC in northern Kenya, while west of Lake Turkana it may extend back into yet earlier times, when domestic animals were apparently still unknown.

**Fig. 103:** Nderit ware pottery bowl from Stable's Drift, Kenya; diameter 21 cm

Since no clear subdivisions (other than Elmenteitan) are apparent, the material relating to the stone-tool-using herders of southern Kenya and northern Tanzania during the last millennium BC must – if only provisionally – be discussed together. There are, in fact, many common features. The dead were buried, without cremation, under stone cairns or in crevices between rocks. Stone bowls occur in settlements as well as on burial sites. There is considerable variation in size of site and in the proportion of the faunal remains represented by domestic animals. It is tempting to suggest that there was some seasonally changing settlement-pattern in which, at certain times of the year, the whole community was dependent upon the produce of the herds, while at others smaller groups obtained their livelihood by more varied means. This is the pattern with several recent pastoralist societies, and there are indications, as noted above for the Khartoum area, that it is one of considerable antiquity (Robertshaw 1989). The most comprehensive picture yet available for East Africa comes from research by Robertshaw (1990b) in the Lemek area of southwestern Kenya, where there is evidence for intensive occupation and where faunal remains support a comprehensive reconstruction of exploitation and management strategies.

It was formerly believed that, within East Africa, only the Rift Valley highlands were settled by stone-tool-using herders. This is now known not to have been the case, traces of comparable and broadly contemporary occupation having been recognised in several surrounding regions including the Lake Victoria Basin and the coastal hinterland from southern Kenya to central Tanzania. Around the western, southern and eastern sides of Lake Victoria, a distinctive type of pottery called Kansyore ware has been reported (Chapman 1967; Soper and Golden 1969). There are indications that it may have originated in the third millennium BC or even earlier (Bower 1991). Its predominantly stamped decoration comprises a variety of motifs, some of which may be derived from earlier pottery styles further to the north. Particularly in view of the fragmentary nature of most of the finds, such conclusions must be regarded as highly tentative, as must claims for sherds of Kansyore ware from far to the east and southeast of Lake Victoria. So far, Kansyore ware has not been found with evidence for the working of iron, and the only indication that its makers may have practised any form of farming is its apparent association with remains of domestic cattle at Gogo Falls in southwestern Kenya (Robertshaw 1991; Karega-Munene 2002).

It will be instructive now briefly to compare the archaeological evidence for the beginnings of farming in East Africa with that which has been deduced from linguistic investigations (cf. Ambrose 1984a). Study of modern linguistic distributions and loanwords indicates that much of highland southern Kenya and northern Tanzania now settled by Nilotic- and Bantu-speakers was formerly occupied by people who spoke languages that may be classified as Southern Cushitic (Ehret 1974). The vocabulary that has been reconstructed indicates that these Southern Cushitic-speakers were herders of domestic stock who milked their cattle and who seem also to have possessed some knowledge of agriculture. Two points require emphasis here. First, although purely linguistic considerations can provide only a very approximate estimate of the time-depth at which these Southern Cushitic languages were spoken, the indications that we possess are that their antiquity is broadly the same as that of the stone-tool-using herders. Secondly, the area where the former presence of the Southern Cushitic-speakers is attested is approximately the same as that covered by the main central distribution of sites which have yielded evidence for domestic animals at this time. It therefore seems reasonable to accept as a working hypothesis the view that most inhabitants of these highland sites may have spoken Southern Cushitic languages. The linguistic affinity of the outlying communities, including the makers of Kansyore ware, remains a matter for speculation pending further research; it is by no means unlikely that some were Nilotic-speakers.

These conclusions have in the past been used to support the view that early East African domestic livestock was derived from Ethiopia. However, it is now known that northern Kenya was itself an important dispersal area for Cushitic speech, being, for example, the region whence the Somali languages were derived (Heine 1978). There is also evidently a very long history of Nilotic/Cushitic contact in the area around Lake Turkana. All this would be fully in keeping with the archaeological indications for the relatively high antiquity of farming in northern Kenya. It suggests that a predominantly Ethiopian origin for East African livestock should not be accepted as proved, and that Sudanese connexions may eventually be shown to have been at least equally important. As noted above, such derivation need not imply large-scale human migration; on the contrary, strong elements of continuity within East Africa have long been recognised (D. W. Phillipson 1979; Karega-Munene 1996).

The evidence of physical anthropology, although far from conclusive, is in keeping with these conclusions. Human skeletons from sites of the early East African herders have been known for some decades; early descriptions, which emphasised their caucasoid features, were misinterpreted as suggesting European affinities. More recent investigations have demonstrated that negroid features are in many cases dominant, and that such non-negroid characteristics as are present would be in keeping with Northeast African caucasoid affinities (Rightmire 1975).

Although the archaeology of central and southern Tanzania remains poorly investigated, there are no indications from sites of the first millennium BC that domestic animals were ever acquired by the stone-tool-using peoples of inland regions to the south of the Serengeti Plain. In more southerly latitudes, indeed, it seems that farming was not practised before the beginning of iron-working. For reasons that are imperfectly understood, the relatively rapid diffusion of farming techniques through the stone-tool-using populations of the northern half of Africa seems here to have come to a temporary halt. Although there is little archaeological evidence from the forested regions of the Congo Basin, it appears that the only parts of sub-equatorial Africa where farming was practised prior to the first millennium AD were in southern Kenya and northern Tanzania and, less certainly (p. 202), in a restricted area around the lower reaches of the Congo River. Possible factors which may have hindered the adoption of farming further to the south at this time include rich and reliable food supplies from wild sources, coupled with very low human population densities. Also relevant are the traditionalism and well-adapted hunter-gatherer life-styles of the KhoiSan-speaking peoples who were probably the exclusive inhabitants of the more southerly latitudes. Later history, as will be described below, shows how reluctant these well-adapted and conservative peoples have often been to adopt alien life-styles and economic practices. Whatever the reasons, the beginning of farming in the southern half of Africa had to await the large-scale population movements which there accompanied the beginning of iron-working.

# Iron-using peoples before AD 1000

## Iron

The greater part of Africa differs from most other regions of the Old World in that there was (except in Egypt and some other areas of northern and northeastern Africa) no distinct 'Bronze Age' or 'Copper Age' during which softer metals, often including gold, were utilised but when techniques of smelting iron had not yet been mastered. In the sub-Saharan latitudes, iron was the first metal to be brought into use; the working of copper and gold began at the same time or somewhat later (van der Merwe 1980; D. Miller 2003). In most of Africa south of the equator, the beginnings of farming and of iron-working took place at approximately the same time. In the latter area there was thus a pronounced contrast between the metal-using farming people and their stone-tool-using hunter-gatherer neighbours and immediate predecessors.

The beginnings of metallurgy cannot be said to have made such a great impact on prehistoric life-styles as did the advent of cultivation and herding. The civilisation of ancient Egypt (pp. 189–95 above) provides a vivid example of the technological achievements that could be attained with virtually no use of iron. Basically, the advantages of iron are ones of increased efficiency. The clearance of forest, the working of wood, the quarrying and carving of stone, the cultivation of ground and the slaughter of enemies may all be accomplished more effectively and with less effort by people who are equipped with iron tools and weapons. These advantages may serve to explain why the knowledge of iron-working techniques spread so rapidly through Africa – as this chapter will demonstrate – in comparison with the slow and often hesitant processes by which cultivation and herding were adopted. They also help to account for the great prestige which, in many African societies, is traditionally associated with the knowledge and ownership of iron (Herbert 1993). The word which the early Bantu-speaking people used to signify iron seems originally to have meant 'a thing of value'.

The technology required to smelt iron – to produce workable metal from the naturally occurring ore – is complex and highly labour-intensive (Wertime 1980; D. Miller 2002). The ore, having been extracted from the ground and broken up, must be heated to a temperature of at least 1100 degrees centigrade under carefully controlled conditions. To achieve such temperatures, aided only by the natural draught of a clay-built furnace and,

**Fig. 104:**
Traditional
African
iron-smelting:
a re-enactment in
Ghana

usually, by hand-operated bellows, is a major task in itself (Fig. 104). Once
smelted, the usable metal has to be separated from the waste-products – the
slag – and brought to its desired shape by repeated heating and hammering. This last process is known as forging. African iron-working technology
(Haaland and Shinnie 1985; D. Miller and van der Merwe 1994; J. Brown 1995;
Schmidt 1997a) did not include the melting and casting of iron although
copper and its alloys, with their much lower melting temperatures, were
successfully cast.

As later sections of this chapter will make clear, the significance of metal-
working for African communities has extended far beyond the technological
sphere. Its cultural and social implications (Herbert 1984, 1993; Schmidt
1996; Vogel 2000) have been at least equally significant and must be given
full weight in any consideration of early African metallurgy.

Knowledge of how to smelt iron on any significant scale seems first to have
been discovered in western Asia early in the second millennium BC (Jean
2001). Iron-working was probably brought to North Africa, west of Egypt, by
Phoenician colonists in about the eighth century BC (van der Merwe 1980).
At about the same time iron objects first came into common use in Egypt
(Nicholson and Shaw 2000). The theory that iron technology spread, with
great rapidity, from these two sources through the rest of the continent has
met with much opposition, not all of it based on archaeological evidence.
Because the associated technology is so complex, and in earlier African
societies no other process involved heating materials to such high

temperatures, we have to consider the possibility of a northerly source for sub-Saharan iron-working knowledge rather than duplicate independent discovery. The radiocarbon dates that are now available for early iron-working in Africa lend only modest support to the view that there could have been an independent development of metal-working technology south of the Sahara (cf. Woodhouse 1998). There is also the problem, rarely considered, of defining exactly what is meant by 'independent'. The question usually posed ignores the need to consider whether, to be truly independent, such a development must be shown to have been made by people who were totally ignorant of related events elsewhere (cf. Gallay 2001). It is perfectly possible that future research will yield evidence which demonstrates that knowledge of iron technology could have been introduced to sub-Saharan Africa from the north. It is particularly difficult to establish a precise chronology for the period which saw the beginning of iron-working because, for most parts of Africa, it is necessary to rely almost exclusively on radiocarbon dates: calibration of such dates (see pp. 5–6) is exceptionally uncertain at just the period – the last millennium BC – with which we are here concerned. It follows that the radiocarbon ages cited in this chapter – although an attempt has been made to calibrate them – should be regarded as approximations. With this proviso, we may now examine the archaeological and other evidence for these processes, and follow the history of the early iron-using societies in Africa up to about the year AD 1000.[1]

## North Africa

During the last millennium BC, the indigenous inhabitants of North Africa west of Egypt were essentially farmers, probably for the most part transhumant herders. Cultivation was concentrated in the river valleys of Libya (Barker *et al.* 1996), Tunisia and the Maghreb. There can be little doubt that, at least in the latter area, these farmers may already be recognised as the ancestors of the modern Berbers (Camps 1982; Brett and Fentress 1996). Such archaeological work as has been done on Berber sites of this period has been concentrated on the stone-built funerary monuments which are by far their most visible component (Camps 1961, 1986), and we know far more about the colonies that were established on the North African coast by a succession of trading peoples from the north and east. A certain amount of information about the early Berbers may, however, be gleaned from the writings of Greek authors, notably Herodotus, whose work dates from the fifth

---

1 This date has been chosen somewhat arbitrarily and is applied loosely in certain regions where a more significant break appears to have occurred rather earlier or later. For example, the Islamic settlements of the East African coast, although traceable back to the eighth century, are all considered in chapter 8.

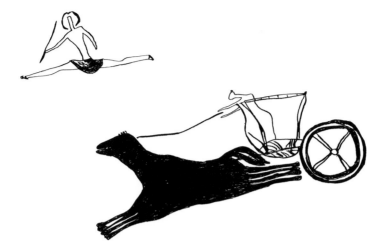

**Fig. 105:** Rock painting of a horse-drawn chariot, Acacus (after Mori 1978)

century BC. Another Saharan people were the Garamantes in Libya (Mattingly *et al.* 1998). The Berbers and Garamantes penetrated much of the Sahara; it has generally been assumed that they used mules as beasts of burden, although Liverani (2000) argues that camels were already in use. There has been much speculation about the use of the horse-drawn chariots which are frequently depicted in Saharan rock paintings (Fig. 105) and engravings and which are also noted by Herodotus (IV.183), who states that they were used by the Garamantes for hunting 'Troglodyte Ethiopians'. It is invariably flimsy two-wheeled vehicles that are shown: they must have carried people rather than heavy goods and it seems highly probable that metal was used in the construction of their wheels. No actual remains of such vehicles have ever been found, so our information about them comes exclusively from the rock art. Attempts to trace trans-Saharan 'chariot routes', based on the distribution of these representations (Mauny 1978), are now widely discounted. It seems likely that the paintings and engravings, which are generally dated to around the first half of the last millennium BC, were done in many areas that were not actually penetrated by such horse-drawn vehicles. Regular traverse of many desert areas, other than on foot, probably did not take place before the arrival of the camel, perhaps during the first half of the last millennium BC. There is good archaeological evidence for the presence of camels in Egyptian Nubia by about the ninth century BC (Rowley-Conwy 1988) and, as shown in chapter 6, possible indications in Ethiopia and East Africa at a significantly earlier date.

Through most of the last millennium BC, metal was a very scarce commodity among the indigenous peoples of North Africa. Knowledge of the working of copper is likely to have reached a limited area of northwestern Africa from

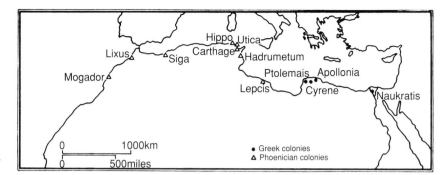

**Fig. 106:** Greek and Phoenician colonies in North Africa

Spain during the second millennium BC, as is suggested by rock engravings in the Atlas Mountains which show metal tools similar to Iberian examples (Malhomme 1959–61; Camps 1974). Elsewhere, although copper and bronze ornaments were occasionally obtained through trade, metal objects generally were very rare; North African warriors of this period were famous in the ancient Mediterranean world for their use of fire-hardened wooden spears without metal points (Herodotus VII.71).

Such were the indigenous peoples amongst whom successive colonists settled. The first to arrive were the Phoenicians who, from their homeland in the coastlands of the eastern Mediterranean, penetrated by sea as far to the west as Mogador in southern Morocco (Markoe 2000). Phoenician expansion into the western Mediterranean may have begun as early as the end of the second millennium BC, but was placed on a firm footing by the foundation of Carthage near the modern Tunis, traditionally dated to the ninth century BC. The map (Fig. 106) shows the location of the principal Phoenician settlements on the African coast. The type of square-rigged ship used by the Phoenicians, which could not sail close into the wind, makes it highly unlikely that any of their vessels would ever have been able to return from a voyage which penetrated further down the coast of northwestern Africa than southernmost Morocco, and this is in fact the limit of well-documented archaeological evidence for a Phoenician presence. The claim mentioned by Herodotus (IV.42), who himself seems to have disbelieved it, for a Phoenician circumnavigation of Africa from the Red Sea to the Atlantic should not be dismissed out of hand (cf. Cary and Warmington 1929); it is incapable of proof or disproof, although objections about the difficulty of a northward voyage along the northwestern coast still apply.

The Phoenicians were great merchants, and their colonies provided a stimulus and end-point for the Berbers' trade with the central Saharan highlands and, perhaps, West Africa. Salt, ivory, animal skins and slaves were the major items that found their way northwards; manufactured goods, including pottery, glass and metalwork, probably went south in exchange. The Phoenician colonies prospered on the profits of this trade, aided by cereal cultivation on the Tunisian plains, most of which was controlled by Carthage from the fifth century BC onwards (Fantar 1993). As a result, the settled Berbers of the coastal regions were drawn into the Phoenician cultural and technological sphere; Berber kingdoms came into existence, nominally independent but often Phoenician clients (Brett and Fentress 1996).

There can be little doubt that both copper and iron were introduced to much of North Africa by the Phoenicians, but conclusive archaeological evidence for this is so far lacking. The only information we have about iron-smelting technology in Punic North Africa dates from as late as the third century BC (Niemeyer 2001), long after the period which is of prime interest if we are to evaluate whether such expertise could have spread from here to more southerly parts of Africa.

While the Phoenicians controlled the maritime trade of the western Mediterranean, including the African coast west of Tripolitania, Greek colonies were established on the coast of Cyrenaica from the late seventh century BC onwards (Boardman 1999). The region takes its name from that of the principal Greek colony, Cyrene. The southernmost point of the Gulf of Sirte was eventually accepted as the boundary between the Greek and Phoenician spheres of influence. The prosperity of Greek Cyrenaica was based on agriculture, the surplus of which was exported.

By the third century BC, Rome was challenging Carthaginian supremacy in the western Mediterranean. Several of the Berber kingdoms were won over as allies of Rome, the most notable being that ruled by Massinissa (201–148 BC) in what is now eastern Algeria (Law 1978). Following the defeat of Carthage by the Romans in 146 BC, these allies were rewarded with tracts of formerly Carthaginian territory. Rome now became the main external power and trading partner in the area, but political annexation followed slowly, and it was some two and a half centuries after the sack of Carthage before Rome established herself as mistress of all the Maghreb north of the Atlas and of the coastal strip further to the east.

The heyday of Roman North Africa was in the second century AD, when major cities were built, public works including roads, aqueducts and irrigation schemes undertaken, and agriculture developed to such an extent that the area became a major economic force in the Roman empire (Fig. 107). The colonists often regarded Africa as their permanent home, and their society fused with that of the Berber élite (Decret and Fantar 1981; Daniels 1987; Raven 1993). The economy of the colonies was firmly based in their agriculture (Mattingly 1989, 1995) and, to a lesser extent, on trans-Saharan

**Fig. 107:** Ruins of the Roman city of Timgad in eastern Algeria. Note the regular street grid centred on forum and theatre.

**Fig. 108:** The Roman emperor Septimius Severus (AD 193–211) was of North African descent

trade (Law 1967). In the third century more than one emperor of Rome was descended from North African stock (Fig. 108). Christianity gained many adherents both in the cities and in rural areas during the second and third centuries. North Africa at this time was a Roman province as effectively colonised as at any subsequent period of the region's history: its economy and industries were essentially those of the empire of which it formed an integral part. However, by the late third century and throughout the fourth, Berber uprisings led to a reduction in Roman influence. North Africa did not escape the collapse of Roman power in the west which came early in the fifth century. In AD 429 Vandals, raiders from the Baltic area, crossed from Spain; Carthage fell to them six years later and they took control of what was left of the urban settlements, while the more distant Roman estates were once again appropriated by the Berbers (Pringle 1981).

## Egypt and the Arab invasion

To the east, the coming of iron meant that Egypt also lost her independence, though in a significantly different manner. The pharaohs of the Twentyfifth Dynasty were the Nubian kings of Kush; they were replaced by an invasion of Assyrians in 671 BC. Despite the fact that the country frequently had tributary status to a succession of foreign powers, the traditional culture of ancient Egypt survived with few important modifications for over six centuries (Lloyd 1983; Nicholson and Shaw 2000). The developing Greek-dominated trade networks of the eastern Mediterranean brought Egypt, through her entrepôt at Naukratis in the Nile Delta, into closer contact with Europe. Herodotus, who visited Egypt in the fifth century BC, has left us (in his Book II) a detailed and informative account both of what he saw and of what he learned about the Egypt of earlier times.

Late in the fourth century BC, the Macedonians from northern Greece under their king, Alexander the Great, destroyed Persian power in the eastern Mediterranean. They conquered Egypt in 332 BC. The succession of pharaohs, after almost three thousand years, was now brought to an end, and one of Alexander's generals was appointed ruler of Egypt as Ptolemy I. He and his descendants controlled Egypt until 30 BC, severing the formal link with Macedon and building the country to a pre-eminent commercial and cultural position in the Greek-speaking world (Bowman 1986) while emphasising, as did Roman emperors in later times, their status as successors to the pharaohs. The Ptolemaic capital at Alexandria (Fraser 1972) became not only a great centre of learning (Fig. 109) but also a port from which traders sailed throughout the Mediterranean as well as through the Red Sea to India and far down the East African coast (Burstein 1989; Salles 1996; see also Manzo 1996).

The Roman conquest of Egypt came in 30 BC. The country's wealth was partly drained in tribute and through taxation, but this did little to shake Alexandria from its position of influence throughout the eastern, Greek-speaking, part of the Roman empire. Extensive archaeological research, complemented by study of the very numerous written documents that have survived in Egypt's arid conditions, gives a uniquely comprehensive picture of everyday life at this time (N. Lewis 1983), illustrating the interplay between traditional and foreign elements. Roman technology modified many earlier practices (e.g. Peacock and Maxfield 1997). After the Jewish revolt late in the first century AD, many refugees settled in Egypt. Among these people and others Christianity rapidly took root (Watterson 1988; Finneran 2002). It was by way of Egypt that Christianity was passed southwards to Nubia and, less directly although at an earlier date, to Ethiopia.

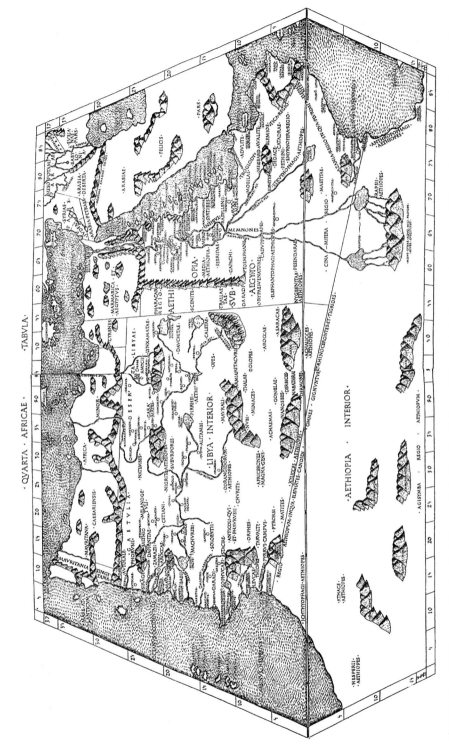

**Fig. 109:** Map of Africa, according to calculations made by Claudius Ptolemy of Alexandria in the second century AD. This version was printed in Rome at the end of the fifteenth century.

**Fig. 110:** The mosque of Sidi Okba at Qayrawan, founded AD 670, rebuilt and enlarged in the ninth century

Following the division of the Roman empire in the fourth century, Egypt was included in the eastern (Byzantine) hegemony, where it remained until the Arab invasion of the seventh century. Byzantine-ruled Egypt was so weakened by internal dissension that it offered little resistance to the invading Arabs in 639. Conversions to Islam proceeded steadily, and Arabic replaced Greek as the language of government. The Arab invasion did not stop in Egypt, but extended rapidly westwards through North Africa (Hitti 1963; Brett 1978). By 647 the Arabs had reached Tunisia and defeated the Byzantine forces, who themselves had ousted the Vandals early in the sixth century. Later in the seventh century the Arab conquest of the area was consolidated, and a local headquarters established at Qayrawan (Fig. 110). In the eighth century the front was pushed further west to Morocco and northwards into Spain. Islam spread more rapidly in North Africa than in Egypt, but some

Christian communities survived for several hundreds of years. Technologically, this period saw the eclipse of Roman skills, and the resurgence of native North African ones. Many aspects of Arab culture were introduced and flourished, advances in architecture, science and literature being particularly noteworthy. As in the days of the Phoenicians, Tunis again became an entrepôt for trade with the south: goods from West Africa and from Europe were to be found in the markets of the North African coast. This trade was now in the hands of itinerant Arabs as well as Berbers, and was institutionalised by the establishment of regular journeys by large camel caravans. Through these, Islam was introduced to the areas south of the desert, as will be described below; and these same areas became known to Arab geographers (Levtzion 1978; Insoll 2003).

## The Sudan

Following the expulsion from Egypt of the kings of Kush after the Assyrian invasion of 671 BC, the Kushites retreated to their former homeland. Their rule in the Sudan continued for another thousand years from a capital which was initially located at Napata near the Fourth Cataract, but which was moved about 600 BC upstream to Meroe, beyond the Nile–Atbara confluence (D. N. Edwards 1996; Shinnie 1996; Welsby 1996; see Fig. 113 below). Meroe lies to the south of the most arid stretch of the Nile Valley, in an area that appears to have been well wooded during the last millennium BC. The transfer of the state's capital to Meroe (Török 1997), for whatever reason it was undertaken, had three important results. It marked an effective break from dependence upon Egypt, it brought the capital within reach of the fuel that was needed to maintain an iron-smelting industry which soon arose, and it provided the town with surroundings that enabled crops and herds to be raised on a scale sufficient to feed its growing population. Millet and sorghum were cultivated; herds consisted primarily of cattle, humpless short-horns being depicted on painted pottery. Horses were in use, but little is yet known about the introduction of the camel, which is attested at Qasr Ibrim in Egyptian Nubia by about the ninth century BC (Rowley-Conwy 1988). Meroe could also take advantage of new trade routes that more than replaced the old Nile Valley route downstream into Egypt. To the east was the way to the Red Sea, while the valley of the Atbara led southeastwards to the highlands of Ethiopia where a distinct urban civilisation was arising during the last millennium BC (see below). To the south the Nile flowed through fertile plains where the mixed farming lifestyle of earlier times continued, and supported substantial settlements such as those at Jebel Moya and Jebel et Tomat (Addison 1949; J. D. Clark and Stemler 1975). Westwards the dry plains stretched away to Darfur and,

**Fig. 111:** The Meroitic temple at Naqa, erected in the reign of King Natakamani and Queen Amanitore (late first century BC / early first century AD)

beyond, to Lake Chad. Egyptian connexions were still emphasised in the monumental architecture (Fig. 111), but Meroe was now able to strengthen its links with peoples to the south of the Sahara and to import luxuries from the north and east via the Red Sea ports. Gradually Meroitic replaced Egyptian as the language of monumental inscriptions. By the last two centuries BC, Egyptian hieroglyphs had been replaced by a local cursive script (Fig. 112). The meaning of these Meroitic inscriptions cannot yet be fully understood.

Archaeologists formerly attached great importance to the evidence for Meroitic iron-working which, to judge from the size of the slag heaps that are to be seen on the site, was at some period carried out on a very substantial scale. Subsequent research (Shinnie and Bradley 1980) has shown that although some smelting may date back close to the seventh or sixth centuries BC – about the time of the establishment of the royal capital – the industry did not reach a massive scale until the last centuries BC or the beginning of the Christian era. The furnaces that have been excavated date from this late period and were cylindrical structures rather over one metre high, fired with the aid of bellows. It appears that much of the iron produced at Meroe was dispersed through trade, since relatively few iron objects – hoes, axes, arrowheads and the like – have been found on the site itself. Despite the large scale of Meroitic iron-working and trade, the late date now demonstrated does not support the view previously held that it played a major role in the transmission of metallurgical knowledge to more

**Fig. 112:** Cursive Meroitic script on a sandstone funerary stela in the shape of an offering table, from el-Maharaqa; width: 34 cm

southerly parts of Africa (cf. Fig. 113). The imposition of Roman rule over Egypt was reflected in the Sudan by luxury imports (Kirwan 1977) and by technological changes, as in methods of quarrying (Harrell 1999).

In the second century AD the prosperity of Meroe began to decline rapidly. Environmental deterioration, perhaps partly brought about by over-grazing and deforestation, may have been a contributing cause; another was the rise to trade-based prosperity of the kingdom of Aksum in northern Ethiopia, discussed below. It may have been King Ezana of Aksum who finally destroyed Meroe in about AD 350 (Kirwan 1960).

Downstream of the Third Cataract, the immediately post-Meroitic centuries are marked by sites attributed to the poorly understood Ballana Culture ('X-Group') – possibly Nubians whom the Romans used as a buffer to protect their southern Egyptian frontier (Kirwan 1974; Welsby 1996, 2002). The sites which have been most intensively investigated are royal graves at Ballana and Qustul in Lower Nubia (Emery and Kirwan 1938) and tumuli at

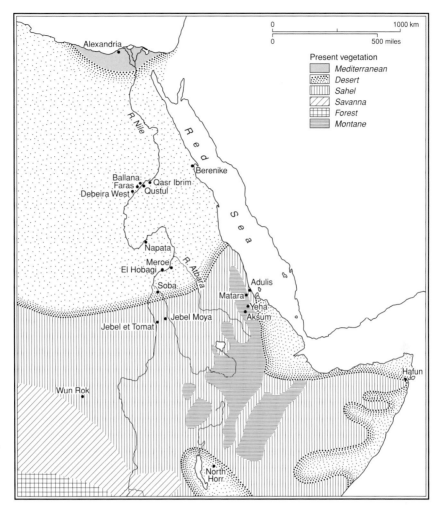

**Fig. 113:** Northeastern Africa, showing some important sites with evidence for early metal-working, with the modern vegetation pattern

El Hobagi in the vicinity of Meroe itself (Lenoble and Sharif 1992; Lenoble *et al.* 1994); at the latter place there is evidence for continuity with Meroitic funerary practices. Early in the sixth century Christianity was introduced, and shortly afterwards Arab expansion cut the Nubians off from their co-religionists in Egypt. Remarkably, the Nubians were able to maintain their Christian culture for some seven hundred years; their artistic accomplishments are best illustrated in the frescoes (Fig. 114) recovered from the cathedral at Faras near Wadi Halfa (Michalowski 1967; Finneran 2002). Similar buildings were erected as far to the south as the modern Khartoum, at Soba which was the capital of the southern Nubian kingdom of Alwa (Welsby and Daniels 1991; Welsby 1998). Village life in Christian Nubia, as illustrated by

**Fig. 114:** Fresco of an archangel from Faras cathedral, tenth century AD

excavations at Debeira West, followed a pattern of irrigation agriculture which has continued into recent times (P. L. and M. Shinnie 1978).

## Ethiopia and adjacent regions

The northern Ethiopian highlands during the last millennium BC saw a gradual influx of Semitic-speaking peoples across the Red Sea from southern Arabia. The new arrivals appear to have encountered a settled, agricultural population, perhaps Cushitic-speaking, such as those illustrated by recent excavations at Kidane Mehret and Beta Giyorgis near Aksum in Tigray (D. W. Phillipson 2000; Bard *et al.* 2000). Dated between the eighth and fourth centuries BC, these settlements comprised clusters of stone buildings whose inhabitants herded cattle, sheep and goats, and cultivated a range of crops including wheat, barley and teff. They made distinctive pottery and mode-5 lithic artefacts; they were familiar with copper but not, it appears, with iron. By the eighth or seventh century BC, the South Arabians established in Tigray a literate urban culture which retained many features – artistic, architectural and technological – derived from their homeland (Anfray 1990; Fattovich 1990). Iron-working was probably introduced into Ethiopia at this time (cf. Mapunda 1997), as were the worship of the South Arabian

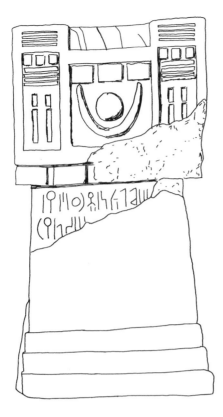

**Fig. 115:** A pre-Aksumite altar from Addi Gelemo, Ethiopia, showing the crescent-and-disc symbol of the moon-god and part of a Himyaritic inscription (after Sergew 1972)

moon-god, symbolised by the crescent and disc, and also writing, in the form of the Himyaritic script (Fig. 115). It seems likely that this culture of South Arabian affinity was originally restricted to a relatively small number of settlements, most notably Yeha near Adwa (Anfray 1963, 1995; Robin and de Maigret 1998), and that it only slowly influenced the lives of the indigenous Cushitic-speaking population.

By the first century AD, Aksum, some 50 kilometres southwest of Yeha, developed as the capital of an extensive state in which there was a fusion of indigenous Ethiopian and South Arabian cultural elements. The farming economy of earlier times continued largely unchanged (Michels 1994). Through its port of Adulis on the Red Sea coast, Aksum was in trade contact with the Roman empire, exporting ivory and skins in exchange for manufactured luxury goods. The Aksumite state incorporated several urban centres in addition to Aksum itself, most notably Matara on the plateau of what is now Eritrea (Anfray 1967). Ge'ez – basically Semitic but with a strong Cushitic element – seems to have been the general language of Aksum, but Greek was also in use for commercial purposes. Coins were struck at Aksum (Fig. 116); on the earlier issues the king's name and titles were given in Greek.

**Fig. 116:** The first Aksumite coinage: a gold coin of King Endybis, late third century AD

In the fourth century AD Aksumite power seems to have reached its peak. It was at this time that King Ezana is believed to have conquered Meroe. It was also in Ezana's reign that Christianity became the state religion of Aksum: on his later coins the crescent and disc of the moon-god were replaced by the cross (Munro-Hay and Juel-Jensen 1995: Hahn 1999).

Aksumite technology and material culture were complex and sophisticated, but the civilisation's indigenous roots are demonstrated by the continuation from earlier times of long-established cultivation and herding practices and of mode-5 lithic technology (L. Phillipson 2000). The monumental architecture and tombs of Aksum are relatively well known (Littmann *et al.* 1913; Munro-Hay 1989; D. W. Phillipson 2000; Fattovich *et al.* 2000). Great stelae – obelisks hewn from a single piece of rock up to 33 metres high and carved as stylised representations of multi-storey buildings – were erected in a burial area on the edge of the town (D. W. Phillipson 1997; Fig. 117). At Aksum, Matara and other sites, large rectangular buildings, sometimes interpreted as palaces, reached heights of several storeys. The architecture of these buildings, like that represented on the stelae, shows several features which may be paralleled in southern Arabia and which have also continued into more recent times in Ethiopian ecclesiastical buildings (Buxton 1970; Garlake 2002). Ethiopian Christian manuscript painting has also been traced back to late Aksumite times (Mercier 2000; D. W. Phillipson 2003b).

Aksum was from early times a major trading and imperial power. With the eclipse of Meroe it effectively controlled the trade between the Red Sea and the rich hunting grounds of the Sudanese Nile Valley, whence came the ivory which was one of Aksum's major exports. In the third century, and again in the sixth, the kings of Aksum held sway also over parts of southern Arabia. When, in the seventh century, Arabs gained control over the Red Sea ports, Aksum was cut off from much of the trade on which its prosperity had depended, and the kingdom rapidly declined into obscurity (Sergew 1972; Munro-Hay 1991; D. W. Phillipson 1998).

**Fig. 117:** The third-largest Aksumite stela (early fourth century AD) still stands, 20.6 metres high

The Red Sea trade of the first few centuries AD was not restricted to Aksumite commerce (Horton 1996a). Most of our information comes from a Greek work, *The Periplus of the Erythraean Sea*, which describes trade, originating in Alexandria, extending into the Indian Ocean (Casson 1989). There, contact was made with sailors from Yemen who penetrated down the East African coast as far as a port called Rhapta. The exact location of this place is unknown (Horton 1990), but it is generally believed to have been somewhere on the coast of modern Tanzania (Chami 2001). The traders brought metal and glass objects which they exchanged for gums, spices, ivory and rhinoceros horn. This commerce continued through the early centuries AD and is well illustrated at Berenike on the Egyptian Red Sea coast (Sidebotham and Wendrich 1998). Excavations at Hafun on the coast of Somalia some 150 kilometres south of Cape Guardafui have revealed traces of a trading settlement which probably dates back to this period (Chittick 1976; M. C. Smith and Wright 1988). To the south, however, no coastal settlements in East Africa that may have been visited by these early seafarers have yet been discovered, although finds of Roman-like pottery and beads on Zanzibar and in the vicinity of Dar es Salaam provide some archaeological evidence for the contacts reported in the written sources (Juma 1996; Chami 1999).

The later archaeology of southern Ethiopia remains largely unknown, investigations having been largely restricted to burials marked by cylindrical stelae (Azaïs and Chambard 1931; Anfray 1982; Joussaume 1995). In the southern Sudan, likewise, research is at such a preliminary stage that few firm conclusions can yet be drawn (Mack and Robertshaw 1982). It appears that iron tools remained extremely scarce until relatively recent times and that in some areas mode-5 lithic technology was practised well into the second millennium AD. At Jebel et Tomat, between the Blue and White Niles not far south of Khartoum, an extensive settlement was occupied through the first five centuries AD. Cattle, sheep and goats were herded, sorghum was cultivated, and food was also obtained through hunting, fowling and fishing. The pottery tradition at this site appears to have been a continuation of that which had prevailed in far earlier times in the Sudanese Nile Valley, and also shows connexions with contemporary Meroitic wares. Iron tools were rare, and backed microliths were in use throughout the occupation (J. D. Clark and Stemler 1975). In the absence of evidence to the contrary, it is tempting to suggest that Jebel et Tomat represents a type of rural settlement that was widespread at this time both in the central Sudan and further to the west and southwest (cf. Fig. 118).

In the southern Sudan, the Wun Rok mounds 150 kilometres north of Wau provide a view of the iron-using communities who inhabited the plains of the Bahr el Ghazal during the first millennium AD. They herded humpless cattle, hunted and fished. Iron was used primarily for personal adornment

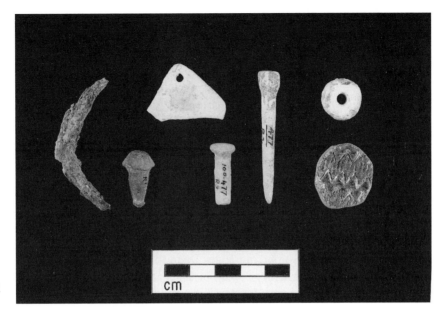

**Fig. 118:** Stone bead, lip-plugs, sherd disc, shell pendant and fragment of iron bangle from Jebel Moya

and many tools were made of bone. Throughout the second half of the first millennium AD these people produced roulette-decorated pottery similar to that made in more recent times by Nilotic-speakers (David *et al.* 1981). Roulette-decorated pottery (Soper 1985; Desmedt 1991) is largely but not exclusively a second-millennium phenomenon; investigation of its possible link with Nilotic-speaking peoples (cf. Ehret 2003) represents a major lacuna in current archaeological research.

In northern Kenya, herding peoples, probably speaking languages of both the Nilotic and Cushitic types, using stone tools and evidently still unfamiliar with iron-working technology, continued the life-style of their predecessors throughout the first millennium AD. Extensive settlements existed beside permanent sources of water, as at North Horr. In more arid areas, nomadic pastoralism was now the only effective means of subsistence. To the south, in the highlands west of the Rift Valley, it seems likely that iron-users of southern Sudanese affinities, speaking Nilotic languages, were established by early in the first millennium AD. The evidence for this is primarily linguistic; and archaeological confirmation is not yet forthcoming (Ehret 1974). In the Rift Valley itself, the herders described in chapter 6 appear to have continued in occupation until late in the first millennium AD, perhaps obtaining some knowledge of iron – which, however, remained very rare – towards the end of that period (Ambrose 1984b; Bower 1991). The coming of iron to the Bantu-speaking parts of East Africa is discussed below;

elsewhere, informative evidence for use of metal prior to AD 1000 remains extremely scanty.

## West Africa

Presentation of a coherent overview of the evidence for early iron-using peoples in West Africa is hampered by the very incomplete and uneven coverage of the research that has yet been undertaken. This is, of course, a difficulty in all areas and periods of African prehistory, but the problems for West Africa are particularly acute. Such research as has taken place has been concentrated on sites which have yielded art objects or which are connected with the trading states mentioned in foreign written accounts. There has been virtually no integrated investigation of technological and economic development, or of state-centralisation processes, although pioneering work around the Inland Niger Delta in Mali (S. K. McIntosh 1999b), in the sahel (Gronenborn 1998) and in Senegal (S. K. McIntosh and Bocoum 2000) amply demonstrates the potential for such research. As a result, whole areas remain effectively unknown archaeologically (cf. S. K. McIntosh 1994).

Two areas of West Africa have received particular attention as providing indications that copper may have been worked there before iron. Near Akjoujt in southwestern Mauritania, copper ore was mined and smelted by the fifth century BC. Around Agadez in Niger, furnaces of elongated plan were used for smelting copper at a similar period (Tylecote 1982). Claims that simple pit furnaces were used at an even earlier time for melting native copper are not supported by more recent research (Killick *et al.* 1988). In both areas copper oxides and carbonates were reduced in simple furnaces and the resultant metal hammered into small tools such as arrowheads and spear-points (Lambert 1971, 1983). At Akjoujt contact with North Africa at this time may be demonstrated archaeologically, and similarities with Agadez suggest that both centres may have derived elements of their metallurgical expertise from that source (S. K. and R. J. McIntosh 1988). It thus appears that the advent of both iron and copper to these areas should be dated around the middle of the first millennium BC, which is in accord with evidence from southern Aïr, also in Niger. Yet further signs of early iron-working in the immediately sub-Saharan latitudes come from Rim in Burkina Faso, in a context of the first centuries AD showing continuity from earlier times. The earliest occupation of the large settlement at Jenne-Jeno, in the Inland Niger Delta of Mali, dates from the last two centuries BC when use of metal tools may have facilitated the first exploitation by farming people of the Inland Delta's heavy clay soils and the cultivation of African rice (R. J. and S. K. McIntosh 1981; R. J. McIntosh 1998). The clear implications of these

**Fig. 119:** Nok terracotta heads

sparse and broadly scattered data are that use of iron in the southernmost Sahara and adjacent northern savanna of West Africa dates back to the last few centuries BC, and was widespread (Posnansky and McIntosh 1976; Calvocoressi and David 1979; Togola 1996). There is no evidence to suggest that any major replacement of population accompanied the beginning of metal-working, although expansion into previously unexploited areas may have been facilitated.

In more southerly parts of West Africa, the earliest evidence for iron so far known is that associated with the Nok 'culture' found in a restricted area on the southern and western slopes of the Jos Plateau in Nigeria (Shaw 1978; Jemkur 1992), and from sites near Nsukka (Okafor and Phillips 1992). Nok artefacts were originally discovered during mining operations in river gravels which, as noted in chapter 4, have also yielded abundant remains from earlier periods. The most striking discoveries were of pottery figures, mostly of humans, some of which are life-size (B. Fagg 1979; de Grunne 1999). These terracottas show great technical competence and an artistically accomplished, though idiosyncratic, style of modelling. Examples are shown in Figure 119. Particularly characteristic are the elaborate hairstyles and the treatment of eyes, which are shown as sub-triangular areas delineated by grooves, with a deep circular hole for the pupil. The faces are unmistakably negroid. The presence of parts of limbs and torsos as well as heads suggests

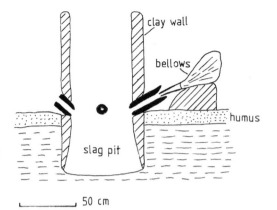

**Fig. 120:**
Reconstruction of
an iron-smelting
furnace at
Taruga (after
Tylecote 1975)

that some specimens were fragments of complete figures, although few of these have survived intact. Particular attention was paid to reproducing physical peculiarities and deformities.

The attributes of some of the Nok figures provide information about their makers' material culture: one man carries a hafted axe, others sit on stools or wear beads and pendants, a fluted pumpkin is represented. Because they came from disturbed contexts, which also yielded archaeological material of several distinct periods, there was initially considerable controversy about the date of the Nok figures, or even as to whether they were earlier or later than the local beginning of iron-working. The situation has now been clarified, because Nok settlement sites at Taruga and Samun Dukiya have been found and investigated. These have yielded radiocarbon dates between the fifth and the third centuries BC, associated with fragments of typical Nok figures, domestic pottery and the remains of furnaces which conclusively demonstrate that iron was worked by the Nok people (A. Fagg 1972; Tylecote 1975). The shallow pit furnaces with cylindrical clay walls are of particular interest for comparison with later examples from other parts of sub-Saharan Africa (Fig. 120). Knives and points for arrows and spears were the principal types of iron artefact produced, together with occasional bangles. The 'Nok culture' continued to flourish into about the second quarter of the first millennium AD.

Unfortunately we know nothing about the local predecessors of the Nok people, and we cannot evaluate the impact which the start of iron-working made on their way of life. It is possible that the Nok tradition of naturalistic clay modelling may have begun before iron was known, but the few early radiocarbon dates come from disturbed contexts and their evidence cannot be regarded as conclusive. In fact, the only excavated sites in West Africa where the beginning of iron-working may be pinpointed in a continuous sequence are in plains bordering Lake Chad in the extreme northeast of Nigeria and in neighbouring states (cf. pp. 200–1 above). Here, only 800 kilometres from the Nok area and a similar distance from Aïr, iron seems not to have been known before the first millennium AD – perhaps as much as eight hundred years later than at Taruga. At Daima, for example, the economy of the early iron-workers, like that of their predecessors, was based on their herds of domestic cattle. Sorghum was cultivated, as it may have been in earlier times. There was no significant change in the associated pottery at the time when iron-working began, but more substantial houses were now built of mud rather than of wood and grass. Some time after the initial appearance of iron a new population seems to have arrived at Daima, and the site became part of a more extended trade system (Connah 1976, 1981). The poorly documented Sao sites (Lebeuf 1962) of southern Chad are probably similar to, and broadly contemporary with, Daima although there are indications that the advent of iron may in this more easterly area have been somewhat earlier (see also Breunig *et al.* 1996; Gronenborn 1998; Holl 2002). In the Koro Toro area of north-central Chad extensive iron-working is attested from the fifth century AD.

In Ghana, iron-working near Begho, as at Atwetwebooso, extends back to around the second century AD, but there is a dearth of other excavated sites that have been dated to the first millennium. In the same general area, sites which are traditionally associated with the origins of Akan groups are dated from the fifth century AD onwards and show a pottery style which developed into those produced by Akan in later times. Rockshelter sites in Ghana, notably Akyekyemabuo, show that microlithic industries and ground-stone artefacts continued in use through the first millennium AD (Anquandah 1982; Stahl 1994).

In more westerly regions only isolated discoveries have so far been reported, and no comprehensive account can be presented. It appears, however, that iron-working was not widely adopted prior to the middle centuries of the first millennium AD, this being the range of the earliest relevant radiocarbon dates from Liberia, Sierra Leone and Senegal. The majority of these dates come from rockshelters or coastal shell middens where there is evidence for continuous occupation from earlier times.

The Nok sites were followed by those of other iron-using communities in various parts of Nigeria later in the first millennium AD, as is shown at several settlements that were investigated in the area now flooded by the waters of the Kainji Dam on the Niger. Near Yelwa, for instance, a small village probably of some eighty inhabitants seems to have been occupied through most of the first seven centuries AD by people who herded domestic animals and made stone beads as well as pottery vessels in two successive styles. They also made clay figurines which, in comparison with those of the Nok 'culture', are small and lack refinement. Stone tools had almost completely fallen out of use, while those of iron – notably axes, knives, fish-hooks and heads for spears and arrows – were abundant (Breternitz 1975). In view of the major developments in art, technology and the socio-political fields which, to judge from the evidence of later times, must have taken place during the first millennium AD, it is unfortunate that the archaeology of this period in Nigeria remains so little known and has been the focus of so little co-ordinated research.

In eastern Nigeria, south of the Benue, there is no evidence that iron was known before the early centuries AD. However, the discoveries from an apparently ninth-century context at Igbo Ukwu near Onitsha show that, by the end of the first millennium, a great concentration of wealth was in the hands (or at the disposal) of a minority who held considerable religious power and perhaps, to judge from later parallels, political authority also. The Igbo Ukwu site was a burial place where persons of great importance had been interred in an elaborate manner and accompanied by rich belongings. Meticulous excavation permitted the principal burial to be reconstructed in considerable detail. The corpse, sitting on a stool, dressed in and surrounded by regalia of office, was placed with three ivory tusks in a deep, earth-dug, wood-lined burial chamber which was then roofed over. In the upper chamber thus created were placed the remains of at least five attendants, the whole grave being then filled with earth. Nearby, two further caches of artefacts were discovered; in one case the objects appeared to have been laid out in a relic house; in the other they had been unceremoniously buried in a pit. There could be little doubt that the whole site represented a single burial complex; radiocarbon dates provide good evidence that it belongs to the ninth century AD, although some archaeologists initially argued for a later date. The excavator has suggested that the person buried at Igbo Ukwu may have held a position analogous to that of the Eze Nri of the recent Ibo people (Shaw 1970).

Without doubt the most remarkable features of the Igbo Ukwu discoveries are the superb bronze castings that were found in all three parts of the site (Fig. 121). They were produced by the 'lost wax' method, in which a wax model is encased in clay to produce a mould, the wax then being replaced by molten metal. The bronzes include a series of elaborate vases with delicate surface decoration, bowls, and models of shells, as well as a breast-ornament, fly-whisk handle and other regalia which accompanied the main burial. Their style and the nature of their elaborate decoration have no close parallels in other West African bronze-casting traditions, although some features do recur on pieces attributed to the later and ill-defined 'Lower Niger'

**Fig. 121:** Lost-wax bronze castings from Igbo Ukwu

group of bronzes (Willett 1967). Despite their technological and stylistic sophistication, the Igbo Ukwu bronzes have no known antecedents. There can, however, be virtually no doubt that they were manufactured locally. There are strong stylistic similarities between the sites' bronzes and pottery, both of which display an iconography which shares features with more recent Ibo symbolism, and it is now known – contrary to previous belief – that the metal from which they were made could have been obtained in the region itself (Chikwendu *et al.* 1989; Craddock *et al.* 1997). The Igbo Ukwu discoveries provide a glimpse of a local development of wealth and crafts-manship within the southeast Nigerian forest region. This had probably been under way for some time before the ninth-century date now accepted for Igbo Ukwu. The extent to which long-distance trade – reflected by the presence of over 150,000 glass beads at Igbo Ukwu – may have stimulated or contributed to this development (Sutton 1991, 2001) remains an open ques-tion, consideration of which will require discussion of contemporary events in the savanna regions to the north.

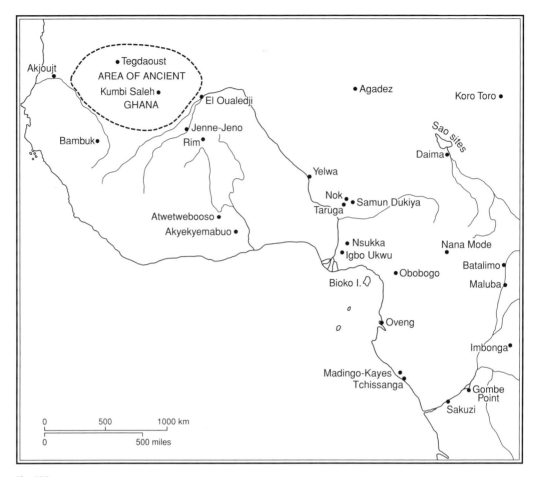

**Fig. 122:**
Principal West and central African sites with evidence for the early use of metal

The Igbo Ukwu discoveries indicate that craft specialisation and the concentration of wealth which are seen in later times, in the Ife and Benin kingdoms for example (see chapter 8), were already taking place by the end of the first millennium AD. It is logical to conclude that state-formation processes were also taking place, at least in some parts of West Africa, during the first millennium, and this is rendered more probable by evidence from further to the north. By the eighth century AD, when Muslim traders first reached the southwestern Sahara, they found that the gold trade with the north was controlled by the powerful kingdom of Ghana, centred between the upper reaches of the Niger and Senegal rivers in the borderlands of the modern southern Mauritania and southwestern Mali (Fig. 122). Ancient Ghana was thus far removed from the modern state which has taken its name. The principal goldfield exploited at this time was located to the south, around Bambuk in the Senegal headwaters, but the kingdom of Ghana controlled its access to the trading centre of Awdaghast, at the southern end of the main camel-caravan route from the north. Its site has now been convincingly identified with the ruins of Tegdaoust, where excavations have revealed prolonged occupation from at least as early as the seventh century, although the main stone buildings are significantly later (Polet 1985; Robert-Chaleix 1989). There has been much controversy surrounding the location of the capital of ancient Ghana (R. J. McIntosh 1998), one candidate being the ruins at Kumbi Saleh in the extreme south of Mauritania, which cover more than 2 square kilometres, the adjacent cemeteries being even more extensive (Thomassey and Mauny 1951, 1956; Berthier 1997). The date of the establishment of this state remains uncertain, but must have been well before the eighth century, when Muslim visitors from the north were impressed by the power and wealth of its ruler (Levtzion 1973). This view is supported by radiocarbon dates from Kumbi Saleh (Sutton 1982) which show that occupation there had begun by the sixth century AD. There can thus be no doubt that the kingdom of Ghana was essentially a local development, based upon local resources (MacDonald 1998), whose resultant wealth subsequently attracted the attention of trans-Saharan traders. The archaeology of Muslim peoples in West Africa is further discussed in chapter 8 (see also Insoll 2003).

Attention has already been drawn (p. 234) to Jenne-Jeno, a mound-site in the flood plain of the Inland Niger Delta. It provides the clearest evidence yet available for the early development of West African urbanism, at a date long before the advent of Muslim traders. Founded late in the first millennium BC as an agricultural village covering a few hectares, Jenne-Jeno rapidly became a true urban centre at the focus of settlement in the Delta region. As the excavators have noted, 'the ability to create food surpluses for export along the river to less favoured regions permitted the inhabitants to procure through trade the raw materials, such as iron, copper and stone, that the Inland Delta lacked' (S. K. and R. J. McIntosh 1984: 87). By AD 300 Jenne-Jeno had expanded to 25 hectares in extent, and excavations have yielded evidence for both herding and fishing, as well as for the cultivation of millet, sorghum and African rice. By the seventh or eighth century, gold was among the items brought from beyond the Delta to the city, which now reached its greatest extent – 33 hectares – and was surrounded by a wall almost 2 kilometres in circumference (Fig. 123). It was at about this time also that many peripheral sites in the flood plain were abandoned, emphasising the emergence of a truly urban system (S. K. and R. J. McIntosh 1980, 1984; S. K. McIntosh 1999b).

Further states arose to the east of ancient Ghana before the close of the first millennium AD. Among these, adjacent to Lake Chad, was Kanem, which grew rich through trade with the north, primarily to Tunis and Tripoli.

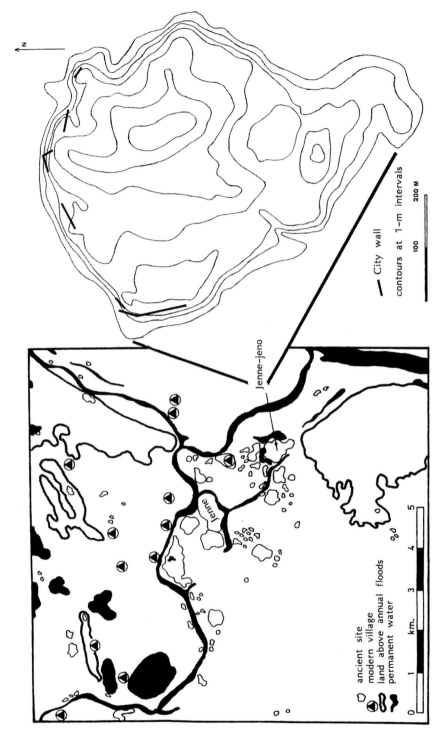

**Fig. 123:** Location and plan of Jenne-Jeno (after S. K. and R. J. McIntosh 1980)

**Fig. 124:**
Megalithic stone
circle at Sine
Saloum, Senegal

Traditions suggest that the Zaghawa rulers of Kanem originated in the southern Sahara. Their penetration southwards to establish themselves as over-
lords of settled farming people in the savanna may have been stimulated by
continuing desiccation of the desert and also by desire to control the source
of the slaves and ivory on which their prosperity depended (H. F. C. Smith
1971). It is tempting to link this process with the change in artefact types
at Daima which, as noted above on pp. 200–1, accompanied evidence for an
expansion and intensification of trade late in the first millennium AD. The
later history of these sudanic states is described in chapter 8.

A remarkable series of megalithic monuments – settings of large, erect
stones (Fig. 124) – in the Gambia, adjacent parts of Senegal and extending
eastwards into Mali, have burials within them that date from the second
half of the first millennium AD (Thilmans *et al.* 1980). It is tempting to link
them with the large burial mounds which occur at numerous places in the
savanna from Mali to Senegal (S. K. and R. J. McIntosh 1993). These clearly
represent non-Islamic interments, some being of very wealthy individuals,
and are best dated between the sixth and fourteenth centuries AD (Connah
2001). At El-Oualedji in Mali a 12-metres-high earthen tumulus was found to
cover a wooden burial chamber containing the remains of two people and a
variety of grave-goods (Desplagnes 1951). As further discussed in chapter 8,
there are close parallels between these graves and the funerary customs
recorded by al-Bakri in the eleventh century.

The more easterly regions of the northern savanna, stretching from Cameroon into the Central African Republic, remain very poorly known archaeologically (Asombang 1999). It was noted in chapter 6 that, probably before the coming of iron, some of the stone-tool-using farming peoples of the eastern Nigeria/Cameroon area had begun to expand southwards into the forest, and probably also eastwards along its northern margin. To the north, at Nana Mode in the Central African Republic, an iron-using settlement in the savanna is dated to about the seventh century AD; the pottery from this site was decorated by means of carved wooden roulettes (David and Vidal 1977).

In attempting a provisional overall picture of cultural trends in West Africa around the beginning of the Christian era, it is essential to bear in mind the very incomplete coverage of the research that has so far been undertaken. An understanding, however provisional, of West African developments is, however, particularly important in view of the indications, to be cited below, that this region played a major role in the transmission of iron technology and associated culture to more southerly parts of the continent.

The first point is that it seems no longer possible to argue that the development of metal-working technology in West Africa was due exclusively to transmission from the north. It now appears that little reliance can be placed on claims that the working of copper in parts of Mauritania and Niger began significantly before iron. There, as in more southerly parts of West Africa, both innovations are now believed to date from around the middle of the first millennium BC. At first sight, the most plausible explanations for the beginning of West African iron-working seem to be either that it was a local invention, or that some relevant knowledge was transmitted south of the Sahara from the north, being then progressed and elaborated in a specifically African manner. These hypotheses are not, of course, mutually exclusive. It is arguably very unlikely that no-one in West Africa had any knowledge of contemporary technological achievements north of the Sahara. This would not mean that the greater part of West African metallurgical expertise was not a local development. Further consideration will have to await the recovery of more detailed evidence as to the smelting methods that were practised in these two regions.

There can be little doubt that iron was adopted in the West African savanna by peoples whose ancestors had lived there for many centuries previously. Savanna–forest contacts at this time have been only cursorily investigated, but continuity of settlement may well have prevailed in the latter area also. This conclusion is supported by the observation that, although metal-working was known from the mid-first millennium BC, some groups retained their stone-tool technology for at least a thousand years afterwards.

Archaeological research in West Africa has been concentrated on sites which illustrate the history of the known states, especially on those which have also yielded art objects. This has tended to obscure the fact that the earliest iron-using communities were composed essentially of peasant farmers, and that such people have probably formed the majority of the West African population throughout the last 2000 years. Very little research has been undertaken on the subsistence economies of these peoples. One must assume that there was a major contrast between the herding and – in places – cereal agriculture of the savanna regions, and the yam cultivation which, with arboriculture, provided the mainstay for life in the more easterly forest and adjacent woodlands. The extent to which African rice was grown at this time remains unknown, the primary evidence being restricted to the Inland Niger Delta. Inter-regional exchange of commodities must be seen as a major factor during this period and one that acted as a significant stimulus to the processes of urbanisation and state-formation, long before the development of formal trans-Saharan trade.

## Central Africa

It is convenient to discuss separately the sparse archaeological evidence for early iron-using peoples that is now available from this vast, largely forested region, the greater part of which lies within the basin of the Congo River. The northwestern part of the region, in the southern half of what is now Cameroon, is contiguous with – and in many respects a part of – the forest belt of southeastern Nigeria which has been discussed above. At Obobogo, near Yaounde, a series of village settlements was occupied during the first millennium BC (de Maret 1989). These sites, each covering an area of about 2 hectares in what was then a forest clearing, are marked by flat-based pottery, ground-stone axe/hoes, grindstones and chipped-stone artefacts. A series of deep pits, of unknown function, contained these characteristic artefacts as well as shells of the edible nut *Canarium schweinfurthii* and of the oil palm *Elaeis guineensis*. Some, but not all, of the pits contained a few pieces of iron slag. It appears that iron came into use on a small scale during the occupation of Obobogo: the date at which this occurred cannot yet be determined precisely but was probably around the fourth century BC. It is noteworthy that ground-stone axe/hoes continued in use after the appearance of iron.

This last point is relevant to an evaluation of discoveries at Batalimo (de Bayle 1975), located in the extreme south of the Central African Republic near the Lobaye-Ubangi confluence, some 500 kilometres east of Obobogo. This extensive site appears to have been a factory for the production of stone axe-hoes. The pottery is flat-based, like that at Obobogo, although the

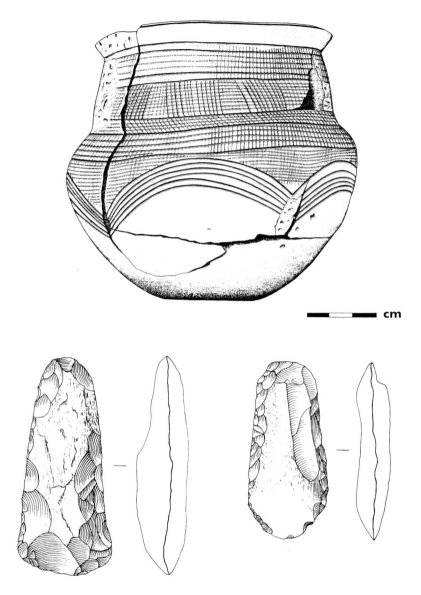

**Fig. 125:** Pottery vessel and stone axes from Batalimo (from Eggert 1987a, after de Bayle)

decoration is distinct (Fig. 125). A date around the fourth century AD is indicated by both thermoluminescence and radiocarbon analyses (de Maret 1985a). Despite this relatively late date, there is no evidence for the use of iron at Batalimo.

The off-shore island of Bioko, Equatorial Guinea, provides additional evidence for the late continuation of stone-tool use, there being no source of metal in its exclusively volcanic rocks. Stone axe/hoes were produced in large numbers on Bioko and, it appears, traded to adjacent areas of the mainland.

**Fig. 126:** Pits at Oveng, Gabon

The known pottery sequence on the island shows certain similarities with that of the mainland, but seems to date only from the second half of the first millennium AD: it is not clear whether the earliest phase has yet been identified (de Maret 1982b; de Maret and Clist 1987).

The beginning of iron-working in the forest regions of Central Africa is best illustrated by recent archaeological investigations in Gabon and Congo. It seems that, at least in the former country, the new technology was adopted in inland regions significantly before it appeared on the coast. There are sites with iron-working dated to the last 500 years BC in all the inland Gabonese provinces, but none near the coast before the first century AD (Clist 1989a). It has been suggested that knowledge of metallurgy may have been introduced from the savanna areas of Congo, subsequently spreading across Gabon by way of the Ogooue River system (Oslisly and Peyrot 1992). Few details of these early sites have yet been published, but the iron-smelting furnaces seem generally to have comprised a clay-lined pit surmounted by a clay shaft. By early in the Christian era several contemporaneous groupings may be recognised among the iron-using inhabitants of what is now Gabon. One of the best known is the Oveng group, named from a site near Libreville (Clist 1989b) where quantities of marine shells indicate a major source of food, and deep pits (Fig. 126) are reminiscent of those at Obobogo. Remains of pole-and-mud buildings suggest that the site was occupied on at least a semi-permanent basis. Despite variations in the decoration, it is significant that the pots in all these groups have flat bases.

Most of our knowledge about Congolese archaeology of this period comes from fieldwork conducted by Denbow (1990) in the vicinity of Pointe Noire. Both open grassland and dense forest environments are represented in this coastal region. At Tchissanga, two phases of occupation have been recognised, both being marked by artefacts of the general type noted above. In the earlier phase, securely dated to the sixth century BC, there is no evidence for the use of iron, but several fragments were recovered from deposits of the later phase which belongs to the late fourth century BC. Although iron may have been brought to Tchissanga from elsewhere, smelting is clearly attested on the Congo coast during the second or third centuries AD at the large village-site of Madingo-Kayes. The technology which they exhibit is identical to that employed in later times further to the south (D. Miller 1998). Ground-stone tools also continued in use throughout this period.

The earliest iron-using peoples in the Lower Congo region of D. R. Congo were those of the so-called Kay Ladio group. At Sakuzi there is evidence for continuity of occupation from the preceding Ngovo group (see p. 202) and, indeed, the pottery of the two groups shows significant similarity. Associations of Kay Ladio pottery with fragments of iron are dated between the mid-first and the early third centuries AD (de Maret 1986). Broadly contemporary settlement by iron-using peoples is known further up the Congo River, at Gombe Point near the modern Kinshasa (Cahen 1981).

The vast interior equatorial forest of D. R. Congo has only recently begun to yield archaeological remains of this general period (Eggert 1992; Wotzka 1995). Pottery very similar to that from Batalimo (see pp. 246–7 above) has been found to extend far into the forest along the Ubangi River. The most informative occurrence, dated to the last two centuries BC, is at Maluba in deep pits where oil palm nuts were also recovered (Eggert 1987a). It seems reasonable to conclude that the Batalimo pottery tradition lasted for some 500 or 600 years, the name-site being a late occurrence. None of the forest sites has yielded traces of iron, but these are unlikely to have survived in the environmental conditions which prevail there. Sites along the southerly Congo tributaries, notably the Momboyo, are marked by another style of flat-based pottery, named Imbonga, which is likewise generally preserved in deep pits containing oil palm and *Canarium* nuts. These sites probably date to the late first millennium BC or early centuries AD. Again, no iron was preserved, although it is likely to have been in use at this time. The far east of the Congo Basin lies within the area, centred on Lake Victoria, which was occupied rather more than 2000 years ago by the iron-working Urewe people, discussed below (pp. 250–2).

There can now be little doubt that the forest regions of the Congo Basin were occupied during the last millennium BC by people who established village settlements marked by the presence of deep pits containing their characteristic pottery, the affinities of which are with the northern and northwestern forest fringe. Some of the sites in the northwest are earlier than those in other parts of the region, and it is in the former area that their antecedents may be recognised. Clear evidence for the use of iron, from about the fifth century BC onwards, is at present only available in the northwest and west, from Cameroon to Bas Congo; it was probably used also in the central forest region but has not survived in the local archaeological record. It is tempting to interpret these sites as evidence for expansion through the Central African forest by the ancestors of the recent Bantu-speaking people (Vansina 1990). This proposed correlation will be discussed and evaluated below (see pp. 261–5).

## Eastern and southern Africa

The earlier iron-using communities over an enormous area of eastern and southern Africa show a very remarkable degree of homogeneity, to the extent that archaeologists generally attribute them to a single complex, here named Chifumbaze.[2] Radiocarbon dates indicate that the complex first appeared on the west side of Lake Victoria around the middle of the last millennium BC, extending by early in the Christian era to the northern and eastern side of the basin. By about the third century AD it had expanded southwards as far as KwaZulu-Natal (D. W. Phillipson 1975). The archaeological sites and artefacts of the Chifumbaze complex make a marked contrast with those that had gone before, and contain the first evidence in these southerly latitudes for the cultivation of crops, for the herding of domestic animals, for settled village life, for metallurgy and, south of Tanzania, for the manufacture of pottery. In each case, these are cultural features for which there is archaeological evidence in the more northerly or northwesterly regions of Africa in earlier times; they were probably more significant in the long term than was metallurgy (cf. Segobye 1998). The fact that so many important aspects of culture were introduced more-or-less together over such a wide area and so rapidly makes it highly probable that these innovations in sub-equatorial Africa were brought about as a result of the physical movement of substantial numbers of people. It cannot be stressed too strongly that, as explained below, these innovations were not

---

2 Following my earlier proposal (D. W. Phillipson 1968a), the interim term 'Early Iron Age' was formerly applied to this complex. However, now that its parameters are relatively well known, and to avoid confusion with contemporary early iron-using societies in other parts of Africa, it is preferable to use a more distinctive designation. The name 'Chifumbaze', from the rockshelter in Mozambique where pottery of this complex was first excavated (D. W. Phillipson 1976), has been widely adopted and is retained here. Other terms that have been proposed, such as 'Early Farming Communities' (Morais 1988) or 'Early Iron-Working' (Chami 1995), are felt to be insufficiently distinctive.

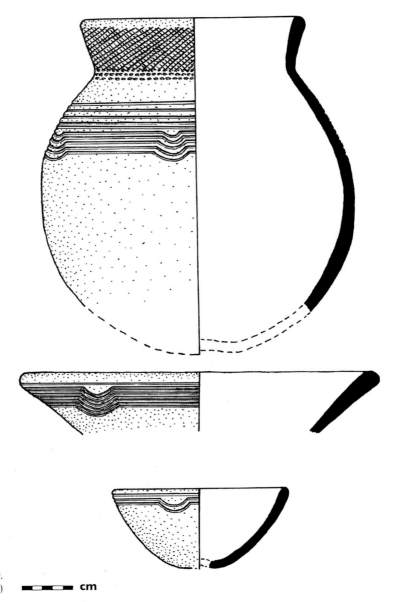

**Fig. 127:** Urewe ware from sites in southwestern Kenya (after M. D. Leakey *et al.* 1948)

cm

inseparably linked in a single 'package'; although often broadly concurrent, they represent separate processes of cultural change.

The first use of iron in the Lake Victoria area is attributed to the Urewe group, named after a site in southwestern Kenya. Its characteristic pottery (Fig. 127), in which several local sub-styles may be recognised, is found in Rwanda and adjacent parts of D. R. Congo, in southern Uganda, northwestern Tanzania and around the Winam Gulf in southwestern Kenya (Van Noten 1979; Van Grunderbeek *et al.* 1983). In Buhaya on the southwestern shore of the lake, extensive settlements and iron-smelting sites, such as Katuruka, date at least to the very beginning of the Christian era and may be several centuries older (Schmidt 1978; Clist 1987). The iron-smelting technology of these sites has attracted considerable attention (Van Grunderbeek *et al.* 2001). Although some claims for its sophistication may have been exaggerated, it was clearly both complex and accomplished (Schmidt and Childs 1985; Eggert 1987b). It produced on a substantial scale what was technically a type of steel, although this may be of little significance since much of the benefit appears to have been lost in the subsequent forging process.

No effective research has yet been undertaken to illustrate the subsistence economy practised by the makers of Urewe ware. There are some indications that they were probably herders of domestic cattle and cultivators of both finger millet and sorghum (Van Noten 1983). Sediments in mountain swamps and on the bed of Lake Victoria contain datable pollen which suggests that there was a significant reduction in forest vegetation around the lake about the middle of the last millennium BC (Kendall and Livingstone 1972; D. Taylor and Marchant 1995). This could, of course, have been brought about by climatic causes or by charcoal-burning for iron-smelting, rather than by ground-clearance for agriculture, as discussed by Schmidt (1997b).

Much more research needs to be done before we shall be able to understand the antecedents of the Urewe group. Their predecessors in parts of the Lake Victoria area appear to have been the makers of Kansyore ware, described in chapter 6, and the relationship, if any, between the two populations remains unknown (cf. MacLean 1996). There can be little doubt that the Urewe sites represent a sharp discontinuity in the local archaeological record, but we are not yet in a position to estimate the extent to which this was due to rapid *in situ* development or to contact with other regions. No close parallels are known for Urewe ware, although some similarities have been suggested with pottery from Chad, far to the northwest (Soper 1971), and also with certain recently discovered material from the equatorial forest region. Linguistic studies may throw some light on this problem, and will be discussed below.

Studies of pottery typology suggest that the earliest iron-using communities of more southerly latitudes may have been derived, at least in part, from those of the Urewe group, and a large number of radiocarbon dates confirm that this is probable on chronological grounds. Although points of controversy remain, there is broad agreement among many archaeologists that the Chifumbaze complex to the south of the Urewe area may best be considered as representing two or three separate facies or 'streams', of which the more easterly probably derived directly from the Urewe group

(D. W. Phillipson 1977a). The ancestry of the western facies also may have had Urewe connexions, but its origins remain less well understood: it probably incorporated local elements from the western D. R. Congo/northern Angola region. The distributions of these facies and of their constituent groups, as currently known, are shown in figure 128.

The easternmost facies extended by about the second century AD to the coastal regions of southeastern Kenya and the adjacent parts of northeastern Tanzania, where it is represented by sites yielding the characteristic type of pottery named Kwale ware, after a site southwest of Mombasa. Settlement seems here to have been restricted to the relatively well-watered hilly country where the villages of the region's present Bantu-speaking farming communities are concentrated (Soper 1967a, 1967b, 1982). It may be noted that in the Rift Valley territory of the stone-tool-using herders no contemporary traces of iron or of Kwale-related pottery have been discovered. Presumably either this comparatively arid country was unsuited to settlement by the Chifumbaze people, or the herders were able to prevent penetration by the newcomers. Whatever the reason, it is probable that the Kwale industry was introduced to the East African coast by a southerly route through what is now central Tanzania, where Chifumbaze sites such as Lelesu have been reported (Smolla 1956; Sutton 1968). Recently discovered sites of the Chifumbaze complex in the vicinity of Dar es Salaam (Chami 1995, 2001) may represent the common source both of Kwale and of its counterparts further to the south.

Around the second century AD there took place an extremely rapid dispersal of iron-using farmers of the Chifumbaze complex through a wide area extending southwards through Mozambique, Malawi, eastern Zambia and Zimbabwe into Swaziland and adjacent parts of South Africa. The easternmost manifestation was largely restricted to the coastal lowlands and clearly sprang from the Kwale group settlements of East Africa. More than 3000 kilometres appear to have been covered in less than two centuries. In the south, the characteristic pottery by which this coastal dispersal may readily be recognised is known as Matola ware, after a site near Maputo (Cruz e Silva 1980; Sinclair 1986). South of the Zambezi, pottery of this general type is now represented at numerous sites in the coastal regions of southern

**Fig. 128:** Sites of the Chifumbaze complex in eastern and southern Africa

| | | | |
|---|---|---|---|
| 1 Benfica | 7 Katuruka | 13 Nakapapula | 19 Silozwane |
| 2 Broederstroom | 8 Kwale | 14 Nkope | 20 Situmpa |
| 3 Chifumbaze | 9 Lelesu | 15 Sakwe | 21 Thandwe |
| 4 Kalundu | 10 Lydenburg | 16 Salumano | 22 Toutswe |
| 5 Kapwirimbwe | 11 Makwe | 17 Sanga | 23 Tzaneen |
| 6 Katoto | 12 Matola | 18 Schroda | 24 Urewe |

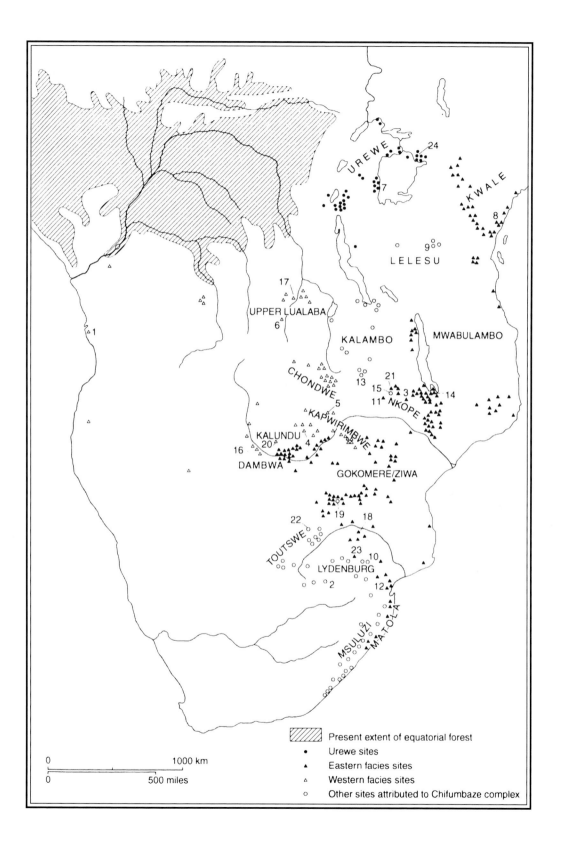

UREWE

KWALE

24

7

8

9
LELESU

17

UPPER LUALABA

6

KALAMBO

MWABULAMBO

CHONDWE

13

21
15    3

5    KAPWIRIMBWE    11  NKOPE    14

KALUNDU
20    4

16

DAMBWA

GOKOMERE/ZIWA

22
TOUTSWE

19    18

23    10

LYDENBURG

2        12

MSULUZI

MATOLA

| 0 | | 1000 km |

| 0 | | 500 miles |

▨ Present extent of equatorial forest
● Urewe sites
▲ Eastern facies sites
△ Western facies sites
○ Other sites attributed to Chifumbaze complex

Mozambique, in the Mpumalanga lowlands, and in KwaZulu-Natal at least as far as latitude 31° south (Maggs 1984). Villages, up to 2 hectares in extent, were generally sited a few kilometres inland of the Indian Ocean shore, in locations suited to the cultivation of cereals. The inhabitants of these short-lived villages exploited iron and other local resources, obtaining most of their protein from shellfish and other marine foods. Domestic animals, if kept, were probably few. Affinities with Kwale ware are particularly striking in the pottery from Tzaneen in Mpumalanga Province (Klapwijk 1974; Klapwijk and Huffman 1996). The archaeology of this time is poorly known in the coastal regions between the Kwale and Matola areas, but comparable material has been reported from the Nampula region of northern Mozambique (D. W. Phillipson 1989a; Sinclair *et al.* 1993a). The involvement of the East African coastal regions in Indian Ocean maritime trade is demonstrable around the first century AD and again from the eighth century onwards; indeed, continuity through the first millennium cannot be ruled out but has not yet been thoroughly investigated (Chami 1995). For convenience, the period of Islamic settlements on the East Coast, beginning in the eighth century, is here discussed in chapter 8.

Further inland, in Malawi, eastern Zambia and much of Zimbabwe, the Chifumbaze complex is represented both by substantial villages and by pottery occurrences in rockshelters that apparently continued to be frequented by stone-tool-using hunter-gatherers throughout the first millennium AD, making only occasional contact with the farming communities (D. W. Phillipson 1976, 1977a; Crader 1984). These inland occurrences are attributed to the Nkope and Gokomere/Ziwa traditions (Fig. 129). Their relationship with the Matola tradition remains unclear and it is uncertain whether they should be regarded as representing coastal and inland manifestations of an eastern facies of the Chifumbaze complex, or as two distinct facies (cf. Huffman 1982, 1989).

The archaeology of the more westerly regions has so far been much less intensively investigated, being well known only in the Katanga Province of D. R. Congo and in central Zambia, where iron was worked as early as the second century AD by villagers who cultivated sorghum and cowpeas. By the fifth century, domestic cattle were kept at Kapwirimbwe near Lusaka, and other settlements had been established close to the rich mineral deposits of the Zambia/Katanga Copperbelt (D. W. Phillipson 1968c, 1972a; Anciaux de Faveaux and de Maret 1985; Robertson 2000). Most of our knowledge of the late first millennium AD in Katanga comes from a series of cemeteries, notably Sanga and Katoto in the valley of the upper Lualaba (Nenquin 1963; Hiernaux *et al.* 1972; de Maret 1985b, 1992). By the closing centuries of the first millennium, copper – which had been worked on a small scale for some

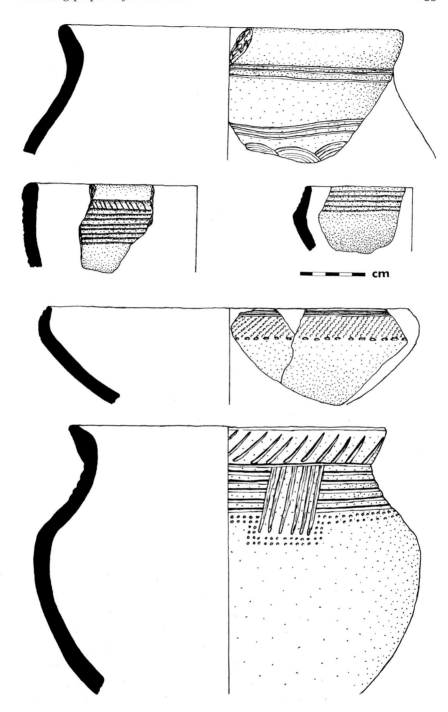

**Fig. 129:** Pottery of the eastern facies of the Chifumbaze complex, from Malawi (after Robinson and Sandelowsky 1968, Robinson 1973)

hundreds of years – was used for a variety of display and prestige purposes. This trend continued and expanded in more recent times, as is discussed in chapter 8 (see also Herbert 1984).

There are indications that pottery which closely resembles that of the Chifumbaze complex was made in parts of northern Angola by the early centuries of the Christian era, as at Benfica near Luanda (dos Santos and Ervedosa 1970). The resultant suggestion that the Chifumbaze complex's beginnings in the western part of the sub-continent may have been at least as early as in the east has been confirmed by investigations in the upper Zambezi Valley (Katanekwa 1981; D. W. Phillipson 1989b). Several sites in this area have yielded pottery which clearly belongs to the Chifumbaze complex, in contexts now dated at Situmpa and Salumano to the third or second centuries BC. These are thus the earliest manifestations of the Chifumbaze complex yet known from the southern savannas. Iron artefacts have not been recovered from the small-scale excavations so far conducted, but the almost complete absence of flaked-stone artefacts suggests that metal was indeed used by these sites' inhabitants. Bones of domestic cattle and, less certainly, ovicaprids at Salumano indicate the practice of herding.

Later manifestations of the Chifumbaze complex are known across northern Botswana (Denbow 1990; Campbell et al. 1996), those in the east and adjacent parts of the Limpopo Valley being particularly significant. In the former area developments from around the seventh century onwards are attributed to the Toutswe tradition, marked by a settlement system with a small number of large easily defended hill-top sites surrounded by many smaller ones generally located close to sources of water (Denbow 1984, 1986). Cattle provided the mainstay of the system's economy and there are good reasons for tracing back to this period the important role played by cattle in the culture of southern Bantu-speaking people. The settlement pattern reflects this emphasis, with dispersed cattle camps located for water and grazing availability, and larger sites serving as foci and centres for the community as a whole, as is still the case with modern Tswana peoples in this area (Segobye 1998). It is clear that the large central sites were subject to prolonged, permanent occupation: this, with the evidence for the herding of very large numbers of cattle, suggests the rise of an élite such as may be recognised also in rather later times at sites in the Limpopo Valley, notably Schroda (Hanisch 1981; Fig. 130). Schroda was a large village of some 12 hectares, occupied between the eighth and the tenth centuries, and comprising a livestock enclosure, circular thatched houses and grain-bins. A particular area of the site was used for the working of ivory, which may have been exchanged for imported glass beads, several hundred of which were recovered. In another, more central, area were found several caches of clay figurines, both human and animal, which strongly resemble those made in

**Fig. 130:**
Schroda, viewed from an overlooking cave. The Limpopo River is visible in the background.

Zimbabwe in later times. Subsequent developments in this Limpopo Valley area are illustrated at the sites of Bambandyanalo and Mapungubwe (Meyer 1998; D. Miller 2001), further discussed in chapter 8; there is evidence for further development of long-distance trade in ivory and, from the eleventh century, in gold (Huffman 1982; Maggs 1984).

The sites of the first millennium AD in the highlands north of the Vaal and in parts of KwaZulu-Natal are for the most part attributed to the Msuluzi/Lydenburg tradition of the Chifumbaze complex. Opinion is divided as to whether this tradition arose, around the fifth century, from the earlier Matola tradition of the Mozambique and KwaZulu-Natal coastlands, or whether its connexions lay further inland, perhaps with the western facies of the Chifumbaze complex (Huffman 1982; Maggs 1984; D. W. Phillipson 1989a). By the seventh century, evidence for early farming settlement in KwaZulu-Natal extended inland into the uKhahlamba/Drakensberg foothills about as far as the 1000-metre contour, and for some 300 kilometres further south than the Matola sites had done, penetrating what is now the Eastern Cape Province in the vicinity of East London at latitude 33° south (Maggs 1980, 1995; Loubser 1993; Whitelaw 1994; Nogwaza 1994; Binneman 1996). Villages were often substantially larger than their earlier counterparts, located on colluvial soils near valley bottoms, and were supported by well-developed mixed farming, with cattle and ovicaprids herded and a variety of crops cultivated including sorghum, finger millet, bulrush millet and pumpkin. The broadly contemporary and analogous occupation in the highland regions north of the Vaal is best known from sites at Broederstroom, west of Pretoria, and near Lydenburg. A large village at the former site was occupied around the sixth century, its inhabitants smelting the local iron ore and relying for their food on the cultivation of cereals and the herding of small stock, with perhaps a few cattle (Mason 1986). Around Lydenburg, the mixed farming economy was more broadly based, but particular interest attaches to the recovery, from a fifth-century context, of a series of life-sized terracotta human heads (Fig. 131), which presumably served some ritual or religious function (Maggs and Davison 1981; Evers 1982; Whitelaw 1995). One of the heads was surmounted by a model of a domestic bovid, suggesting both that herds occupied an important position in the lives of the site's inhabitants, and also that the heads may have been in some way linked with practices intended to ensure the maintenance of the herds. Fragments of similar objects have been found at other sites nearby and in KwaZulu-Natal, but the Lydenburg heads are without parallel elsewhere south of the equator.

Throughout the area inhabited by the Chifumbaze people, iron-working was practised on a scale adequate to ensure that they only rarely, if ever, used stone tools. In regions where the appropriate mineral deposits occur, copper and gold were also worked. Mining appears to have been restricted to small-scale operations during the first millennium AD; we have as yet little reliable information concerning the types of smelting-furnaces that were used, except in the interlacustrine region. Iron artefacts were mainly utilitarian: axes, hoes, arrowheads and the like. Copper was used for bangles and items of personal adornment; by AD 1300 in Katanga it was being cast into small cross-shaped ingots which may have served as a form of currency (Bisson 1975; see also chapter 8). Gold-working, effectively restricted to Zimbabwe, is attested only from the end of the first millennium AD and seems largely to have been geared to an export trade through the ports of the Indian Ocean coast, whence imported glass beads and, perhaps, other more perishable items found their way inland (Summers 1969; Swan 1994).

Detailed evidence concerning the farming economies of the Chifumbaze communities, and the plant and animal species on which they were based, has only rarely been recovered. While the presence of iron hoes and of numerous grindstones may indicate agriculture, conclusive proof of this in the form of specifically identifiable plant remains comes from disappointingly few sites, mostly in Zambia, Zimbabwe and South Africa. The species for which we so far have evidence include bulrush and finger millet, sorghum, cowpeas and varieties of squash and beans. There can be little doubt that most, if not all, of these crops were ultimately derived from

**Fig. 131:**
Terracotta head
from Lydenburg

those which, as shown above in chapter 6, were originally brought under cultivation in the areas to the north of the equatorial forest. More detailed botanical studies will be needed before this statement can be amplified.

A small number of crops, notably the banana, appear to have been introduced to eastern Africa from across the Indian Ocean. The date or dates at which this took place remains effectively unknown, those most frequently suggested being in the first millennium AD. Bananas are most widely grown in the Lake Victoria Basin (Schoenbrun 1993, 1998) and in parts of western Africa. The recent demonstration (p. 202 above) that they were present in Cameroon in the mid-first millennium BC now suggests that their antiquity further east may be greater than was previously supposed. We do not yet know to what extent people of the Chifumbaze complex grew these and other vegetatively propagated crops, but they are likely to have been significant, particularly in the better-watered areas.

The evidence for domestic livestock is somewhat more comprehensive, although of such uneven distribution that it is probably dangerous to generalise. Sheep and/or goats, together with cattle, are attested on sites covering virtually the whole time-span of the Chifumbaze complex: cattle seem to have become much more numerous in southeastern Africa from around the seventh or eighth century AD. The breed or breeds of these cattle is still a matter for speculation (Grigson 1996, 2000); the extent to which they were humped has not been ascertained and the possibility that cattle of Indian origin were introduced through the Swahili coastal settlements remains to be evaluated. Domestic fowl (MacDonald 1992; MacDonald and Edwards 1993) appear in eastern and southeastern Africa during the mid-first millennium AD, in Chifumbaze-complex contexts. Whether they derived from more northerly parts of Africa or more directly from their Asian homeland remains unknown.

Throughout this period, the hunting of wild animals retained considerable economic importance. Iron arrowheads and spearpoints (which need not, of course, have been used exclusively for hunting) have been recovered from many sites, and those from which bones of wild animals have been excavated are appreciably more numerous than those that have yielded remains of domestic stock. At Kalundu, in southern Zambia, the faunal remains from successive layers show the gradual replacement of wild by domestic species (Fagan 1967). The wild animals represented include wildebeest and buffalo, as well as many of the smaller antelope. Fish bones are rarely preserved, but have been recorded in Malawi, notably at Nkope.

The appearance and lay-out of houses and settlements represents an aspect of the Chifumbaze complex that has only rarely been addressed by the research so far undertaken. Elucidation of these matters requires far more extensive excavation than has generally proved practicable, but will undoubtedly be a focus for future investigation. Many sites have yielded fragments of clay house-walls bearing impressions of vertical stakes and interwoven withies; together with traces of clay floors and of burnt thatch, these indicate that the general type of house erected in Chifumbaze-complex villages was not dissimilar to those used in many rural areas of eastern and southern Africa during recent times. Whether these houses were round or rectangular is, however, rarely apparent; we generally have little information about their internal arrangements. In recent times such features have shown significant variation between different areas, and clear correlations may be seen with the general life-style, economy and socio-political system of the inhabitants (Huffman 1989, 1993, 2001). People in southeastern Africa whose lives centre around their herds of cattle, for example, often live in villages where houses, usually round, are arranged around a central corral. In southern parts of D. R. Congo, on the other hand, the predominantly agricultural people live in rectangular houses set in straight lines beside a street. The extent to which these distinctive patterns may be traced back in the archaeological sequence is clearly of considerable significance. In fact, there is growing evidence that the former pattern, that of the southern cattle-herders, had originated by late in the first millennium AD, when it is attested at Toutswe and related sites in northeastern Botswana and adjacent parts of South Africa. It is, however, important to recognise that cultural continuity cannot be assumed: practices and their rationale (cf. Huffman 1998) can both change, and do so independently.

By the tenth century a clear distinction may be seen between Chifumbaze communities in the central and western savannas and those of southeastern Africa. In the former region, metal clearly formed a medium for the accumulation and exchange of wealth, a function served in the southeast by cattle (Vansina 1984; D. W. Phillipson 1989a). This important distinction is one which rose to even greater prominence in subsequent centuries.

## The contribution of Bantu linguistic studies

In order that maximum use may be made of the evidence afforded by linguistic studies, it is necessary to consider the possibility of a correlation between the archaeological picture described above and the processes of the dispersal of the Bantu languages. In the eastern and southern savanna the geographical distribution of the Chifumbaze complex is almost identical with the area occupied in more recent times by people speaking languages of the closely interrelated Bantu type. This observation lends support to the widely held belief that this complex represents the archaeological manifestation of the initial eastward and southward dispersal of Bantu-speakers beyond the equatorial forest. The view that the people responsible for the Chifumbaze complex were the first local speakers of Bantu languages is widely accepted (Ehret and Posnansky 1982; Ehret 1998; Holden 2002; Bellwood and Renfrew 2003) but has not gone undisputed (see, most recently, Robertson and Bradley 2000), particularly by those who have paid relatively little attention to linguistic studies. The Bantu languages, which are today spoken by upwards of 250 million people spread over an area of nearly 9 million square kilometres, show a remarkable degree of inter-comprehensibility; there can be no reasonable doubt that they have attained their present wide distribution as a result of dispersal from a localised ancestral language within the comparatively recent past – certainly within the last 3000 or 4000 years. Linguists are virtually unanimous in the belief that this ancestral Bantu language was spoken close to the northwestern border of the present Bantu-speaking area – in what is now Cameroon and eastern Nigeria (cf. Dalby 1975). It is likewise widely agreed that the modern Bantu languages, considered together, may be divided into at least two major groups, spoken respectively in the western and eastern parts of Bantu Africa (Vansina 1984, 1995; but see Nurse 1982; Holden 2002). The modern boundary between the two groups closely follows the eastern edge of the equatorial forest and the western branch of the Rift Valley from Lake Albert southwards to the southern end of Lake Tanganyika, but is less clearly defined in the savanna further to the south where there seems to have been much movement and interaction (Bastin *et al.* 1983; Vansina 1984).

It has recently been emphasised that a direct linguistic comparison between western and eastern Bantu may be misleading (Ehret 2001): while the latter is indeed a clear entity, the former is far more heterogeneous, effectively definable only as 'the rest' or 'non-eastern Bantu'. This view, here accepted, had in fact been foreseen by Vansina (1984, 1990), who had emphasised the distinction between the Bantu languages of the northwest and the equatorial forest on the one hand and, on the other, those of the southwestern savanna which are much less sharply distinguished from eastern Bantu than are their forest counterparts.

The earliest dispersal of Bantu-speakers appears to have been that of the western group in the equatorial forest (Vansina 1990; Bastin *et al.* 1999), with lexicostatistical studies indicating several stages successively to Bioko, Gabon, northern and central D. R. Congo (Fig. 132). In much of the savanna to the south of the forest, the affinities of the recent languages are less clearly understood; those in more westerly regions, while clearly related to those of the forest, suggest that much interaction and linguistic development took place following contact with speakers of eastern Bantu.

The eastern Bantu languages show much less diversity than do those of the western group. This implies that their differentiation and expansion may have been comparatively recent, but it also makes the elucidation of these processes correspondingly difficult (Nurse 1982). The problem is compounded by the long history of linguistic borrowing that must have taken place between populations living in close proximity and interaction with one another (Bennett 1983). Studies of loanwords from non-Bantu sources have, however, suggested that most of the modern Bantu languages of

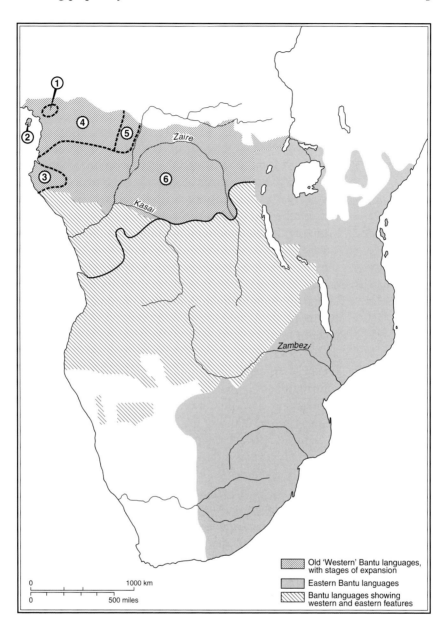

**Fig. 132:** The distribution of Bantu languages (modified from Vansina 1984, 1990)

eastern and southern Africa may be derived from a form that was spoken in the area north of Lake Tanganyika (Ehret 1973).

A large majority of the known sites of the Chifumbaze complex are in the area where eastern Bantu languages are now spoken. While this may be due to the fact that the more westerly regions have seen substantially less archaeological research, the possibility remains that the Chifumbaze complex may prove to be the archaeological signature specifically of eastern Bantu and its influences.

It is now appropriate to compare the conclusions of historical linguistic studies with the picture that emerges from archaeological research. The methodological problems inherent to such an exercise have been set out in chapter 1 (pp. 6–9): here it must be stressed once again that the two approaches have totally different aims, emphases and data-bases, so no absolute correlation between their conclusions should be either assumed or expected. The comparison is nevertheless a perfectly valid exercise in historical reconstruction since each study may supplement or expand the results of the other. An account of this stage in African prehistory, presented in primarily linguistic terms, has been published by Ehret (1998).

The first point which emerges is that, as noted above, it is specifically with the eastern Bantu languages, including those of the southern savanna interaction zone, that the Chifumbaze complex shares its distribution. Archaeological evidence that the Urewe sites represent the earliest manifestation of the Chifumbaze complex is mirrored by the linguists' suggestion that the modern eastern Bantu dialects are derived from a language that was formerly spoken in the area north of Lake Tanganyika. There is, however, no reason to argue that a forest origin is inherently unlikely or to belittle the contribution of indigenous East African elements to the development of the Urewe group and the Chifumbaze complex as a whole.

The economic bases of life in the equatorial forest are markedly different from those of the East African savannas. The herding of domestic animals other than goats is effectively impossible in the former area. Likewise, agriculture in the forest is based upon vegetatively propagated crops, whilst in the savanna cereals are of major importance. It is hardly surprising to find these differences reflected linguistically. Some words for 'goat' in both eastern Bantu and its antecedents can be traced to a common ancestral form. Many of the terms used in eastern Bantu languages to designate cattle and sheep, on the other hand, were borrowed from non-Bantu sources that are also represented in more northerly areas, and the same is true for words connected specifically with the cultivation or processing of cereals (Ehret 1973). The concurrence in the southern savanna of farming practices derived from the forest zone as well as from more easterly regions is reflected in the linguistic evidence in that area for interaction between Bantu-speakers of the eastern savannas and those whose origins lay in the forests to the north. We may conclude that there is strong circumstantial evidence that the beginning of farming in central, eastern and southern Africa was connected with the dispersal of people who spoke Bantu languages (Ehret and

Posnansky 1982; D. W. Phillipson 2003a). In very broad terms, there is some similarity between the regional divisions of the early farming cultures and the linguistically defined stages of Bantu expansion.

We have stressed above how the Chifumbaze complex represents a major archaeological discontinuity in almost all parts of its distribution area. Its settlements, economic practices and technology were all very significantly different from those which had gone before, and were all known during earlier times in more northerly parts of Africa. There can be little doubt that the dispersal of the Chifumbaze complex was largely due to the expansion of a new population element. The apparent link with a linguistic dispersal adds strength to the argument, but no one-to-one correlation should be assumed: there is no reason to suggest that all farmers in these regions spoke Bantu languages, or that all Bantu-speakers were necessarily farmers. It is, however, highly likely that the beginnings both of farming and of metal-working in these regions were due at least in part to the activities of people who spoke Bantu languages. On that basis, we may now turn to consider how these processes may have taken place.

## Mode of dispersal

From the data which have been summarised above, there can be little doubt that the Chifumbaze complex was introduced into sub-equatorial Africa as a result of a substantial and rapid movement of population. The entire culture represented on sites of this complex can be shown to be foreign to the areas in which it occurs, and most of its constituent features may be traced to a source or sources in the northern savanna. The large number of available radiocarbon dates accords with this view, and linguistic evidence also lends it a considerable degree of support. More problematic is seeking to understand how this process may have occurred (cf. Collett 1982).

Despite the novelty of the metal-using farmers' life-style, economy and technology, it is clear that these were not rapidly or totally accepted by the indigenous populations. In several areas, indeed, there is plentiful evidence both from archaeology and from oral traditions for the survival of people who continued to practise the old microlithic technology long after the appearance of metallurgy. In some parts of south-central Africa this continued until only two or three centuries ago, although the degree of this survival obviously varied according to the intensity of farming settlement in the various areas. The best-studied of these very late microlithic industries are those of northern and eastern Zambia. Here, detailed analyses of industrial successions covering the last three millennia, such as those from Nakapapula, Thandwe and Makwe, indicate no significant discernible typological changes such as might be expected had there been any major change in the hunter-gatherer economy and life-style of the stone-tool-makers as a result of cultural contact with their farming contemporaries (D. W. Phillipson 1976, 1977a). That some form of contact did in fact take place between the indigenes and the immigrant food-producers is indicated by the presence in nearly all the microlithic assemblages of this period of varying numbers of sherds of characteristic Chifumbaze pottery (Musonda 1987). The persistence of the mode-5 industries, showing only gradual typological development following trends that were already apparent before the first arrival of farmers, suggests that such contact between the two groups was usually minimal. By contrast, in areas where farming settlement at an early date was relatively dense, there seems to have been fairly rapid displacement of the hunter-gatherer populations as, for example, in much of southern Zambia. One plausible reconstruction of the interactions which may have taken place between hunter-gatherers and farmers is that of a temporary client relationship, such as has been recorded in recent times both in southern Africa and further to the north (Barnard 1992; Mercader *et al.* 2000). This analogy also suggests that, in some areas, relations between the two population groups were characterised by aloofness or mutual avoidance (Musonda 1987). It must be remembered that virtually all our evidence for interaction comes from the territory of the Chifumbaze complex's eastern facies; we have as yet no reliable means of knowing whether the processes were similar in more westerly areas.

The final absorption, conquest or displacement of the stone-tool-using hunting peoples in south-central Africa may be attributed to the expanding population of the early second millennium, which was marked by increased emphasis on the herding of domestic animals, notably cattle. With the passage of time, continued expansion would have brought the cattle-keeping farmers and the hunters into intensified competition. Except where stable symbiosis was established, the ultimate result was apparently the disappearance of the stone-tool-making traditions in all but those few areas which were unsuitable for farming settlement. An example of the former situation is provided by the pygmies of the eastern equatorial forest (d'Hertefelt 1965; Turnbull 1965; Mercader *et al.* 2000). The early history of these small-statured hunting people is completely unknown, as is the language or languages which they originally spoke. Today, most pygmy groups are involved in a client relationship with their agricultural neighbours whose language, whether Bantu, Sudanic or Ubangian, they have adopted. What is now abundantly clear is that the process was not one of simple conquest.

The arrival of the farming peoples in the territories of the indigenous hunter-gatherers of southern Africa also appears to have been recorded

by the latter in rock paintings. The representation of a group of people
at Silozwane Cave in the Matopo Hills of Zimbabwe is believed to show
grain-grinding and other activities of agriculturalists; the people themselves are quite different in appearance from the hunters represented in the
earlier paintings (Fig. 133). Elsewhere, fat-tailed sheep are clearly recognisable (Summers 1959). Later paintings and occasional engravings, consisting
mainly of geometric and schematic designs (Fig. 134), are best attributed
to the farmers themselves. In some areas, including Malawi and eastern
Zambia, they may be linked with art forms associated with religious practices that have continued into recent times (D. W. Phillipson 1972b, 1976;
Gutierrez 1996). Similar instances have been discerned in South Africa
(Prins and Hall 1994), where there is evidence that much of the non-
representational art was the work of herding peoples (B. W. Smith and
Ouzman in press).

Although there can be little doubt that the inception of farming in Africa
south of the equator was brought about through movement of population, it
is not easy to suggest what may have been its causes and motivation. While
the number of people involved at any one time may not have been very
large, it was evidently sufficient to sustain the migrants' distinctive life-style
and customs. It is most probable that entire family groups were involved in
the movements. While population pressure in the original Bantu homeland
in what is now Cameroon and eastern Nigeria may have been one of several causal factors, it would not explain why they moved over such a vast

**Fig. 134:**
Schematic rock painting at Sakwe, Zambia

and sparsely inhabited area so rapidly – the eastern facies appears to have expanded southwards at an average rate of some 15 kilometres a year: about 350 kilometres per generation. The advantages conferred by the knowledge of metallurgy, stock rearing and, probably to a lesser extent, agriculture would greatly have facilitated this expansion (Vogel 1987), but there are likely to have been other factors also of which we are as yet unaware. It is useful to speculate on the reasons why the first-millennium-AD expansion of the Chifumbaze complex, which proceeded with such remarkable rapidity as far to the south as the Vaal River and KwaZulu-Natal, was arrested so abruptly just beyond the Kei River. Although the site distribution remains very imperfectly known, especially in the west, it is nevertheless reasonably clear that its southern limit broadly coincides with the northern edge of the southwest African zone of desert vegetation and that of the long-grass veld of South Africa's Free State Province. On the eastern side of the continent the southernmost extent of the Chifumbaze complex is restricted to the west by the uKhahlamba/Drakensberg and to the south by the Cape winter-rainfall zone. Recent societies have demonstrated that this frontier presents no barrier to herding communities; it is none the less an effective southern limit for the cultivation of traditional African cereals and other food crops. It seems reasonable to suppose, therefore, that agricultural potential limited the initial expansion of farming people into southern Africa. It was not until the development of the more pastorally oriented societies of the early second millennium AD that further southward expansion took place, resulting in the settlement by Bantu-speaking peoples of such marginal lands as those of the Free State Province and parts of Namibia.

## Madagascar and the Comoro Islands

The huge island of Madagascar and the small Comoro archipelago require consideration, albeit briefly. Human settlement of these islands has an antiquity of less than two thousand years (Dewar and Wright 1993; Dewar 1996; Allibert and Vérin 1996; Rakotoarisoa 1998). Throughout this time, they have maintained varying degrees of contact with the African mainland, and this is reflected in certain aspects of their culture and language. Today, the population of the Comoro Islands is essentially Swahili, although there is evidence – primarily but not exclusively linguistic – that this situation was preceded by one when connexions with Madagascar were dominant. The Malagasy culture, on the other hand, has little in common with those of the mainland and the language is Austronesian, being apparently derived most directly from the speech of Borneo, although it includes numerous loanwords and other evidence for contact with speakers of African Bantu languages. There is historical evidence for the presence of Bantu-speaking enclaves on the west and northwest coasts; it is likely that at least some elements of the Austronesian population settled for a while on the East African coast before moving to Madagascar, although no clear archaeological indication of this has yet been recognised (cf. Blench 1996). The connexion between these processes and the advent to East Africa of cultural elements originating across the Indian Ocean remains to be demonstrated.

The oldest evidence for the human settlement of Madagascar is essentially circumstantial, there being no definite archaeological traces which are securely dated before the late first millennium AD. However, major changes in vegetation and in the animal population suggest that there may have been a human presence, perhaps intermittent and restricted to coastal regions, since around the beginning of the Christian era. The first urban development on Madagascar took place at Mahilaka on the northwest coast around the twelfth century. Between the fourteenth and the sixteenth centuries, there is evidence for the growth of social hierarchies, followed by the formation of states.

## Stone-tool-using herders of southwestern Africa

Beyond the area that was settled by the farmers of the Chifumbaze complex, principally in Namibia and in the Northern and Western Cape Provinces of South Africa, use of lithic technology continued throughout the first millennium AD and even into more recent centuries (Klein 1986; Kinahan

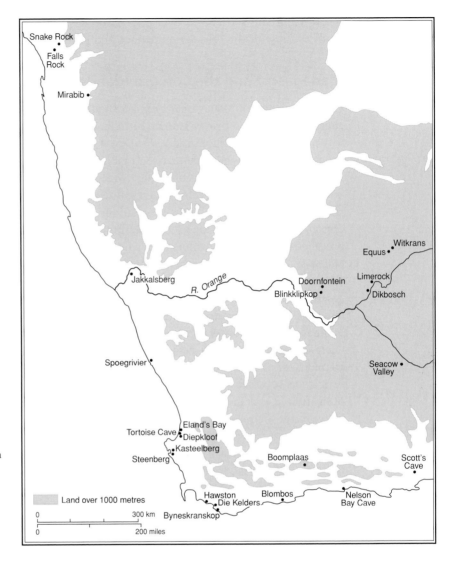

**Fig. 135:**
Principal sites in southwestern Africa which have yielded remains of domestic sheep in precolonial contexts

1991; Brink and Webley 1996; Webley 1997; Bousman 1998). There can be little doubt that the people responsible for these stone industries were KhoiSan-speakers, ancestors of the more recent Khoi ('Hottentots') and San ('Bushmen') of southern and southwestern Africa. At an early date some of these stone-tool-using people (Fig. 135) obtained access to domestic sheep and – although this is less certain – cattle. Bones of domestic animals make their appearance on sites in Namibia and the Western Cape which are dated to the first or second century AD. Pottery first occurs in the local archaeological sequence at approximately the same time, but there remains some

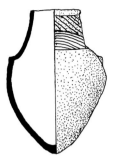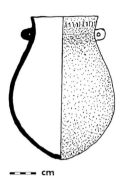

**Fig. 136:** Cape coastal pottery (after Rudner 1968)

uncertainty as to whether the two innovations were intimately linked. The pottery shows no particular similarity to wares in adjacent regions from which it could have been derived, the earliest material being usually thin and well made; later vessels, especially in coastal regions, comprised pointed-based jars and beakers (Fig. 136; Rudner 1968; Schweitzer 1979). The latter wares seem also to have been used by communities who did not have access to domestic stock and who continued their traditional reliance on gathering wild vegetable foods, collecting shellfish, hunting and fishing (A. B. Smith *et al.* 1991). There has been much controversy over the nature of the cultural processes which these archaeological manifestations represent: it has frequently been assumed that the distinction between hunting and herding KhoiSan-speaking populations recorded by European visitors from the fifteenth century onwards could be projected back to the beginning of the Christian era when their ancestors had entered southwestern Africa along routes which might, it was sometimes proposed, be demonstrated archaeologically. A related assumption was that some hunting peoples may have obtained varying numbers of sheep (perhaps as prey rather than as livestock) from neighbouring herding populations whose remains have not yet been recognised archaeologically.

Recent research makes such interpretations seem increasingly unlikely. A complicated pattern of local seasonal resource-exploitation has been revealed, but does not include any clear distinction between hunters and herders except in parts of the Northern Cape where variation in lithic technology has been attributed to such a division (Parsons 2003). At least in some areas, such as the west coast north of the Cape of Good Hope (Fig. 137), this seasonal pattern seems to have involved movement of population between, on the one hand, the inland regions where wild vegetable foods were plentiful during the summer and where the diet could then readily be supplemented by the meat of small animals and, on the other hand, the caves and open sites near the coast where shellfish were exploited

**Fig. 137:** The early herder site of Kasteelberg, Western Cape

during the winter (Parkington and Hall 1987). This appears not only to have been the main regimen of life during the centuries which preceded the advent of domestic sheep, but also to have continued into relatively recent centuries in several areas without significant discernible modification (Kinahan 1996). It is now considered likely that some level of sheep-herding was adopted by some of these seasonally migrating groups, and that herders *per se* did not form a distinct population element (cf. A. B. Smith 1990, 1998b; Sadr 2003).

There are no local wild ancestors for domestic sheep or cattle in the relatively well-studied South African faunal assemblages of the last millennia BC, so there can be no reasonable doubt that the first domestic animals in southernmost Africa were introduced into the region from more northerly latitudes. Links with the stone-tool-using herder peoples of East Africa were at one time considered but have not proved easy to demonstrate. Recent research has located a potential source in much greater proximity.

In the Matopo Hills and neighbouring parts of southwestern Zimbabwe, pottery of the idiosyncratic type known as Bambata ware occurs in the upper levels of several rockshelter deposits (K. R. Robinson 1966a): it appears to have been the first pottery produced in this particular area and to be associated not with the working of iron but with the production of mode-5 lithic artefacts. At Bambata Cave it is also associated with bones of domestic sheep and dated around the second century BC (N. J. Walker 1983). Although typologically distinct, at least in its earlier occurrences, Bambata ware shows some affinity with pottery of the Chifumbaze complex, although its fine, thin fabric is particularly distinctive. Analogous material is now reported from several sites in north-central Botswana and in Namibia (Jacobsen 1984; Denbow 1986; Huffman 1994; Reid *et al.* 1998). It was noted above that the earliest pottery in the Western Cape, as at Die Kelders (Schweitzer 1979), may also be distinguished from the later wares by its exceptionally thin, fine fabric.

The presence of domestic animals in southwestern Zimbabwe during the last centuries BC is no longer surprising in view of the evidence cited above (p. 256) for the very early establishment of the Chifumbaze complex in the upper Zambezi Valley. If, as is now indicated, this region was penetrated in about the third century BC by pioneers of the main dispersal of farming economy into southern Africa, we can understand how, shortly afterwards, certain technological and economic traits were adopted from this source by people living further to the south, in what is now Botswana and southwestern Zimbabwe (D. W. Phillipson 1989b). The relevant traits were, primarily, the herding of sheep and (possibly later) cattle and the manufacture of pottery. Metal-working and cultivation, if practised in the upper Zambezi Valley at this time, were probably not adopted further to the south until significantly later. The potential for cultivation was, in any event, severely restricted by the arid climatic conditions of southwestern Africa. It was from these central regions of southern Africa that herding and pottery manufacture probably spread to the southwestern coastal regions by very early in the Christian era (Sadr 1998; A. B. Smith 1998a). This conclusion is concordant with linguistic arguments (Ehret 1982; Elphick 1985) which also suggest that domestic stock was acquired by KhoiSan-speakers in northern Botswana or a neighbouring area, and thence transmitted southwards. Thus it was that herding was introduced into southwesternmost Africa some two centuries before the farmers of the Chifumbaze complex penetrated the coastlands of KwaZulu-Natal.

# The second millennium AD in sub-Saharan Africa

## The last 1000 years

In many parts of Africa the last 1000 years comprise a period for which archaeology, although still of considerable importance, is by no means our only source of information. Linguistic reconstructions which, when taken together with the results of archaeology, have been valuable for illuminating earlier times, now become less speculative. For the more recent periods the oral historical traditions of many African societies preserve a great deal of valuable information, even though their interpretation is exposed to many pitfalls. In some areas of the continent, written records are also available. For much of northern Africa, indeed, the last 1000 years fall fully within the period of written history, and for that reason this chapter is concerned only with the regions lying to the south of the Sahara. Here, some areas, such as those of the sudanic kingdoms and parts of the East African coast, were in more-or-less regular contact with people from literate communities in whose records much useful historical detail has been preserved. These writings may be used in conjunction with information from other sources in the building up of a composite picture of the period's events and developments. Elsewhere, we have no significant written records pre-dating contact with the European traders and colonisers who gradually established control over most of Africa between the fifteenth and the nineteenth centuries. With this process the subject-matter of this book comes to an ill-defined end; and the study of the African past enters the field of conventional history (Iliffe 1995).

To a large extent interest in the archaeology of sub-Saharan Africa after AD 1000 has, until recently, focussed on evidence for the progress of long-distance trade and the development of states (cf. Garlake 1978a; Connah 2001). In many areas the two processes may have been to some extent con-current and dependent on one another. Trade has been seen as both a stimulus and a mechanism for state-formation through the opportunities it provided for individuals or groups to monopolise or control the distri-bution of wealth. However, as will be shown below, it is in several areas becoming increasingly apparent that essentially local resource exploitation and exchange systems often provided the necessary basis. Political centrali-sation made it possible for the products of a region to be gathered together for organised redistribution. These factors have had a significant effect on our sources of historical information. State centres or capitals provide many attractions for the archaeologist; such sites, because of their size, wealth or monumental architecture, may be readily recognised, leading to a tendency to ignore less conspicuous sites that were inhabited by peasants or subject communities. Thus trade and political power have tended to be over-emphasised in archaeological studies. Likewise, as was shown in chapter 1, oral traditions often serve to record and to support the position of ruling groups or dynasties, which may therefore tend to be stressed at the expense of other aspects of the past. One result of this bias in our available sources is that we tend to know far more about the history of those peoples who developed centralised state-systems than of those who did not, and more about activities relating to long-distance trade than about those connected with domestic economy. One of the strengths of archaeology as a data-source for African history and later prehistory is its ability to throw light on aspects of past societies which are not stressed by studies rooted in other disciplines. Archaeology is of particular relevance also to the study of the development of acephalous societies.

## West Africa

Some account was given in chapter 7 of the early stages of urbanism and socio-political centralisation in the savanna country of West Africa before AD 1000, with particular reference to Jenne-Jeno and to the kingdoms of Ghana and Kanem. Later centuries saw the further development and proliferation of such kingdoms as well as the establishment of comparable institutions further to the south. For the sudanic kingdoms, much of our information now comes from written Arabic sources, which are in some areas beginning to be supplemented by the testimony of archaeology (Levtzion 1973, 1977; Levtzion and Pouwels 2000; Connah 2001). Indeed, throughout the period with which this chapter is concerned, the widespread adoption of Islam has been a major factor in African history, archaeology and culture, especially in the northern half of the continent and along the Indian Ocean coast (Adahl and Sahlström 1995; Insoll 2003).

To the second half of the eleventh century belongs al-Bakri's description of Ghana. He commented on the near-divine status of the ruler, who was succeeded, not by his son, but by his sister's son; on his death he was buried beneath a large earth mound, accompanied by the bodies of his retainers. A large armed force enabled the king to maintain control over many tributary chiefdoms. The capital of ancient Ghana was divided into two areas. One, surrounding the royal residence, was built in the local African style with predominantly round houses of mud; while the other, inhabited mainly by

Muslim traders and other migrants from the north, was built of stone and included several mosques (Levtzion and Hopkins 1981).

These observations may be paralleled by evidence from archaeology. Interments under tumuli are known from a wide area of the West African savanna from Nigeria to Senegal; several examples have been excavated (Desplagnes 1903, 1951; Joire 1955; Saliège *et al.* 1980; Gallay *et al.* 1982; S. K. and R. J. McIntosh 1993; Connah 2001). Some of these burials, notably those at Rao in Senegal which yielded fine gold ornaments of the fourteenth century (Joire 1943), clearly belonged to very powerful and/or rich individuals, but mound-burial was by no means restricted to this class. What the excavations do show is that traditional burial customs continued to be practised long after the introduction of Islam. The apparent slowness by which the new religion was adopted is not otherwise reflected in the results of archaeological research, largely because so much attention has been focussed on sites mentioned in Islamic records. At Kumbi Saleh (see p. 241, above), a wide central avenue and market area are lined by the remains of two-storey stone buildings; the site's population has been estimated at between 15,000 and 20,000 people and the artefacts indicate the North African connexions and long-distance trade of the inhabitants (Mauny 1978). It is noteworthy, however, that excavation seems to have been restricted to the traders' area, and that the presumed royal quarter has not been investigated. The bias in our archaeological information is thus not surprising. To the north, a broadly contemporary settlement at Tegdaoust in south-central Mauritania has been more thoroughly excavated (Robert 1970; Robert-Chaleix 1989; Fig. 138).

The trade which contributed so significantly to the prosperity of ancient Ghana was conducted chiefly in gold and presumably slaves from the south, in salt from the Sahara and in copper and a variety of manufactured goods from the north. These items are only very selectively preserved in the archaeological record: one particularly informative discovery is that of an abandoned caravan at Majabat al-Koubra in the Mauritanian Sahara (Monod 1969). Copper-alloy bars and cowrie shells were the principal objects carried, presumably southwards, at a date now confidently placed in the twelfth century. Trade in these commodities was controlled and taxed by the rulers of ancient Ghana, although none was actually produced within the territory that was subject to their jurisdiction, the source of gold being around Bambuk on the upper Senegal far to the southwest. (Exploitation of the Akan gold deposits in modern Ghana probably did not begin until later.) Ancient Ghana was in a strong position to exploit its intermediary position between the suppliers and the trans-Saharan traders (Brett 1983). The majority of the people of the kingdom of Ghana were probably of northern Mande stock. Oral traditions recorded in Timbuktu during the sixteenth century

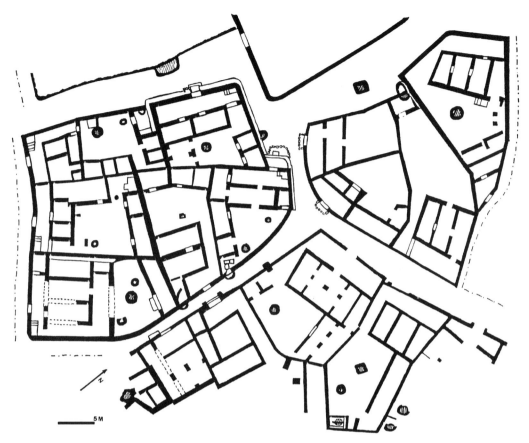

**Fig. 138:** Plan of stone-built houses at Tegdaoust (after Robert-Chaleix 1989)

suggest that its founding rulers may have been of Saharan Berber Sanhaja (ancestral Tuareg) origin, although by the time of al-Bakri's account in the mid-eleventh century this dynasty had apparently been replaced by one with more southerly affinities.

By the eleventh century several of the Berber peoples of the western Sahara had converted to Islam. They then united as the Almoravids, a militant group which expanded rapidly both to the north and to the south, coming in the process into conflict with the kingdom of Ghana. The stability of the kingdom was severely weakened and it never fully reverted to its former prosperity (R. J. McIntosh 1998). More southerly Mande groups now rose to prominence, and by early in the thirteenth century the empire of Mali came into being as the effective successor to Ghana. Mali had a richer agricultural base than its predecessor and exercised more direct control over the gold-fields. By the fourteenth century its rulers held sway, from their capital on

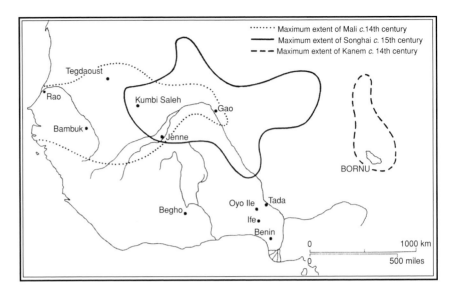

**Fig. 139:** West African sites and kingdoms discussed in chapter 8

the upper Niger, over an extensive territory (Fig. 139), stretching from the southern Sahara to the northern edge of the forest.

Downstream along the Niger the Songhai had, by the end of the first millennium AD, formed their own riverine kingdom, with its capital at Gao, east of the still-flourishing Jenne (Insoll 1996, 1997, 2000; Insoll and Shaw 1997). They also had strong trade links with the Mediterranean world, the most striking evidence for which is a series of inscribed twelfth-century tombstones near Gao (Flight 1975), which appear to have been made to order in Spain and transported thence across the Sahara by camel. It is noteworthy how the West African savanna's centres of greatest prosperity arose in places where goods were transferred from one mode of transport to another, as from the camels used to cross the Sahara to the donkeys and, increasingly, horses of the savanna or the canoes of the Niger River.

Before the end of the thirteenth century the Mande had established control over the Songhai kingdom, greatly increasing the power and prosperity of Mali. Not long afterwards, Musa, ruler of Mali, went on a pilgrimage to Mecca; the wealth and size of his entourage created a lasting impression and served to consolidate Mali's position in the Islamic world (Sutton 1997). The works of North African writers now become major sources for our knowledge of the sudanic kingdoms; unfortunately, neither they nor the archaeology provide adequate information about the trans-Saharan slave trade which undoubtedly took place over a long period, although its scale may sometimes have been exaggerated. The power of Mali was broken in the late fifteenth century by the Songhai sultan, Ali, who extended his rule eastwards through Hausaland and northwards to Aïr. Mali was by then restricted to a small area west of the upper Niger. The enlarged Songhai empire was short-lived, being destroyed at the end of the sixteenth century by a force from Morocco.

To the east, the rulers of Kanem were converted to Islam late in the eleventh century. For some hundreds of years, Kanem did not receive the attentions of trans-Saharan contacts on the same scale as did ancient Ghana and Mali; its exports, although valuable, lacked the lure of the gold of Bambuk. Eventually, after a long period of internecine strife among the rulers, the former Bornu province southwest of Lake Chad became the centre of a new empire, with Kanem reduced to tributary status. Troops of cavalry were important in maintaining the power of the state. By the sixteenth century the main trans-Saharan trade had shifted eastwards: the Hausa states and Bornu were established as major markets where the products both of the sudan and of more southerly regions were exchanged for goods from North Africa and beyond. The direct successors to these states, and their urban centres such as Hamdallahi (Gallay *et al.* 1990), played an important part in the more recent history of the area into the twentieth century. Future archaeological research may be expected to throw much light on their chronology and on the economic processes which underlay their development.

To the south, in the West African forests and on their northern fringes, a contrasting situation prevailed, for here the events of the period between AD 1000 and the arrival of the first European voyagers at the end of the fifteenth century are known only from archaeology, supplemented to some extent with the oral traditions preserved by more recent peoples. Only very indirectly are events of these southerly regions recorded in the Arabic writings which have proved such useful sources for the history of the sudanic kingdoms. Unfortunately, archaeological investigation of the second millennium AD in the West African forest regions is still in its infancy, and has so far been largely restricted to parts of modern Ghana and Nigeria. Research has been concentrated at sites which have yielded important works of art in terracotta or copper alloy, with the result that little comprehensive information is yet available relating to the growth of states or the development of the urbanism which has been such a prominent characteristic of the Yoruba and neighbouring peoples in recent times.

In what is now Ghana, a series of small states arose by the fourteenth century in an area between the Akan goldfield and the entrepôts of the middle Niger (Posnansky 1973; S. K. and R. J. McIntosh 1980). The best known of these states was that centred on Begho near the Volta River, just north of the forest margin. Excavations at Begho have demonstrated both the relevance of recent oral traditions concerning the early history of the town, and also the cultural continuity which has prevailed between the first

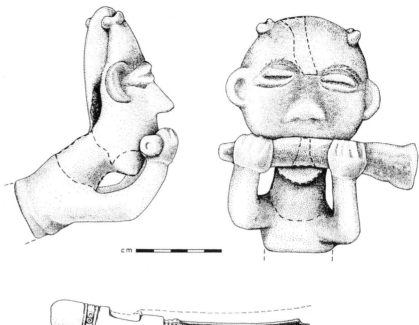

**Fig. 140:** Begho: terracotta figure of a trumpet-blower, and part of an ivory side-blown trumpet (after Posnansky 1976)

inhabitants and the modern Brong (Fig. 140). The separate quarters of Begho that were inhabited by artisans and by visiting traders may still be identified (Posnansky 1973, 1976). Imported materials confirm the close connexions with Jenne. Begho was finally eclipsed by the rise of the Asante kingdom, probably at the beginning of the eighteenth century (Anquandah 1982); before this the flow of gold northwards had been significantly reduced, because the European traders who had arrived on the coast were also trading in gold. Knowledge of the subsequent history of the Ghanaian forest area is, for the most part, derived from the oral traditions of the Asante and their neighbours and from the records of European visitors to the coast (DeCorse 1992, 2001).

In southern Nigeria, processes of urbanisation can be traced back to about the beginning of the second millennium, but have been the subject of remarkably little specific archaeological research. Such work is, of course, hindered by dense forest, intensive cultivation and the growth of modern cities like Ife and Benin. One of the few early urban centres not obliterated by modern building is Oyo Ile (Soper and Darling 1980; Soper 1993), although disappointingly little archaeological information has yet been made available about its growth and development.

**Fig. 141:**
Terracotta heads
from Ife

Probably the most significant archaeological discoveries of early second-millennium date in this region have been made at Ife (Willett 1967; Eyo 1974; Garlake 1974, 1977, 2002). The site had evidently been occupied in earlier times, but little is yet known about its initial phases. By about the eleventh century more intensive settlement is indicated, marked archaeologically by pavements made of large numbers of potsherds set on edge. These pavements evidently formed open-air courtyards that were used for domestic purposes, although in one case there were also the remains of an altar, likewise decorated with sherds. Of the associated buildings, which were made of sun-dried mud, few traces have survived. The greatest attention in archaeological work at Ife has been devoted to a remarkable series of highly realistic figures in terracotta (Fig. 141) or copper alloy, which are thought by most art historians to represent a tradition derived – albeit perhaps indirectly – from that of the much earlier 'Nok culture' described in chapter 7. These figures apparently had a religious significance and were on occasion kept in shrines or on altars, which formed part of domestic houses. They occur in several different areas of Ife, including those away from the royal palace quarter, so it appears that they were not a prerogative of the ruler. Although the archaeological arguments are tenuous, they suggest that the Ife figures were created for a variety of ritual situations, which may be paralleled in more recent Yoruba traditional practices.

**Fig. 142:** Part of the linear earthworks in the region of Benin (after Darling 1984)

Whilst Ife may be seen as heir to ancient urban and artistic traditions, it probably owed much of its prosperity to its location, which enabled it to participate in exchange between the products of the forest and luxuries derived from or beyond the savanna. The copper used in its metalwork was almost certainly derived from the east or the north, presumably by way of the Niger Valley; connexions with the latter are attested by the presence there, as at Tada, of copper-alloy castings in an Ife-related style (Eyo and Willett 1980). Glass beads were imported in large numbers and were

**Fig. 143:** Benin 'bronzes': left – a head in early style; right – fragment of a plaque depicting a Portuguese

then melted down and re-worked. Virtually no information has survived concerning the domestic economy of early Ife, but it is reasonable to assume that yam cultivation, then as now, contributed significantly to its food supply.

The 'lost-wax bronzes' – they are actually made of brass – of Ife are few in number in comparison with the terracottas. Brass-working was carried out on a far greater scale at Benin, where archaeological excavation shows that there was, from at least the thirteenth century, a town where the human sacrifices for which the place subsequently became notorious were conducted (Connah 1975). Archaeological survey in the environs of Benin has revealed the presence of a vast network of linear earthworks (Darling 1984; Fig. 142). It is suggested that the earliest of these date from the end of the first millennium AD, and that by the twelfth century a territory several thousands of square kilometres in extent had been delineated and subdivided, including the city zones of Benin and Udo. The growth of Benin itself may also be illustrated by the successive extensions to its surrounding walls and earthworks. The earliest Benin 'bronzes', which probably date to the fifteenth century, show some stylistic connexions with those of Ife (Fig. 143). At Benin, brass-working was carried out for the ruler, the Oba; and it is relevant to note that the Obas of Benin originally had strong ties with Ife. The history of Benin is fairly well known both from oral traditions and from written sources, for the city was in contact with Portuguese traders from the sixteenth century (Dark 1973; Connah 1975; see also Willett 1967). Although most of the recorded history of Benin falls outside the period of time covered by this book, archaeology is now beginning to illustrate the growth of the city and set it in a comparative context.

In conclusion, it must be admitted that archaeology has so far contributed rather little to our understanding of events in West Africa during the earlier centuries of the second millennium AD. The concentration on sites that are already known from written sources has had a stultifying effect on archaeological research, as has the emphasis on investigating artistic traditions, especially those based on the working of terracotta and copper alloy. Since wooden sculpture, which is of paramount importance in the art history of more recent periods, hardly ever survives for longer than two or three centuries, even this aspect of research has been noticeably incomplete. Despite these problems, some important points do emerge from the archaeological investigations outlined above. Long-distance trade seems to have been a sequel, rather than a causative factor, to the development of states and cities both in the West African savanna and in the forest. Prosperity in both zones originated in the exploitation of local resources. The emphasis of some earlier writers on foreign elements, whether religious or material, should be attributed to their focus and methodology. This revised viewpoint offers a much-needed stimulus to further integrated research in West African archaeology.

Further to the east, in the equatorial forests of the Congo Basin and in the savanna country to their north, the recent archaeology remains almost completely unknown. The information about past events that we can derive from other sources suggests that in the first half of the second millennium AD there continued to be small-scale settlement of Bantu-speaking peasant communities in the forest and of Ubangian-speakers on its northern fringes, some of the latter still expanding eastwards, following the pattern that had been established in earlier times (David 1980). The end result of this process was the establishment in what is now the extreme southwestern Sudan and adjacent parts of D. R. Congo and the Central African Republic of the Ubangian-speaking Zande as rulers of a cluster of peoples of varied Bantu, Sudanic and Nilotic antecedents.

## Ethiopia, the southern Sudan and adjacent regions

Elsewhere in the southern Sudan, in the Bahr el Ghazal territory of the Nilotic-speakers, peasant farming continued, with emphasis on the herding of cattle. The most significant economic development of this time, as we see at the Wun Rok mound-sites early in the second millennium AD, was the replacement of the earlier humpless cattle by humped ones, which may have been obtained from Arabic-speaking peoples further to the north (David *et al.* 1981). The pottery, decorated with twisted-cord roulettes as in earlier times, continued with no significant change. Indeed, the general picture which emerges from the limited research so far undertaken is one of basic continuity from the first millennium AD into recent times. The first half of the second millennium was, however, a period of major southward expansion by Nilotic-speakers into East Africa, as will be further discussed below. In parts of the southeastern Sudan, as in much of northern Kenya and, probably, Uganda, iron remained extremely rare; use of stone tools continued into the last few centuries (Fig. 144).

In highland Ethiopia, the history of this period is marked by the southward shift in the centre of Christian culture from Aksum into the Lasta and Shoa regions, the spread of Islamic culture in the east and southeast, and the continued obscurity of events in the south. In the seventh century, the kingdom of Aksum was in decline and its capital had probably been moved to a new location. By this time, the inhabitants of the mountainous Lasta area east of Lake Tana had adopted much of the earlier Christian culture. Here, around the beginning of the twelfth century, if not before, the Zagwe dynasty arose and established its political authority over the area. Like the written records, the surviving sites of this period are exclusively ecclesiastical. Pride of place goes to the rock-cut churches at Lalibela, the Zagwe capital (Fig. 145). Hewn on both the exterior and the interior from solid rock, these churches show several architectural features that may be traced back to Aksumite buildings (Gerster 1970). Indeed, the degree of continuity between ancient Aksum and the Christian civilisation of highland Ethiopia has, until recently, been underestimated (D. W. Phillipson 2003b). Numerous less elaborate rock-cut churches are widespread in Tigray. Towards the end of the thirteenth century the Semitic-speaking Amhara of Shoa, south of the Blue Nile, replaced the Zagwe ruling dynasty and the centre of political power shifted still further southwards (Sergew 1972); this pattern of authority survived, albeit in modified form, into the twentieth century.

After the decline and eventual eclipse of Christian Nubia from the late thirteenth century onwards, their co-religionists in Ethiopia became largely cut off from the outside world. Islamic culture, by the beginning of the second millennium AD, was reaching large areas of eastern Ethiopia from the port of Zeila near the mouth of the Red Sea. So far, our knowledge comes primarily from written records, but there are also extensive sites of ruined towns which await archaeological investigation (Wilding 1980). To the south, the later archaeology of southern Ethiopia remains almost totally unknown apart from the presence of varied megalithic monuments,

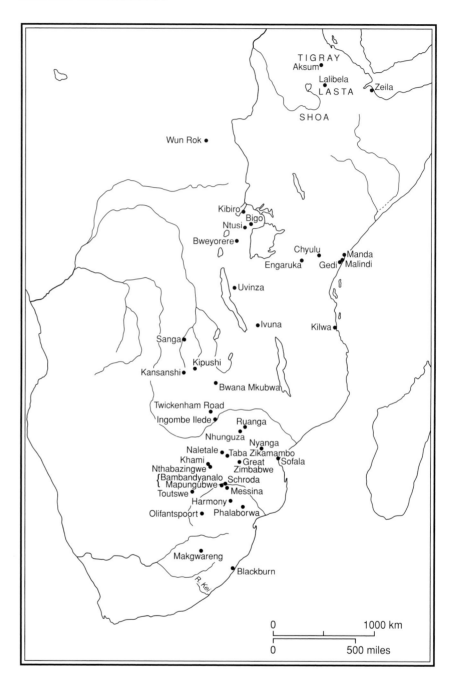

**Fig. 144:**
Principal
archaeological
sites of the
second
millennium AD
in eastern and
southern Africa

**Fig. 145:** The rock-cut church of Abba Libanos, Lalibela

some at least of which date within the last one thousand years (Azaïs and Chambard 1931; Joussaume 1974, 1995; Anfray 1982). In northern Kenya and much of Somalia stone tools probably continued in use until the last few centuries: archaeological traces of nomadic pastoralist populations such as the present Eastern Cushitic-speaking peoples of this area are notoriously sparse and difficult to interpret. The surviving oral traditions (H. S. Lewis 1966; Turton 1975) mostly relate to a southward expansion of the Oromo at the expense of the Rendille and Somali, a process which has continued into recent times.

In the better-watered areas of Kenya's western highlands and parts of Uganda, settled cattle-herders are attested from the beginning of the second millennium. They built stone-walled semi-subterranean stock enclosures and, at least in later times, practised irrigation agriculture (Sutton 1973, 1998c). There are good reasons for believing that these people were Nilotic-speakers ancestral to the modern Kalenjin. Several later penetrations of Nilotic-speakers southwards into East Africa are attested (Oliver 1977). One incursion brought the Maasai into the Rift Valley country which had been occupied by stone-tool-using herders during the last millennium BC. Another introduced the Luo to their present territory on the northeastern shore of Lake Victoria. The extensive stone-built terraces and irrigation works at Engaruka in northern Tanzania (Sutton 1998a) may also be attributed, albeit tentatively, to an early Nilotic-speaking population. To the south lay the territory of the Bantu-speaking peoples, discussed below.

## The east coast of Africa

Mention was made in chapter 7 of the written evidence, contained in *The Periplus of the Erythraean Sea*, for trading voyages along the East African coast as early as the first centuries of the Christian era. Only slight archaeological evidence for such trade has yet been found (Chami 1999). It is not until the early eighth century AD that we have clear traces of the coastal settlements that were frequented by the Indian Ocean traders, who penetrated as far to the south as the Maputo area of Mozambique (Sinclair 1982; Horton 1996b). Indeed, we have virtually no information about any type of settlement on the coast prior to the eighth century. Research has until recently been concentrated on the remains of stone buildings, and traces of more ephemeral occupation of mud-and-thatch structures, perhaps extending back into earlier times, have received comparatively little attention (Fleisher and Laviolette 1999). The distribution along the coast of Kwale-derived pottery in the early centuries of the Christian era has been noted above (pp. 252–4). Late in the first millennium a similar continuum is apparent for the pottery of the so-called Tana tradition which is found from the Lamu Archipelago of Kenya southwards to Vilanculos Bay in Mozambique, as well as on Zanzibar, Pemba, the Comoro Islands and perhaps in northern Madagascar (Fig. 146). Tana pottery (Horton 1987; see also Chami 1998) has affinities inland, but it cannot yet be linked more precisely with any particular population or area. Its extensive coastal distribution does, however, demonstrate a degree of cultural unity along the Indian Ocean seaboard which was independent of overseas traders and their activities.

Excavations at Shanga in the Lamu Archipelago (Horton 1996b) indicate that there was probably a brief period of occupation before the introduction of imported pottery from the Arabian Gulf area provides evidence for overseas trade, probably around the beginning of the eighth century. A very small wooden building of this time has been interpreted as a mosque, suggesting that only a few of the site's inhabitants were Muslims. There are good reasons to believe that conversion of local people to Islam did not often take place until around the tenth or eleventh centuries, when the Shanga mosque, still on the same site, was substantially larger and built of coral. By this time overseas trade had expanded considerably and tiny silver coins were in use, their Arabic inscriptions clearly demonstrating the Islamic faith of the rulers.

Much of our information about the trading cities of the East African coast comes from excavations on two off-shore islands: Manda in the Lamu Archipelago of Kenya and Kilwa in Tanzania, some 350 kilometres to the south of Dar es Salaam (Chittick 1974, 1984). At the more northerly settlement, Manda, a massive sea-wall protected stone-built houses with plastered walls. Imported pottery and glass were in frequent use, much of it

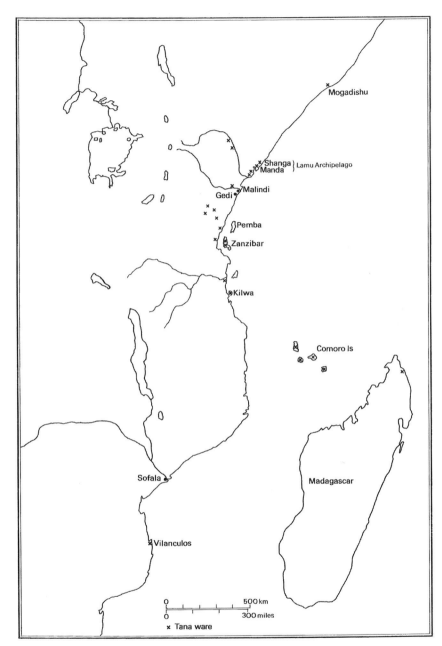

**Fig. 146:**
Principal sites on
the East African
coast, and the
distribution of
Tana-tradition
pottery (after
Horton 1987)

apparently brought from the eastern shore of the Arabian Gulf, where the
port of Siraf is known to have flourished at this time. The contemporary occupation of Kilwa shows weaker foreign influences: most of the houses were of
local wood-and-mud construction and imported goods were less numerous.
It may be concluded that settlements on the East African coast re-established

overseas trading contacts in about the eighth century. Settlements of foreigners were initially few, and the majority of the coast's inhabitants were of indigenous African stock. In later centuries these elements progressively combined to form the modern urban Swahili culture, but it must be emphasised that many non-African facets of this culture appear to be comparatively recent additions (Allen 1974, 1993). A similar picture emerges from studies of the Swahili language which is basically, grammatically and structurally Bantu, although with a significant number of loanwords from Arabic and other Indian Ocean sources, many of which have been added only within the past two centuries (Nurse and Spear 1985).

The chief items of export trade from eastern Africa were ivory, horn and skins (Wright 1993). Slaves must also have been carried away; the evidence comes mainly from written accounts of slave communities in lands beside the Arabian Gulf, notably from the ninth century (Trimingham 1975). In the south, as will be shown below, gold from the Zimbabwe mines was of paramount importance. Beads, pottery, glass, cloth and other luxury manufactures were the principal imports, together with much of the skills and learning which contributed to the coastal culture at this time. Some of the beads appear to have been produced at Fustat, Cairo (Saitowitz *et al.* 1996). Iron, which the *Periplus* indicates had been imported in earlier times, was now produced locally, as is shown both by archaeological discoveries at Manda and by contemporary Arabic writings. From the tenth-century record of al-Mas'udi we get further information: he refers to the indigenous coastal people as 'Zenj' and implies that, even in the towns, few of them were yet Muslims. They used domestic cattle as beasts of burden, and cultivated millet and bananas (the latter introduced from Indonesia). Ivory, obtained inland by Zenj hunters and collectors, was brought by them to the ports and then shipped to Oman and on to India and China. It was by similar means that the coastal traders obtained gold from what they called 'the land of Sofala and the Waqwaq' (Freeman-Grenville 1962).

During the eleventh and twelfth centuries the coastal settlements increased in prosperity. This was particularly true in the case of towns on the Benadir coast of the modern Somalia, notably Mogadishu (Brobeng 1995; Dualeh 1996), and also in the south, as at Kilwa (Sutton 1998b). In the latter place, the so-called Shirazi dynasty of rulers was established, and the town's importance grew rapidly; elaborate stone buildings were erected, pottery and glass were imported, and coins were issued. The greatest prosperity of the East African coast came in the late thirteenth and fourteenth centuries, which saw the foundation of many new towns, such as Gedi (Fig. 147) in Kenya, and the erection of the finest stone buildings at Kilwa. In 1331 the coast was visited by ibn Battuta, who has left a vivid eye-witness description. By this time the rulers of Kilwa controlled the coast as far to the south as

**Fig. 147:** Ruins of a mosque at Gedi

Sofala, near the modern Beira on the coast of Mozambique. As will be shown below, the trade in Zimbabwean gold reached its peak in the period around AD 1400, Sofala being its main point of export (Chittick 1977).

It is now generally accepted that this coastal civilisation, which flourished from at least the early eighth century until the beginning of the fifteenth, was ancestral to that of the Swahili (Chami 1998; C. Kusimba 1999; Horton and Middleton 2000). As such, it is rightly seen as an essentially African, outward-looking society, the overseas connexions of which have in the past been stressed at the expense of those which linked it to the African hinterland (Abungu 1998; cf also Mutoro 1998).

Europe knew little about the civilisation of the East African coastal towns until the Portuguese rounded the Cape of Good Hope, reaching Sofala in 1497. To guard their sea-route to India, they rapidly established forts at both Sofala and Kilwa. The gold-rich interior then attracted their attention, and control of the coastal trade, with many of the settlements on which that trade depended, passed into European hands. Both the trade and the urban settlements of the East African coast have survived into post-colonial times.

## Bantu-speakers north of the Zambezi

In the interior of East Africa, the areas that had been settled by the people responsible for the Chifumbaze complex, described in chapter 7, saw accelerated cultural change around 1000 years ago. In some more southerly

Bantu-speaking regions, this development is fairly securely dated to about the eleventh century, but in East Africa neither the archaeological sequence nor the chronology is properly understood. It is commonly believed that in much of Bantu Africa the second millennium AD was marked by increased cattle-herding (Oliver 1982), and the contribution of Nilotic-speaking peoples in East Africa has been emphasised. At the same time, it is important not to underestimate the very real cultural unity of the last two thousand years in the Bantu-speaking regions and the many lines of continuity which extend from early in the first millennium AD into recent times (D. W. Phillipson 1985a).

In much of southern Uganda, the archaeological occurrences of the second millennium AD feature pottery decorated by means of a roulette made of cord (Soper 1985; Desmedt 1991). The affinities of this pottery are with more northerly areas, where it is particularly associated with speakers of Nilotic languages. It is attested in Rwanda from about the ninth century, but its period of manufacture in Uganda cannot yet be shown to have begun at such an early date (Sinclair 1991). It has been widely believed that this development was in some way linked with the establishment of the major kingdoms of the interlacustrine region, including those of Buganda, Bunyoro and Ankole (Robertshaw 1994). Although Bantu-speaking, at least in more recent times, these kingdoms preserve traditions which attribute their foundation to a group called the Bachwezi, who appear to have been cattle-herders, perhaps from Nilotic-speaking areas to the north.

These traditions need not be taken at face value, and there is much controversy concerning the date, identity and activities of the Bachwezi. If they were indeed a distinct group, the most likely interpretation of the available evidence is that they were the alien founders of ruling dynasties who came to dominate sections of a pre-existing Bantu-speaking population. It should be noted that control of long-distance trade was apparently not the major stimulus for the formation of the interlacustrine states (Oliver 1977; Connah 2001). On the contrary, local resources – notably herds of cattle – provided their economic basis, as is emphasised by some of their rulers' regalia (Sassoon 1983). While the populations of these states made and used roulette-decorated pottery, there is no reason to link the two developments. The widespread appearance of this pottery in Uganda should occasion no surprise in view of the readiness with which it has been adopted by Bantu-speaking peoples in more easterly and southerly parts of East Africa. Although this process is still continuing today, it is one for which the reasons are not at all clear, and it provides an excellent example of a major change in artefact style that is not accompanied by any significant shift in population or, indeed, by any apparent economic or practical advantage.

**Fig. 148:** Salt crystallising on the surface of a 'salt-garden', Kibiro, 1990

The archaeology of the interlacustrine kingdoms has been investigated at the capital sites of Bigo, Bweyorere and Ntusi (Posnansky 1968, 1969; Reid and Robertshaw 1987; Reid 1996). Extensive dams and earthworks – those at Bigo total more than 10 kilometres in length – indicate the scale of organisation that was achieved. Remains of large circular houses resemble the royal residences of more recent times. Salt was evidently an important commodity at this time in East Africa, as elsewhere, and major workings have been investigated at Kibiro (Fig. 148) on Lake Albert and at Uvinza in western Tanzania, as well as at Ivuna further south (Hiernaux and Maquet 1968; Fagan and Yellen 1968; Sutton and Roberts 1968; Connah 1996).

Elsewhere in East Africa our knowledge of this period is even less comprehensive. In parts of the eastern Kenya highlands pottery derived from the Kwale tradition may have continued to be made as late as the thirteenth or fourteenth centuries, before being replaced by a style, still practised by the modern Kamba and Gikuyu, which may have originated in the Chyulu area of southern Kenya. In both Kenya and Tanzania there is evidence, early in the present millennium, for peasant farmers owning domestic cattle and sheep/goats and cultivating sorghum. Except in the immediate hinterland, glass beads and other items imported from the coast remained rare until recent times (Odner 1971; Soper 1976, 1979).

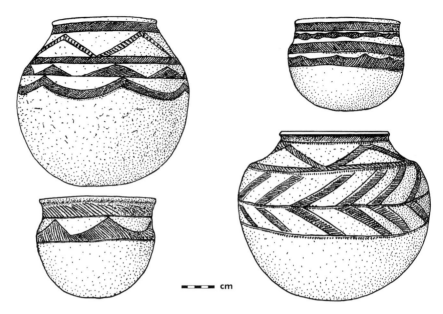

**Fig. 149:**
Luangwa-
tradition pottery
(after D. W.
Phillipson 1977a)

A similar situation appears to have prevailed in most areas of the modern Zambia and Malawi. Here, however, as in a wide area further to the south, there was a series of pronounced and apparently sudden changes in pottery styles around the eleventh century AD. The main exception to this is in the Upper Zambezi region of western Zambia, which seems to belong to a western culture area, extending into Angola, where there is evidence for greater continuity in pottery style from the first millennium AD into more recent times (D. W. Phillipson 1974). In eastern and much of northern and central Zambia the main pottery style of the second millennium AD has been called the Luangwa tradition (Fig. 149). Its appearance around the eleventh century represents a sharp break with its predecessors of both the eastern and the western facies of the Chifumbaze complex, and it has continued with relatively little modification ever since. The contrast is well seen at the site known as Twickenham Road in Lusaka (D. W. Phillipson 1970). The antecedents of the Luangwa-tradition pottery remain unknown but may lie in the direction of Katanga in southeastern D. R. Congo (cf. Huffman 1989). Today, Luangwa-tradition pottery is traditionally made by women. In more westerly areas, vessels of the Lungwebungu tradition, apparently derived from the Chifumbaze complex, are made by men. This suggests that the contrast between the pottery of the Chifumbaze complex and that of the Luangwa tradition may have been due to the establishment of communities amongst whom potting was undertaken by women. Luangwa-tradition pottery is today made by people of many different societies, including the

Bemba, Chewa and Nsenga. It was clearly established long before these societies became differentiated from each other following the arrival of chiefly dynasties (which claim an origin in what is now D. R. Congo) in about the fifteenth and sixteenth centuries (D. W. Phillipson 1974).

By the fourteenth/fifteenth century copper mining, which had begun on a small scale about one thousand years earlier, became much intensified, resulting in enormous workings such as those at Kipushi, Bwana Mkubwa and Kansanshi in the Zambia/Katanga Copperbelt area. Cross-shaped ingots were cast in closely standardised sizes and widely traded; they probably served as a form of currency (Bisson 1975, 2000; de Maret 1981). It is probably not coincidence that the development of copper mining and trading is indicated at the same general time as the local rise of centralised states, and that the chiefly dynasties of surrounding areas trace their origin to southeastern D. R. Congo, which saw the greatest development of the copper trade. As shown in chapter 7, the local use of metal as an embodiment of wealth may be traced back to the first millennium AD. A further feature of later metal-working in this area was the tall natural-draught iron-smelting furnace fired without the use of bellows (D. W. Phillipson 1968b; Sutton 1985).

The southern Congo Basin region appears to have contributed significantly to the cultural development of a very large part of central Africa during the second millennium AD. It is thus particularly unfortunate that its archaeology for this period remains virtually unknown (Ervedosa 1980). A considerable amount of research has been undertaken on the oral traditions relating to the kingdoms which flourished in this area, especially along the southern and eastern margins of the forest. Further evidence has been obtained through historical linguistic studies, but it is not easy to correlate these results with those obtained by archaeologists in neighbouring areas (Vansina 1966, 1984, 1990).

Archaeologically, the only well-documented late sequence in the whole of this vast area is that based on excavations around Lake Kisale near the southeastern corner of the forest (de Maret 1977, 1985b, 1992). The great cemetery of Sanga was noted in chapter 7: although the sequence began late in the first millennium, its main period of use is dated by radiocarbon to the eleventh and twelfth centuries. Already by this Classic Kisalian period considerable metal-based wealth had been accumulated; flange-welded iron gongs, of a type which – at least in later times – served as symbols of kingship (Vansina 1969), were found in some of the richer graves (Fig. 150). Later use of the cemetery, attributed to the Kabambian phase, continued at least into the sixteenth century. There is no good reason for regarding the Kabambian as other than a descendant of the Kisalian, although there are important differences between them, most pertinently in the much greater frequency

**Fig. 150:** A Kisalian grave at Sanga

of copper cross-ingots in the Kabambian graves. The most recent graves at Sanga are attributed to the Luba and probably date within the last two centuries.

Three important points emerge from this discussion. One is that, as suggested above, there was a greater degree of continuity from the Chifumbaze complex into later times in some more westerly areas than there was further east. The second is that certain cultural items which became prevalent in eastern areas during the second millennium AD may have had a greater antiquity in the west. This view is supported by oral traditions which, as we have seen, derive the ruling dynasties of many states in Zambia, Malawi and adjacent regions from a Congo Basin origin. One interpretation of these traditions places the rise of the savanna kingdoms of southern D. R. Congo and northern Angola at least as far back as the thirteenth century (J. C. Miller 1976), and this is not contradicted by the scanty archaeological evidence. Lastly, although the region clearly saw the interplay of several cultural traditions, and although its natural resources and economic potential were diverse, particular and widespread emphasis appears to have been placed on the working of metal and its use not only for everyday utilitarian objects but also for items intended for display, symbolism, exchange and conspicuous consumption. Metal as an embodiment of an individual's or a society's wealth may thus be seen as a characteristic feature of the western Bantu region, and one which may be traced back into the archaeological record of the first millennium AD (D. W. Phillipson 1985a; cf. Volavka 1998). As in the interlacustrine region, both the accumulation of wealth and the centralisation of political authority may be seen as local processes which, contrary to previous opinion, began well before long-distance trading contacts were developed. In this western part of the sub-continent overseas contacts did not develop on any scale before the arrival of the Portuguese in Angola late in the fifteenth century. More precise information about these processes must await further archaeological research in Angola and D. R. Congo.

## Southeastern Africa

To the south of the Zambezi, in what is now Zimbabwe, eastern Botswana, northern South Africa and KwaZulu-Natal, a significantly greater amount of research into the archaeology of the present millennium has taken place than has been the case further to the north. These and contiguous areas are discussed here, followed by a separate section on the southwesternmost part of the African continent.

Schroda in the Limpopo Valley, noted above in chapter 7 (p. 257), is one of few sites which appear truly intermediate between the Chifumbaze complex and its successors. Its material culture, including the pottery, shows several features that later became prominent in the Leopard's Kopje industry of Zimbabwe. The suggestion has accordingly been made (Huffman 1978, 1984b) that this industry may have originated south of the Limpopo.

In southeastern Zimbabwe, the Leopard's Kopje industry was established in about AD 1000. At the site of Nthabazingwe (Leopard's Kopje) itself, near Bulawayo, the people lived in circular pole-and-clay houses some 3 metres in diameter. There were rare domestic tools of iron, and copper was mainly used for personal adornment. Some contact with the coastal trade is indicated by the presence of occasional glass beads. Large numbers of cattle were herded, with some ovicaprids. Clay figurines of cattle show that these animals were of a humped, long-horned variety. Cultivated crops included sorghum, finger millet, ground beans and cowpeas (Huffman 1974). In a second phase of the Leopard's Kopje industry, dated to the thirteenth/fourteenth century, cotton cloth began to be made and there is evidence for the construction of dry-stone walling. The Leopard's Kopje people were by this time engaged in the mining and working of gold, for pieces of their characteristic pottery have been recovered from several ancient workings, and a crucible from a site of this period at Taba Zikamambo was found to contain traces of gold (K. R. Robinson 1966b; see also Swan 1994; D. Miller *et al.* 2000).

In the Limpopo Valley, excavation has illustrated a parallel process of development from those at Schroda and the early sites of the Toutswe tradition, which were discussed in chapter 7. At Bambandyanalo, close to the

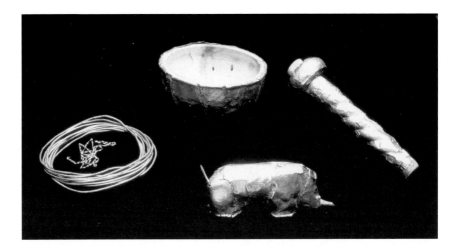

**Fig. 151:** Gold artefacts from Mapungubwe

Shashi–Limpopo confluence, a substantial village was established shortly after AD 1000. Its cattle-herding inhabitants worked extensively in ivory, which was evidently exchanged for large quantities of imported glass beads, presumably obtained through the trading settlements which are attested from this time on the coast of southern Mozambique (Eloff and Meyer 1981; Sinclair 1982; Meyer 1998). Around AD 1220, occupation was transferred from the valley-bottom Bambandyanalo site to the adjacent steep-sided hill of Mapungubwe. This abrupt shift appears to have accompanied significant economic and socio-political developments (Huffman 1982, 1986). Cattle-herding remained the mainstay of the subsistence economy (Voigt 1983), but overall prosperity increased markedly. Iron tools were more numerous and, as in the Bulawayo region, cotton cloth was produced (Davison and Harries 1980). Stone walling was used to demarcate parts of the hill-top which were probably associated with a wealthy élite group holding some form of political authority. Thirteenth-century burials on the summit of Mapungubwe Hill provide clear indications of this, being richly adorned with glass beads and with copper and gold ornaments. Gold foil was laid over carved wooden animal figures, bowls and staffs (Fouché 1937; D. Miller *et al.* 2000; Fig. 151); the beginning of gold-working seems to have been accompanied by a reduction in the use of ivory. There can be little doubt that wealth, and presumably influence and political power, were becoming concentrated in the hands of a minority.

The occupation of Mapungubwe declined and ceased by the end of the thirteenth century, when this part of the Limpopo Valley appears to have been largely depopulated. It is a marginal area for farming; and over-grazing, perhaps with a minor shift in rainfall patterns (Tyson and Lindesay 1992; Huffman 1996a), may have destroyed its viability. To continue the story it

**Fig. 152:**
Remains of a
clay-walled house
excavated amidst
the stone walls at
Great Zimbabwe

is necessary to move north to the central regions of Zimbabwe where, near
the modern town of Masvingo, is situated the remarkable archaeological
site which has become known as the Great Zimbabwe or simply as Great
Zimbabwe (Garlake 1973a; Huffman and Vogel 1991). (The word *zimbabwe*,
in the language of the Shona, means either 'stone houses' or 'venerated
houses'.) The site is renowned as the place where the indigenous southern African tradition of dry-stone architecture reached its most impressive
achievement. After an initial Chifumbaze-complex occupation, during which
there is no evidence for building in stone, the main sequence at Great Zimbabwe started with the Gumanye phase in about the late tenth century. At
that time the economy of the site's inhabitants was probably similar to that
described above from the Bulawayo region, but significantly simpler than
that which prevailed at the same time at Bambandyanalo and Mapungubwe.
By about 1250–80, simple stone walling was erected at Great Zimbabwe
to form enclosures and platforms which supported pole-and-mud houses
(Fig. 152): gold came into use at this period. It seems significant that these
developments had taken place somewhat earlier at Mapungubwe, and that
their appearance at Great Zimbabwe occurred at the time when the former
site was abandoned. It is thus plausible to suggest that the rise to prominence of Great Zimbabwe was in some way connected with a northward
movement by the rulers of Mapungubwe and the establishment of their
hegemony over a new or enlarged area (Huffman 1982). The famous carved
stone figures of birds have been found at Great Zimbabwe but at no other
site; their significance remains uncertain (Matenga 1998).

**Fig. 153:** Inside the great enclosure, with the conical tower, Great Zimbabwe

All the finest and most elaborate stone buildings at Great Zimbabwe are now known to have been erected during a relatively brief period between the late thirteenth and mid-fifteenth centuries. At this time the place was a large town, covering an area of some 78 hectares and with a population plausibly estimated at some 18,000 people (Huffman 1986). While most of the site was covered with pole-and-mud houses with thatched roofs, the stone buildings fall into two groups. Those on a steep-sided rocky hill consist of lengths of well-coursed walling linking the natural boulders of the hill-top to form a series of easily defended enclosures. In the adjacent valley is a series of larger, free-standing walled enclosures in some of which stood circular pole-and-mud houses joined together by short lengths of similar walling (Collett *et al.* 1992). One enclosure stands out through its size and complexity: its perimeter wall reaches a height of over 10 metres, as does a solid stone tower which stands within (Fig. 153). Despite its massive scale and excellence of execution, the stone architecture at Great Zimbabwe is basically simple. There were no domes or arches; doorways were narrow and roofed with stone lintels over which the upper courses of stonework were laid without interruption. Internal structures were of puddled mud, sun-baked to great hardness and durability, in which material also the builders were masters of their techniques (Chipunza 1993).

There can be little reasonable doubt that the inhabitants of Great Zimbabwe, from at least the Gumanye phase onwards, were directly ancestral to the modern Shona (Beach 1980, 1994). This connexion has stimulated attempts to determine the uses to which the various parts of the Great

Zimbabwe site, particularly the stone constructions, were put. The resultant claims (Huffman 1984a, 1996b) remain controversial, being largely based on unsubstantiated oral traditions and poorly recorded information from more recent times (cf. Beach *et al.* 1998). Such research has clear potential but it would not at present be wise to place reliance on suggestions that the main stone-walled enclosure was a place for female initiation, or that a certain area was inhabited by the royal wives. We should restrict our credence to the view that the site was the capital of rulers who controlled major territories and resources. Great Zimbabwe must have been a centre of political authority, and the presence of large numbers of imported items indicates that this authority was linked with the control of trade. Imported objects – glass beads, Persian and Chinese pottery, Near Eastern glass, even a coin minted in the name of the ruler of Kilwa – are far more numerous here than on contemporary sites elsewhere in Zimbabwe. Gold and copper objects from other parts of the interior have also been found at Great Zimbabwe (Herbert 1996), so we may conclude that the products of outlying regions were collected there either through patronage, or as gifts or tribute; from here trade for coastal imports was presumably organised. Great Zimbabwe's period of greatest prosperity coincided not only with its architectural florescence, but also with the peak in the export of gold via the Indian Ocean coast. Indeed, it may be shown archaeologically that Great Zimbabwe was the centre of a widespread network of related sites (Sinclair 1987; Sinclair *et al.* 1993b; Pikirayi 2001), for near-identical pottery is found in stone buildings of comparable style as far afield as Manekweni on the coastal plain of southern Mozambique and at Ruanga and Nhunguza in northern Zimbabwe (Garlake 1973b, 1976). In the latter area the Great Zimbabwe people apparently settled in control over a peasant community with a distinct pottery tradition. One house within the Nhunguza stone enclosure seems to have served as an audience chamber (Fig. 154).

Cattle-herding was of major importance at Great Zimbabwe and related sites (Garlake 1978b). The livestock was often kept at a distance from the main settlements, and transhumance seems to have been practised in some areas (Sinclair 1984). Study of bones recovered from different areas of the Great Zimbabwe site suggests that prime young animals were slaughtered for the ruling élite (Thorp 1995).

The decline of Great Zimbabwe in the fifteenth century came at a time when political power was transferred to a more northerly site, near the Zambezi Valley, which was then replacing the Sabi as the major route to the coast (Pikirayi 1993). This development may have been linked with an increase in the importance of copper from the northern mines as a valuable trade item (Fig. 155). A site of this period has been excavated at Ingombe Ilede, on the bank of the Zambezi near Kariba (Fagan *et al.* 1969; D. W.

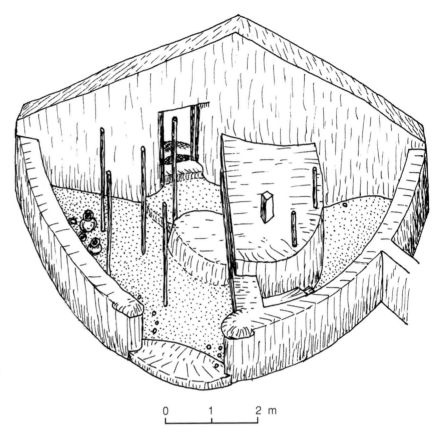

**Fig. 154:**
Reconstruction of
the main
building at
Nhunguza (after
Garlake 1973b)

0        1        2 m

Phillipson and Fagan 1969). By the middle of the sixteenth century the Portuguese had penetrated the Zambezi Valley route to the interior. To the southwest, sites such as Naletale and Khami (K. R. Robinson 1959), where elaborately decorated stone walling faced massive terraces (Fig. 156), belong to this late period and may be attributed to the kingdom of Guruhuswa, which traded with the Portuguese during the seventeenth and eighteenth centuries (Beach 1994). Archaeology thus serves to confirm the evidence of oral tradition for the essential continuity between the inhabitants of sites related to Great Zimbabwe and the modern Shona-speaking peoples.

Broadly contemporary with these developments, in the eastern highlands of Zimbabwe near the border with Mozambique, the extensive remains of stone terraces and associated structures around Nyanga (Soper 2002) have long attracted attention. They may now be dated between the twelfth and the nineteenth centuries, with most intensive use during the second half of this period. It has not proved possible to link these developments with those known from more westerly regions. The Nyanga structures are now

**Fig. 155:** Copper cross-ingot from Ingombe Ilede

**Fig. 156:** Elaborate stone walling at Naletale

seen as essentially agricultural, comprising elaborate terrace systems with some capacity for irrigation and associated pens for dwarf cattle. The few apparently defensive structures in more northerly parts of the area are probably of late date and may not be connected with the other features (Fig. 157).

In more southerly regions, we are here concerned both with the areas noted in chapter 7 as having been inhabited by people of the Chifumbaze complex, and with those to which Bantu-speaking people subsequently expanded. By the seventeenth century, when written records for this part of the continent effectively begin, it appears that Bantu-speakers occupied most of the territory lying northeast of a line extending roughly from the Windhoek area of Namibia to Port Alfred on the southeast

**Fig. 157:** Nyanga: above, dense terracing, Hambuka Valley; below, lintelled entrance to a 'fort', Tanda

coast of South Africa. Beyond this line, the indigenous populations were KhoiSan-speaking, using stone and bone tools together with metal items which they obtained by trade with their northern and eastern neighbours or with European colonists. Some of these KhoiSan-speakers were hunter-gatherers, others pastoralists (Wilson 1969). They are discussed below.

As was the case further to the north, there seems to have been a significant acceleration of change in the Bantu-speaking regions of South Africa around the eleventh century, although these developments were probably not so fundamental as was formerly believed. The most important changes may be linked with an increased scale of cattle herding which, *inter alia*, contributed to the expansion of settlement into the high grasslands of the Free State as well as into parts of Botswana and Namibia not previously inhabited by Bantu-speaking people. There is controversy over the extent to which this trend – which had, of course, begun before the close of the first millennium AD – was facilitated by bush clearance at the hands of earlier cultivators. It is, however, clear that the increasing scale of herding has been important in setting the distinctive course of subsequent South African history (M. Hall 1987; Feely 1987). It has been argued that the development of a socio-economic system based upon the herding of cattle, with its opportunities for the accumulation of personal wealth, was at least as great a shift as the beginning of farming had been several centuries earlier (M. Hall 1987; Segobye 1998).

In the Northern (Limpopo) Province of South Africa, the Soutpansberg area is marked by a series of stone-walled sites which bear many resemblances to those of Zimbabwe. They may be attributed to the ancestors of the present Venda, and indicate a formal settlement hierarchy linked with a centralised system of political authority (Huffman and Hanisch 1987). The clearest picture of a village site of the first half of the present millennium north of the Vaal comes from Olifantspoort in North-West Province. Here, about twenty circular pole-and-mud houses were set around an open area where cattle were kept (Mason 1974, 1986). Such a site plan may be seen as a characteristic feature of many southern African societies, and one which has been traced tentatively back into the first millennium AD (Huffman 1982).

Ancient mines for iron, copper, tin and gold are reported from several northern areas of South Africa, but most were destroyed by modern mining operations before archaeological investigations could be undertaken. Fortunately this does not apply to the copper workings around Messina in the Limpopo Valley and those for both iron and copper in the Phalaborwa area of Mpumalanga. At Phalaborwa both shafts and horizontal passages were excavated for the recovery of copper ore, but iron ore was collected or quarried from the surface. The pottery sequence at Phalaborwa is continuous from the eleventh century and leads up to wares of the type made by northeastern Sotho peoples (van der Merwe and Scully 1971). At Harmony, also in the Mpumalanga Lowveld, soapstone bowls were used for evaporating brine.

Archaeological survey, much of it carried out by aerial photography, has revealed the presence in highland areas north and south of the Vaal of numerous enclosures of dry-stone walling incorporating circular structures,

**Fig. 158:**
Stone-walled
structures at
Makgwareng,
Free State

many of which were evidently houses or stock pens (Fig. 158). The majority of these sites probably date to the period between the fifteenth and the very beginning of the nineteenth centuries. In Free State Province, the earliest settlement by iron-using peoples is marked by several distinct types of stone enclosures which may be attributed to populations ancestral to certain Tswana and Sotho groups (Maggs 1976), providing links between peoples recognised in the archaeological record and those whose history has been investigated from oral and written sources. Parallel evidence comes from eastern Botswana where, as indicated in chapter 7, the early stages of these developments had taken place during the closing centuries of the first millennium AD.

The region of East London marks the southernmost settlement of iron-using people in pre-colonial times. At least in some areas, the structures that were in use were insubstantial and may have been of dome-shaped grass-covered type, as at Blackburn near Durban (Davies 1971). Evidently, between the eleventh and the sixteenth centuries, iron-using peoples intensified their settlement through KwaZulu-Natal and into the Eastern Cape as far as the Kei River (Maggs 1980). In the uKhahlamba/Drakensberg foothills more permanent villages were constructed, and the farming economy appears to have been based on the herding of cattle and the cultivation of sorghum. These archaeological reconstructions are in keeping with Zulu and Xhosa traditions.

Before concluding this survey of the second millennium AD in the Bantu-speaking regions, certain points require emphasis. The transition from the Chifumbaze complex to its successors cannot be seen as a clear break: there are many indications of continuity in culture and in population. Regional trends, notably the emphasis on cattle herds in the southeast and on metal-working to the north and west, were continued and amplified. Population densities seem rapidly to have increased, to judge from the number of visible sites, the distribution of which now extended into less favourable regions, and the remnant populations from earlier times seem finally to have been absorbed. In many areas there are strong indications of cultural continuity into recent times. It follows, therefore, that many of the peoples who inhabit this part of Africa can regard themselves as having roots which extend back to the early centuries AD (cf. Garlake 1982).

## Southwestern Africa

Beyond the Bantu-speaking zone, in the territory of the KhoiSan-speakers, the varied life-styles noted for first-millennium times in chapter 7 continued, at first with little perceptible change. The first European colonists at the Cape of Good Hope divided the indigenous inhabitants into three categories. There were the 'strandlopers', who were gatherers of shellfish and wild vegetable foods, there were herders of cattle and sheep, and there were fishermen who also owned herds of cattle. It is not clear whether these groups represented three separate populations or representatives of a single society following different economic patterns at different seasons. Archaeology in this instance provides no clear means of distinguishing between separate populations, but the balance of probability now suggests that, at least in the Western Cape, herders and foragers were largely distinct from one another, pottery manufacture being generally the prerogative of the former (A. B. Smith *et al.* 1991). This picture probably holds good for much of the coastal region from Namibia to the Eastern Cape.

One aspect of the culture of the second-millennium KhoiSan-speakers of southern Africa which has been studied in particular detail by prehistorians is the rock art, which is essentially a continuation of that executed in earlier times (see chapter 4; also Lewis-Williams 1983). The large number of paintings which appear to belong to the present millennium may be due to increased population stress as foragers, herders and, latterly, European settlers competed for resources and land (Parkington *et al.* 1986). In the Western Cape several representations of fat-tailed sheep have been discovered but, interestingly, paintings of cattle only occur in the latest stylised series. Rare paintings of European-style ships must be later than the end of the fifteenth century. Human figures are shown in dress akin to that of the eighteenth- and nineteenth-century settlers, as are ox- or horse-drawn wagons (Fig. 159). The finest and most abundant paintings occur in the uKhahlamba/Drakensberg, as noted above. Many are apparently of late date, but domestic animals are not shown except in the most recent series which

**Fig. 159:** Rock painting of an ox-wagon in the uKhahlamba/ Drakensberg, KwaZulu-Natal

broadly correlates with the advent of European settlement (Vinnicombe 1976).

In the drier interior regions of South Africa, backed microliths continued to be made well into the second millennium AD, perhaps as late as the seventeenth century. The presence at sites of this period of glass beads, pottery and occasional metal objects probably indicates some degree of contact with iron-using peoples further to the north. From about the sixteenth century, peoples of the southwestern Free State and adjacent areas of the Northern Cape began to adopt a more settled pastoralist life-style, erecting stone-walled enclosures apparently inspired by those of their Bantu-speaking neighbours (Maggs 1971). The characteristic stone tools, in place of backed microliths, were now varied types of edge-retouched flakes. It is not surprising that rivalry eventually developed between the two groups. Along much of the 'frontier', raiding, stock theft and open hostility became the order of the day. In Lesotho, KwaZulu-Natal and the Free State the process is vividly recorded in a number of rock paintings. Nor were the European colonists excluded from these events. Their herds likewise received the attentions of the raiders. As a result of European counter-measures and aggression, the KhoiSan-speaking population of much of South Africa was, by the early nineteenth century, destroyed or reduced to serfdom.

## Epilogue

I have attempted in this chapter to outline the many connexions which may be made in sub-Saharan Africa between the evidence of archaeology and that of other historical sources for the events and processes which have taken place during the second millennium AD. As archaeological and other research in these regions passes increasingly into the hands of indigenous scholars, whose own cultural roots are in the societies under study, such links can only be strengthened, to the benefit of mankind's understandings and appreciation of the African past and its heritage.

Such trends are, in fact, paralleled throughout the long time-span covered in this book. First published in 1985, it has now been subject to two major revisions. In preparing this third edition, I have been struck by several recent developments. The first is the extremely rapid growth in the number of relevant publications; unfortunately, this reflects not only an increased tempo of research and understanding, but also pressures for scholars to publish in a world where quantity and quality are less clearly differentiated than formerly. Secondly, although this book is focussed primarily on archaeology, the range of adjunct disciplines to which reference must be made is steadily increasing both in number and in the significance of their contribution to understanding. Nowhere is this more apparent than in the contribution of genetic studies throughout the African archaeological sequence. This trend will undoubtedly continue, with the result that study of the African past is becoming increasingly collaborative; no longer can any individual command the range of expertise fully to understand, much less co-ordinate, the increasing complexity, variety and quantity of the available data. Third, African archaeology is now accepted internationally as a study not only of local interest, but also of world-wide relevance. It is being studied not only by those whose primary interests lie in Africa itself, but by many other members of the international community of archaeologists. This is an extremely welcome development, which can only benefit international understanding in fields which include, but extend far beyond, archaeology.

# Bibliographic guide

The text of this book is fully referenced to the published supporting and explanatory evidence. For each significant topic a primary reference is given, together with citations for major current controversies and the most recent available overview of which the author is aware. In some cases, a single definitive statement is available, but often reference must be made to numerous publications of a preliminary nature. Research and discovery proceed so fast that it is neither practicable nor desirable to exclude such sources. Where a choice is available between languages, English has been chosen as most likely to be accessible to the majority of readers. United Kingdom imprints are generally cited, although many works are also published in the United States of America, occasionally with variant titles. In view of the highly detailed nature of many of the sources cited, readers may find it useful to have a brief guide to some more general works that provide up-to-date interpretative surveys of particular regions or topics.

Much current research is first published in journals. The relevant papers can be widely scattered and it is not easy to track them all down. The journals which often include African material include *Nature*, the *Journal of Archaeological Science*, the *Journal of World Prehistory* and the *Journal of Human Evolution*. The *African Archaeological Review* has been, until very recently, the only title devoted to the archaeology of the entire continent. As this book goes to press, the *Journal of African Archaeology* and *Afrique: Archéologie et Arts* are making their appearance. There are numerous national and regional journals such as the *South African Archaeological Bulletin*, *Azania*, the *West African Journal of Archaeology*, *Sahara*, *Archéologie du Nil Moyen*, and *Sudan & Nubia*. Much important material is also recorded in the various volumes of *Proceedings of the Panafrican Congress on Prehistory*.

For the early periods of human evolution and cultural development, on a world-wide rather than an exclusively African stage, the survey by Klein (1999) is invaluable. For Africa itself, much useful information on all periods in the sub-Saharan regions has been assembled by Vogel (1997). Later periods in Africa are considered in archaeological terms by Connah (2001) and against an essentially linguistic framework by Ehret (2002). A useful attempt to view African socio-political developments is by S. K. McIntosh (1999a). Africa's role in the development and dissemination of world monotheistic religion is surveyed by Insoll (2003) for Islam (see also Adahl and Sahlström 1995) and by Finneran (2002) for Christianity. Garlake (2002) has provided a selective but finely illustrated overview of art and architecture.

Regional studies are of variable quality. Many parts of the continent lack an up-to-date survey, perhaps because research has proliferated in some areas or because it has stagnated in others. Overviews with comprehensive bibliographies include the following: on the development of farming in the Sahara and adjacent regions – Hassan 2002; on ancient Egypt – Kemp 1989 and Nicholson & Shaw 2000; on later periods in the Sudan – Welsby 1996, 2002; on Ethiopia – D. W. Phillipson 1998; on the East African coast – C. Kusimba 1999; on Botswana – Lane *et al.* 1998; on southern Africa – H. J. and J. Deacon 1999; Mitchell 2002.

# Bibliographic references

Abbate, E. *et al.* 1998. A one-million-year-old *Homo* cranium from the Danakil (Afar). *Nature* 393: 458–60.

Abungu, G. H. O. 1998. City states of the East African coast and their maritime contacts, pp. 204–18 in G. Connah (ed.) *Transformations in Africa: Essays on Africa's Later Past*. London: Leicester University Press.

Adahl, K. and B. Sahlström (eds.) 1995. *Islamic Art and Culture in Sub-Saharan Africa*. Uppsala: University of Uppsala.

Adams, W. M. *et al.* (eds.) 1996. *The Physical Geography of Africa*. Oxford: Oxford University Press.

Adams, W. Y. 1977. *Nubia: Corridor to Africa*. London: Lane.

Adamson, D. *et al.* 1974. Barbed bone points from central Sudan and the age of the Early Khartoum tradition. *Nature* 249: 120–3.

Addison, F. 1949. *Jebel Moya*. London: Oxford University Press.

Agazi Negash 1997a. Temben's place in the neolithic of northern Ethiopia, pp. 389–98 in K. Fukui *et al.* (eds.) *Ethiopia in Broader Perspective*, vol. 1. Kyoto: Shukado Book Sellers.

  1997b. Ethiopia and the Horn: rock art, pp. 357–61 in J. O. Vogel (ed.) *Encyclopedia of Precolonial Africa*. Walnut Creek, CA: Altamira Press.

Aiello, L. 1996. Hominine preadaptations for language and cognition, pp. 89–99 in P. Mellars and K. Gibson (eds.) *Modelling the Early Human Mind*. Cambridge: McDonald Institute for Archaeological Research.

Aiello, L. and P. Wheeler 1995. The expensive tissue hypothesis. *Current Anthropology* 36: 199–222.

Alimen, M. 1978. *L'Evolution de l'Acheuléen au Sahara nord-occidental (Saoura, Ougarta, Tabelbala)*. Meudon: CNRS.

Allen, J. de V. 1974. Swahili culture reconsidered: some historical implications of the material culture of the northern Kenya coast in the eighteenth and nineteenth centuries. *Azania* 9: 105–38.

  1993. *Swahili Origins*. London: Currey.

Allibert, C. and P. Vérin 1996. The early pre-Islamic history of the Comores Islands: links with Madagascar and Africa, pp. 461–70 in J. Reade (ed.) *The Indian Ocean in Antiquity*. London: Kegan Paul.

Allsworth-Jones, P. 1986. Middle Stone Age and Middle Palaeolithic: the evidence from Nigeria and Cameroon, pp. 153–68 in G. Bailey and P. Callow (eds.) *Stone Age Prehistory*. Cambridge: Cambridge University Press.

  1987. The earliest human settlement in West Africa and the Sahara. *West African Journal of Archaeology* 17: 87–129.

  2001. Diamonds, alluvials and artefacts: the Stone Age in Sierra Leone and the Cotton Tree Museum, pp. 47–62 in S. Milliken and J. Cook (eds.) *A Very Remote Period Indeed: Papers on the Palaeolithic Presented to Derek Roe*. Oxford: Oxbow.

Amblard, S. 1996. Agricultural evidence and its interpretation on the Dhars Tichitt and Oualata, southeastern Mauritania, pp. 421–7 in G. Pwiti and R. Soper (eds.) *Aspects of African Archaeology*. Harare: University of Zimbabwe Publications.

Ambrose, S. H. 1984a. The introduction of pastoral adaptations to the highlands of East Africa, pp. 212–39 in J. D. Clark and S. A. Brandt (eds.) *From Hunters to Farmers: The Causes and Consequences of Food Production in Africa*. Berkeley, CA: University of California Press.

1984b. Excavations at Deloraine, Rongai, 1978. *Azania* 19: 79–104.

1998a. Late Pleistocene human population bottleneck, volcanic winter, and differentiation of modern humans. *Journal of Human Evolution* 34: 623–51.

1998b. Chronology of the Later Stone Age and food production in East Africa. *Journal of Archaeological Science* 25: 377–92.

2002. Small things remembered: origins of early microlithic industries in sub-Saharan Africa, pp. 9–29 in R. G. Elston and S. L. Kuhn (eds.) *Thinking Small: Global Perspectives on Microlithization*. New York: American Anthropological Association.

Ambrose, S. H. *et al.* 1980. The taxonomic status of the Kenya Capsian, pp. 248–52 in R. E. Leakey and B. A. Ogot (eds.) *Proceedings of the 8th Panafrican Congress of Prehistory*. Nairobi: Louis Leakey Memorial Institute.

2002. The emergence of modern human behavior in the Kenya Rift Valley. *Journal of Human Evolution* 42(3): A3–A4.

Anati, E. 1986. The rock art of Tanzania and the East African sequence. *Bolletino del Centro Camuno di Studi Preistorici* 23: 15–68.

Anciaux de Faveaux, F. and P. de Maret 1985. Premières datations pour la fonte du cuivre au Shaba (Zaïre). *Bulletin de la Société Royale Belge d'Anthropologie et de Préhistoire* 95: 5–21.

Andah, B. W. and F. Anozie 1980. Preliminary report on the prehistoric site of Afikpo, Nigeria. *West African Journal of Archaeology* 10: 83–102.

d' Andrea, A. C. and J. Casey 2002. Pearl millet and Kintampo subsistence. *African Archaeological Review* 19: 147–73.

Anfray, F. 1963. Une campagne de fouilles à Yéha. *Annales d'Ethiopie* 5: 171–232.

1967. Matara. *Annales d'Ethiopie* 7: 33–88.

1982. Les stèles du sud: Shoa et Sidamo. *Annales d'Ethiopie* 12: 1–229.

1990. *Les anciens Ethiopiens: siècles d'histoire*. Paris: Armand Colin.

1995. Les ruines de Grat Be'al Gebri – recherches archéologiques. *Rassegna di Studi Etiopici* 39: 5–24.

Anquandah, J. 1982. *Rediscovering Ghana's Past*. Accra: Sedco.

Anthony, B. 1972. The Stillbay question, pp. 80–2 in H. Hugot (ed.) *Actes du 6e Congrès panafricain de Préhistoire*. Chambéry: Les Imprimeries Réunies de Chambéry.

Arambourg, C. and L. Balout 1952. Du nouveau à l'Ain Hanech. *Bulletin de la Société d'Histoire Naturelle de l'Afrique du Nord* 43: 152–9.

1955. L'ancien lac de Tihodaine et ses gisements préhistoriques, pp. 281–92 in L. Balout (ed.) *Actes du 2e Congrès panafricain de préhistoire*. Paris: Arts and Métiers Graphiques.

Arkell, A. J. 1949. *Early Khartoum*. London: Oxford University Press for Sudan Government.

1953. *Esh Shaheinab*. London: Oxford University Press for Sudan Government.

1954. Four occupation sites at Agordat. *Kush* 2: 33–62.

1964. *Wanyanga and an Archaeological Reconnaissance of the South-West Libyan Desert.* London: Oxford University Press.

1975. *The Prehistory of the Nile Valley.* Leiden: Brill.

Asfaw, B. *et al.* 1992. The earliest Acheulean from Konso-Gardula. *Nature* 360: 732–5.

1999. *Australopithecus garhi*: a new species of early hominid from Ethiopia. *Science* 284: 629–35.

2002. Remains of *Homo erectus* from Bouri, Middle Awash, Ethiopia. *Nature* 416: 317–20.

Asombang, R. N. 1999. Sacred centers and urbanization in west-central Africa, pp. 80–7 in S. K. McIntosh (ed.) *Beyond Chiefdoms: Pathways to Complexity in Africa.* Cambridge: Cambridge University Press.

Atherton, J. H. 1972. Excavations at Kamabai and Yagala rockshelters, Sierra Leone. *West African Journal of Archaeology* 2: 39–74.

Azaïs, [B.] and R. Chambard 1931. *Cinq années de recherches archéologiques en Ethiopie.* Paris: Geuthner.

Backwell, L. R. and F. d'Errico 2000. A new functional interpretation of the Swartkrans early hominid bone tools. *Journal of Human Evolution* 38 (3): A4–A5.

Bailloud, G. 1959. La préhistoire de l'Ethiopie. *Cahiers de l'Afrique et de l'Asie* 5: 15–43.

1969. L'évaluation des styles céramiques en Ennedi, République du Tchad, pp. 31–45 in *Actes du premier Colloque international d'archéologie africaine.* Fort Lamy: Institut National Tchadien pour les Sciences Humaines.

Balout, L. 1967. Procédés d'analyse et questions de terminologie dans l'étude des ensembles industriels du Paléolithique inférieur en Afrique du Nord, pp. 701–35 in W. W. Bishop and J. D. Clark (eds.) *Background to Evolution in Africa.* Chicago: University of Chicago Press.

Balout, L. *et al.* 1967. L'Acheuléen de Ternifine (Algérie): gisement de l'Atlanthrope. *L'Anthropologie* 71: 217–38.

Bamford, M. K. and Z. L. Henderson 2003. A reassessment of the wooden fragment from Florisbad, South Africa. *Journal of Archaeological Science* 30: 637–50.

Banks, K. M. 1984. *Climates, Cultures and Cattle: The Holocene Archaeology of the Eastern Sahara.* Dallas, TX: Southern Methodist University.

Barakat, H. N. 2002. Regional pathways to agriculture in northeast Africa, pp. 111–22 in F. Hassan (ed.) *Drought, Food and Culture: Ecological Change and Food Security in Africa's Later Prehistory.* New York: Kluwer/Plenum.

Bard, K. A. *et al.* 2000. The environmental history of Tigray (northern Ethiopia) in the Middle and Late Holocene: a preliminary outline. *African Archaeological Review* 17: 65–86.

Barham, L. S. 2000. *The Middle Stone Age of Zambia, South-Central Africa.* Bristol: Western Academic and Specialist Press.

2001. Central Africa and the emergence of regional identity in the Middle Pleistocene, pp. 65–80 in L. S. Barham and K. Robson-Brown (eds.) *Human Roots: Africa and Asia in the Middle Pleistocene.* Bristol: Western Academic and Specialist Press.

2002a. Systematic pigment use in the Middle Pleistocene of central Africa. *Current Anthropology* 43: 181–90.

2002b. Backed tools in Middle Pleistocene central Africa and their evolutionary significance. *Journal of Human Evolution* 43: 585–603.

Barich, B. E. 1987. *Archaeology and Environment in the Libyan Sahara: Excavations in the Tadrart Acacus 1978–83.* Oxford: British Archaeological Reports.

1992. Holocene communities of western and central Sahara: a reappraisal, pp. 185–204 in F. Klees and R. Kuper (eds.) *New Light on the Northeast African Past.* Cologne: Heinrich-Barth-Institut.

1998. *People, Water and Grain: The Beginnings of Domestication in the Sahara and the Nile Valley.* Rome: L'Erma di Bretschneider.

Barich, B. E. and M. C. Gatto (eds.) 1997. *Dynamics of Populations: Movements and Responses to Climatic Change in Africa.* Rome: Bonsignori.

Barker, G. 2003. Transitions to farming and pastoralism in North Africa, pp. 151–62 in P. Bellwood and C. Renfrew (eds.) *Examining the Farming/Language Dispersal Hypothesis.* Cambridge: McDonald Institute for Archaeological Research.

Barker, G. *et al.* (eds.) 1996. *Farming the Desert: The UNESCO Libyan Valleys Archaeological Survey.* London: Society for Libyan Studies.

Barnard, A. 1992. *Hunters and Herders of Southern Africa.* Cambridge: Cambridge University Press.

Barnett, T. 1999. *The Emergence of Food Production in Ethiopia.* Oxford: British Archaeological Reports.

Barthelme, J. W. 1985. *Fisher-Hunters and Neolithic Pastoralists of East Turkana, Kenya.* Oxford: British Archaeological Reports.

Barton, R. N. E. *et al.* 2001. Bridging the gap: new fieldwork in northern Morocco. *Antiquity* 75: 489–90.

Barut, S. 1994. Middle and Later Stone Age lithic technology and land use in East African savannas. *African Archaeological Review* 12: 43–72.

Bar Yosef, O. 1987. Pleistocene connexions between Africa and Southwest Asia: an archaeological perspective. *African Archaeological Review* 5: 29–38.

2003. The Natufian culture and the Early Neolithic: social and economic trends in southwestern Asia, pp. 113–26 in P. Bellwood and C. Renfrew (eds.) *Examining the Farming/Language Dispersal Hypothesis.* Cambridge: McDonald Institute for Archaeological Research.

Bar Yosef, O. and S. L. Kuhn 1999. The big deal about blades: laminar technologies and human evolution. *American Anthropologist* 101: 322–38.

Bastin, Y. *et al.* 1983. Classification lexicostatistique des langues bantoues (214 relevés). *Bulletin de l'Académie Royale des Sciences d'Outre-Mer* 27: 173–99.

1999. *Continuity and Divergence in the Bantu Languages: Perspectives from a Lexicostatistical Study.* Tervuren: Musée Royal de l'Afrique Centrale.

Baumgartel, E. J. 1955. *The Cultures of Prehistoric Egypt.* Oxford: Oxford University Press for Griffith Institute.

de Bayle des Hermens, R. 1975. *Recherche préhistorique en République centrafricaine.* Paris: Labethno.

Beach, D. N. 1980. *The Shona and Zimbabwe 900–1850.* London: Heinemann.

1994. *The Shona and Their Neighbours.* Oxford: Blackwell.

Beach, D. N. *et al.* 1998. Cognitive archaeology and imaginary history at Great Zimbabwe. *Current Anthropology* 39: 47–72.

Beaumont, P. B. 1973. Border Cave – a progress report. *South African Journal of Science* 69: 41–6.

1980. On the age of Border Cave hominids 1–5. *Palaeontologia Africana* 23: 21–33.

1990. Wonderwerk Cave, pp. 101–34 in P. B. Beaumont and D. Morris (eds.) *Guide to Archaeological Sites in the Northern Cape*. Kimberley: McGregor Museum for the Southern African Association of Archaeologists.

Beaumont, P. B. and J. C. Vogel 1972. On a new radiocarbon chronology for Africa south of the equator. *African Studies* 31: 67–89, 155–82.

Beaumont, P. B. *et al.* 1978. Modern man in sub-Saharan Africa prior to 49,000 years B.P. *South African Journal of Science* 74: 409–19.

Behrensmeyer, K. 1976. Fossil assemblages in relation to sedimentary environments in the East Rudolf succession, pp. 388–401 in Y. Coppens *et al.* (eds.) *Earliest Man and Environments in the Lake Rudolf Basin*. Chicago: University of Chicago Press.

Bellwood, P. and C. Renfrew (eds.) 2003. *Examining the Farming/Language Dispersal Hypothesis*. Cambridge: McDonald Institute for Archaeological Research.

Benefit, B. R. and M. L. McCrossin 1995. Miocene hominoids and hominid origins. *Annual Review of Anthropology* 24: 237–56.

Bennett, P. R. 1983. Patterns in linguistic geography and the Bantu origins controversy. *History in Africa* 10: 35–51.

Berger, L. R. and R. J. Clarke 1995. Eagle involvement in accumulation of the Taung child fauna. *Journal of Human Evolution* 29: 275–99.

Berthier, S. 1997. *Recherches archéologiques sur la capitale de l'empire de Ghana: étude d'un secteur d'habitat à Koumbi Saleh, Mauritanie*. Oxford: British Archaeological Reports.

Beyries, S. and H. Roche 1982. Technologie et traces d'utilisation à des industries acheuléens (Carrières Thomas, Casablanca, Maroc). *Studia Prehistorica Belgica* 2: 267–77.

Biberson, P. 1961. *Le paléolithique inférieur du Maroc atlantique*. Rabat: Service des Antiquités du Maroc.

1967. Some aspects of the Lower Palaeolithic of North-West Africa, pp. 447–75 in W. W. Bishop and J. D. Clark (eds.) *Background to Evolution in Africa*. Chicago: University of Chicago Press.

1971. Index cards on the marine and continental cycles of the Moroccan Quaternary. *Quaternaria* 13: 1–76.

Binford, L. R. 1981. *Bones: Ancient Men and Modern Myths*. New York: Academic Press.

1984. *Faunal Remains from Klasies River Mouth*. New York: Academic Press.

Binneman, J. N. F. 1994. A unique stone-tipped arrowhead from Adam's Kranz Cave, Eastern Cape. *South African Field Archaeology* 3: 58–60.

1996. Preliminary report on the investigations at Kulubele, an Early Iron Age farming settlement in the Great Kei River Valley, Eastern Cape. *Southern African Field Archaeology* 5: 28–35.

Binneman, J. N. F. and P. B. Beaumont 1992. Use-wear analysis of two Acheulean handaxes from Wonderwerk Cave, Northern Cape. *Southern African Field Archaeology* 1: 92–7.

Binneman, J. N. F. and P. J. Mitchell 1997. Microwear analysis of Robberg bladelets from Sehonghong Shelter, Lesotho. *Southern African Field Archaeology* 6: 42–9.

Bisson, M. S. 1975. Copper currency in central Africa: the archaeological evidence. *World Archaeology* 6: 272–92.

2000. Precolonial copper metallurgy: socio-political context, pp. 83–145 in J. O. Vogel (ed.) *Ancient African Metallurgy: The Socio-Political Context*. Walnut Creek, CA: Altamira Press.

Blench, R. M. 1996. The ethnographic evidence for long-distance contacts between Oceania and East Africa, pp. 417–38 in J. Reade (ed.) *The Indian Ocean in Antiquity*. London: Kegan Paul.

    1999. The languages of Africa: macrophyla proposals and implications for archaeological interpretation, pp. 29–47 in R. Blench and M. Spriggs (eds.) *Archaeology and Language*, vol. 4. London: Routledge.

    2000. A history of donkeys, wild asses and mules in Africa, pp. 339–54 in R. M. Blench and K. C. MacDonald (eds.) *The Origins and Development of African Livestock*. London: UCL Press.

Blench, R. M. and K. C. MacDonald (eds.) 2000. *The Origins and Development of African Livestock: Archaeology, Genetics, Linguistics and Ethnography*. London: UCL Press.

Blumenschine, R. J. and F. T. Masao 1991. Living sites at Olduvai Gorge, Tanzania? *Journal of Human Evolution* 21: 451–62.

Boardman, J. 1999. *The Greeks Overseas*. London: Thames and Hudson.

Boaz, N. T. *et al.* 1992. A new evaluation of the significance of the late Neogene Lusso Beds, Upper Semlike Valley, Zaïre. *Journal of Human Evolution* 22: 505–17.

Boesch, C. and H. Boesch 1990. Tool use and tool making in wild chimpanzees. *Folia Primatologia* 54: 86–99.

Bohannan, L. *et al.* (eds.) 1958. *Tribes without Rulers: Studies in African Segmentary Systems*. London: Routledge.

Bonnefille, R. 1999. Evolution du cadre botanique et climatique du grand rift africain, pp. 199–230 in A. Gallay (ed.) *Comment l'homme?* Paris: Editions Errance.

Bonnefille, R. *et al.* 1995. Glacial/interglacial record from intertropical Africa: high-resolution pollen and carbon data at Rusaka, Burundi. *Quaternary Science Review* 14: 917–36.

Bonnet, C. 1991. Upper Nubia from 3000 to 1000 BC, pp. 112–17 in W. V. Davies (ed.) *Egypt and Africa: Nubia from Prehistory to Islam*. London: British Museum Press.

    1992. Excavations at the Nubian royal town of Kerma, 1975–91. *Antiquity* 66: 611–25.

Bonnet, C. *et al.* 1990. *Kerma: royaume de Nubie*. Geneva: Musée d'Art et d'Histoire.

Bousman, C. B. 1998. The chronological evidence for the introduction of domestic stock into southern Africa. *African Archaeological Review* 15: 133–50.

Bower, J. R. F. 1991. The pastoral neolithic of East Africa. *Journal of World Prehistory* 5: 49–82.

    1995. Early food production in Africa. *Evolutionary Anthropology* 4: 130–9.

Bower, J. R. F. and C. M. Nelson 1978. Early pottery and pastoral cultures of the Central Rift Valley, Kenya. *Man (N.S.)* 13: 554–66.

Bower, J. R. F. *et al.* 1977. The University of Massachusetts Later Stone Age/Pastoral Neolithic comparative study in central Kenya. *Azania* 12: 119–46.

Bowman, A. K. 1986. *Egypt after the Pharaohs*. London: British Museum Press.

Bowman, A. K. and E. Rogan (eds.) 1999. Agriculture in Egypt from Pharaonic to modern times. *Proceedings of the British Academy* 96.

Brain, C. K. 1967. Hottentot food remains and their bearing on the interpretation of fossil bone assemblages. *Scientific Papers of the Namib Desert Research Station* 32: 1–11.

    1969. New evidence for climatic change during Middle and Late Stone Age times in Rhodesia. *South African Archaeological Bulletin* 24: 127–43.

1981. *The Hunters or the Hunted?* Chicago: University of Chicago Press.

(ed.) 1993. *Swartkrans: A Cave's Chronicle of Early Man.* Pretoria: Transvaal Museum.

Brandt, S. A. 1984. New perspectives on the origins of food production in Ethiopia, pp. 173–90 in J. D. Clark and S. A. Brandt (eds.) *From Hunters to Farmers: The Causes and Consequences of Food Production in Africa.* Berkeley: University of California Press.

1986. The Upper Pleistocene and early Holocene prehistory of the Horn of Africa. *African Archaeological Review* 4: 41–82.

1996. The ethnoarchaeology of flaked stone tool use in southern Ethiopia, pp. 733–8 in G. Pwiti and R. Soper (eds.) *Aspects of African Archaeology.* Harare: University of Zimbabwe Publications.

Brandt, S. A. and N. Carder 1987. Pastoral rock art in the Horn of Africa: making sense of udder chaos. *World Archaeology* 19: 194–213.

Bräuer, G. 1984. A craniological approach to the origin of anatomically modern *Homo sapiens* in Africa, pp. 327–410 in F. H. Smith and F. Spencer (eds.) *The Origins of Modern Humans: A World Survey of the Fossil Record.* New York: Liss.

Bräuer, G. and M. J. Mehlman 1988. Hominid molars from a Middle Stone Age level at Mumba Rock Shelter, Tanzania. *American Journal of Physical Anthropology* 75: 69–76.

Bräuer, G. *et al.* 1997. Modern human origins backdated. *Nature* 386: 337.

Breasted, J. 1906. *Ancient Records of Egypt*, vol. 1. Chicago: University of Chicago Press.

Breternitz, D. A. 1975. Rescue archaeology in the Kainji Reservoir area, 1968. *West African Journal of Archaeology* 5: 91–151.

Brett, M. 1978. The Arab conquest and the rise of Islam in North Africa, pp. 490–555 in J. D. Fage (ed.) *Cambridge History of Africa*, vol. 2. Cambridge: Cambridge University Press.

1983. Islam and trade in the Bilad al-Sudan, 10th–11th century AD. *Journal of African History* 24: 431–40.

Brett, M. and E. Fentress 1996. *The Berbers.* Oxford: Blackwell.

Breunig, P. 1996. The 8000-year-old dugout canoe from Dufuna (N.E. Nigeria), pp. 461–8 in G. Pwiti and R. Soper (eds.) *Aspects of African Archaeology.* Harare: University of Zimbabwe Publications.

Breunig, P. and K. Neumann 2002. From hunters and gatherers to food producers: new archaeological and archaeobotanical evidence from the West African sahel, pp. 123–56 in F. Hassan (ed.) *Drought, Food and Culture: Ecological Change and Food Security in Africa's Later Prehistory.* New York: Kluwer/Plenum.

Breunig, P. *et al.* 1996. New research on the Holocene settlement and environment of the Chad basin in Nigeria. *African Archaeological Review* 13: 111–45.

Brewer, D. J. 1989. *Fishermen, Hunters and Herders: Zooarchaeology in the Fayum, Egypt 8200–5000 bp.* Oxford: British Archaeological Reports.

Brink, J. and L. Webley 1996. Faunal evidence for pastoralist settlement at Jakkalsberg, Richtersveld, Northern Cape Province. *Southern African Field Archaeology* 5: 70–8.

Brobeng, A. 1995. New aspects of the medieval towns of Benadir in southern Somalia, pp. 111–22 in K. Adahl and B. Sahlström (eds.) *Islamic Art and Culture in Sub-Saharan Africa.* Uppsala: University of Uppsala.

Bromage, T. G. *et al.* 1995. Paleoanthropology of the Malawi Rift: an early hominid mandible from the Chiwondo Beds, northern Malawi. *Journal of Human Evolution* 28: 71–108.

Brook, G. A. *et al.* 1992. Evidence of a shallow lake at Tsodilo Hills, Botswana, 17500–15000 BP: further confirmation of a widespread Late Pleistocene humid period in the Kalahari Desert. *Palaeoecology of Africa* 23: 165–75.

Brooks, A. S. and P. T. Robertshaw 1990. The glacial maximum in tropical Africa, pp. 121–69 in C. Gamble and O. Soffer (eds.) *The World at 18000 BP: Low Latitudes.* London: Unwin Hyman.

Brooks, A. S. and C. C. Smith 1987. Ishango revisited: new age determinations and cultural interpretations. *African Archaeological Review* 5: 65–78.

Brooks, A. S. *et al.* 1984. Food production and culture change among the !Kung San: implications for prehistoric research, pp. 293–310 in J. D. Clark and S. A. Brandt (eds.) *From Hunters to Farmers: The Causes and Consequences of Food Production in Africa.* Berkeley: University of California Press.

    1995. Dating and context of three Middle Stone Age sites with bone points in the upper Semliki Valley, Zaïre. *Science* 268: 548–53.

Brothwell, D. R. 1971. The skeletal remains from Gwisho B and C, pp. 37–47 in B. M. Fagan and F. L. Van Noten *The Hunter-Gatherers of Gwisho.* Tervuren: Musée Royal de l'Afrique Centrale.

Brothwell, D. R. and T. Shaw 1971. A late Upper Pleistocene proto-West African Negro from Nigeria. *Man (N.S.)* 6: 221–7.

Brown, F. H. 1975. Barbed bone points from the lower Omo Valley, Ethiopia. *Azania* 10: 144–8.

    1994. Development of Pliocene and Pleistocene chronology in the Turkana Basin, East Africa, and its relation to other sites, pp. 285–312 in R. S. Corruccini and R. L. Ciochon (eds.) *Integrative Paths to the Past: Paleoanthropological Advances in Honor of F. Clark Howell.* Englewood Cliffs, NJ: Prentice Hall.

Brown, J. 1990. Horn-shaping ground-stone axe-hammers. *Azania* 25: 57–67.

    1995. *Traditional Metalworking in Kenya.* Oxford: Oxbow.

Brunet, M. *et al.* 1996. *Australopithecus bahrelghazali,* une nouvelle espèce d'hominidé ancien de la région de Koro Toro (Tchad). *Comptes-rendus des Séances de l'Académie des Sciences de Paris, sér. 2A,* 322: 907–13.

    2002. A new hominid from the Upper Miocene of Chad, Central Africa. *Nature* 418: 145–51.

Bunn, H. T. and E. M. Kroll 1986. Systematic butchery by Plio/Pleistocene hominids at Olduvai Gorge, Tanzania. *Current Anthropology* 27: 431–52.

Bunn, H. T. *et al.* 1980. FxJj50: an early Pleistocene site in northern Kenya. *World Archaeology* 12: 109–36.

Burstein, S. M. (ed.) 1989. *Agatharchides of Cnidus on the Erythraean Sea.* London: Hakluyt Society.

de Busk, G. H. 1998. A 37,500-year pollen record from Lake Malawi and implications for the biogeography of afromontane forests. *Journal of Biogeography* 25: 479–500.

Butzer, K. W. 1971. *Recent History of an Ethiopian Delta.* Chicago: University of Chicago Press.

    1974. Paleoecology of South African australopithecines: Taung revisited. *Current Anthropology* 15: 367–82, 413–16.

    1980. The Holocene lake plain of North Rudolf, East Africa. *Physical Geography* 1: 42–58.

Butzer, K. W. and G. L. Isaac (eds.) 1975. *After the Australopithecines*. The Hague: Mouton.

Butzer, K. W. *et al.* 1978. Lithostratigraphy of Border Cave, KwaZulu, South Africa: a Middle Stone Age sequence beginning *c.* 195,000 BP. *Journal of Archaeological Science* 5: 317–41.

1979. Dating and context of rock engravings in southern Africa. *Science* 203: 1201–14.

Buxton, D. 1970. *The Abyssinians*. London: Thames and Hudson.

Bye, B. A. *et al.* 1987. Increased age estimate for the Lower Palaeolithic hominid site at Olorgesailie, Kenya. *Nature* 329: 237–9.

Cachel, S. and J. W. K. Harris 1998. The lifeways of *Homo erectus* inferred from archaeology and evolutionary ecology: a perspective from East Africa, pp. 108–32 in M. D. Petraglia and R. Korisettar (eds.) *Early Human Behaviour in Global Context*. London: Routledge.

Cadénat, P. and J. Tixier 1960. Une faucille préhistorique à Columnata. *Libyca* 8: 239–58.

Cahen, D. 1975. *Le site archéologique de la Kamoa (région du Shaba, République du Zaïre) de l'âge de la pierre ancien à l'âge du fer*. Tervuren: Musée Royal de l'Afrique Centrale.

1978. Vers une revision de la nomenclature des industries préhistoriques de l'Afrique centrale. *L'Anthropologie* 82: 5–36.

1981. Contribution à la chronologie de l'âge du fer dans la région de Kinshasa, pp. 127–37 in C. Roubet *et al.* (eds.) *Préhistoire africaine: mélanges offerts au doyen Lionel Balout*. Paris: ADPF.

Cahen, D. and J. Moeyersons 1977. Subsurface movements of stone artefacts and their implications for the prehistory of Central Africa. *Nature* 266: 812–15.

Cahen, D. and G. Mortelmans 1973. *Un site Tshitolien sur le plateau des Batéké*. Tervuren: Musée Royal de l'Afrique Centrale.

Caligari, G. 1993. *L'Arte e l'ambiente del Sahara preistorico: dati e interpretazioni*. Milan: Museo Civico di Storia Naturale.

Calvocoressi, D. and N. David 1979. A new survey of radiocarbon and thermoluminescence dates for West Africa. *Journal of African History* 20: 1–29.

Campbell, A. *et al.* 1996. Variation in the Early Iron Age of southeastern Botswana. *Botswana Notes and Records* 28: 1–22.

Camps, G. 1961. *Aux origines de la Berbérie: monuments et rites funéraires protohistoriques*. Paris: Arts and Métiers Graphiques.

1969. *Amekni: néolithique ancien du Hoggar*. Paris: Arts and Métiers Graphiques.

1974. *Les civilisations préhistoriques de l'Afrique du Nord et du Sahara*. Paris: Doin.

1975. The prehistoric cultures of North Africa: radiocarbon chronology, pp. 182–92 in F. Wendorf and A. E. Marks (eds.) *Problems in Prehistory – North Africa and the Levant*. Dallas, TX: Southern Methodist University Press.

1982. Beginnings of pastoralism and cultivation in north-west Africa and the Sahara: origins of the Berbers, pp. 548–623 in J. D. Clark (ed.) *Cambridge History of Africa*, vol. 1. Cambridge: Cambridge University Press.

1986. Funerary monuments with attached chapels from the northern Sahara. *African Archaeological Review* 4: 151–64.

Caneva, I. (ed.) 1983. Pottery-using gatherers and hunters at Saggai (Sudan): preconditions for food production. *Origini* 12: 7–278.

(ed.) 1988. *El-Geili: The History of a Middle Nile Environment 7000 BC–AD 1500*. Oxford: British Archaeological Reports.

Caneva, I. *et al.* 1993. Pre-pastoral cultures along the central Sudanese Nile. *Quaternaria Nova* 3: 177–252.

Cann, R. *et al.* 1987. Mitochondrial DNA and human evolution. *Nature* 325: 31–6.

Carbonell, E. *et al.* 1999. Out of Africa: the dispersal of the earliest technical systems reconsidered. *Journal of Anthropological Archaeology* 18: 119–36.

Carter, P. L. 1970. Late Stone Age exploitation patterns in southern Natal. *South African Archaeological Bulletin* 25: 55–8.

Carter, P. L. and J. D. Clark 1976. Adrar Bous and African cattle, pp. 487–93 in Berhanou Abebe *et al.* (eds.) *Proceedings of the 7th Panafrican Congress on Prehistory*. Addis Ababa: Antiquities Administration.

Carter, P. L. and J. C. Vogel 1974. The dating of industrial assemblages from stratified sites in eastern Lesotho. *Man (N.S.)* 9: 577–70.

Carter, P. L. *et al.* 1988. *Sehonghong: The Middle and Later Stone Age Industrial Sequence at a Lesotho Rock-Shelter*. Oxford: British Archaeological Reports.

Cary, M. and E. H. Warmington 1929. *The Ancient Explorers*. London: Methuen.

Casey, J. 2000. *The Kintampo Complex: The Late Holocene on the Gambaga Escarpment, Northern Ghana*. Oxford: British Archaeological Reports.

Cassinello, J. 1998. *Ammotragus lervia*: a review on systematics, biology, ecology and distribution. *Annales Zoologici Fennici* 35: 149–62.

Casson, L. 1989. *The Periplus Maris Erythraei*. Princeton, NJ: Princeton University Press.

Caton-Thompson, G. and E. W. Gardner 1934. *The Desert Fayum*. London: Royal Anthropological Institute.

Chami, F. 1995. The first millennium AD on the East Coast: a new look at the cultural sequence and interactions. *Azania* 29–30: 232–7.

1998. A review of Swahili archaeology. *African Archaeological Review* 15: 199–218.

1999. Roman beads from the Rufiji Delta, Tanzania: first incontrovertible archaeological link with the *Periplus*. *Current Anthropology* 40: 237–41.

2001. The archaeology of the Rufiji region: coastal and interior dynamics from AD 0–500, pp. 7–20 in F. Chami *et al.* (eds.) *People, Contacts and the Environment in the African Past*. Dar es Salaam: University of Dar es Salaam.

2003. Neolithic pottery traditions from the islands, the coast and the interior of East Africa. *African Archaeological Review* 20: 65–80.

Chamla, M. C. 1978. Le peuplement de l'Afrique du Nord de l'epipaléolithique à l'époque actuelle. *L'Anthropologie* 82: 385–430.

Chapman, S. 1967. Kantsyore Island. *Azania* 2: 165–91.

Chavaillon, J. 1979. From the Oldowan to the Middle Stone Age at Melka Kunturé, Ethiopia: understanding cultural changes. *Quaternaria* 21: 87–114.

Chenorkian, R. 1983. Ivory Coast prehistory: recent developments. *African Archaeological Review* 1: 127–42.

Chikwendu, V. E. and C. E. A. Okezie 1989. Factors responsible for the ennoblement of African yams: inferences from experiments in yam domestication, pp. 344–57 in D. R. Harris and G. C. Hillman (eds.) *Foraging and Farming*. London: Unwin Hyman.

Chikwendu, V. E. *et al.* 1989. Nigerian sources of copper, lead and tin for the Igbo-Ukwu bronzes. *Archaeometry* 31: 27–36.

Childs, S. T. 1991. Style, technology and iron-smelting furnaces in Bantu-speaking Africa. *Journal of Anthropological Archeology* 10: 332–59.

Chipunza, K. T. 1993. *A Diachronic Analysis of the Architecture of the Hill Complex at Great Zimbabwe*. Uppsala: Societas Archaeologica Upsalensis.

Chittick, N. 1974. *Kilwa: An Islamic Trading City on the East African Coast*. Nairobi: British Institute in Eastern Africa.

1976. An archaeological reconnaissance in the Horn: the British-Somali expedition, 1975. *Azania* 11: 117–33.

1977. The east coast, Madagascar and the Indian Ocean, pp. 183–231 in R. Oliver (ed.) *Cambridge History of Africa*, vol. 3. Cambridge: Cambridge University Press.

1984. *Manda: Excavations at an Island Port on the Kenya Coast*. Nairobi: British Institute in Eastern Africa.

Chmielewski, W. 1968. Early and Middle Palaeolithic sites near Arkin, Sudan, pp. 110–93 in F. Wendorf (ed.) *The Prehistory of Nubia*. Dallas, TX: Southern Methodist University Press.

Clark, A. M. B. 1997. The MSA/LSA transition in southern Africa: new technological evidence. *South African Archaeological Bulletin* 52: 113–21.

1999. Late Pleistocene technology at Rose Cottage Cave: a search for modern behavior in an MSA context. *African Archaeological Review* 16: 93–120.

Clark, J. D. 1950. *The Stone Age Cultures of Northern Rhodesia*. Cape Town: South African Archaeological Society.

1954. *Prehistoric Cultures of the Horn of Africa*. Cambridge: Cambridge University Press.

1958. Some Stone Age woodworking tools in southern Africa. *South African Archaeological Bulletin* 13: 144–52.

1959. Further excavations at Broken Hill, Northern Rhodesia. *Journal of the Royal Anthropological Institute* 89: 201–32.

1963. *Prehistoric Cultures of Northeast Angola and Their Significance in Tropical Africa*. Lisbon: Companhia de Diamantes de Angola.

1964. The influence of environment in inducing culture change at the Kalambo Falls prehistoric site. *South African Archaeological Bulletin*. 20: 93–101.

1967. *Atlas of African Prehistory*. Chicago: University of Chicago Press.

1969. *Kalambo Falls Prehistoric Site*, vol. 1. Cambridge: Cambridge University Press.

1970. *The Prehistory of Africa*. London: Thames and Hudson.

1971. A re-examination of the evidence for agricultural origins in the Nile Valley. *Proceedings of the Prehistoric Society* 37 (2): 34–79.

1974. *Kalambo Falls Prehistoric Site*, vol. 2. Cambridge: Cambridge University Press.

1980. Human populations and cultural adaptations in the Sahara and Nile during prehistoric times, pp. 527–82 in M. A. J. Williams and H. Faure (eds.) *The Sahara and the Nile*. Rotterdam: Balkema.

1982a. The cultures of the Middle Palaeolithic/Middle Stone Age, pp. 248–341 in J. D. Clark (ed.) *The Cambridge History of Africa*, vol. 1. Cambridge: Cambridge University Press.

(ed.) 1982b. *Cambridge History of Africa*, vol. 1. Cambridge: Cambridge University Press.

1987. Transitions: *Homo erectus* and the Acheulian, the Ethiopian sites of Gadeb and the Middle Awash. *Journal of Human Evolution* 16: 809–26.

1989. Shabona: an Early Khartoum settlement on the White Nile, pp. 387–410 in L. Krzyzaniak and M. Kobusiewicz (eds.) *Late Prehistory of the Nile Basin and the Sahara*. Poznan: Poznan Archaeological Museum.

1990. Stone Age man at the Victoria Falls, pp. 32–50 in D. W. Phillipson (ed.) *Mosi-oa-Tunya: A Handbook to the Victoria Falls Region (Second Edition)*. Harare: Longman Zimbabwe.

1992. The Earlier Stone Age/Lower Palaeolithic in North Africa and the Sahara, pp. 17–37 in F. Klees and R. Kuper (eds.) *New Light on the Northeast African Past*. Cologne: Heinrich-Barth-Institut.

1996. Decision-making and variability in the Acheulean, pp. 93–8 in G. Pwiti and R. Soper (eds.) *Aspects of African Archaeology*. Harare: University of Zimbabwe Publications.

2001a. *Kalambo Falls Prehistoric Site*, vol. 3. Cambridge: Cambridge University Press.

2001b. Variability in primary and secondary technologies of the later Acheulian in Africa, pp. 1–18 in S. Milliken and J. Cook (eds.) *A Very Remote Period Indeed: Papers on the Palaeolithic Presented to Derek Roe*. Oxford: Oxbow.

Clark, J. D. and K. Brown 2001. The Twin Rivers kopje, Zambia: stratigraphy, fauna and artefact assemblages from the 1954 and 1956 excavations. *Journal of Archaeological Science* 28: 305–30.

Clark, J. D. and J. W. K. Harris 1985. Fire and its roles in early hominid lifeways. *African Archaeological Review* 3: 3–27.

Clark, J. D. and C. V. Haynes 1970. An elephant butchery site at Mwanganda's village, Karonga, Malawi. *World Archaeology* 1: 390–411.

Clark, J. D. and A. Stemler 1975. Early domesticated sorghum from central Sudan. *Nature* 254: 588–91.

Clark, J. D. and M. A. J. Williams 1978. Recent archaeological research in southeastern Ethiopia, 1974–5. *Annales d'Ethiopie* 11: 19–42.

Clark, J. D. *et al.* 1950. New studies on Rhodesian Man. *Journal of the Royal Anthropological Institute* 77: 7–32.

1973. The geomorphology and archaeology of Adrar Bous, Central Sahara: a preliminary report. *Quaternaria* 17: 245–98.

1974. Interpretations of prehistoric technology from Ancient Egyptian and other sources: I – Ancient Egyptian bows and arrows and their relevance for African prehistory. *Paléorient* 2: 323–88.

1994. African *Homo erectus*: old radiometric ages and young Oldowan assemblages in the middle Awash Valley, Ethiopia. *Nature* 264: 1907–10.

1995. Papers concerning research on the Chiwondo Beds, northern Malawi. *Journal of Human Evolution* 28: 3–120.

2003. Stratigraphic, chronological and behavioural contexts of Pleistocene *Homo sapiens* from Middle Awash, Ethiopia. *Nature* 423: 747–52.

Clark, J. G. D. 1961. *World Prehistory: An Outline*. Cambridge: Cambridge University Press.

1969. *World Prehistory: A New Outline*. Cambridge: Cambridge University Press.

1977. *World Prehistory in New Perspective*. Cambridge: Cambridge University Press.

Clarke, R. J. 1976. New cranium of *Homo erectus* from Lake Ndutu, Tanzania. *Nature* 262: 485–7.

1985. A new reconstruction of the Florisbad cranium, with notes on the site, pp. 301–5 in E. Delson (ed.) *Ancestors: The Hard Evidence*. New York: Liss.

1988. Habiline handaxes and Paranthropine pedigree at Sterkfontein. *World Archaeology* 20: 1–12.

1990. The Ndutu cranium and the origin of *Homo sapiens. Journal of Human Evolution* 19: 699–736.

1998. First ever discovery of a well preserved skull and associated skeleton of *Australopithecus. South African Journal of Science* 94: 460–3.

1999. Discovery of complete arm and hand of the 3.3-million-year-old *Australopithecus* skeleton from Sterkfontein. *South African Journal of Science* 95: 477–80.

Clist, B. 1986. Le néolithique en Afrique centrale: état de la question et perspectives d'avenir. *L'Anthropologie* 90: 217–32.

1987. A critical reappraisal of the chronological framework of the Urewe Early Iron Age industry. *Muntu* 6: 35–62.

1989a. Archaeology in Gabon 1886–1988. *African Archaeological Review* 7: 59–95.

1989b. La campagne de fouilles 1989 du site âge du fer ancien d'Oveng, province de l'Estuaire, Gabon. *Nsi* 5: 15–18.

Close, A. E. 1986. The place of Haua Fteah in the late Palaeolithic of North Africa, pp. 169–80 in G. Bailey and P. Callow (eds.) *Stone Age Prehistory.* Cambridge: Cambridge University Press.

1992. Holocene occupation of the eastern Sahara, pp. 155–83 in F. Klees and R. Kuper (eds.) *New Light on the Northeast African Past.* Cologne: Heinrich-Barth-Institut.

1995. Few and far between: early ceramics in North Africa, pp. 23–37 in W. K. Barnett and J. W. Hooper (eds.) *The Emergence of Pottery.* Washington, DC: Smithsonian Institution Press.

Close, A. and F. Wendorf 1992. The beginnings of food production in the eastern Sahara, pp. 63–72 in A. B. Gebauer and T. D. Price (eds.) *Transitions to Agriculture in Prehistory.* Madison, WI: Prehistory Press.

Clottes, J. 2002. *World Rock Art.* Los Angeles, CA: Getty Trust.

Cole, G. H. 1967. The later Acheulian and Sangoan of southern Uganda, pp. 481–528 in W. W. Bishop and J. D. Clark (eds.) *Background to Evolution in Africa.* Chicago: University of Chicago Press.

Cole, S. 1964. *The Prehistory of East Africa.* London: Weidenfeld and Nicolson.

Collett, D. P. 1982. Models of the spread of the Early Iron age, pp. 182–98 in C. Ehret and M. Posnansky (eds.) *The Archaeological and Linguistic Reconstruction of African History.* Berkeley: University of California Press.

Collett, D. P. *et al.* 1992. The chronology of the Valley Enclosures: implications for the interpretation of Great Zimbabwe. *African Archaeological Review* 10: 139–61.

Connah, G. [1964] *Polished Stone Axes in Benin.* Lagos: [Federal Department of Antiquities].

1975. *The Archaeology of Benin.* Oxford: Oxford University Press.

1976. The Daima sequence and the prehistoric chronology of the Lake Chad region of Nigeria. *Journal of African History* 17: 321–52.

1981. *Three Thousand Years in Africa.* Cambridge: Cambridge University Press.

1996. *Kibiro: The Salt of Bunyoro, Past and Present.* London: British Institute in Eastern Africa.

2001. *African Civilisations (Second Edition).* Cambridge: Cambridge University Press.

Conroy, G. C. *et al.* 1978. Newly discovered fossil hominid skull from the Afar Depression, Ethiopia. *Nature* 275: 67–70.

Cooke, C. K. 1963. Report on excavations at Pomongwe and Tshangula Caves, Matopo Hills, Southern Rhodesia. *South African Archaeological Bulletin* 18: 73–151.

1969. A re-examination of the 'Middle Stone Age' industries of Rhodesia. *Arnoldia* 4: no. 7.

1971. Excavation in Zombepata Cave, Sipolilo District, Mashonaland, Rhodesia. *South African Archaeological Bulletin* 25: 104–27.

1973. The Middle Stone Age in Rhodesia and South Africa. *Arnoldia* 6: no. 20.

1978. The Redcliff Stone Age site, Rhodesia. *Occasional Papers, National Museums of Rhodesia* 4a (2): 45–73.

Cooke, H. B. S. 1974. The fossil mammals of Cornelia, O.F.S., South Africa. *Memoirs van die Nasionale Museum Bloemfontein* 9: 63–84.

Coon, C. S. 1968. *Yengema Cave Report.* Philadelphia: University of Pennsylvania Museum.

Coppens, Y. *et al.* (eds.) 1976. *Earliest Man and Environments in the Lake Rudolf Basin.* Chicago: University of Chicago Press.

Cornelissen, E. 1992. *Site GnJh-17 and Its Implications for the Archaeology of the Middle Kapthurin Formation, Baringo, Kenya.* Tervuren: Musée Royal de l'Afrique Centrale.

2002. Human responses to changing environments in Central Africa between 40,000 and 12,000 BP. *Journal of World Prehistory* 16: 197–235.

2003. On microlithic quartz industries at the end of the Pleistocene in Central Africa: the evidence from Shum Laka, NW Cameroon. *African Archaeological Review* 20: 1–24.

Cornelissen, E. *et al.* 1990. The Kapthurin formation revisited. *African Archaeological Review* 8: 23–75.

Coursey, D. G. 1976. The origins and domestication of yams in Africa, pp. 383–408 in J. Harlan *et al.* (eds.) *Origins of African Plant Domestication.* The Hague: Mouton.

Craddock, P. T. *et al.* 1997. Metal sources and the bronzes from Igbo Ukwu, Nigeria. *Journal of Field Archaeology* 24: 405–29.

Crader, D. C. 1984. *Hunters in Iron Age Malawi.* Lilongwe: Malawi Antiquities Department.

Cremaschi, M. 2002. Late Pleistocene and Holocene climatic changes in the central Sahara: the case study of the southwestern Fezzan, Libya, pp. 65–81 in F. Hassan (ed.) *Drought, Food and Culture: Ecological Change and Food Security in Africa's Later Prehistory.* New York: Kluwer/Plenum.

Cremaschi, M. and S. di Lernia 1999. Holocene climatic changes and cultural dynamics in the Libyan Sahara. *African Archaeological Review* 16: 211–38.

Cremaschi, M. *et al.* 1998. Some insights on the Aterian in the Libyan Sahara: chronology, environment and archaeology. *African Archaeological Review* 15: 261–86.

Crow, T. J. (ed.) 2002. *The Speciation of Modern* Homo sapiens. Oxford: Oxford University Press for The British Academy.

Cruz e Silva, T. 1980. First indications of Early Iron Age in southern Mozambique: Matola IV 1/68, pp. 349–50 in R. E. Leakey and B. A. Ogot (eds.) *Proceedings of the 8th Panafrican Congress of Prehistory.* Nairobi: Leakey Memorial Institute.

Dagan, T. 1956. Le site préhistorique de Tiémassas. *Bulletin de l'Institut Fondamental de l'Afrique Noire* 18B: 432–61.

1972. Les gisements préhistoriques de Tiémassas et de pointe Sarène, Sénégal. pp. 92–4 in H. Hugot (ed.) *Actes du 6e Congrès panafricain de préhistoire.* Chambéry: Les Imprimeries Réunies de Chambéry.

Dahl, G. and A. Hjort 1976. *Having Herds.* Stockholm: University of Stockholm Department of Social Anthropology.

Dalby, D. 1975. The prehistorical implications of Guthrie's Comparative Bantu: problems of internal relationship. *Journal of African History* 16: 481–501.

Daniels, C. M. 1987. Africa, pp. 223–65 in J. Wacher (ed.) *The Roman World,* vol. 1. London: Routledge.

Dark, P. J. C. 1973. *An Introduction to Benin Art and Technology.* Oxford: Clarendon Press.

Darling, P. J. 1984. *Archaeology and History in Southern Nigeria: The Ancient Linear Earthworks of Benin and Ishan.* Oxford: British Archaeological Reports.

Dart, R. A. 1925. *Australopithecus africanus*: the ape-man of South Africa. *Nature* 115: 195–9.

1957. *The Osteodontokeratic Culture of* Australopithecus prometheus. Pretoria: Transvaal Museum.

Darwin, C. 1859. *On the Origin of Species through Natural Selection.* London: Murray.

Dauvois, M. 1981. De la simultanéité des concepts Kombéwa et Levallois dans l'Acheuléen du Maghreb et du Sahara nord-occidental, pp. 313–21 in C. Roubet *et al.* (eds.) *Préhistoire africaine: mélanges offerts au doyen Lionel Balout.* Paris: ADPF.

David, N. 1980. Early Bantu expansion in the context of central African prehistory, pp. 609–44 in L. Bouquiaux (ed.) *L'expansion bantoue.* Paris: SELAF.

1982. Tazunu: megalithic monuments of Central Africa. *Azania* 17: 43–77.

David, N. and C. Kramer 2001. *Ethnoarchaeology in Action.* Cambridge: Cambridge University Press.

David, N. and P. Vidal 1977. The Nana-Mode village site and the prehistory of the Ubangian-speaking peoples. *West African Journal of Archaeology* 7: 17–56.

David, N. *et al.* 1981. Excavations in the southern Sudan, 1979. *Azania* 16: 7–54.

Davies, O. 1964. *The Quaternary of the Coastlands of Guinea.* Glasgow: Jackson.

1967. *West Africa before the Europeans.* London: Methuen.

1971. Excavations at Blackburn. *South African Archaeological Bulletin* 26: 165–78.

Davison, P. and P. Harries 1980. Cotton weaving in south-east Africa: its history and technology. *Textile History* 11: 175–92.

Day, M. H. and C. B. Stringer 1991. Les restes craniens d'Omo-Kibish et leur classification à l'intérieur du genre *Homo*. *L'Anthropologie* 95: 573–94.

Day, M. H. *et al.* 1980. On the status of *Australopithecus afarensis*. *Science* 207: 1102–5.

1991. Les vestiges post-craniens d'Omo I (Kibish). *L'Anthropologie* 95: 595–610.

Deacon, H. J. 1966. Note on the x-ray of two mounted implements from South Africa. *Man (N.S.)* 1: 87–90.

1970. The Acheulian occupation at Amanzi Springs, Uitenhage District, Cape Province. *Annals of the Cape Provincial Museums* 8: 89–189.

1976. *Where Hunters Gathered.* Cape Town: South African Archaeological Society.

1979. Excavations at Boomplaas Cave – a sequence through the Upper Pleistocene and Holocene in South Africa. *World Archaeology* 10: 241–57.

1989. Late Pleistocene palaeoecology and archaeology in the southern Cape, South Africa, pp. 547–64 in P. Mellars and C. Stringer (eds.) *The Human Revolution: Behavioural and Biological Perspectives on the Origins of Modern Humans.* Edinburgh: Edinburgh University Press.

1995. Two late Pleistocene–Holocene archaeological depositories from the southern Cape, South Africa. *South African Archaeological Bulletin* 50: 121–31.

1998. Elandsfontein and Klasies River revisited, pp. 23–8 in N. Ashton *et al. Stone Age Archaeology.* Oxford: Oxbow Books.

Deacon, H. J. and J. Deacon 1999. *Human Beginnings in South Africa.* Cape Town: Philip.

Deacon, H. J. and V. B. Geleijnse 1988. The stratigraphy and sedimentology of the main site sequence, Klasies River, South Africa. *South African Archaeological Bulletin* 42: 5–14.

Deacon, H. J. and R. Schuurman 1992. The origins of modern people: the evidence from Klasies River, pp. 121–9 in G. Bräuer and F. H. Smith (eds.) *Continuity or Replacement: Controversies in* Homo sapiens *Evolution.* Rotterdam: Balkema.

Deacon, H. J. and S. Wurz 2001. Middle Pleistocene populations of southern Africa and the emergence of modern behaviour, pp. 55–63 in L. S. Barham and K. Robson-Brown (eds.) *Human Roots: Africa and Asia in the Middle Pleistocene.* Bristol: Western Academic and Specialist Press.

Deacon, J. 1972. Wilton – a re-assessment after fifty years. *South African Archaeological Bulletin* 27: 10–48.

1974. Patterning in the radiocarbon dates for the Wilton/Smithfield complex in southern Africa. *South African Archaeological Bulletin* 29: 3–18.

1978. Changing patterns in the Late Pleistocene/Early Holocene prehistory of southern Africa as seen from the Nelson Bay Cave stone artifact sequence. *Quaternary Research* 10: 84–111.

1984. *The Later Stone Age of Southernmost Africa.* Oxford: British Archaeological Reports.

1995. An unsolved mystery at the Howieson's Poort name site. *South African Archaeological Bulletin* 50: 110–20.

Deacon, J. and N. Lancaster 1988. *Late Quaternary Palaeoenvironments of Southern Africa.* Oxford: Oxford University Press.

Debénath, A. 2000. Le peuplement préhistorique du Maroc: données récentes et problèmes. *L'Anthropologie* 104: 131–45.

Debénath, A. *et al.* 1986. Stratigraphie, habitat, typologie et devenir de l'Atérien marocain: données récentes. *L'Anthropologie* 90: 233–46.

DeCorse, C. R. 1992. Culture contact, continuity and change on the Gold Coast, 1400–1900. *African Archaeological Review* 10: 159–92.

2001. *An Archaeology of Elmina: Africans and Europeans on the Gold Coast, 1400–1900.* Washington, DC: Smithsonian Institution Press.

Decret, F. and M. Fantar 1981. *L'Afrique du Nord dans l'antiquité: histoire et civilisation.* Paris: Payot.

Deino, A. and S. McBrearty 2002. 40Ar/39Ar chronology for the Kapthurin Formation, Baringo, Kenya. *Journal of Human Evolution* 42: 1–10.

De Langhe, E. *et al.* 1994–5. Plantain in the early Bantu world. *Azania* 29–30: 147–60.

Denbow, J. R. 1984. Cows and kings: a spatial and economic analysis of a hierarchical Early Iron Age settlement system in eastern Botswana, pp. 24–39 in M. Hall *et al.*

(eds.) *Frontiers: Southern African Archaeology Today*. Oxford: British Archaeological Reports.

1986. A new look at the later prehistory of the Kalahari. *Journal of African History* 27: 3–28.

1990. Congo to Kalahari: data and hypotheses about the political economy of the western stream of the Early Iron Age. *African Archaeological Review* 8: 139–76.

Desmedt, C. 1991. Poteries anciennes décorées à la roulette dans la Région des Grands Lacs. *African Archaeological Review* 9: 161–96.

Desplagnes, L. 1903. Etude sur les tumuli du Killi, dans la région de Goundam. *L'Anthropologie* 14: 151–72.

1951. Fouilles du tumulus d'El Oualedji (Soudan). *Bulletin de l'Institut Français d'Afrique Noire* 13: 1159–73.

Dewar, R. E. 1996. The archaeology of the early settlement of Madagascar, pp. 471–86 in J. Reade (ed.) *The Indian Ocean in Antiquity*. London: Kegan Paul.

Dewar, R. E. and H. T. Wright 1993. The culture history of Madagascar. *Journal of World Prehistory* 7: 417–66.

Dibble, H. and O. Bar Yosef (eds.) 1995. *The Definition and Interpretation of Levallois Technology*. Madison, WI: Prehistory Press.

Dickson, D. B. and G.-Y. Gang 2002. Evidence for the emergence of 'modern' behavior in the Middle and Later Stone Age lithic assemblages of Sharmai Rockshelter and Kakura Lelan Rockshelter in the Makogodo Hills of north-central Kenya. *African Archaeological Review* 19: 1–26.

Dombrowski, J. 1970. Preliminary report on excavations in Lalibela and Natchabiet Caves, Begemeder. *Annales d'Ethiopie* 8: 21–9.

1980. Earliest settlements in Ghana: the Kintampo industry, pp. 261–2 in R. E. Leakey and B. A. Ogot (eds.) *Proceedings of the 8th Panafrican Congress of Prehistory*. Nairobi: Leakey Memorial Institute.

Dominguez-Rodrigo, M. *et al.* 2001. Woodworking activities by early humans: a plant residue analysis of Acheulean stone tools from Peninj (Tanzania). *Journal of Human Evolution* 40: 289–99.

Dowson, T. A. 1992. *Rock Engravings of Southern Africa*. Johannesburg: Witwatersrand University Press.

Dowson, T. A. and D. Lewis-Williams (eds.) 1994. *Contested Images: Diversity in Southern African Rock Art Research*. Johannesburg: Witwatersrand University Press.

Dreyer, T. F. 1935. A human skull from Florisbad, Orange Free State. *Verhandelingen der Koninklijke Nederlandse Akademie van Wetenschappen* 38: 3–12.

Dualeh, A. 1996. *The Origins and Development of Mogadishu AD 1000–1850: A Study in Urban Growth along the Benadir Coast of Southern Somalia*. Uppsala: Uppsala University.

Dunham, D. 1982. *Excavations at Kerma*, vol. 6. Boston, MA: Museum of Fine Arts.

Dupont, L. M. *et al.* 2000. Vegetation changes in equatorial West Africa: time-slices for the last 150 ka. *Palaeogeography, Palaeoclimatology, Palaeoecology* 155: 95–122.

Dupuy, C. 1993. Primauté du masculin dans les arts gravés du Sahara, pp. 193–207 in R. Chenorkian (ed.) *L'homme méditerranéen: mélanges offerts à Gabriel Camps*. Aix-en-Provence: Publications de l'Université.

Dutour, O. 1989. *Hommes fossiles du Sahara: peuplements holocènes du Mali septentrional*. Paris: CNRS.

Edwards, A. W. F. 2003. Human genetic diversity: Lewontin's fallacy. *BioEssays* 25: 798–801.

Edwards, D. N. 1996. *The Archaeology of the Meroitic State: New Perspectives on its Social and Political Organisation*. Oxford: British Archaeological Reports.

Eggert, M. K. H. 1987a. Imbonga and Batalimo: ceramic evidence for early settlement of the equatorial forest. *African Archaeological Review* 5: 129–45.

1987b. On the alleged complexity of early and recent smelting in Africa. *Journal of Field Archaeology* 14: 377–82.

1992. The central African rain forest: historical speculation and archaeological facts. *World Archaeology* 24: 1–24.

Ehret, C. 1973. Patterns of Bantu and Central Sudanic settlement in central and southern Africa. *Transafrican Journal of History* 3: 1–71.

1974. *Ethiopians and East Africans*. Nairobi: East African Publishing House.

1980. On the antiquity of agriculture in Ethiopia. *Journal of African History* 20: 161–77.

1982. The first spread of food production to southern Africa, pp. 158–81 in C. Ehret and M. Posnansky (eds.) *The Archaeological and Linguistic Reconstruction of African History*. Berkeley: University of California Press.

1993. Nilo-Saharans and the Saharo-Sudanese neolithic, pp. 104–25 in T. Shaw *et al.* (eds.) *The Archaeology of Africa: Foods, Metals and Towns*. London: Routledge.

1998. *An African Classical Age*. Charlottesville: University Press of Virginia.

2001. Bantu expansions: re-envisioning a central problem of early African History. *International Journal of African Historical Studies* 34: 5–41.

2002. *Civilizations of Africa*. London: Currey.

2003. Language family expansions: broadening our understandings of cause from an African perspective, pp. 163–76 in P. Bellwood and C. Renfrew (eds.) *Examining the Farming/Language Dispersal Hypothesis*. Cambridge: McDonald Institute for Archaeological Research.

Ehret, C. and M. Posnansky (eds.) 1982. *The Archaeological and Linguistic Reconstruction of African History*. Berkeley: University of California Press.

Elenga, H. *et al.* 1994. Pollen evidence of Late Quaternary vegetation and inferred climatic changes in Congo. *Palaeogeography, Palaeoclimatology, Palaeoecology* 109: 345–56.

Eloff, J. F. and A. Meyer 1981. The Greefswald sites, pp. 7–22 in E. A. Voigt (ed.) *Guide to Archaeological Sites in the Northern and Eastern Transvaal*. Pretoria: Transvaal Museum for South African Association of Archaeologists.

Elphick, R. 1985. *Khoikhoi and the Founding of White South Africa*. Johannesburg: Ravan Press.

Emery, W. B. and L. P. Kirwan 1938. *The Royal Tombs of Ballana and Qustul*. Cairo: Government Printer.

Ennouchi, E. 1962. Un néanderthalien: l'homme du Jebel Irhoud (Maroc). *L'Anthropologie* 66: 279–99.

Epstein, H. 1971. *The Origin of the Domestic Animals of Africa*. New York: Africana.

d'Errico, F. *et al.* 2001. An engraved bone fragment from c. 75 kyr Middle Stone Age levels at Blombos Cave, South Africa: implications for the origin of symbolism. *Antiquity* 75: 309–18.

Ervedosa, C. 1980. *Arqueologia Angolana*. Lisbon: Ediçoes 70.

Evernden, J. F. and G. H. Curtis 1965. The potassium-argon dating of late Caenozoic rocks in East Africa and Italy. *Current Anthropology* 6: 343–64.

Evers, T. M. 1982. Excavations at the Lydenburg Heads site, eastern Transvaal, South Africa. *South African Archaeological Bulletin* 37: 16–33.

Eyo, E. 1974. Odo Ogbe Street and Lafogido: contrasting archaeological sites at Ile Ife, Western Nigeria. *West African Journal of Archaeology* 4: 99–109.

Eyo, E. and F. Willett 1980. *Treasures of Ancient Nigeria*. London: Royal Academy of Arts.

Fagan, B. M. 1967. *Iron Age Cultures in Zambia*, vol. 1. London: Chatto and Windus.

Fagan, B. M. and F. L. Van Noten 1971. *The Hunter-Gatherers of Gwisho*. Tervuren: Musée Royal de l'Afrique Centrale.

Fagan, B. M. and J. Yellen 1968. Ivuna: ancient salt-working in southern Tanzania. *Azania* 3: 1–43.

Fagan, B. M. *et al.* 1969. *Iron Age Cultures in Zambia*, vol. 2. London: Chatto and Windus.

Fagg, A. 1972. A preliminary report on an occupation site in the Nok Valley, Nigeria. *West African Journal of Archaeology* 2: 75–9.

Fagg, B. 1979. *Nok Terracottas*. London: Ethnographica.

Fagg, B. *et al.* 1972. Four papers on the Rop rockshelter. *West African Journal of Archaeology* 2: 1–38.

Fantar, M. 1993. *Carthage: approche d'une civilisation*. Tunis.

Fattovich, R. 1990. Remarks on the Pre-Aksumite period in northern Ethiopia. *Journal of Ethiopian Studies* 23: 3–33.

   1994. The contribution of the recent field work at Kassala (eastern Sudan) to Ethiopian archaeology. *Etudes Ethiopiennes* 1: 43–51.

   1996. The Afro-Arabian circuit: contacts between the Horn of Africa and southern Arabia in the third–second millennia BC, pp. 395–402 in L. Krzyzaniak *et al.* (eds.) *Inter-regional Contacts in the Later Prehistory of North-Eastern Africa*. Poznan: Poznan Archaeological Museum.

Fattovich, R. *et al.* 2000. *The Aksum Archaeological Area: A Preliminary Assessment*. Naples: Istituto Universitario Orientale.

Feathers, J. K. and D. A. Bush 2000. Luminescence dating of Middle Stone Age deposits at Die Kelders. *Journal of Human Evolution* 38: 91–119.

Feely, J. M. 1987. *The Early Farmers of Transkei, Southern Africa*. Oxford: British Archaeological Reports.

Fiedler, L. and J. Preuss 1985. Stone tools from the inner Zaïre Basin (Région de l'Equateur, Zaïre). *African Archaeological Review* 3: 179–87.

Finneran, N. 2000. A new perspective on the LSA of the N. Ethiopian highlands: excavations at Anqqer Baahti, Aksum, 1996. *Azania* 35: 21–51.

   2002. *The Archaeology of Christianity in Africa*. Stroud: Tempus.

Fleisher, J. and A. Laviolette 1999. Elusive wattle-and-daub: finding the elusive majority in the archaeology of the Swahili. *Azania* 34: 87–108.

Flight, C. 1975. Gao 1972, first interim report: a preliminary investigation of the cemetery at Sane. *West African Journal of Archaeology* 5: 81–90.

Fock, G. J. 1968. Rooidam, a sealed site of the First Intermediate. *South African Journal of Science* 64: 153–9.

Foley, R. A. 1991. How many species of hominid should there be? *Journal of Human Evolution* 20: 413–29.

   1994. Speciation, extinction and climatic change in hominid evolution. *Journal of Human Evolution* 26: 275–89.

2002. Parallel tracks in time: human evolution and archaeology, pp. 3–42 in B. Cunliffe *et al.* (eds.) *Archaeology: The Widening Debate*. Oxford: Oxford University Press for The British Academy.

Foley, R. A. and M. M. Lahr 1997. Mode 3 technologies and the evolution of modern humans. *Cambridge Archaeological Journal* 7: 3–36.

Fosbrooke, H. A. *et al.* 1950. Tanganyika rock paintings. *Tanganyika Notes and Records* 29: 1–61.

Fouché, L. (ed.) 1937. *Mapungubwe: Ancient Bantu Civilisation on the Limpopo*. Cambridge: Cambridge University Press.

Frank, T. *et al.* 2001. The Chaîne de Gobnangou, southeast Burkina Faso: archaeological, archaeobotanical, archaeozoological and geomorphological studies. *Beiträge zur Allgemeinen und Vergleichenden Archäologie* 21: 127–90.

Fraser, P. M. 1972. *Ptolemaic Alexandria*. Oxford: Clarendon Press.

Freeman-Grenville, G. S. P. 1962. *The East African Coast: Select Documents from the First to the Earlier Nineteenth Century*. Oxford: Clarendon Press.

Gabunia, L. *et al.* 2000. Earliest Pleistocene hominid cranial remains from Dmanisi, Republic of Georgia: taxonomy, geological setting and age. *Science* 288: 1019–25.

Gagneux, P. *et al.* 1999. Mitochondrial sequences show diverse evolutionary histories of African hominids. *Proceedings of the National Academy of Sciences (U.S.A.)* 96: 5077–82.

Gallay, A. 1966. Quelques gisements néolithiques du Sahara malien. *Journal de la Sociétédes Africanistes* 36: 167–208.

2001. Diffusion ou invention: un faux débat pour l'archéologie? *Mediterranean Archaeology* 14: 13–24.

Gallay, A. *et al.* 1982. Mbolop Tobé (Santhiou Kohel, Sénégal): contribution à la connaissance du mégalithisme sénégambien. *Archives Suisses d'Anthropologie Générale* 46: 217–59.

1990. *Hamdallahi, capitale de l'empire peul du Massina, Mali.* Stuttgart: Steiner.

Gamble, C. and G. Marshall 2001. The shape of handaxes: the structure of the Acheulian world, pp. 19–27 in S. Milliken and J. Cook (eds.) *A Very Remote Period Indeed: Papers on the Palaeolithic Presented to Derek Roe*. Oxford: Oxbow.

Gamble, C. and O. Soffer (eds.) 1990. *The World at 18000 BP: Low Latitudes*. London: Unwin Hyman.

Garcea, E. A. A. 1993. *Cultural Dynamics in the Saharo-Sudanese Prehistory*. Rome: Gruppo Editoriale Internazionale.

(ed.) 2001. *Uan Tabu in the Settlement History of the Libyan Sahara*. Florence: Edizioni all'Insegna del Giglio.

Garlake, P. S. 1973a. *Great Zimbabwe*. London: Thames and Hudson.

1973b. Excavations at the Nhunguza and Ruanga Ruins in Northern Mashonaland. *South African Archaeological Bulletin* 27: 107–43.

1974. Excavations at Obalara's Land, Ife: an interim report. *West African Journal of Archaeology* 4: 111–48.

1976. An investigation of Manekweni, Mozambique. *Azania* 11: 25–47.

1977. Excavations on the Woye Asiri family land in Ife, western Nigeria. *West African Journal of Archaeology* 7: 57–96.

1978a. *The Kingdoms of Africa*. Oxford: Elsevier-Phaidon.

1978b. Pastoralism and Zimbabwe. *Journal of African History* 19: 479–93.

1982. Prehistory and ideology in Zimbabwe. *Africa* 52 (3): 1–19.

1995. *The Hunter's Vision: The Prehistoric Art of Zimbabwe*. London: British Museum Press.

2002. *Early Art and Architecture of Africa*. Oxford: Oxford University Press.

Gau, F. C. 1822. *Antiquités de la Nubie, ou monuments inédits des bords du Nil*. Stuttgart: Cotta.

Gautier, A. 1987. Prehistoric men and cattle in North Africa: a dearth of data and a surfeit of models, pp. 163–87 in A. E. Close (ed.) *The Prehistory of Arid North Africa*. Dallas, TX: Southern Methodist University Press.

2002. The evidence for the earliest livestock in North Africa: or adventures with large bovids, ovicaprids, dogs and pigs, pp. 195–207 in F. Hassan (ed.) *Drought, Food and Culture: Ecological Change and Food Security in Africa's Later Prehistory*. New York: Kluwer/Plenum.

Geraadś, D. *et al.* 1986. The Pleistocene hominid site of Ternifine, Algeria: new results on the environment, age and human industries. *Quaternary Research* 25: 380–6.

Gerster, G. 1970. *Churches in Rock: Early Christian Art in Ethiopia*. London: Phaidon.

Gibert, J. *et al.* 1998. Two 'Oldowan' assemblages in the Plio-Pleistocene deposits of the Orce region, southeast Spain. *Antiquity* 72: 17–25.

Gibson, K. R. and T. Ingold (eds.) 1993. *Tools, Language and Cognition in Human Evolution*. Cambridge: Cambridge University Press.

Gifford-Gonzalez, D. 1998. Early pastoralists in East Africa: ecological and social dimensions. *Journal of Anthropological Archaeology* 17: 166–200.

2000. Animal disease challenges to the emergence of pastoralism in sub-Saharan Africa. *African Archaeological Review* 17: 95–139.

2003. The fauna from Ele Bor: evidence for the persistence of foragers into the later Holocene of arid North Kenya. *African Archaeological Review* 20: 81–119.

Goodman, M. *et al.* 1990. Primate evolution at the DNA level and a classification of the hominoids. *Journal of Molecular Evolution* 30: 260–6.

Goren-Inbar, N. and I. Saragusti 1996. An Acheulian biface assemblage from Gesher Benot Ya'aqov, Israel: indications of African affinities. *Journal of Field Archaeology* 23: 15–30.

Gowlett, J. A. J. 1978. Kilombe: an Acheulian site complex in Kenya, pp. 337–60 in W. W. Bishop (ed.) *Geological Background to Fossil Man*. Edinburgh: Edinburgh University Press.

1986. Culture and conceptualisation: the Oldowan–Acheulian gradient, pp. 243–60 in G. Bailey and P. Callow (eds.) *Stone Age Prehistory*. Cambridge: Cambridge University Press.

1996. Mental abilities of early *Homo*, pp. 191–215 in P. Mellars and K. Gibson (eds.) *Modelling the Early Human Mind*. Cambridge: McDonald Institute for Archaeological Research.

Gowlett, J. A. J. *et al.* 1981. Early archaeological sites, hominid remains and traces of fire from Chesowanja, Kenya. *Nature* 294: 125–9.

Gramly, R. M. 1976. Upper Pleistocene archaeological occurrences at site GvJm/22, Lukenya Hill, Kenya. *Man (N.S.)* 11: 319–44.

Gramly, R. M. and G. P. Rightmire 1973. A fragmentary cranium and dated later Stone Age assemblage from Lukenya Hill, Kenya. *Man (N.S.)* 8: 571–9.

Greenberg, J. H. 1963. *The Languages of Africa*. The Hague: Mouton.

Grigson, C. 1991. An African origin for African cattle? – some archaeological evidence. *African Archaeological Review* 9: 119–44.

1996. Early cattle around the Indian Ocean, pp. 41–74 in J. Reade (ed.) *The Indian Ocean in Antiquity*. London: Kegan Paul.

2000. *Bos africanus* (Brehm)? Notes on the archaeozoology of the native cattle of Africa, pp. 38–60 in R. M. Blench and K. C. MacDonald (eds.) *The Origins and Development of African Livestock*. London: UCL Press.

Grine, F. E. (ed.) 1988. *The Evolutionary History of the Robust Australopithecines*. New York: Aldine de Gruyter.

2000. Middle Stone Age human fossils from Die Kelders Cave 1, Western Cape Province, South Africa. *Journal of Human Evolution* 38: 129–45.

Grine, F. E. and C. S. Henshilwood 2002. Additional human remains from Blombos Cave, South Africa. *Journal of Human Evolution* 42: 293–302.

Grine, F. E. *et al.* 2000. Human remains from Blombos Cave, South Africa (1997–98 excavations). *Journal of Human Evolution* 38: 755–65.

Gronenborn, D. 1998. Archaeological and ethnohistorical investigations along the southern fringes of Lake Chad, 1993–96. *African Archaeological Review* 15: 225–59.

Grove, A. T. 1993. Africa's climate in the Holocene, pp. 32–42 in T. Shaw *et al.* (eds.) *The Archaeology of Africa: Foods, Metals and Towns*. London: Routledge.

Grün, R. and P. B. Beaumont 2001. Border Cave revisited: a revised ESR chronology. *Journal of Human Evolution* 40: 467–82.

Grün, R. *et al.* 1996. Direct dating of Florisbad hominid. *Nature* 382: 500–1.

de Grunne, B. 1999. *The Birth of Art in Africa: Nok Statuary in Nigeria*. Paris: Biro.

Guérin, C. *et al.* 1996. Mission archéologique et paléontologique dans le Pléistocene ancien d'Oubédiyeh (Israel): résultats 1992–94. *Comptes-rendus des Séances de l'Académie des Sciences de Paris, sér. 2A*, 322: 709–12.

Gutierrez, M. 1996. *L'art pariétal de l'Angola*. Paris: L'Harmattan.

Haaland, R. 1987. *Socio-Economic Differentiation in the Neolithic Sudan*. Oxford: British Archaeological Reports.

1992. Fish, pots and grain: early and mid-Holocene adaptations in the central Sudan. *African Archaeological Review* 10: 43–69.

Haaland, R. and A. Abdul Magid (eds.) 1995. *Aqualithic Sites along the Rivers Nile and Atbara, Sudan*. Bergen: Alma Mater.

Haaland, R. and P. Shinnie (eds.) 1985. *African Iron Working: Ancient and Traditional*. Oslo: Norwegian University Press.

Hahn, W. 1999. Symbols of pagan and Christian worship on Aksumite coins. *Nubica et Aethiopica* 4/5: 43–66.

Hall, M. 1983. Tribes, traditions and numbers: the American model in southern African Iron Age studies. *South African Archaeological Bulletin* 38: 51–61.

1987. *The Changing Past: Farmers, Kings and Traders in Southern Africa*. Cape Town: Philip.

2002. Timeless time: Africa and the world, pp. 439–64 in B. Cunliffe *et al.* (eds.) *Archaeology: The Widening Debate*. Oxford: Oxford University Press for The British Academy.

Hall, S. L. 2000. Burial sequence in the Later Stone Age of the Eastern Cape Province, South Africa. *South African Archaeological Bulletin* 55: 137–46.

Hall, S. L. and J. N. F. Binneman 1987. Later Stone Age burial variability in the Cape: a social interpretation. *South African Archaeological Bulletin* 42: 140–52.

Hall, S. L. and B. W. Smith 2000. Empowering places: rock shelters and ritual control in farmer–forager interaction in the Northern Province, South Africa. *South African Archaeological Society Goodwin Series* 8: 30–46.

Hamilton, A. C. and D. Taylor 1991. History of climate and forests in tropical Africa during the last 8 million years. *Climatic Change* 19: 65–78.

Hanisch, E. O. M. 1981. Schroda: a Zhizo site in the northern Transvaal, pp. 37–54 in E. A. Voigt (ed.) *Guide to Archaeological Sites in the Northern and Eastern Transvaal*. Pretoria: Transvaal Museum for the Southern African Association of Archaeologists.

Hansen, C. L. and C. M. Keller 1971. Environment and activity patterning at Isimila *karongo*, Tanzania. *American Anthropologist* 73: 1201–11.

Harlan, J. R. 1969. Ethiopia: a centre of diversity. *Economic Botany* 23: 309–14.

1971. Agricultural origins: centers and non-centers. *Science* 174: 468–74.

1989. Wild grass harvesting in the Sahara and sub-Sahara, pp. 79–95 in D. R. Harris and G. C. Hillman (eds.) *Foraging and Farming*. London: Unwin Hyman.

1992. Indigenous African agriculture, pp. 59–70 in C. W. Cowan and P. J. Watson (eds.) *The Origins of Agriculture*. Washington, DC: Smithsonian Institution Press.

Harper, P. T. 1997. The Middle Stone Age sequences at Rose Cottage Cave: a search for continuity and discontinuity. *South African Journal of Science* 93: 470–5.

Harrell, J. 1999. Ancient stone quarries at the Third and Fourth Nile Cataracts, northern Sudan. *Sudan and Nubia* 3: 21–7.

Harris, J. M. *et al.* 1988. Pliocene and Pleistocene hominid-bearing sites from west of Lake Turkana, Kenya. *Science* 239: 27–33.

Harris, J. R. (ed.) 1971. *The Legacy of Egypt*. Oxford: Clarendon Press.

Harris, J. W. K. 1983. Cultural beginnings: Plio/Pleistocene archaeological occurrences from the Afar, Ethiopia. *African Archaeological Review* 1: 3–31.

Harris, J. W. K. and G. L. Isaac 1976. The Karari industry. *Nature* 262: 102–7.

Harris, J. W. K. *et al.* 1987. Late Pliocene hominid occupation of the Senga 5A site, Zaïre. *Journal of Human Evolution* 16: 701–28.

Harvey, P. and A. T. Grove 1982. A prehistoric source of the Nile. *Geographical Journal* 148: 327–36.

Hassan, F. A. 1980. Prehistoric settlements along the main Nile, pp. 421–50 in M. A. J. Williams and H. Faure (eds.) *The Sahara and the Nile*. Rotterdam: Balkema.

1986a. Chronology of the Khartoum Mesolithic and Neolithic and related sites in the Sudan: statistical analysis and comparisons with Egypt. *African Archaeological Review* 4: 83–102.

1986b. Desert environment and origins of agriculture in Egypt. *Norwegian Archaeological Review* 19: 63–76.

1988a. The Predynastic of Egypt. *Journal of World Prehistory* 2: 135–85.

1988b. Holocene Nile floods and their implications for the origins of Egyptian agriculture, pp. 1–17 in J. R. F. Bower and D. Lubell (eds.) *Prehistoric Cultures and Environments in the Late Quaternary of Africa*. Oxford: British Archaeological Reports.

1997. Holocene palaeoclimates of Africa. *African Archaeological Review* 14: 213–30.

(ed.) 2002. *Drought, Food and Culture: Ecological Change and Food Security in Africa's Later Prehistory*. New York: Kluwer/Plenum.

Hawass, Z. *et al.* 1988. Chronology, sediments and subsistence at Merimda Beni Salama. *Journal of Egyptian Archaeology* 74: 31–8.

Hay, R. L. 1976. *The Geology of Olduvai Gorge.* Berkeley: University of California Press.

Hays, T. R. 1974. Wavy line pottery: an element of Nilotic diffusion. *South African Archaeological Bulletin* 29: 27–32.

Heine, B. 1978. The Sam languages. *Afro-Asiatic Linguistics* 6 (2): 1–93.

Heine, B. and D. Nurse (eds.) 2000. *African Languages: An Introduction.* Cambridge: Cambridge University Press.

Heinzelin, J. de 1957. *Les Fouilles d'Ishango.* Brussels: Institut des Parcs Nationaux du Congo Belge.

Heinzelin, J. de *et al.* 1999. Environment and behavior of 2.5-million-year-old Bouri hominids. *Science* 284: 625–9.

  (eds.) 2000. *The Acheulean and the Plio-Pleistocene Deposits of the Middle Awash Valley, Ethiopia.* Tervuren: Musée Royal de l'Afrique Centrale.

Helgren, D. M. and A. S. Brooks 1983. Geoarchaeology at Gi, a Middle Stone Age and Later Stone Age site in the north-west Kalahari. *Journal of Archaeological Science* 10: 181–97.

Hendey, Q. B. 1981. Palaeoecology of the Late Tertiary fossil occurrences in 'E' Quarry, Langebaanweg, South Africa, and a reinterpretation of their geological context. *Annals of the South African Museum* 84: 1–104.

Henige, D. P. 1974. *The Chronology of Oral Tradition.* Oxford: Clarendon Press.

Henshilwood, C. and J. Sealy 1997. Bone artefacts from the Middle Stone Age at Blombos Cave, Southern Cape, South Africa. *Current Anthropology* 38: 890–5.

Henshilwood, C. S. *et al.* 2001a. Blombos Cave, southern Cape, South Africa: preliminary report on the 1992–99 excavations of the Middle Stone Age levels. *Journal of Archaeological Science* 28: 421–48.

  2001b. An early bone tool industry from the Middle Stone Age at Blombos Cave, South Africa: implications for the origins of modern human behaviour, symbolism and language. *Journal of Human Evolution* 41: 631–78.

  2002. Emergence of modern human behaviour: Middle Stone Age engravings from South Africa. *Science* 295: 1278–80.

Herbert, E. W. 1984. *Red Gold of Africa: Copper in Precolonial History and Culture.* Madison: University of Wisconsin Press.

  1993. *Iron, Gender and Power: Rituals of Transformation in African Societies.* Bloomington: Indiana University Press.

  1996. Metals and power at Great Zimbabwe, pp. 641–7 in G. Pwiti and R. Soper (eds.) *Aspects of African Archaeology.* Harare: University of Zimbabwe Publications.

d'Hertefelt, M. 1965. The Rwanda of Rwanda, pp. 405–40 in J. L. Gibbs (ed.) *Peoples in Africa.* New York: Holt, Rinehart and Winston.

Hiernaux, J. 1968. *La diversité humaine en Afrique sub-saharienne.* Brussels: Institut de Sociologie, Université Libre de Bruxelles.

Hiernaux, J. and E. Maquet 1968. *L'Age du Fer à Kibiro, Uganda.* Tervuren: Musée Royal de l'Afrique Centrale.

Hiernaux, J. *et al.* 1972. Le cimetière protohistorique de Katoto, Vallée du Lualaba, Congo-Kinshasa, pp. 148–58 in H. Hugot (ed.) *Actes du 6e Congrès panafricain de préhistoire.* Chambéry: Les Imprimeries Réunies de Chambéry.

Hillman, G. C. 1989. Late Palaeolithic plant foods from Wadi Kubbaniya in Upper Egypt, pp. 207–39 in D. R. Harris and G. C. Hillman (eds.) *Foraging and Farming*. London: Unwin-Hyman.

Hitti, P. K. 1963. *History of the Arabs*. London: Macmillan.

Hoffman, M. A. 1980. *Egypt before the Pharaohs*. London: Routledge.

Holden, C. J. 2002. Bantu language trees reflect the spread of farming across sub-Saharan Africa: a maximum-parsimony analysis. *Proceedings of the Royal Society of London B* 269: 793–9.

Holl, A. 1985a. Subsistence patterns of the Dhar Tichitt neolithic, Mauretania. *African Archaeological Review* 3: 151–62.

1985b. Background to the Ghana Empire: archaeological investigation on the transition to statehood in the Dhar Tichitt region, Mauretania. *Journal of Anthropological Archaeology* 4: 73–115.

1989. Habitat et sociétés préhistoriques du Dhar Tichitt (Mauritanie). *Sahara* 2: 49–60.

1995. Pathways to elderhood. *Origini* 18: 69–113.

2002. *The Land of Houlouf: genesis of a Chadic polity 1900 BC–AD 1800*. Ann Arbor: University of Michigan Museum of Anthropology.

Horton, M. C. 1987. Early Muslim trading settlements on the East African coast: new evidence from Shanga. *Antiquaries Journal* 67: 290–323.

1990. The *Periplus* and East Africa. *Azania* 25: 95–9.

1996a. Early maritime trade and settlement along the coasts of eastern Africa, pp. 439–59 in J. Reade (ed.) *The Indian Ocean in Antiquity*. London: Kegan Paul.

1996b. *Shanga: The Archaeology of a Muslim Trading Community on the Coast of East Africa*. London: British Institute in Eastern Africa.

Horton, M. and J. Middleton 2000. *The Swahili: The Social Landscape of a Mercantile Society*. Oxford: Blackwell.

Hours, F. 1973. Le Middle Stone Age de Melka-Kunture: résultats acquis en 1971. *Documents pour Servir à l'Histoire des Civilisations Ethiopiennes* 4: 19–29.

Howell, F. C. 1976. An overview of the Pliocene and earlier Pleistocene of the lower Omo Basin, southern Ethiopia, pp. 227–68 in G. L. Isaac and E. McCown (eds.) *Human Origins: Louis Leakey and the East African Evidence*. Menlo Park, CA: Benjamin.

1982. Origins and evolution of African Hominidae, pp. 70–156 in J. D. Clark (ed.) *Cambridge History of Africa*, vol. 1. Cambridge: Cambridge University Press.

Howell, F. C. *et al.* 1962. Isimila: an Acheulian occupation site in the Iringa highlands, pp. 43–80 in G. Mortelmans (ed.) *Actes du 4e Congrès panafricain de Préhistoire*. Tervuren: Musée Royal de l'Afrique Centrale.

1987. Depositional environments, archaeological occurrences and hominids from Members E and F of the Shungura Formation (Omo Basin, Ethiopia). *Journal of Human Evolution* 16: 665–700.

Hublin, J.-J. 1985. Human fossils from the North African Middle Pleistocene and the origin of *Homo sapiens*, pp. 283–8 in E. Delson (ed.) *Ancestors: The Hard Evidence*. New York: Liss.

1993. Recent human evolution in northwestern Africa, pp. 118–31 in M. J. Aitken *et al.* (eds.) *The Origin of Modern Humans and the Impact of Chronometric Dating*. Princeton, NJ: Princeton University Press.

2001. Northwestern African Middle Pleistocene hominids and their bearing on the emergence of *Homo sapiens*, pp. 99–121 in L. S. Barham and K. Robson-Brown (eds.) *Human Roots: Africa and Asia in the Middle Pleistocene*. Bristol: Western Academic and Specialist Press.

Huffman, T. N. 1974. *The Leopard's Kopje Tradition*. Salisbury: National Museums of Rhodesia.

1978. The origins of Leopard's Kopje: an 11th-century Difaqane. *Arnoldia* 8: no. 23.

1982. Archaeology and ethnohistory of the African Iron Age. *Annual Review of Anthropology* 11: 133–50.

1984a. Expressive space in the Zimbabwe culture. *Man (N.S.)* 19: 593–612.

1984b. Leopard's Kopje and the nature of the Iron Age in Bantu Africa. *Zimbabwea* 1: 28–35.

1986. Iron Age settlement patterns and the origins of class distinction in southern Africa. *Advances in World Archaeology* 5: 291–338.

1989. *Iron Age Migrations*. Johannesburg: Witwatersrand University Press.

1993. Broederstroom and the Central Cattle Pattern. *South African Journal of Science* 89: 220–6.

1994. Toteng pottery and the origins of Bambata. *South African Field Archaeology* 3: 3–9.

1996a. Archaeological evidence for climatic change during the last 2000 years in southern Africa. *Quaternary International* 33: 55–60.

1996b. *Snakes and Crocodiles: Power and Symbolism in Ancient Zimbabwe*. Johannesburg: Witwatersrand University Press.

1998. The antiquity of *lobola. South African Archaeological Bulletin* 53: 57–62.

2001. The Central Cattle Pattern and interpreting the past. *Southern African Humanities* 13: 19–35.

Huffman, T. N. and E. O. M. Hanisch 1987. Settlement hierarchies in the northern Transvaal: Zimbabwe ruins and Venda history. *African Studies* 46: 79–116.

Huffman, T. N. and J. C. Vogel 1991. The chronology of Great Zimbabwe. *South African Archaeological Bulletin* 46: 61–70.

Humphreys, A. J. B. 1970. The role of raw material and the concept of the Fauresmith. *South African Archaeological Bulletin* 35: 139–44.

Iliffe, J. 1995. *Africans: The History of a Continent*. Cambridge: Cambridge University Press.

Ingold, T. 1988. Notes on the foraging mode of production, pp. 269–85 in T. Ingold *et al.* (eds.) *Hunters and Gathers: History, Evolution and Social Change*. Oxford: Berg.

Inskeep, R. R. 1962. The age of the Kondoa rock paintings in the light of recent excavations at Kisese II rock shelter, pp. 249–56 in G. Mortelmans (ed.) *Actes du 4e Congrès panafricain de préhistoire*. Tervuren: Musée Royal de l'Afrique Centrale.

1987. *Nelson Bay Cave, Cape Province, South Africa: The Holocene Levels*. Oxford: British Archaeological Reports.

Insoll, T. 1996. *Islam, Archaeology and History, a Complex Relationship: The Gao Region (Mali) ca. AD 900–1250*. Oxford: British Archaeological Reports.

1997. Iron Age Gao: an archaeological contribution. *Journal of African History* 38: 1–30.

2000. *Urbanism, Archaeology and Trade: Further Observations on the Gao Region (Mali)*. Oxford: British Archaeological Reports.

2003. *The Archaeology of Islam in Sub-Saharan Africa*. Cambridge: Cambridge University Press.

Insoll, T. and T. Shaw 1997. Gao and Igbo-Ukwu: beads, inter-regional trade, and beyond. *African Archaeological Review* 14: 9–23.

Irish, J. D. 1994. The African dental complex: diagnostic morphological variants of modern sub-Saharan populations. *American Journal of Physical Anthropology* 18: 112.

Irish, J. D. and C. G. Turner 1990. West African dental affinity of Late Pleistocene Nubians. *Homo* 41: 42–53.

Isaac, G. L. 1967. The stratigraphy of the Peninj Group, pp. 229–57 in W. W. Bishop and J. D. Clark (eds.) *Background to Evolution in Africa*. Chicago: University of Chicago Press.

1972. Chronology and the tempo of cultural change during the Pleistocene, pp. 381–430 in W. W. Bishop and J. A. Miller (eds.) *Calibration of Hominoid Evolution*. Edinburgh: Edinburgh University Press.

1976. Stages of cultural elaboration in the Pleistocene: possible archaeological indicators of the development of language capabilities. *Annals of the New York Academy of Sciences* 280: 275–88.

1977. *Olorgesailie*. Chicago: University of Chicago Press.

1978. The food-sharing behaviour of protohuman hominids. *Scientific American* 238 (4): 90–9.

(ed.) 1997. *Koobi Fora Research Project*, vol. 5: *Plio-Pleistocene Archaeology*. Oxford: Clarendon Press.

Isaac, G. L. and G. H. Curtis 1974. The age of early Acheulian industries from the Peninj group, Tanzania. *Nature* 249: 62–7.

Isaac, G. L. and J. W. K. Harris 1978. Archaeology, pp. 64–85 in M. G. and R. E. Leakey (eds.) *Koobi Fora Research Project*, vol. 1. Oxford: Clarendon Press.

Isaac, G. L. *et al.* 1972. Stratigraphic and archaeological studies in the Lake Nakuru basin, Kenya. *Palaeoecology of Africa* 6: 225–32.

1976. Archaeological evidence from the Koobi Fora formation, pp. 533–51 in Y. Coppens *et al.* (eds.) *Earliest Man and Environments in the Lake Rudolf Basin*. Chicago: Chicago University Press.

Jablonski, N. G. and L. C. Aiello (eds.) 1998. *The Origin and Diversification of Language*. San Francisco: California Academy of Sciences.

Jacobsen, L. 1984. Comments on Bambata pottery. *South African Archaeological Bulletin* 39: 142.

James, T. G. H. (ed.) 1979. *An Introduction to Ancient Egypt*. London: British Museum.

Jean, E. 2001. Le fer chez les Hittites: au bilan des donnés archéologiques. *Mediterranean Archaeology* 14: 163–88.

Jemkur, J. F. 1992. *Aspects of the Nok Culture*. Zaria: Ahmadu Bello University Press.

Jodin, A. 1959. Les grottes d'El Khril à Achakar, Province de Tangier. *Bulletins d'Archéologie Marocain* 3: 249–313.

Johanson, D. C. and M. A. Edey 1981. *Lucy, the Beginnings of Humankind*. London: Granada.

Johanson, D. C. and T. White 1979. A systematic assessment of early African hominids. *Science* 203: 321–30.

Johanson, D. C. *et al.* 1987. New partial skeleton of *Homo habilis* from Olduvai Gorge, Tanzania. *Nature* 327: 205–9.

Joire, J. 1943. Archaeological discoveries in Senegal. *Man* 43: 49–52.

  1955. Découvertes archéologiques dans la région de Rao (Bas-Sénégal). *Bulletin de l'Institut Français d'Afrique Noire* 17B: 249–333.

Jones, M. 2001. *The Molecule Hunt.* Harmondsworth: Penguin Books.

Jones, P. R. 1980. Experimental butchery with modern stone tools and its relevance for Palaeolithic archaeology. *World Archaeology* 12: 153–75.

Joussaume, R. 1974. *Le mégalithisme en Ethiopie: monuments funéraires protohistoriques du Harar.* Paris: Museum National d'Histoire Naturelle.

  1995. *Tiya: l'Ethiopie des mégalithes.* Paris: Association des Publications Chauvinoises.

Juma, A. M. 1996. The Swahili and the Mediterranean world: pottery of the late Roman period from Zanzibar. *Antiquity* 70: 147–54.

Kalb, J. E. *et al.* 1982. Preliminary geology, paleontology and paleoecology of a Sangoan site at Andalee, Middle Awash Valley, Ethiopia. *Journal of Archaeological Science* 9: 349–63.

Karega-Munene 1996. The East African Neolithic: an alternative view. *African Archaeological Review* 13: 247–54.

  2002. *Holocene Foragers, Fishers and Herders of Western Kenya.* Oxford: British Archaeological Reports.

Katanekwa, N. 1981. Upper Zambezi Iron Age Research Project: phase II preliminary report. *Archaeologia Zambiana* 20: 12–14.

Kaufulu, Z. M. and N. Stern 1987. The first stone artefacts found *in situ* within the Plio-Pleistocene Chiwondo Beds in northern Malawi. *Journal of Human Evolution* 27: 159–71.

Keding, B. 1998. The Yellow Nile: new data on settlement and environment in the Sudanese eastern Sahara. *Sudan and Nubia* 2: 2–12.

Keeley, L. H. 1980. *Experimental Determination of Stone Tool Uses.* Chicago: University of Chicago Press.

Keeley, L. H. and N. J. Toth 1981. Microwear polishes on early stone tools from Koobi Fora, Kenya. *Nature* 293: 464–5.

Keller, C. M. 1969. Mossel Bay: a re-description. *South African Archaeological Bulletin* 23: 131–40.

  1973. *Montagu Cave in Prehistory.* Berkeley: University of California Press.

Kemp, B. J. 1989. *Ancient Egypt: Anatomy of a Civilisation.* London: Routledge.

Kendall, R. L. and D. A. Livingstone 1972. Palaeoecological studies on the East African plateau, pp. 386–8 in H. Hugot (ed.) *Actes du 6e Congrès panafricain de préhistoire.* Chambéry: Les Imprimeries Réunies de Chambéry.

Kibunjia, M. 1994. Pliocene archaeological occurrences in the Lake Turkana Basin. *Journal of Human Evolution* 16: 729–40.

Killick, D. *et al.* 1988. Reassessment of the evidence for early metallurgy in Niger, West Africa. *Journal of Archaeological Science* 15: 367–94.

Kimbel, W. H. *et al.* 1996. Late Pliocene *Homo* and Oldowan tools from the Hadar Formation (Kada Hadar Member), Ethiopia. *Journal of Human Evolution* 31: 549–61.

Kinahan, J. 1991. *Pastoral Nomads of the Central Namib Desert.* Windhoek: New Namibia Books.

  1996. A new archaeological perspective on nomadic pastoralist expansion in south-western Africa. *Azania* 29/30: 211–26.

Kingston, J. D. *et al.* 2002. Stratigraphy and environments of the late Miocene Mpesida Beds, Tugen Hills, Kenya. *Journal of Human Evolution* 42: 95–116.

Kirwan, L. P. 1960. The decline and fall of Meroe. *Kush* 8: 163–5.

1974. Nuba and Nubian origins. *Geographical Journal* 140: 43–51.

1977. Rome beyond the southern Egyptian frontier. *Proceedings of the British Academy* 63: 13–31.

Kitchen, K. A. 1993. The land of Punt, pp. 587–608 in T. Shaw *et al.* (eds.) *The Archaeology of Africa: Food, Metals and Towns*. London: Routledge.

Kittles, R. and S. O. Y. Keita 1999. Interpreting African genetic diversity. *African Archaeological Review* 16: 87–91.

Klapwijk, M. 1974. A preliminary report on pottery from the north-eastern Transvaal. *South African Archaeological Bulletin* 29: 19–23.

Klapwijk, M. and T. N. Huffman 1996. Excavations at Silver Leaves: a final report. *South African Archaeological Bulletin* 51: 84–93.

Klein, R. G. 1973. Geological antiquity of Rhodesian man. *Nature* 244: 311–12.

1974. Environment and subsistence of prehistoric man in the southern Cape Province, South Africa. *World Archaeology* 5: 249–84.

1978. Stone age predation on large African bovids. *Journal of Archaeological Science* 5: 195–217.

1986. The prehistory of Stone Age herders in the Cape Province of South Africa. *South African Archaeological Society Goodwin Series* 5: 5–12.

1988. The archaeological significance of animal bones from Acheulian sites in southern Africa. *African Archaeological Review* 6: 3–26.

1995. Anatomy, behavior and modern human origins. *Journal of World Prehistory* 9: 167–98.

1999. *The Human Career: Human Biological and Cultural Origins (Second Edition)*. Chicago: University of Chicago Press.

2000a. Archaeology and the evolution of human behavior. *Evolutionary Anthropology* 9: 17–36.

2000b. The Earlier Stone Age of southern Africa. *South African Archaeological Bulletin* 55: 107–22.

Klein, R. G. and K. Scott 1986. Re-analysis of faunal assemblages from the Haua Fteah and other Late Quaternary archaeological sites in Cyrenaican Libya. *Journal of Archaeological Science* 3: 515–42.

Klein, R. G. *et al.* 1999. Duinefontein 2: an Acheulean site in the Western Cape Province of South Africa. *Journal of Human Evolution* 37: 153–90.

Kleindienst, M. R. 2001. What is the Aterian? The view from Dakhleh Oasis and the Western Desert, Egypt, pp. 1–14 in C. A. Marlow and A. J. Mills (eds.) *The Oasis Papers 1: Proceedings of the First International Symposium of the Dakhleh Oasis Project*. Oxford: Oxbow Books.

Knight, A. *et al.* 2003. African Y-chromosome and mtDNA divergence provides insight into the history of click languages. *Current Biology* 13: 464–73.

Kohn, M. and S. Mithen 1999. Handaxes: products of sexual selection? *Antiquity* 73: 518–26.

Krings, M. *et al.* 1999. mtDNA analysis of Nile River Valley populations: a genetic corridor or a barrier to migration? *American Journal of Human Genetics* 64: 1166–76.

Krzyzaniak, L. 1978. New light on early food-production in the central Sudan. *Journal of African History* 19: 159–72.

1984. The neolithic habitation at Kadero, pp. 309–16 in L. Krzyzaniak and M. Kobusiewicz (eds.) *Origin and Early Development of Food-Producing Cultures in North-East Africa*. Poznan: Polish Academy of Sciences.

Kuman, K. 1994. The archaeology of Sterkfontein – past and present. *Journal of Human Evolution* 27: 471–95.

1996. The Oldowan industry from Sterkfontein: raw materials and core forms, pp. 139–46 in G. Pwiti and R. Soper (eds.) *Aspects of African Archaeology*. Harare: University of Zimbabwe Publications.

1998. The earliest South African industries, pp. 151–86 in M. D. Petraglia and R. Korisettar (eds.) *Early Human Behaviour in Global Context*. London: Routledge.

2001. An Acheulean factory site with prepared-core technology near Taung, South Africa. *South African Archaeological Bulletin* 56: 8–22.

Kuman, K. and R. J. Clarke 1986. Florisbad: new investigations at a Middle Stone Age site in South Africa. *Geoarchaeology* 1: 103–25.

2000. Stratigraphy, artefact industries and hominid associations for Sterkfontein, Member 5. *Journal of Human Evolution* 38: 827–47.

Kuman, K. *et al.* 1997. Discovery of new artefacts at Kromdraai. *South African Journal of Science* 93: 187–93.

1999. Palaeoenvironments and cultural sequence of the Florisbad Middle Stone Age hominid site, South Africa. *Journal of Archaeological Science* 26: 1409–25.

Kusimba, C. M. 1999. *The Rise and Fall of Swahili States*. Walnut Creek, CA: Altamira Press.

Kusimba, S. B. 2001. The Early Later Stone Age in East Africa: excavations and lithic assemblages from Lukenya Hill. *African Archaeological Review* 18: 77–123.

Kyule, M. D. *et al.* 1997. Pliocene and Pleistocene sites in southern Narok District, southwest Kenya. *Journal of Human Evolution* 32 (4): A9–10.

Lahr, M. 1994. The multiregional model of modern human origins. *Journal of Human Evolution* 26: 33–56.

Lahr, M. and R. Foley 1994. Multiple dispersals and modern human origins. *Evolutionary Anthropology* 3: 48–60.

2001. Mode 3, *Homo helmei* and the pattern of human evolution in the Middle Pleistocene, pp. 23–39 in L. S. Barham and K. Robson-Brown (eds.) *Human Roots: Africa and Asia in the Middle Pleistocene*. Bristol: Western Academic and Specialist Press.

Lalueza Fox, C. 1997. mtDNA analysis in ancient Nubians supports the existence of gene flow between sub-Sahara and North Africa in the Nile Valley. *Annals of Human Biology* 24 (3): 217–27.

Lambert, N. 1971. Les industries sur cuivre dans l'ouest saharien. *West African Journal of Archaeology* 1: 9–21.

1983. Nouvelle contribution à l'étude du Chalcolithique de Mauritanie, pp. 63–87 in N. Echard (ed.) *Métallurgies africaines: nouvelles contributions*. Paris: Sociétédes Africanistes.

Lane, P. *et al.* (eds.) 1998. *Ditswa Mmung: The Archaeology of Botswana*. Gaborone: Pula Press and the Botswana Society.

Lanfranchi, R. 1996. Une industrie MSA de stone-line en forêt dense: le site de Mokeko (Congo), pp. 165–75 in G. Pwiti and R. Soper (eds.) *Aspects of African Archaeology.* Harare: University of Zimbabwe Publications.

Lanfranchi, R. and D. Schwartz (eds.) 1990. *Paysages quaternaires de l'Afrique centrale atlantique.* Paris: ORSTOM.

Larsson, L. 1996. The Middle Stone Age of Zimbabwe: some aspects of former research, pp. 201–6 in G. Pwiti and R. Soper (eds.) *Aspects of African Archaeology.* Harare: University of Zimbabwe Publications.

Lavachery, P. 2001. The Holocene archaeological sequence of Shum Laka rock shelter (Grassfields, Cameroon). *African Archaeological Review* 18: 213–47.

Law, R. C. 1967. The Garamantes and trans-Saharan enterprise in classical times. *Journal of African History* 8: 181–200.

   1978. North Africa in the Hellenistic and Roman periods, pp. 148–209 in J. D. Fage (ed.) *Cambridge History of Africa*, vol. 2. Cambridge: Cambridge University Press.

Leakey, D. M. *et al.* 1969. An Acheulian industry with prepared core technique and the discovery of a contemporary hominid mandible at Lake Baringo, Kenya. *Proceedings of the Prehistoric Society* 35: 48–76.

Leakey, L. S. B. 1931. *The Stone Age Cultures of Kenya Colony.* Cambridge: Cambridge University Press.

   1943. Industries of the Gorgora rock shelter, Lake Tana. *Journal of the East Africa and Uganda Natural History Society* 17: 199–203.

   1951. *Olduvai Gorge.* Cambridge: Cambridge University Press.

   1965. *Olduvai Gorge*, vol. 1. Cambridge: Cambridge University Press.

Leakey, M. D. 1945. Report on the excavations at Hyrax Hill, Nakuru, Kenya Colony. *Transactions of the Royal Society of South Africa* 30: 271–409.

   1971. *Olduvai Gorge*, vol. 3. Cambridge: Cambridge University Press.

   1975. Cultural patterns in the Olduvai sequence, pp. 477–94 in K. W. Butzer and G. L. Isaac (eds.) *After the Australopithecines.* The Hague: Mouton.

   1976. A summary and discussion of the archaeological evidence from Bed I and Bed II, Olduvai Gorge, Tanzania, pp. 431–59 in G. L. Isaac and E. McCown (eds.) *Human Origins: Louis Leakey and the East African Evidence.* Menlo Park, CA: Benjamin.

   1983. *Africa's Vanishing Art: The Rock Paintings of Tanzania.* New York: Doubleday.

Leakey, M. D. and J. M. Harris 1987. *Laetoli: A Pliocene Site in Northern Tanzania.* Oxford: Clarendon Press.

Leakey, M. D. and R. L. Hay 1982. The chronological position of the fossil hominids of Tanzania, pp. 753–65 in M.-A. de Lumley (ed.) *L'Homo erectus et la place de l'homme de Tautavel parmi les hominidés fossiles.* Nice: Premier Congrès internationale de paléontologie humaine.

Leakey, M. D. and L. S. B. Leakey 1950. *Excavations at Njoro River Cave.* Oxford: Oxford University Press.

Leakey, M. D. with D. A. Roe 1994. *Olduvai Gorge*, vol. 5: *Excavations in Beds III, IV and the Masek Beds.* Cambridge: Cambridge University Press.

Leakey, M. D. *et al.* 1948. *Dimple-Based Pottery from Central Kavirondo, Kenya Colony.* Nairobi: Coryndon Memorial Museum.

1972. Stratigraphy, archaeology and age of the Ndutu and Naisiusiu Beds, Olduvai Gorge, Tanzania. *World Archaeology* 3: 328–41.

Leakey, M. G. and R. E. Leakey (eds.) 1978. *Koobi Fora Research Project*, vol. 1. Oxford: Clarendon Press.

Leakey, M. G. *et al.* 1995. New four-million-year-old hominid species from Kanapoi and Allia Bay, Kenya. *Nature* 376: 565–71.

Lebeuf, J. P. 1962. *Archéologie tchadienne*. Paris: Actualités Scientifiques et Industrielles (1295).

Lee, R. B. 1963. The population ecology of man in the early Upper Pleistocene of southern Africa. *Proceedings of the Prehistoric Society* 29: 235–57.

1968. What hunters do for a living, pp. 30–48 in R. B. Lee and I. DeVore (eds.) *Man the Hunter*. Chicago: Aldine.

Lee-Thorp, J. A. *et al.* 1994. Diet of *Australopithecus robustus* at Swartkrans from stable carbon isotopic analysis. *Journal of Human Evolution* 27: 361–72.

Lenoble, P. and N. M. Sharif 1992. Barbarians at the gates? The royal mounds of El Hobagi and the end of Meroe. *Antiquity* 66: 626–35.

Lenoble, P. *et al.* 1994. La fouille du tumulus à enceinte à El Hobagi. *Meroitic Newsletter* 25: 53–88.

Le Quellec, J.-L. 1987. *L'art rupestre du Fezzan*. Oxford: British Archaeological Reports.

1993. *Symbolisme et art rupestre au Sahara*. Paris: L'Harmattan.

di Lernia, S. 1998. Cultural control over wild animals during the early Holocene: the case of Barbary sheep in central Sahara, pp. 113–26 in S. di Lernia and G. Manzi (eds.) *Before Food Production in North Africa*. Forlì: Abaco.

(ed.) 1999. *The Uan Afuda Cave: Hunter-Gatherer Societies of Central Sahara*. Florence: Edizioni all'Insegna del Giglio.

di Lernia, S. and G. Manzi (eds.) 1998. *Before Food Production in North Africa: Questions and Tools Dealing with Resource Exploitation and Population Dynamics 12,000–7,000 bp*. Forlì: Abaco.

di Lernia, S. and A. Palombini 2002. Desertification, sustainability and archaeology: indications from the past for an African future. *Origini* 24: 303–33.

Levtzion, N. 1973. *Ancient Ghana and Mali*. London: Methuen.

1977. The western Maghrib and Sudan, pp. 331–462 in R. Oliver (ed.) *Cambridge History of Africa*, vol. 3. Cambridge: Cambridge University Press.

1978. The Sahara and the Sudan from the Arab conquest of the Maghrib to the rise of the Almoravids, pp. 637–84 in J. D. Fage (ed.) *Cambridge History of Africa*, vol. 2. Cambridge: Cambridge University Press.

Levtzion, N. and J. F. P. Hopkins 1981. *Corpus of Early Arabic Sources for West African History*. Cambridge: Cambridge University Press.

Levtzion, N. and R. Pouwels (eds.) 2000. *The History of Islam in Africa*. Oxford: Currey.

Lewis, H. S. 1966. The origins of the Galla and Somali. *Journal of African History* 7: 27–46.

Lewis, N. 1983. *Life in Egypt under Roman Rule*. Oxford: Clarendon Press.

Lewis-Williams, J. D. 1981. *Believing and Seeing*. London: Academic Press.

1983. *The Rock Art of Southern Africa*. Cambridge: Cambridge University Press.

Lewis-Williams, J. D. and T. A. Dowson 1988. The signs of all times: entoptic phenomena in Upper Palaeolithic art. *Current Anthropology* 29: 201–45.

1989. *Images of Power: Understanding Bushman Rock Art*. Johannesburg: Southern Book Publishers.

Lieberman, D. E. *et al.* 1996. Homoplasy and early *Homo*: an analysis of the evolutionary relationships of *H. habilis sensu stricto* and *H. rudolfensis*. *Journal of Human Evolution* 30: 97–120.

Linares de Sapir, O. 1971. Shell middens of Lower Casamance and problems of Diola protohistory. *West African Journal of Archaeology* 1: 23–54.

Linnaeus, C. 1735. *Systema Naturae*. Leiden: Haak.

Littmann, E. *et al.* 1913. *Deutsche Aksum-Expedition*. Berlin: Reimer.

Liverani, M. 2000. The Libyan caravan road in Herodotus IV. 181–5. *Journal of the Economic and Social History of the Orient* 43: 496–520.

Lloyd, A. B. 1983. The Late Period 664–323 BC, pp. 279–348 in B. G. Trigger *et al. Ancient Egypt: A Social History*. Cambridge: Cambridge University Press.

Loubser, J. 1993. Ndondondwane: the significance of features and finds from a ninth-century site on the lower Thukela River, Natal. *Natal Museum Journal of Humanities* 5: 109–51.

Lubell, D. 1974. *The Fakhurian: A Late Palaeolithic Industry from Upper Egypt*. Cairo: Geological Survey of Egypt.

Ludwig, B. V. and J. W. K. Harris 1998. Towards a technological reassessment of East African Plio-Pleistocene lithic assemblages, pp. 84–107 in M. D. Petraglia and R. Korisettar (eds.) *Early Human Behaviour in Global Context*. London: Routledge.

McBrearty, S. 1987. Une évaluation du Sangoen: son âge, son environnement et son rapport avec l'origine de l'*Homo sapiens*. *L'Anthropologie* 91: 497–510.

1988. The Sangoan-Lupemban and Middle Stone Age sequence at the Muguruk site, western Kenya. *World Archaeology* 19: 388–420.

1999. The archaeology of the Kapthurin Formation, pp. 143–56 in P. Andrews and P. Banham (eds.) *Late Cenozoic Environments and Hominid Evolution*. London: Geological Society.

2001. The Middle Pleistocene of East Africa, pp. 81–98 in L. S. Barham and K. Robson-Brown (eds.) *Human Roots: Africa and Asia in the Middle Pleistocene*. Bristol: Western Academic and Specialist Press.

McBrearty, S. and A. S. Brooks 2000. The revolution that wasn't: a new interpretation of the origin of modern human behaviour. *Journal of Human Evolution* 39: 453–563.

McBrearty, S. *et al.* 1996. Variability in traces of Middle Pleistocene hominid behaviour in the Kapthurin Formation, Baringo, Kenya. *Journal of Human Evolution* 30: 563–80.

McBurney, C. B. M. 1960. *The Stone Age of Northern Africa*. Harmondsworth: Penguin Books.

1967. *The Haua Fteah (Cyrenaica)*. Cambridge: Cambridge University Press.

1975. The archaeological context of the Hamitic languages in northern Africa, pp. 495–515 in J. Bynon and T. Bynon (eds.) *Hamito-Semitica*. The Hague: Mouton.

MacCalman, H. R. 1963. The Neuhoff-Kowas Middle Stone Age, Windhoek district. *Cimbebasia* 7.

MacCalman, H. R. and H. Viereck 1967. Peperkorrel, a factory site of Lupemban affinities from central South West Africa. *South African Archaeological Bulletin* 22: 41–50.

McDermott, F. *et al.* 1996. New Late-Pleistocene uranium-thorium and ESR dates for the Singa hominid (Sudan). *Journal of Human Evolution* 31: 507–16.

MacDonald, K. C. 1992. The domestic chicken (*Gallus gallus*) in sub-Saharan Africa: a background to its introduction and its osteological differentiation from indigenous fowls. *Journal of Archaeological Science* 19: 303–18.

1997. Kourounkorokale revisited: the Pays Mande and the West African microlithic technocomplex. *African Archaeological Review* 14: 161–200.

1998. Before the Empire of Ghana: pastoralism and the origins of cultural complexity in the sahel, pp. 71–103 in G. Connah (ed.) *Transformations in Africa: Essays on Africa's Later Past*. London: Leicester University Press.

MacDonald, K. C. and P. Allsworth-Jones 1994. A reconsideration of the West African macrolithic conundrum: new factory sites and an associated settlement in the Vallée du Serpent, Mali. *African Archaeological Review* 12: 73–104.

MacDonald, K. C. and D. N. Edwards 1993. Chickens in Africa: the importance of Qasr Ibrim. *Antiquity* 67: 584–90.

McDonald, M. M. A. 1991. Technological organisation and sedentism in the Epipalaeolithic of Dakhleh Oasis, Egypt. *African Archaeological Review* 9: 81–109.

McHenry, H. M. 1988. New estimates of body weight in early hominids and their significance to encephalization and megadontia in robust australopithecines, pp. 133–46 in F. E. Grine (ed.) *The Evolutionary History of the Robust Australopithecines*. New York: Aldine de Gruyter.

McIntosh, R. J. 1998. *The Peoples of the Middle Niger*. Oxford: Blackwell.

McIntosh, R. J. and S. K. McIntosh 1981. The inland Niger delta before the empire of Mali: evidence from Jenne-Jeno. *Journal of African History* 22: 1–22.

McIntosh, S. K. 1994. Changing perceptions of West Africa's past: archaeological research since 1988. *Journal of Archaeological Research* 2: 165–98.

(ed.) 1999a. *Beyond Chiefdoms: Pathways to Complexity in Africa*. Cambridge: Cambridge University Press.

1999b. Modelling political organisation in large-scale settlement clusters: a case study from the Inland Niger Delta, pp. 66–79 in S. K. McIntosh (ed.) *Beyond Chiefdoms: Pathways to Complexity in Africa*. Cambridge: Cambridge University Press.

McIntosh, S. K. and H. Bocoum 2000. New perspectives on Sinan Baras, a first millennium [A.D.] site in the Senegal Valley. *African Archaeological Review* 17: 1–43.

McIntosh, S. K. and R. J. McIntosh 1980. *Prehistoric Investigations in the Region of Jenne, Mali*. Oxford: British Archaeological Reports.

1984. The early city in West Africa: towards an understanding. *African Archaeological Review* 2: 73–98.

1988. From stone to metal: new perspectives on the later prehistory of West Africa. *Journal of World Prehistory* 2: 89–133.

1993. Field survey in the tumulus zone of Senegal. *African Archaeological Review* 11: 73–107.

Mack, J. and P. Robertshaw (eds.) 1982. *Culture History in the Southern Sudan*. Nairobi: British Institute in Eastern Africa.

McKee, J. K. 1993. Faunal dating of the Taung hominid fossil deposit. *Journal of Human Evolution* 23: 363–76.

MacLean, M. R. 1996. Socio-political development in the Early Iron Age of the Interlacustrine region, pp. 497–503 in G. Pwiti and R. Soper (eds.) *Aspects of African Archaeology*. Harare: University of Zimbabwe Publications.

McNabb, J. 2001. The shape of things to come: a speculative essay on the role of the Victoria West phenomenon at Canteen Koppie during the South African Earlier Stone Age, pp. 37–46 in S. Milliken and J. Cook (eds.) *A Very Remote Period Indeed: Papers on the Palaeolithic Presented to Derek Roe*. Oxford: Oxbow.

McPherron, S. P. 2000. Handaxes as a measure of the mental capacities of early hominids. *Journal of Archaeological Science* 27: 655–63.

Maggs, T. M. O'C. 1971. Pastoral settlements on the Riet River. *South African Archaeological Bulletin* 26: 37–63.

1976. *Iron Age Communities of the Southern Highveld.* Pietermaritzburg: Natal Museum.

1980. The Iron Age sequence south of the Vaal and Pongola Rivers. *Journal of African History* 21: 1–15.

1984. The Iron Age south of the Zambezi, pp. 329–60 in R. G. Klein (ed.) *Southern African Prehistory and Palaeoenvironments.* Rotterdam: Balkema.

1995. The Early Iron Age in the extreme south: some patterns and problems. *Azania* 29/30: 171–8.

Maggs, T. M. O'C. and P. Davison 1981. The Lydenburg heads. *African Arts* 14: 28–33.

Magori, C. C. and M. H. Day 1983. Laetoli Hominid 18: an early *Homo sapiens* skull. *Journal of Human Evolution* 12: 747–53.

Malhomme, J. 1959–61. *Corpus des gravures rupestres du Grand Atlas.* Rabat: Service des Antiquités du Maroc.

Manzo, A. 1996. *Culture ed ambiente: l'Africa nord-orientale nei dati archeologici e nella letteratura geografica ellenistica.* Naples: Istituto Universitario Orientale.

Mapunda, P. B. B. 1997. Patching up evidence for ironworking in the Horn. *African Archaeological Review* 14: 107–24.

de Maret, P. 1977. Sanga: new excavations, more data and some related problems. *Journal of African History* 18: 321–37.

1981. L'évolution monétaire du Shaba central entre le 7e et le 18e siècle. *African Economic History* 10: 117–49.

1982. The 'Neolithic' problem in the West and South, pp. 59–65 in F. Van Noten *The Archaeology of Central Africa.* Graz: Akademische Druck-u. Verlagsanstalt.

1985a. Recent archaeological research and dates from central Africa. *Journal of African History* 26: 129–48.

1985b. *Fouilles archéologiques dans le vallée du Haut-Lualaba, Zaïre: Sanga et Katongo.* Tervuren: Musée Royal de l'Afrique Centrale.

1986. The Ngovo Group: an industry with polished stone tools and pottery in Lower Zaïre. *African Archaeological Review* 4: 103–33.

1989. Le contexte archéologique de l'expansion Bantu en Afrique centrale, pp. 118–38 in T. Obenga (ed.) *Les peuples bantu: migrations, expansion et identité culturelle.* Paris: L'Harmattan.

1992. *Fouilles archéologiques dans le vallée du Haut-Lualaba, Zaïre: Kamilamba, Kikulu et Malemba-Nkulu.* Tervuren: Musée Royal de l'Afrique Centrale.

de Maret, P. and B. Clist 1987. Mission de fouilles 1987 en Guinée-Equatoriale insulaire. *Nsi* 2: 32–5.

de Maret, P. *et al.* 1987. Résultats des premiers fouilles dans les abris de Shum Laka et d'Abéké. *L'Anthropologie* 91: 559–84.

Markoe, G. E. 2000. *The Phoenicians.* London: British Museum Press.

Marks, A. E. 1968. The Khormusan and the Halfan, pp. 315–460 in F. Wendorf (ed.) *The Prehistory of Nubia.* Dallas, TX: Southern Methodist University Press.

Marks, A. E. and A. Mohammed-Ali (eds.) 1991. *The Late Prehistory of the Eastern Sahel: The Mesolithic and Neolithic of Shaqadud, Sudan.* Dallas, TX: Southern Methodist University Press.

Marshall, F. 1989. Rethinking the role of *Bos indicus* in Africa. *Current Anthropology* 30: 235–40.

    2000. The origins and spread of domestic animals in East Africa, pp. 191–221 in R. M. Blench and K. C. MacDonald (eds.), *The Origins and Development of African Livestock*. London: UCL Press.

Marshall, F. *et al.* 1984. Early domestic stock at Dongodien. *Azania* 19: 120–7.

Masao, F. T. 1979. *The Later Stone Age and the Rock Paintings of Central Tanzania*. Wiesbaden: Steiner.

Mason, R. J. 1962. *The Prehistory of the Transvaal*. Johannesburg: Witwatersrand University Press.

    1974. Background to the Transvaal Iron Age: discoveries at Olifantspoort and Broederstroom. *Journal of the South African Institute of Mining and Metallurgy* 74: 211–16.

    1986. *Origins of Black People of Johannesburg and the Southern Western Central Transvaal*. Johannesburg: University of the Witwatersrand.

Matenga, E. 1998. *The Soapstone Birds of Great Zimbabwe: Symbols of a Nation*. Harare: African Publishing Group.

Mattingly, D. J. 1989. Farmers and frontiers: exploiting and defending the countryside of Roman Tripolitania. *Libyan Studies* 20: 135–53.

    1995. *Tripolitania*. London: Batsford.

Mattingly, D. J. *et al.* 1998. The Fezzan Project 1998: preliminary report. *Libyan Studies* 29: 115–44.

Mauny, R. 1973. Datation au carbone 14 d'amas de coquillages des lagunes de Basse Côte d'Ivoire. *West African Journal of Archaeology* 3: 207–14.

    1978. Trans-Saharan contacts and the Iron Age in West Africa, pp. 272–341 in J. D. Fage (ed.) *Cambridge History of Africa*, vol. 2. Cambridge: Cambridge University Press.

Mazel, A. D. and A. L. Watchman 2003. Dating rock paintings in the uKhahlamba/ Drakensberg and the Biggarsberg, KwaZulu-Natal, South Africa. *Southern African Humanities* 15: 59–73.

Mbida, C. M. *et al.* 2000. Evidence for banana cultivation and animal husbandry during the first millennium BC in the forest of southern Cameroon. *Journal of Archaeological Science* 27: 151–62.

Mehlman, M. J. 1977. Excavations at Nasera Rock, Tanzania. *Azania* 12: 111–18.

    1987. Provenience, age and associations of archaic *Homo sapiens* crania from Lake Eyasi, Tanzania. *Journal of Archaeological Science* 14: 133–62.

    1991. Context for the emergence of modern man in eastern Africa: some new Tanzanian evidence, pp. 177–96 in J. D. Clark (ed.) *Cultural Beginnings*. Bonn: Habelt.

Mellars, P. 1993. Archaeology and modern human origins. *Proceedings of the British Academy* 82: 1–35.

    2002. Archaeology and the origins of modern humans: European and African perspectives, pp. 31–47 in T. J. Crow (ed.) *The Speciation of Modern* Homo sapiens. Oxford: Oxford University Press for The British Academy.

Mellars, P. and K. Gibson (eds.) 1996. *Modelling the Early Human Mind*. Cambridge: McDonald Institute for Archaeological Research.

de Menocal, P. B. 1995. Plio-Pleistocene African climate. *Science* 270: 53–9.

Mercader, J. and A. S. Brooks 2001. Across forests and savannas: later Stone Age assemblages from Ituri and Semliki, Democratic Republic of Congo. *Journal of Anthropological Research* 5: 197–217.

Mercader, J. and R. Marti 2003. The hunter-gatherer occupation of Atlantic central Africa, pp. 64–92 in J. Mercader (ed.) *Under the Canopy: The Archaeology of Tropical Rainforests*. New Brunswick, NJ: Rutgers University Press.

Mercader, J. *et al.* 2000. Shared technology: forager–farmer interaction and ancient iron metallurgy in the Ituri rainforest. *Azania* 35: 107–22.

Mercier, J. 2000. La peinture éthiopienne à l'époque axoumite et au XVIII siècle. *Comptes-Dendus des Séances de l'Académie des Inscriptions et Belles-Lettres, Année 2000*: 35–71.

Merrick, H. V. and F. H. Brown 1984. Obsidian sources and patterns of source utilization in Kenya and northern Tanzania: some initial findings. *African Archaeological Review* 2: 129–52.

Merrick, H. V. and J. P. S. Merrick 1976. Archaeological occurrences of earlier Pleistocene age from the Shungura formation, pp. 574–84 in Y. Coppens *et al.* (eds.) *Earliest Man and Environments in the Lake Rudolf Basin*. Chicago: University of Chicago Press.

Merrick, H. V. *et al.* 1994. Use and movement of obsidian in the Early and Middle Stone Ages of Kenya and northern Tanzania, pp. 29–44 in S. T. Childs (ed.) *Society, Culture and Technology in Africa*. Philadelphia: University of Pennsylvania Museum.

van der Merwe, N. J. 1980. The advent of iron in Africa, pp. 463–506 in T. A. Wertime and J. D. Muhly (eds.) *The Coming of the Age of Iron*. New Haven, CT: Yale University Press.

van der Merwe, N. J. and R. T. K. Scully 1971. The Phalaborwa story: archaeological and ethnographic investigation of a South African Iron Age group. *World Archaeology* 3: 178–96.

Meyer, A. 1998. *The Archaeological Sites at Greefswald*. Pretoria: University of Pretoria.

Michalowski, K. 1967. *Faras: die Kathedrale aus dem Wustensand*. Zurich: Benziger.

Michels, J. W. 1994. Regional political organisation in the Axum–Yeha area during the Pre-Axumite and Axumite eras. *Etudes Ethiopiennes* 1: 61–80.

Miller, D. 1998. Metal artefacts and slags from archaeological sites on the Congo coast. *Southern African Field Archaeology* 7: 26–34.

2001. Metal assemblages from Greefswald areas K2, Mapungubwe Hill and Mapungubwe Southern Terrace. *South African Archaeological Bulletin* 56: 83–103.

2002. Smelter and smith: metal fabrication technology in the southern African Early and Late Iron Age. *Journal of Archaeological Science* 29: 1083–1131.

2003. Indigenous copper mining and smelting in pre-colonial southern Africa, pp. 101–10 in P. T. Craddock and J. Lang (eds.) *Mining and Metal Production through the Ages*. London: British Museum Press.

Miller, D. and N. J. van der Merwe 1994. Early metal working in sub-Saharan Africa: a review of recent research. *Journal of African History* 33: 1–36.

Miller, D *et al.* 2000. Indigenous gold mining in southern Africa: a review. *South African Archaeological Society Goodwin Series* 8: 91–9.

Miller, J. C. 1972. The Imbangala and the chronology of early Central African history. *Journal of African History* 13: 549–74.

1976. *Kings and Kinsmen*. Oxford: Clarendon Press.

Miller, S. F. 1971. The age of the Nachikufan industries in Zambia. *South African Archaeological Bulletin* 26: 143–6.

1972. The archaeological sequence of the Zambian later Stone Age, pp. 565–72 in H. Hugot (ed.) *Actes du 6e Congrès Panafricain de Préhistoire*. Chambéry: Les Imprimeries Réunies de Chambéry.

1988. Patterns of environment utilization by late prehistoric cultures in the southern Congo basin, pp. 127–44 in J. Bower and D. Lubell (eds.) *Prehistoric Cultures and Environments in the Late Quaternary of Africa*. Oxford: British Archaeological Reports.

Milliken, S. 2002. Out of Africa and Out of Asia? New light on early hominid dispersal. *Review of Archaeology* 23 (2): 21–35.

Milo, R. 1998. Evidence for hominid predation at Klasies River Mouth, South Africa, and its implications for the behaviour of early modern humans. *Journal of Archaeological Science* 25: 99–133.

Mitchell, P. J. 1988. *The Early Microlithic Assemblages of Southern Africa*. Oxford: British Archaeological Reports.

1994. Understanding the MSA/LSA transition: the pre-20,000 BP assemblages from new excavations at Sehonghong rock shelter, Lesotho. *Southern African Field Archaeology* 3: 15–25.

1996. The late Quaternary of the Lesotho highlands, southern Africa: preliminary results and future potential of ongoing research at Sehonghong Shelter. *Quaternary International* 33: 35–44.

1997. Holocene Later Stone Age hunter-gatherers south of the Limpopo River *ca.* 10,000–2000 BP. *Journal of World Prehistory* 11: 15–25.

2002. *The Archaeology of Southern Africa*. Cambridge: Cambridge University Press.

Miyamoto, M. M. and M. Goodman 1990. DNA systematics and evolution of primates. *Annual Review of Ecology and Systematics* 2: 197–220.

Mohammed-Ali, A. S. 1982. *The Neolithic Period in the Sudan, c. 6000–2500 BC*. Oxford: British Archaeological Reports.

Mohammed-Ali, A. S. and A.-R. M. Khabir 2003. The wavy line and the dotted wavy line pottery in the prehistory of the central Nile and the Sahara-Sahel belt. *African Archaeological Review* 20: 25–58.

Monod, T. 1969. Le Maden Ijafen: une épave caravanière ancienne dans la Majabat al-Koubra, pp. 286–320 in *actes du premier Colloque international d'archéologie africaine*. Fort-Lamy: Institut National Tchadien pour les Sciences Humaines.

Morais, J. 1988. *The Early Farming Communities of Southern Mozambique*. Stockholm: Central Board of National Antiquities.

Mori, F. 1965. *Tadrart Acacus: arte rupestre e culture del Sahara preistorico*. Turin: Einaudi.

1974. The earliest Saharan rock engravings. *Antiquity* 48: 87–92.

1978. Zur Chronologie der Sahara-Felsbilder, pp. 253–61 in P. Stehli (ed.) *Sahara*. Cologne: Museen der Stadt Köln.

Morris, A. G. 2003. The myth of the East African 'Bushmen'. *South African Archaeological Bulletin* 58: 85–90.

Mortelmans, G. 1962. Vue d'ensemble sur la préhistoire du Congo occidental, pp. 129–64 in G. Mortelmans (ed.) *Actes du 4e Congrès panafricain de préhistoire*. Tervuren: Musée Royal de l'Afrique Centrale.

Mountain, J. L. *et al.* 1993. Evolution of modern humans: evidence from nuclear DNA polymorphisms, pp. 69–83 in M. J. Aitken *et al.* (eds.) *The Origin of Modern Humans and the Impact of Chronometric Dating.* Princeton, NJ: Princeton University Press.

Mturi, A. 1976. New hominid from Lake Ndutu, Tanzania. *Nature* 262: 484–5.

Munro-Hay, S. 1989. *Excavations at Aksum.* London: British Institute in Eastern Africa.

  1991. *Aksum: An African Civilisation of Late Antiquity.* Edinburgh: Edinburgh University Press.

Munro-Hay, S. and B. Juel-Jensen 1995. *Aksumite Coinage.* London: Spink.

Munson, P. J. 1976. Archaeological data on the origins of cultivation in the south-western Sahara and their implications for West Africa, pp. 187–210 in J. Harlan *et al.* (eds.) *Origins of African Plant Domestication.* The Hague: Mouton.

Musonda, F. B. 1984. Late Pleistocene and Holocene microlithic industries from the Lunsemfwa Basin, Zambia. *South African Archaeological Bulletin* 39: 24–36.

  1987. The significance of pottery in Zambian later Stone Age sites. *African Archaeological Review* 5: 147–58.

Mutoro, H. W. 1998. Precolonial trading systems of the East African interior, pp. 186–203 in G. Connah (ed.) *Transformations in Africa: Essays on Africa's Later Past.* London: Leicester University Press.

Muzzolini, A. 1986. *L'art rupestre préhistorique des massifs centraux sahariens.* Oxford: British Archaeological Reports.

  1991. Proposals for up-dating the rock-drawing sequence of the Acacus. *Libyan Studies* 22: 7–30.

  1993. The emergence of a food-producing economy in the Sahara, pp. 227–39 in T. Shaw *et al.* (eds.) *The Archaeology of Africa: Foods, Metals and Towns.* London: Routledge.

  1995. *Les images rupestres du Sahara.* Toulouse: the author.

Naville, E. 1898. *The Temple of Deir el Bahari.* London: Egypt Exploration Fund.

Nelson, C. M. and M. Posnansky 1970. The stone tools from the re-excavation of Nsongezi rock shelter. *Azania* 5: 119–72.

Nenquin, J. 1963. *Excavations at Sanga, 1957.* Tervuren: Musée Royal de l'Afrique Centrale.

  1967. *Contributions to the Study of the Prehistoric Cultures of Rwanda and Burundi.* Tervuren: Musée Royal de l'Afrique Centrale.

Nicholson, P. T. and I. Shaw (eds.) 2000. *Ancient Egyptian Materials and Technology.* Cambridge: Cambridge University Press.

Niemeyer, H. G. 2001. Archaeological evidence of early iron technology at Carthage and other Phoenician settlements. *Mediterranean Archaeology* 14: 83–94.

Noble, W. and I. Davidson 1996. *Human Evolution, Language and Mind: A Psychological and Archaeological Enquiry.* Cambridge: Cambridge University Press.

Nogwaza, T. 1994. Early Iron Age pottery from Canasta Place, East London district. *Southern African Field Archaeology* 3: 103–6.

Nordström, H. A. 1972. *Neolithic and A-Group Sites.* Stockholm: Scandinavian Joint Expedition to Sudanese Nubia.

Nurse, H. A. 1982. Bantu expansion into East Africa: linguistic evidence, pp. 199–222 in C. Ehret and M. Posnansky (eds.) *The Archaeological and Linguistic Reconstruction of African History.* Berkeley: University of California Press.

1997. The contribution of linguistics to the study of history in Africa. *Journal of African History* 38: 359–91.

Nurse, D. and T. Spear 1985. *The Swahili: Reconstructing the History and Language of an African Society, 800–1500.* Philadelphia: University of Pennsylvania Press.

Oakley, K. P. 1952. *Man the Tool-Maker.* London: British Museum (Natural History).

O'Brien, T. P. 1939. *The Prehistory of the Uganda Protectorate.* Cambridge: Cambridge University Press.

O'Connor, D. 1993a. *Ancient Nubia: Egypt's Rival in Africa.* Philadelphia: University of Pennsylvania Museum of Archaeology and Anthropology.

1993b. Urbanism in Bronze-Age Egypt and northeast Africa, pp. 570–86 in T. Shaw *et al.* (eds.) *The Archaeology of Africa: Food, Metals and Towns.* London: Routledge.

O'Connor, D. and A. Reid (eds.) 2003. *Ancient Egypt in Africa.* London: UCL Press.

Odner, K. 1971. Usangi Hospital and other archaeological sites in the North Pare mountains, north-eastern Tanzania. *Azania* 6: 89–130.

Okafor, E. E. and P. Phillips 1992. New 14-C ages from Nsukka, Nigeria, and the origin of African metallurgy. *Antiquity* 66: 686–8.

Oliver, R. 1977. The East African interior, pp. 621–69 in R. Oliver (ed.) *Cambridge History of Africa*, vol. 3. Cambridge: Cambridge University Press.

1982. The Nilotic contribution to Bantu Africa. *Journal of African History* 23: 433–42.

Opperman, H. 1996. Excavation of a Later Stone Age deposit in Strathalan Cave A, Maclear District, northeastern Cape, South Africa, pp. 335–42 in G. Pwiti and R. Soper (eds.) *Aspects of African Archaeology.* Harare: University of Zimbabwe Publications.

Opperman, H. and B. Heydenrych 1990. A 22,000 year-old Middle Stone Age camp site with plant food remains from the north-eastern Cape. *South African Archaeological Bulletin* 45: 93–9.

Oslisly, R. and B. Peyrot 1992. L'arrivée des premiers métallurgistes sur l'Ogooué, Gabon. *African Archaeological Review* 10: 129–38.

Ouzman, S. and L. Wadley 1997. A history in paint and stone from Rose Cottage Cave, South Africa. *Antiquity* 71: 386–404.

Owen, R. B. *et al.* 1982. Palaeolimnology and archaeology of Holocene deposits northeast of Lake Turkana, Kenya. *Nature* 298: 523–9.

Panchen, A. L. 1992. *Classification, Evolution, and the Nature of Biology.* Cambridge: Cambridge University Press.

Paradis, G. 1980. Découverte d'une industrie paléolithique d'âge sangoen dans les sables argileux 'néogenes' (ou 'terre de barre') de la basse Côte d'Ivoire. *Comptes-Rendus des Séances de l'Académie des Sciences de Paris, sér. D* 290: 1393–5.

Parkington, J. E. 1986. Stone tool assemblages, raw material distributions and prehistoric subsistence activities: the Late Stone Age of South Africa, pp. 181–94 in G. Bailey and P. Callow (eds.) *Stone Age Prehistory.* Cambridge: Cambridge University Press.

2001. Mobility, seasonality and southern African hunter-gatherers. *South African Archaeological Bulletin* 56: 1–7.

Parkington, J. E. and M. Hall (eds.) 1987. *Papers in the Prehistory of the Western Cape, South Africa.* Oxford: British Archaeological Reports.

Parkington, J. E. *et al.* 1986. The social impact of pastoralism in the south-western Cape. *Journal of Anthropological Archaeology* 5: 313–29.

Parsons, I. 2003. Lithic expressions of Later Stone Age lifeways in the Northern Cape. *South African Archaeological Bulletin* 58: 33–7.

Partridge, T. C. *et al.* 1999. The new hominid skeleton from Sterkfontein, South Africa: age and preliminary assessment. *Journal of Quaternary Science* 14: 293–8.

Passariño, G. *et al.* 1998. Different genetic components in the Ethiopian population, identified by mtDNA and Y-chromosome polymorphisms. *American Journal of Human Genetics* 62: 420–34.

Peabody, F. E. 1954. Travertines and cave deposits of the Kaap escarpment of South Africa and the type locality of *Australopithecus africanus. Bulletin of the Geological Society of America* 65: 671–705.

Peacock, D. P. S. and V. A. Maxfield 1997. *Mons Claudianus: survey and excavation.* Cairo: Institut Français d'Archéologie Orientale.

van Peer, P. 1991. Inter-assemblage variability and Levallois styles: the case of the northern African Middle Palaeolithic. *Journal of Anthropological Archaeology* 10: 107–51.

Pereira, L. *et al.* 2001. Prehistoric and historic traces in the mtDNA of Mozambique: insights into the Bantu expansions and the slave trade. *Annals of Human Genetics* 65: 439–58.

Peters, J. 1986. A revision of the faunal remains from two central Sudanese sites: Khartoum Hospital and Esh Shaheinab. *Archaeozoologia (Mélanges)* 11–33.

Petit-Maire, N. 1988. Climatic change and man in the Sahara, pp. 19–42 in J. Bower and D. Lubell (eds.) *Prehistoric Cultures and Environments in the Late Quaternary of Africa.* Oxford: British Archaeological Reports.

   1991. Recent climatic change and man in the Sahara. *Journal of African Earth Sciences* 12: 125–32.

Phillips, J. S. 1997. Punt and Aksum: Egypt and the Horn of Africa. *Journal of African History* 38: 423–57.

Phillipson, D. W. 1968a. The Early Iron Age in Zambia: regional variants and some tentative conclusions. *Journal of African History* 9: 191–211.

   1968b. Cewa, Leya and Lala iron-smelting furnaces. *South African Archaeological Bulletin* 23: 102–13.

   1968c. The Early Iron Age site at Kapwirimbwe, Lusaka. *Azania* 3: 87–105.

   1970. Excavations at Twickenham Road, Lusaka. *Azania* 5: 77–118.

   1972a. Early Iron Age sites on the Zambian Copperbelt. *Azania* 7: 93–128.

   1972b. Zambian rock paintings. *World Archaeology* 3: 313–27.

   1974. Iron Age history and archaeology in Zambia. *Journal of African History* 15: 1–25.

   1975. The chronology of the Iron Age in Bantu Africa. *Journal of African History* 16: 321–42.

   1976. *The Prehistory of Eastern Zambia.* Nairobi: British Institute in Eastern Africa.

   1977a. *The Later Prehistory of Eastern and Southern Africa.* London: Heinemann Educational Books.

   1977b. The excavation of Gobedra rockshelter, Axum: an early occurrence of cultivated finger millet in northern Ethiopia. *Azania* 12: 53–82.

   1977c. Lowasera. *Azania* 12: 1–32.

   1979. The origin of prehistoric farming in East Africa, pp. 41–63 in B. Ogot (ed.) *Ecology and History in East Africa.* Nairobi: East African Publishing House.

1984. Aspects of early food production in northern Kenya, pp. 489–95 in L. Krzyzaniak and M. Kobusiewicz (eds.) *Origin and Early Development of Food-Producing Cultures in North-East Africa*. Poznan: Poznan Archaeological Museum.

1985a. An archaeological reconsideration of Bantu expansion. *Muntu* 2: 69–84.

1985b. *African Archaeology*. Cambridge: Cambridge University Press.

1989a. Bantu-speaking people in southern Africa: an archaeological perspective, pp. 145–64 in T. Obenga (ed.) *Les peuples bantu: migrations, expansion et identité culturelle*. Paris: L'Harmattan.

1989b. The first South African pastoralists and the Early Iron Age. *Nsi* 6: 127–34.

1993a. The antiquity of cultivation and herding in Ethiopia, pp. 344–57 in T. Shaw *et al.* (eds.) *The Archaeology of Africa: Foods, Metals and Towns*. London: Routledge.

1993b. *African Archaeology (Second Edition)*. Cambridge: Cambridge University Press.

1997. *The Monuments of Aksum*. Addis Ababa: Addis Ababa University Press and British Institute in Eastern Africa.

1998. *Ancient Ethiopia: Aksum, Its Antecedents and Successors*. London: British Museum Press.

2000. *Archaeology at Aksum, Ethiopia, 1993–97*. London: British Institute in Eastern Africa and Society of Antiquaries.

2003a. Language and farming dispersals in sub-Saharan Africa, with particular reference to the Bantu-speaking peoples, pp. 177–87 in P. Bellwood and C. Renfrew (eds.) *Examining the Farming/Language Dispersal Hypothesis*. Cambridge: McDonald Institute for Archaeological Research.

2003b. *Archaeology in Africa and in Museums (an Inaugural Lecture)*. Cambridge: Cambridge University Press.

Phillipson, D. W. and B. M. Fagan 1969. The date of the Ingombe Ilede burials. *Journal of African History* 10: 199–204.

Phillipson, L. 1978. *The Stone Age Archaeology of the Upper Zambezi Valley*. Nairobi: British Institute in Eastern Africa.

1997. Edge modification as an indicator of function and handedness of Acheulian handaxes from Kariandusi, Kenya. *Lithic Technology* 22: 171–83.

2000. Aksumite lithic industries. *African Archaeological Review* 17: 49–63.

Phillipson, L. and D. W. Phillipson 1970. Patterns of edge damage on the Late Stone Age industry from Chiwemupula, Zambia. *Zambia Museums Journal* 1: 40–75.

Pickford, M. 1983. Sequence and environments of the Lower and Middle Miocene hominoids of western Kenya, pp. 421–39 in R. L. Ciochon and R. S. Corruccini (eds.) *New Interpretations of Ape and Human Ancestry*. New York: Plenum Press.

1986. A reappraisal of *Kenyapithecus*, pp. 163–71 in J. G. Else and P. C. Lee (eds.) *Primate Evolution*. Cambridge: Cambridge University Press.

Pikirayi, I. 1993. *The Archaeological Identity of the Mutapa State*. Uppsala: Societas Archaeologica Upsalensis.

2001. *The Zimbabwe Culture*. Walnut Creek, CA: Altamira Press.

Piperno, D. R. 1988. *Phytolith Analysis: An Archaeological and Geological Perspective*. London: Academic Press.

Polet, J. 1985. *Tegdaoust IV: fouille d'un quartier de Tegdaoust*. Paris: Editions Recherche sur les Civilisations.

Posnansky, M. 1968. The excavation of an Ankole capital site at Bweyorere. *Uganda Journal* 32: 165–82.

1969. Bigo bya Mugenyi. *Uganda Journal* 33: 125–50.

1973. Aspects of early West African trade. *World Archaeology* 5: 149–62.

1976. Archaeology and the origins of the Akan society in Ghana, pp. 49–59 in G. de G. Sieveking *et al.* (eds.) *Problems in Economic and Social Archaeology*. London: Duckworth.

Posnansky, M. and R. McIntosh 1976. New radiocarbon dates for northern and western Africa. *Journal of African History* 17: 161–95.

Potts, R. B. 1984. Home bases and early hominids. *American Scientist* 72: 338–47.

1986. Temporal span of bone accumulations at Olduvai Gorge and implications for early hominid foraging behaviour. *Paleobiology* 12: 25–31.

1989. Olorgesailie: new excavations and findings in Early and Middle Pleistocene contexts, southern Kenya Rift Valley. *Journal of Human Evolution* 18: 477–84.

Pringle, D. 1981. *The Defence of Byzantine Africa from Justinian to the Arab Conquest*. Oxford: British Archaeological Reports.

Prins, F. E. and S. Hall 1994. Expressions of fertility in the rock art of Bantu-speaking agriculturalists. *African Archaeological Review* 12: 171–203.

Pycraft, W. P. *et al.* 1928. *Rhodesian Man and Associated Remains*. London: British Museum (Natural History).

Quintana-Murci, L. *et al.* 1999. Genetic evidence of an early exit of *Homo sapiens* from Africa through eastern Africa. *Nature Genetics* 23: 437–41.

Rakotoarisoa, J.-A. 1998. *Mille ans d'occupation humaine dans le sud-est de Madagascar*. Paris: L'Harmattan.

Ranov, V. A. 2001. Cleavers: their distribution, chronology and typology, pp. 105–13 in S. Milliken and J. Cook (eds.) *A Very Remote Period Indeed: Papers on the Palaeolithic Presented to Derek Roe*. Oxford: Oxbow.

Raven, S. 1993. *Rome in Africa (Third Edition)*. London: Routledge.

Ravisé, A. 1970. Industrie néolithique en os de la région de S. Louis, Sénégal. *Notes Africaines* 128: 97–102.

Raynal, J. P. and J.-P. Texier 1989. Découverte d'Acheuléen ancien dans la carrière Thomas à Casablanca et problème de l'anciennetéde la présence humaine au Maroc. *Comptes-Rendus des Séances de l'Académie des Sciences de Paris, sér. 2, 308:* 1743–9.

Raynal, J. P. *et al.* 1990. Un nouveau gisement paléontologique plio-pléistocene en Afrique du Nord: Ahl Al Oughlam (ancienne carrière Deprez) à Casablanca (Maroc). *Comptes-Rendus des Séances de l'Académie des Sciences de Paris, sér. 2, 310:* 315–20.

1995. The earliest occupation of Atlantic Morocco: the Casablanca evidence, pp. 255–62 in W. Roebroeks and T. van Kolfschoten (eds.) *The Earliest Occupation of Europe*. Leiden: University of Leiden.

Rayner, R. J. *et al.* 1993. The Makapansgat australopithecine environment. *Journal of Human Evolution* 24: 219–31.

Reed, K. E. 1997. Early hominid evolution and ecological change through the African Plio-Pleistocene. *Journal of Human Evolution* 32: 289–322.

Reid, A. 1996. Ntusi and the development of social complexity in southern Uganda, pp. 621–7 in G. Pwiti and R. Soper (eds.) *Aspects of African Archaeology*. Harare: University of Zimbabwe Publications.

Reid, A. and P. Robertshaw 1987. A new look at Ankole capital sites. *Azania* 22: 83–8.

Reid, A. *et al.* 1998. Herding traditions, pp. 81–100 in P. Lane *et al.* (eds.) *Ditswa Mmung: The Archaeology of Botswana.* Gaborone: Pula Press and the Botswana Society.

Reisner, G. A. 1923. *Excavations at Kerma* (Harvard African Studies 5–6). Cambridge, MA: Harvard University Paris.

Reygasse, M. 1935. Découverte d'ateliers de technique acheuléenne dans les Tassili des Ajjers (Erg Tihodaïne). *Bulletin de la Société Préhistorique Française* 32: 358–62.

Ribot, I. *et al.* 2001. *The Prehistoric Burials of Shum Laka Rockshelter (North-West Cameroon).* Tervuren: Musée Royal de l'Afrique Centrale.

Richmond, B. G. and W. L. Jungers 1995. Size variation and sexual dimorphism in *Australopithecus afarensis* and living hominoids. *Journal of Human Evolution* 29: 229–45.

Richter, J. 1989. Neolithic sites in the Wadi Howar, western Sudan, pp. 431–42 in L. Krzyzaniak and M. Kobusiewicz (eds.) *The Late Prehistory of the Nile Basin and the Sahara.* Poznan: Polish Academy of Sciences.

van Riet Lowe, C. 1952. The Vaal River chronology. *South African Archaeological Bulletin* 7: 135–49.

Rightmire, G. P. 1972. Cranial measurements and discrete traits compared in distance studies of African negro skulls. *Human Biology* 44: 263–73.

   1975. New studies of post-Pleistocene human skeletal remains from the Rift Valley, Kenya. *American Journal of Physical Anthropology* 42: 351–70.

   1978. Human skeletal remains from the southern Cape Province and their bearing on the Stone Age prehistory of South Africa. *Quaternary Research* 9: 219–30.

   1979a. Implications of Border Cave skeletal remains for later Pleistocene human evolution. *Current Anthropology* 20: 23–35.

   1979b. Cranial remains of *Homo erectus* from Beds II and IV, Olduvai Gorge, Tanzania. *American Journal of Physical Anthropology* 51: 99–115.

   1990. *The Evolution of* Homo erectus. Cambridge: Cambridge University Press.

   1996. The human cranium from Bodo, Ethiopia: evidence for speciation in the Middle Pleistocene. *Journal of Human Evolution* 31: 21–39.

   1998. Human evolution in the Middle Pleistocene: the role of *Homo heidelbergensis*. *Evolutionary Anthropology* 6: 218–27.

   2001. Comparison of Middle Pleistocene hominids from Africa and Asia, pp. 123–33 in L. S. Barham and K. Robson-Brown (eds.) *Human Roots: Africa and Asia in the Middle Pleistocene.* Bristol: Western Academic and Specialist Press.

Rightmire, G. P. and H. J. Deacon 1991. Comparative studies of Late Pleistocene human remains from Klasies River Mouth, South Africa. *Journal of Human Evolution* 20: 131–56.

Robbins, L. H. 1974. *The Lothagam Site.* East Lansing: Michigan State University Museum.

Robbins, L. H. *et al.* 1980. *Lopoy and Lothagam.* East Lansing: Michigan State University Museum.

   1994. Barbed bone points, paleoenvironment and the antiquity of fish exploitation in the Kalahari Desert. *Journal of Field Archaeology* 21: 257–64.

   2000. Archaeology, paleoenvironment and chronology of the Tsodilo Hills White Paintings Rock Shelter, northwest Kalahari Desert, Botswana. *Journal of Archaeological Science* 27: 1085–113.

Robert, D. 1970. Les fouilles de Tegdaoust. *Journal of African History* 11: 471–93.

Robert-Chaleix, D. 1989. *Tegdaoust V: une concession mediévale à Tegdaoust.* Paris: Editions Recherche sur les Civilisations.

Roberts, D. L. and L. Berger 1997. Last interglacial (*c.* 117 kyr) human footprints in South Africa. *South African Journal of Science* 93: 349–50.

Robertshaw, P. 1988. The Elmenteitan: an early food-producing culture in East Africa. *World Archaeology* 20: 57–69.

    1989. The development of pastoralism in East Africa, pp. 207–12 in J. Clutton-Brock (ed.) *The Walking Larder.* London: Unwin Hyman.

    (ed.) 1990a. *A History of African Archaeology.* London: Currey.

    (ed.) 1990b. *Early Pastoralists in South-Western Kenya.* Nairobi: British Institute in Eastern Africa.

    1991. Gogo Falls: a complex site east of Lake Victoria. *Azania* 26: 63–195.

    1994. Archaeological survey, ceramic analysis, and state formation in western Uganda. *African Archaeological Review* 12: 105–31.

Robertshaw, P. and D. Collett 1983. A new framework for the study of early pastoral communities in East Africa. *Journal of African History* 24: 289–301.

Robertson, J. H. 2000. Early Iron Age archaeology in central Zambia. *Azania* 35: 147–82.

Robertson, J. H. and R. Bradley 2000. A new paradigm: the African Early Iron Age without Bantu migrations. *History in Africa* 27: 287–323.

Robin, C. and A. de Maigret 1998. Le grand temple de Yéha (Tigray, Ethiopie) après la première campaigne de fouilles de la Mission française (1998). *Comptes-Rendus des Séances de l'Académie des Inscriptions et Belles-Lettres, année 1998*: 737–98.

Robinson, K. R. 1959. *Khami Ruins.* Cambridge: Cambridge University Press.

    1966a. Bambata ware: its position in the Rhodesian Iron Age in the light of recent evidence. *South African Archaeological Bulletin* 21: 81–5.

    1966b. The Leopard's Kopje culture: its position in the Iron Age in Southern Rhodesia. *South African Archaeological Bulletin* 21: 5–51.

    1973. *The Iron Age of the Upper and Lower Shire.* Zomba: Malawi Antiquities Department.

Robinson, K. R. and B. Sandelowsky 1968. The Iron Age in northern Malawi: recent work. *Azania* 3: 107–46.

Roche, H. and J. J. Tiercelin 1980. Industries lithiques de la formation plio-pléistocène d'Hadar, Ethiopie, pp. 194–9 in R. E. Leakey and B. A. Ogot (eds.) *Proceedings of the 8th Panafrican Congress of Prehistory.* Nairobi: Louis Leakey Memorial Institute.

Roche, H. *et al.* 1988. Isenya: état des recherches sur un nouveau site acheuléen d'Afrique orientale. *African Archaeological Review* 6: 27–55.

    1999. Early hominid stone tool production and technical skill 2.34 myr ago in West Turkana, Kenya. *Nature* 399: 57–60.

Roche, J. 1971. La grotte de Taforalt. *Bulletin de la Société Historique de Maroc* 3: 7–14.

Rolland, N. 2001. The initial peopling of Eurasia and the early occupation of Europe in its Afro-Asian context: major issues and current perspectives, pp. 78–94 in S. Milliken and J. Cook (eds) *A Very Remote Period Indeed: Papers on the Palaeolithic Presented to Derek Roe.* Oxford: Oxbow.

Rose, L. and F. Marshall 1996. Meat eating, hominid sociality and home bases revisited. *Current Anthropology* 37: 307–38.

Roset, J.-P. 1987. Paleoclimatic and cultural conditions of neolithic development in the Early Holocene of northern Niger (Aïr and Ténéré), pp. 211–34 in A. E. Close (ed.) *Prehistory of Arid North Africa*. Dallas, TX: Southern Methodist University Press.

Roubet, C. 1979. *Economie pastorale préagricole en Algérie orientale: le néolithique de tradition capsienne*. Paris: CNRS.

Rowley-Conwy, P. 1988. The camel in the Nile Valley: new radiocarbon accelerator (AMS) dates for Qasr Ibrim. *Journal of Egyptian Archaeology* 74: 245–8.

Rudner, J. 1968. Strandloper pottery from South and South West Africa. *Annals of the South African Museum* 49: 441–663.

   1971. Painted burial stones from the Cape. *South African Journal of Science* special issue 2: 54–61.

Russell, T. 2000. The application of the Harris Matrix to San rock art at Main Caves North, KwaZulu-Natal. *South African Archaeological Bulletin* 55: 60–70.

Ruvulo, M. *et al.* 1993. Mitochondrial COII sequences and modern human origins. *Molecular Biology and Evolution* 10: 1115–35.

Sadr, K. 1991. *The Development of Nomadism in Ancient Northeast Africa*. Philadelphia: University of Pennsylvania Press.

   1998. The first herders at the Cape of Good Hope. *African Archaeological Review* 15: 101–32.

   2003. The neolithic of southern Africa. *Journal of African History* 44: 195–209.

Sahnouni, M. 1998. *The Lower Palaeolithic of the Maghreb: excavations and analyses at Ain Hanech, Algeria*. Oxford: British Archaeological Reports.

Saitowitz, S. J. *et al.* 1996. Glass bead trade from Islamic Egypt to South Africa. *South African Journal of Science* 92: 101–4.

Salas, A. *et al.* 2002. The making of the African mtDNA landscape. *American Journal of Human Genetics* 71: 1082–111.

Saliège, J. F. *et al.* 1980. Premières datations de tumulus pré-islamiques au Mali: site mégalithique de Tondidarou. *Comptes-Rendus des Séances de l'Académie des Sciences de Paris, sér. D*, 291: 981–4.

Salles, J.-F. 1996. Achaemenid and Hellenistic trade in the Indian Ocean, pp. 251–67 in J. Reade (ed.) *The Indian Ocean in Antiquity*. London: Kegan Paul.

Sampson, C. G. 1974. *The Stone Age Archaeology of Southern Africa*. New York: Academic Press.

   2001. An Acheulian settlement pattern in the Upper Karoo region of South Africa, pp. 28–36 in S. Milliken and J. Cook (eds.) *A Very Remote Period Indeed: Papers on the Palaeolithic Presented to Derek Roe*. Oxford: Oxbow.

Sandford, K. 1934. *Palaeolithic Man and the Nile Valley in Upper and Middle Egypt*. Chicago: Oriental Institute.

Sandford, K. and W. J. Arkell 1933. *Palaeolithic Man and the Nile Valley in Nubia and Upper Egypt*. Chicago: Oriental Institute.

dos Santos Junior, J. R. and C. M. Ervedosa 1970. A estaçao arquelogica de Benfica. *Estudos de Biologia (Luanda)* 1: 31–51.

Sassoon, H. 1983. Kings, cattle and blacksmiths. *Azania* 18: 93–106.

Sausse, F. 1975. La mandibule atlanthropienne de la carrière Thomas I (Casablanca). *L'Anthropologie* 79: 81–112.

Saxon, E. *et al.* 1974. Results of recent investigations at Tamar Hat. *Libyca* 22: 49–91.

Schepartz, L. A. 1988. Who were the later Pleistocene eastern Africans? *African Archaeological Review* 6: 57–72.

Schick, K. D. and N. Toth 1995. *Making Silent Stones Speak*. London: Phoenix.

Schild, R. and F. Wendorf 1977. *The Prehistory of Dakhla Oasis and the Adjacent Desert*. Warsaw: Polish Academy of Sciences.

Schlanger, N. 1996. Understanding Levallois. *Cambridge Archaeological Journal* 6: 231–54.

Schmidt, P. R. 1978. *Historical Archaeology*. Westport, CT: Greenwood Press.

1995. Using archaeology to remake history in Africa, pp. 119–47 in P. R. Schmidt and T. C. Patterson (eds.) *Making Alternative Histories*. Santa Fe, NM: School of American Research Press.

(ed.) 1996. *The Culture and Technology of African Iron Production*. Gainesville: University of Florida Press.

1997a. *Iron Technology in East Africa: Symbolism, Science and Archaeology*. Bloomington: Indiana University Press.

1997b. Archaeological views on a history of landscape change in East Africa. *Journal of African History* 38: 260–88.

Schmidt, P. R. and T. Childs 1985. Innovation and industry during the Early Iron Age in East Africa. *African Archaeological Review* 3: 53–94.

Schoenbrun, D. L. 1993. We are what we eat: ancient agriculture between the Great Lakes. *Journal of African History* 34: 1–31.

1998. *A Green Place, a Good Place: Agrarian Change, Gender and Social Identity in the Great Lakes Region to the 15th Century*. Oxford: Currey.

Schuck, W. 1989. From lake to well: 5000 years of settlement in Wadi Shaw (Northern Sudan), pp. 421–9 in L. Krzyzaniak and M. Kobusiewicz (eds.) *Late Prehistory of the Nile Basin and the Sahara*. Poznan: Poznan Archaeological Museum.

Schwabe, C. W. 1984. A unique surgical operation on the horns of African bulls in ancient and modern times. *Agricultural History* 58: 138–56.

Schwarcz, H. P. 2001. Chronometric dating of the Middle Pleistocene, pp. 41–53 in L. S. Barham and K. Robson-Brown (eds.) *Human Roots: Africa and Asia in the Middle Pleistocene*. Bristol: Western Academic and Specialist Press.

Schweitzer, F. R. 1979. Excavations at Die Kelders, Cape Province, South Africa: the Holocene deposits. *Annals of the South African Museum* 78: 101–233.

Segobye, A. 1998. Daughters of Cattle: the significance of herding in the growth of complex societies in southern Africa between the 10th and 15th centuries AD, pp. 227–33 in S. Kent (ed.) *Gender in African Archaeology*. Walnut Creek, CA: Altamira Press.

Semaw, S. 2000. The earliest archaeology: the world's oldest stone artifacts from Gona, Ethiopia and their implications for the understanding of stone technology and patterns of human evolution. *Journal of Archaeological Science* 27: 1197–1214.

Senut, B. *et al.* 2001. First hominid from the Miocene Lukeino formation, Kenya. *Comptes-Rendus des Séances de l'Académie des Sciences de Paris, sér. terre et planètes* 332; 137–44.

Sergew Hable Sellassie 1972. *Ancient and Medieval Ethiopian History*. Addis Ababa: United Printers [for the author?].

Shackley, M. 1985. *Palaeolithic Archaeology of the Central Namib Desert*. Windhoek: State Museum.

Shaw, T. 1944. Report on excavations carried out in the cave known as Bosumpra at Abetifi, Kwahu, Gold Coast Colony. *Proceedings of the Prehistoric Society* 10: 1–67.

1970. *Igbo Ukwu.* London: Faber.

1971. Africa in prehistory: leader or laggard? *Journal of African History* 12: 143–53.

1977. Hunters, gatherers and first farmers in West Africa, pp. 69–126 in J. V. S. Megaw (ed.) *Hunters, Gatherers and First Farmers beyond Europe.* Leicester: Leicester University Press.

1978. *Nigeria: its archaeology and early history.* London: Thames and Hudson.

1981. The Late Stone Age in West Africa and the beginnings of African food production, pp. 213–35 in C. Roubet *et al. Préhistoire africaine: mélanges offerts au doyen Lionel Balout.* Paris: ADPF.

1985. The prehistory of West Africa, pp. 48–86 in J. F. A. Ajayi and M. Crowder (eds.) *History of West Africa*, vol. 1. Harlow: Longman.

Shaw, T. and S. G. H. Daniels 1984. Excavations at Iwo Eleru, Ondo State, Nigeria. *West African Journal of Archaeology* 14: 1–269.

Sheppard, P. J. and M. R. Kleindienst 1996. Technological change in the Earlier and Middle Stone Age of Kalambo Falls, Zambia. *African Archaeological Review* 13: 171–96.

Sheppard, P. J. and D. Lubell 1990. Early Holocene Maghreb prehistory: an evolutionary approach. *Sahara* 3: 63–9.

Shinnie, P. L. 1996. *Ancient Nubia.* London: Kegan Paul.

Shinnie, P. L. and R. Bradley 1980. *The Capital of Kush*, vol. 1. Berlin: Akademie Verlag.

Shinnie, P. L. and M. Shinnie 1978. *Debeira West.* Warminster: Aris and Phillips.

Shipman, P. 1986. Scavenging or hunting in early hominids: theoretical framework and tests. *American Anthropologist* 88: 27–43.

Shipman, P. and J. Rose 1983. Early hominid hunting, butchering and carcass-processing behaviors: approaches to the fossil record. *Journal of Anthropological Archaeology* 2: 57–98.

Sidebotham, S. E. and W. Z. Wendrich 1998. Berenike: archaeological fieldwork at a Ptolemaic-Roman port on the Red Sea coast of Egypt. *Sahara* 10: 85–96.

Simons, E. L. 1990. Discovery of the oldest known anthropoidean skull from the Paleogene of Egypt. *Science* 247: 1567–9.

Simons, E. L. and D. T. Rasmussen 1994. A whole new world of ancestors: Eocene anthropoideans from Africa. *Evolutionary Anthropology* 3: 128–38.

Simoons, F. J. 1965. Some questions on the economic prehistory of Ethiopia. *Journal of African History* 6: 1–13.

Sinclair, P. J. J. 1982. Chibuene – an early trading site in southern Mozambique. *Paideuma* 28: 149–64.

1984. Some aspects of the economic level of the Zimbabwe state. *Zimbabwea* 1: 48–53.

Sinclair, P. J. J. 1986. *Pottery from Matola 2531 Cdl, Southern Mozambique.* Stockholm: Central Board of National Antiquities.

1987. *Space, Time and Social Formation: A Territorial Approach to the Archaeology and Anthropology of Zimbabwe and Mozambique, c. 0–1700 A.D.* Uppsala: Societas Archaeologica Upsalensis.

1991. Archaeology in eastern Africa: an overview of current chronological issues. *Journal of African History* 32: 179–219.

Sinclair, P. J. J. *et al.* 1993a. A perspective on archaeological research in Mozambique, pp. 409–31 in T. Shaw *et al.* (eds.) *The Archaeology of Africa: Foods, Metals and Towns.* London: Routledge.

    1993b. Urban trajectories on the Zimbabwe plateau, pp. 705–31 in T. Shaw *et al.* (eds.) *The Archaeology of Africa: Foods, Metals and Towns.* London: Routledge.

Singer, R. J. and J. Wymer 1968. Archaeological investigations at the Saldanha skull site in South Africa. *South African Archaeological Bulletin* 23: 63–74.

    1969. Radiocarbon date for two painted stones from a coastal cave in South Africa. *Nature* 224: 508–10.

    1982. *The Middle Stone Age at Klasies River Mouth in South Africa.* Chicago: University of Chicago Press.

Smith, A. B. 1974. Preliminary report of excavations at Karkarichinkat, Mali. *West African Journal of Archaeology* 4: 33–55.

    1975. Radiocarbon dates from Bosumpra Cave, Abetifi, Ghana. *Proceedings of the Prehistoric Society* 41: 179–82.

    1976. A microlithic industry from Adrar Bous, Tenere Desert, Niger, pp. 181–96 in Berhanou Abebe *et al.* (eds.) *Proceedings of the 7th Panafrican Congress of Prehistory and Quaternary Studies.* Addis Ababa: Antiquities Administration.

    1980a. The neolithic tradition in the Sahara, pp. 451–65 in M. A. J. Williams and H. Faure (eds.) *The Sahara and the Nile.* Rotterdam: Balkema.

    1980b. Domesticated cattle in the Sahara and their introduction into West Africa, pp. 489–501 in M. A. J. Williams and H. Faure (eds.) *The Sahara and the Nile.* Rotterdam: Balkema.

    1990. On becoming herders: Khoikhoi and San ethnicity in southern Africa. *African Studies* 49: 51–73.

    1993a. New approaches to Saharan rock art of the bovidean period, pp. 77–89 in L. Krzyzaniak *et al.* (eds.) *Environmental Change and Human Culture in the Nile Basin and Northern Africa until the Second Millennium BC.* Poznan: Poznan Archaeological Museum.

    1993b. Terminal palaeolithic industries of the Sahara: a discussion of new data, pp. 69–75 in L. Krzyzaniak *et al.* (eds.) *Environmental Change and Human Culture in the Nile Basin and Northern Africa until the Second Millennium BC.* Poznan: Poznan Archaeological Museum.

    1998a. Early domestic stock in southern Africa: a commentary. *African Archaeological Review* 15: 151–6.

    1998b. Keeping people on the periphery: the ideology of social hierarchies between hunters and herders. *Journal of Anthropological Archaeology* 17: 201–15.

Smith, A. B. *et al.* 1991. Excavations in the south-western Cape, South Africa, and the archaeological identity of prehistoric hunter-gatherers within the last 2000 years. *South African Archaeological Bulletin* 46: 71–91.

Smith, B. W. and S. Ouzman 2004. Taking stock: identifying Khoekhoen herder rock art in southern Africa. *Current Anthropology* 45: 479–526.

Smith, B. W. and J. A. Van Schalkwyk 2002. The white camel of the Makgabeng. *Journal of African History* 43: 235–54.

Smith, H. F. C. 1971. The early states of the central Sudan, pp. 158–201 in J. F. A. Ajayi and M. Crowder (eds.) *History of West Africa*, vol. 1. London: Longman.

Smith, H. S. 1991. The development of the 'A-Group' culture in northern lower Nubia, pp. 92–111 in W. V. Davies (ed.) *Egypt and Africa: Nubia from Prehistory to Islam.* London: British Museum Press.

Smith, M. C. and H. T. Wright 1988. The ceramics from Ras Hafun in Somalia: notes on a classical maritime site. *Azania* 23: 115–41.

Smith, P. E. L. 1967. New investigations in the late Pleistocene archaeology of the Kom Ombo Plain, Upper Egypt. *Quaternaria* 9: 141–52.

1968. Problems and possibilities of the prehistoric rock art of northern Africa. *African Historical Studies* 1: 1–39.

1982. The late palaeolithic and epipalaeolithic of northern Africa, pp. 342–409 in J. D. Clark (ed.) *Cambridge History of Africa*, vol. 1. Cambridge: Cambridge University Press.

Smolla, G. 1956. Prähistorische Keramik aus Ostafrika. *Tribus* 6: 35–64.

Sohnge, P. G. *et al.* 1937. Geology and archaeology of the Vaal River Basin. *Memoirs of the Geological Survey of the Union of South Africa* 35: 1–184.

Solomon, A. 1997. The myth or ritual origins? Ethnography, mythology and interpretation of San rock art. *South African Archaeological Bulletin* 52: 3–13.

Soper, R. C. 1965. The Stone Age in Northern Nigeria. *Journal of the Historical Society of Nigeria* 3: 175–94.

1967a. Kwale: an Early Iron Age site in south-eastern Kenya. *Azania* 2: 1–17.

1967b. Iron Age sites in north-eastern Tanzania. *Azania* 2: 19–36.

1971. A general review of the Early Iron Age in the southern half of Africa. *Azania* 6: 5–37.

1976. Archaeological sites in the Chyulu Hills, Kenya. *Azania* 11: 83–116.

1979. Iron Age archaeology and traditional history in Embu, Mbeere and Chuka areas of central Kenya. *Azania* 14: 31–59.

1982. Bantu expansion into eastern Africa: archaeological evidence, pp. 223–38 in C. Ehret and M. Posnansky (eds.) *The Archaeological and Linguistic Reconstruction of African History.* Berkeley: University of California Press.

1985. Roulette decoration on African pottery: technical considerations, dating and distributions. *African Archaeological Review* 3: 29–51.

1993. The palace at Oyo Ile, western Nigeria. *West African Journal of Archaeology* 22: 295–311.

2002. *Nyanga: Ancient Fields, Settlements and Agricultural History in Zimbabwe.* London: British Institute in Eastern Africa.

Soper, R. C. and P. Darling 1980. The walls of Oyo Ile. *West African Journal of Archaeology* 10: 61–81.

Soper, R. C. and B. Golden 1969. An archaeological survey of Mwanza region, Tanzania. *Azania* 4: 15–79.

Sowunmi, M. A. 2002. Environmental and human responses to climatic events in West and West-central Africa during the Late Holocene, pp. 95–104 in F. Hassan (ed.) *Drought, Food and Culture: Ecological Change and Food Security in Africa's Later Prehistory.* New York: Kluwer/Plenum.

Spencer, A. J. 1993. *Early Egypt: The Rise of Civilisation in the Nile Valley.* London: British Museum Press.

Speth, J. D. and D. D. Davis 1976. Seasonal variability in early hominid predation. *Science* 192: 441–5.

Stahl, A. B. 1985. Reinvestigation of Kintampo 6 rock shelter, Ghana: implications for the nature of culture change. *African Archaeological Review* 3: 117–50.

1994. Innovation, diffusion and culture contact: the Holocene archaeology of Ghana. *Journal of World Prehistory* 8: 51–112.

2001. *Making History in Banda: Anthropological Visions of Africa's Past.* Cambridge: Cambridge University Press.

Stehli, P. (ed.) 1978. *Sahara.* Cologne: Muzeen der Stadt Köln.

Stewart, K. M. 1989. *Fishing Sites of North and East Africa in the Late Pleistocene and Holocene.* Oxford: British Archaeological Reports.

Stiles, D. 1991. Early hominid behaviour and culture tradition: raw material studies in Bed II, Olduvai Gorge. *African Archaeological Review* 9: 1–19.

1998. Raw material as evidence for human behaviour in the Lower Pleistocene: the Olduvai case, pp. 133–50 in M. D. Petraglia and R. Korisettar (eds.) *Early Human Behaviour in Global Context.* London: Routledge.

Stokes, S. *et al.* 1998. Punctuated aridity in southern Africa during the last glacial cycle: the chronology of linear dune construction in the northeastern Kalahari. *Palaeogeography, Palaeoclimatology, Palaeoecology* 137: 305–32.

Stoneking, M. and R. L. Cann 1989. African origin of human mitochondrial DNA, pp. 17–30 in P. Mellars and C. Stringer (eds.) *The Human Revolution: Behavioural and Biological Perspectives on the Origins of Modern Humans.* Edinburgh: Edinburgh University Press.

Stringer, C. 1979. A re-evaluation of the fossil hominid calvaria from Singa (Sudan). *Bulletin of the British Museum of Natural History (Geology)* 32: 77–83.

2001. Modern human origins: distinguishing the models. *African Archaeological Review* 18: 67–75.

2002a. The morphological and behavioural origins of modern humans, pp. 23–30 in T. J. Crow (ed.) *The Speciation of Modern* Homo sapiens. Oxford: Oxford University Press for The British Academy.

2002b. Modern human origins: progress and prospects. *Philosophical Transactions of the Royal Society of London B* 357: 563–79.

Stringer, C. and R. McKie 1996. *African Exodus.* London: Cape.

Stringer, C. *et al.* 1985. Preparation and further study of the Singa skull from Sudan. *Bulletin of the British Museum of Natural History (Geology)* 38: 347–58.

Stuiver, M. and R. S. Kra (eds.) 1986. Radiocarbon calibration issue: Proceedings of the Twelfth International Radiocarbon Conference. *Radiocarbon* 28: 805–1030.

Stuiver, M. *et al.* 1998. INTCAL98 radiocarbon age calibration 24,000–0 cal. BP. *Radiocarbon* 40: 1041–84.

Summers, M. (ed.) 1959. *Prehistoric Rock Art of the Federation of Rhodesia and Nyasaland.* Salisbury, Southern Rhodesia: National Publications Trust.

1969. *Ancient Mining in Rhodesia.* Salisbury, Southern Rhodesia: National Museums of Rhodesia.

Susman, R. L. 1998. Hand function and tool behavior in early hominids. *Journal of Human Evolution* 35: 23–46.

Sutton, J. E. G. 1968. Archaeological sites in Usandawe. *Azania* 3: 167–74.

1973. *The Archaeology of the Western Highlands of Kenya.* Nairobi: British Institute in Eastern Africa.

1974. The aquatic civilization of middle Africa. *Journal of African History* 15: 527–46.

1982. Archaeology in West Africa: a review of recent work and a further list of radiocarbon dates. *Journal of African History* 23: 291–313.

1985. Temporal and spatial variability in African iron furnaces, pp. 164–96 in R. Haaland and P. Shinnie (eds.) *African Iron Working: Ancient and Traditional.* Oslo: Norwegian University Press.

1991. The international factor at Igbo-Ukwu. *African Archaeological Review* 9: 145–60.

1997. The African lords of the intercontinental gold trade before the Black Death: al-Hasan bin Sulaiman of Kilwa and Mansa Musa of Mali. *Antiquaries Journal* 77: 221–42.

1998a. Engaruka: an irrigation-agriculture community in northern Tanzania before the Maasai. *Azania* 33: 1–37.

1998b. Kilwa: a history of the ancient Swahili town with a guide to the monuments of Kilwa Kisiwani and adjacent islands. *Azania* 33: 113–69.

1998c. Hyrax Hill and the later archaeology of the Central Rift Valley of Kenya. *Azania* 33: 73–112.

2001. Igbo-Ukwu and the Nile. *African Archaeological Review* 18: 49–62.

Sutton, J. E. G. and A. D. Roberts 1968. Uvinza and its salt industry. *Azania* 3: 45–86.

Suwa, G. *et al.* 1997. The first skull of *Australopithecus boisei*. *Nature* 389: 489–92.

Swan, L. 1994. *Early Gold Mining on the Zimbabwe Plateau.* Uppsala: Societas Archaeologica Upsalensis.

Swisher, C. C. *et al.* 1994. Age of the earliest known hominids in Java, Indonesia. *Science* 263: 1118–21.

Szumowski, G. 1956. Fouilles de l'abri sous roche de Kourounkorokalé, Soudan français. *Bulletin de l'Institut Fondamental de l'Afrique Noire* 18: 462–508.

Taylor, D. and R. Marchant 1995. Human impact in the Interlacustrine region: long-term pollen records from the Rukiga Highlands. *Azania* 29/30: 283–95.

Taylor, J. H. 1991. *Egypt and Nubia.* London: British Museum Press.

Templeton, A. R. 2002. Out of Africa again and again. *Nature* 416: 45–51.

Thackeray, A. I. 1989. Changing fashions in the Middle Stone Age: the stone artefact sequence from Klasies River main site, South Africa. *African Archaeological Review* 7: 33–57.

1992. The Middle Stone Age south of the Limpopo River. *Journal of World Prehistory* 6: 385–439.

2000. Middle Stone Age artefacts from the 1993 and 1995 excavations of Die Kelders Cave 1, South Africa. *Journal of Human Evolution* 38: 147–68.

Thackeray, A. I. and A. J. Kelly 1988. A technological and typological analysis of Middle Stone Age assemblages antecedent to the Howieson's Poort at Klasies River main site. *South African Archaeological Bulletin* 43: 15–26.

Thackeray, A. I. *et al.* 1981. Dated rock engravings from Wonderwerk Cave, South Africa. *Science* 214: 64–7.

Thilmans, G. *et al.* 1980. *Protohistoire du Senegal: 1 – Les sites mégalithes.* Dakar: Institut Fondamental d'Afrique Noire.

Thomas, D. S. G. *et al.* 2000. Dune activity as a record of Late Quaternary aridity in the northern Kalahari: new evidence from northern Namibia interpreted in the context of regional arid and humid chronologies. *Palaeogeography, Palaeoclimatology, Palaeoecology* 156: 243–59.

Thomas, H. 1979. Géologie et paléontologie du gisement acheuléen de l'erg Tihodaïne. *Mémoires du Centre de Recherches Anthropologiques, Préhistoriques et Ethnographiques* 27: 1–122.

Thomassey, P. and R. Mauny 1951. Campagne de fouilles à Koumbi Saleh. *Bulletin de l'Institut Français d'Afrique Noire* 13: 438–62.

1956. Campagne de fouilles à Koumbi Saleh. *Bulletin de l'Institut Français d'Afrique Noire* 18: 117–40.

Thorp, C. 1995. *Kings, Commoners and Cattle at Great Zimbabwe Tradition Sites.* Harare: National Museums and Monuments.

Tillet, T. 1985. The Palaeolithic and its environment in the northern part of the Chad basin. *African Archaeological Review* 3: 163–77.

Tobias, P. V. 1949. The excavation of Mwulu's Cave, Potgietersrust district. *South African Archaeological Bulletin* 4: 2–13.

1978a. The South African australopithecines in time and hominid phylogeny with special reference to the dating and affinities of the Taung skull, pp. 45–84 in C. Jolly (ed.) *Early Hominids of Africa.* London: Duckworth.

1978b. *The Bushmen.* Cape Town: Human and Rousseau.

1980. *Australopithecus* and early *Homo*, pp. 161–5 in R. E. Leakey and B. A. Ogot (eds.) *Proceedings of the 8th Panafrican Congress of Prehistory.* Nairobi: Louis Leakey Memorial Institute.

1991. The emergence of spoken language in hominid evolution, pp. 67–78 in J. D. Clark (ed.) *Approaches to Understanding Early Hominid Lifeways in the African Savanna.* Bonn: Habelt.

Togola, T. 1996. Iron Age occupation in the Méma region, Mali. *African Archaeological Review* 13: 91–110.

Török, L. 1997. *Meroe City, an Ancient African Capital: John Garstang's Excavations in the Sudan.* London: Egypt Exploration Society.

Toth, N. 1985a. The Oldowan reassessed: a close look at early stone artifacts. *Journal of Archaeological Science* 12: 101–20.

1985b. Archaeological evidence for preferential right-handedness in the lower and middle Pleistocene, and its possible implications. *Journal of Human Evolution* 14: 607–14.

Toth, N. and K. Schick 1986. The first million years: the archaeology of proto-human culture. *Advances in Archaeological Method and Theory* 9: 1–96.

Toth, N. *et al.* 1993. *Pan* the tool-maker. *Journal of Archaeological Science* 20: 81–91.

Trigger, B. 1976. *Nubia under the Pharaohs.* London: Thames and Hudson.

2003. *Understanding Early Civilizations.* Cambridge: Cambridge University Press.

Trimingham, J. S. 1975. The Arab geographers and the East African coast, pp. 115–46 in H. N. Chittick and R. I. Rotberg (eds.) *East Africa and the Orient.* New York: Africana.

Turnbull, C. 1965. The Mbuti pygmies of the Congo, pp. 279–318 in J. L. Gibbs (ed.) *Peoples in Africa.* New York: Holt, Rinehart and Winston.

Turner, A. 1999. Assessing earliest human settlement of Eurasia: Late Pliocene dispersions from Africa. *Antiquity* 73: 563–70.

Turton, E. R. 1975. Bantu, Galla and Somali migrations in the Horn of Africa. *Journal of African History* 16: 519–37.

Tylecote, R. F. 1975. The origin of iron smelting in Africa. *West African Journal of Archaeology* 5: 1–9.

1982. Early copper slags and copper-base metal from the Agadez region of Niger. *Journal of the Historical Metallurgy Society* 16: 58–64.

Tyson, P. D. 1999. Late Quaternary and Holocene palaeoclimates of southern Africa: a synthesis. *South African Journal of Geology* 102: 335–49.

Tyson, P. D. and J. A. Lindesay 1992. The climate of the last 2000 years in southern Africa. *Holocene* 2: 271–8.

Unger-Hamilton, R. 1988. *Method in Microwear Analysis: Prehistoric Sickles and Other Stone Tools from Arjoune, Syria.* Oxford: British Archaeological Reports.

Van Campo, M. 1975. Pollen analyses in the Sahara, pp. 45–64 in F. Wendorf and A. E. Marks (eds.) *Problems in Prehistory – North Africa and the Levant.* Dallas, TX: Southern Methodist University Press.

Van Grunderbeek, M.-C. *et al.* 1983. *Le premier âge du fer au Rwanda et au Burundi: archéologie et environnement.* Brussels: IFAQ.

2001. Type de fourneau de fonte de fer associé à la culture urewe (âge du fer ancien) au Rwanda et au Burundi. *Mediterranean Archaeology* 14: 271–97.

Van Moorsel, H. 1968. *Atlas de préhistoire de la Plaine de Kinshasa.* Kinshasa: Université Lovanium.

Van Neer, W. 1989. Fishing along the prehistoric Nile, pp. 49–56 in L. Krzyzaniak and M. Kobusiewicz (eds.) *Late Prehistory of the Nile Basin and the Sahara.* Poznan: Poznan Archaeological Museum.

2002. Food security in western and central Africa during the Late Holocene: the role of domestic stock-keeping, hunting and fishing, pp. 251–74 in F. Hassan (ed.) *Drought, Food and Culture: Ecological Change and Food Security in Africa's Later Prehistory.* New York: Kluwer/Plenum.

Van Noten, F. L. 1971. Excavations at Munyama Cave. *Antiquity* 45: 56–8.

1977. Excavations at Matupi Cave. *Antiquity* 51: 35–40.

1978. *Rock Art of the Jebel Uweinat (Libyan Sahara).* Graz: Akademische Druck-u. Verlagsanstalt.

1979. The Early Iron Age in the Interlacustrine Region: the diffusion of iron technology. *Azania* 14: 61–80.

1982. *The Archaeology of Central Africa.* Graz: Akademische Druck-u. Verlagsanstalt.

1983. *Histoire archéologique du Rwanda.* Tervuren: Musée royal de l'Afrique Centrale.

Vansina, J. 1966. *Kingdoms of the Savanna.* Madison: University of Wisconsin Press.

1969. The bells of kings. *Journal of African History* 10: 187–97.

1984. Western Bantu expansion. *Journal of African History* 25: 129–45.

1985. *Oral Tradition as History.* London: Currey.

1990. *Paths in the Rainforests.* London: Currey.

1995. New linguistic evidence and the Bantu expansion. *Journal of African History* 36: 173–95.

van der Veen, M. (ed.) 1999. *The Exploitation of Plant Resources in Ancient Africa.* Dordrecht: Kluwer.

Vermeersch, P. M. 1992. The Upper and Late Palaeolithic of northern and eastern Africa, pp. 99–153 in F. Klees and R. Kuper (eds.) *New Light on the Northeast African Past.* Cologne: Heinrich-Barth-Institut.

(ed.) 2002. *Palaeolithic Quarrying Sites in Upper and Middle Egypt.* Leuven: Leuven University Press.

Vermeersch, P. M. *et al.* 1990. Palaeolithic chert exploitation in the limestone stretch of the Egyptian Nile Valley. *African Archaeological Review* 8: 77–102.

1996. Neolithic occupation of the Sodmein area, Red Sea Mountains, Egypt, pp. 411–19 in G. Pwiti and R. Soper (eds.) *Aspects of African Archaeology*. Harare: University of Zimbabwe Publications.

1998. A Middle Palaeolithic burial of a modern human at Taramsa Hill, Egypt. *Antiquity* 72: 475–84.

Vernet, R. 1995. *Les Paléoenvironnements du nord de l'Afrique depuis 600 000*. Meudon: CNRS.

2002. Climate during the Late Holocene in the Sahara and the Sahel: evolution and consequences on human settlement, pp. 47–63 in F. Hassan (ed.) *Drought, Food and Culture: Ecological Change and Food Security in Africa's Later Prehistory*. New York: Kluwer/Plenum.

Vinnicombe, P. 1976. *People of the Eland*. Pietermaritzburg: University of Natal Press.

Vogel, J. O. 1987. Iron Age farmers in southwestern Zambia: some aspects of spatial organisation. *African Archaeological Review* 5: 159–70.

(ed.) 1997. *Encyclopedia of Precolonial Africa: Archaeology, History, Languages, Cultures and Environments*. Walnut Creek, CA: Altamira Press.

(ed.) 2000. *Ancient African Metallurgy: The Socio-Political Context*. Walnut Creek, CA: Altamira Press.

Vogelsang, R. 1996. The Middle Stone Age in south-western Namibia, pp. 207–11 in G. Pwiti and R. Soper (eds.) *Aspects of African Archaeology*. Harare: University of Zimbabwe Publications.

1998. *MSA Fundstellen in Südwest Namibia*. Cologne: Heinrich-Barth-Institut.

Voigt, E. A. 1983. *Mapungubwe: An Archaeozoological Interpretation of an Iron Age Community*. Pretoria: Transvaal Museum.

Volavka, Z. (ed.) 1998. *Crown and Ritual: The Royal Insignia of Ngoyo*. Toronto: University of Toronto Press.

Volman, T. P. 1984. Early prehistory of southern Africa, pp. 169–220 in R. G. Klein (ed.) *Southern African Prehistory and Palaeoenvironments*. Rotterdam: Balkema.

Vrba, E. S. *et al.* 1992. *Palaeoclimate and Evolution with Emphasis on Human Origins*. New Haven, CT: Yale University Press.

Wadley, L. 1987. *Later Stone Age Hunters and Gatherers of the Southern Transvaal*. Oxford: British Archaeological Reports.

1993. The Pleistocene Later Stone Age south of the Limpopo River. *Journal of World Prehistory* 7: 243–96.

1996. The Robberg industry of Rose Cottage Cave, eastern Free State: the technology, spatial patterns and environment. *South African Archaeological Bulletin* 51: 64–74.

1997. Rose Cottage Cave: archaeological work 1987 to 1997. *South African Journal of Science* 93: 439–44.

2001a. What is cultural modernity? A general view and a South African perspective from Rose Cottage Cave. *Cambridge Archaeological Journal* 11: 201–21.

2001b. Preliminary report on excavations at Sibudu Cave, KwaZulu-Natal. *Southern African Humanities* 13: 1–17.

Wadley, L. and J. N. F. Binneman 1995. Arrowheads or pen knives? A microwear analysis of mid-Holocene stone segments from Jubilee Shelter, Transvaal. *South African Journal of Science* 91: 153–5.

Wai-Ogusu, B. 1973. Was there a Sangoan industry in West Africa? *West African Journal of Archaeology* 3: 191–6.

Walker, A. C. and R. E. F. Leakey (eds.) 1993. *The Nariokotome* Homo erectus *Skeleton*. Cambridge, MA: Harvard University Press.

Walker, A. C. *et al.* 1986. 2.5 myr *Australopithecus boisei* from west of Lake Turkana, Kenya. *Nature* 322: 517–22.

   1993. A new species of Proconsul from the early Miocene of Rusinga/Mfangano Islands, Kenya. *Journal of Human Evolution* 25: 43–56.

Walker, N. J. 1983. The significance of an early date for pottery and sheep in Zimbabwe. *South African Archaeological Bulletin* 38: 88–92.

   1995. *Late Pleistocene and Holocene Hunter-Gatherers of the Matopos*. Uppsala: Societas Archaeologia Upsalensis.

Walter, R. C. and J. L. Aronson 1982. Revisions of K/Ar ages for the Hadar hominid site, Ethiopia. *Nature* 296: 122–7.

Wandibba, S. 1980. The application of attribute analysis to the study of Later Stone Age/Neolithic pottery ceramics in Kenya, pp. 283–5 in R. E. Leakey and B. A. Ogot (eds.) *Proceedings of the 8th Panafrican Congress of Prehistory*. Nairobi: Leakey Memorial Institute.

Wasylikowa, K. 1992. Exploitation of wild plants by prehistoric peoples in the Sahara. *Würzburger Geographische Arbeiten* 84: 247–62.

Watson, E. *et al.* 1997. Mitochondrial footprints of human expansions in Africa. *American Journal of Human Genetics* 61: 691–704.

Watterson, B. 1988. *Coptic Egypt*. Edinburgh: Edinburgh University Press.

Webley, L. 1997. Jakkalsberg A and B: The Cultural material from two pastoralist sites in the Richtersveld, Northern Cape. *South African Field Archaeology* 6: 3–19.

Weiner, J. S. and J. Huizinga (eds.) 1972. *The Assessment of Population Affinities in Man*. Oxford: Clarendon Press.

Welsby, D. A. 1996. *The Kingdom of Kush: The Napatan and Meroitic Empires*. London: British Museum Press.

   1998. *Soba II: Renewed Excavations within the Metropolis of the Kingdom of Alwa in Central Sudan*. London: British Museum Press and British Institute in Eastern Africa.

   2002. *The Medieval Kingdoms of Nubia*. London: British Museum Press.

Welsby, D. A. and C. M. Daniels 1991. *Soba: Archaeological Research at a Medieval Capital on the Blue Nile*. London: British Institute in Eastern Africa.

Wendorf, F. (ed.) 1968. *The Prehistory of Nubia*. Dallas, TX: Southern Methodist University Press.

Wendorf, F. and F. A. Hassan 1980. Holocene ecology and prehistory in the Egyptian Sahara, pp. 407–19 in M. A. J. Williams and H. Faure (eds.) *The Sahara and the Nile*. Rotterdam: Balkema.

Wendorf, F. and R. Schild 1974. *A Middle Stone Age Sequence from the Central Rift Valley, Ethiopia*. Warsaw: Polish Academy of Sciences.

   1976. *Prehistory of the Nile Valley*. New York: Academic Press.

   2003. Review of Hassan 2002. *African Archaeological Review* 20: 121–33.

Wendorf, F. *et al.* (eds.) 1989. *The Prehistory of Wadi Kubbaniya*. Dallas, TX: Southern Methodist University Press.

   1993. *Egypt during the Last Interglacial: the Middle Palaeolithic of Bir Tarfawi and Bir Sahara East*. New York: Plenum.

   1998. The use of plants during the early Holocene in the Egyptian Sahara: early neolithic food economies, pp. 71–8 in S. di Lernia and G. Manzi (eds.) *Before Food Production in North Africa*. Forli: Abaco.

2001. *Holocene Settlements of the Egyptian Sahara*, vol. 1: *The Archaeology of Nabta Playa*. New York: Kluwer/Plenum.

Wendt, W. E. 1966. Two prehistoric archaeological sites in Egyptian Nubia. *Postilla* 102: 1–46.

1972. Preliminary report on an archaeological research programme in South West Africa. *Cimbebasia* B2: 1–61.

1976. Art mobilier from the Apollo 11 Cave, South West Africa: Africa's oldest dated works of art. *South African Archaeological Bulletin* 31: 5–11.

Wertime, T. A. 1980. The pyrotechnologic background, pp. 1–24 in T. A. Wertime and J. D. Muhly (eds.) *The Coming of the Age of Iron*. New Haven, CT: Yale University Press.

Wetterstrom, W. 1993. Foraging and farming in Egypt: the transition from hunting and gathering to horticulture in the Nile Valley, pp. 165–226 in T. Shaw *et al.* (eds.) *The Archaeology of Africa: foods, metals and towns*. London: Routledge.

1998. The origins of agriculture in Africa, with particular reference to sorghum and pearl millet, pp. 30–46 in O. Bar Yosef (ed.) *The Transition to Agriculture in the Old World*. (*Review of Archaeology* 19.)

White, T. D. 1986. Cutmarks on the Bodo cranium: a case of prehistoric defleshing. *American Journal of Physical Anthropology* 69: 503–9.

1987. Cannibalism at Klasies? *Sagittarius* 2: 6–9.

White, T. D. *et al.* 1994. *Australopithecus ramidus*, a new species of early hominid from Aramis, Ethiopia. *Nature* 371: 306–33.

2003. Pleistocene *Homo sapiens* from Middle Awash, Ethiopia. *Nature* 423: 742–7.

Whitelaw, G. 1994. KwaGandaganda: settlement patterns in the Natal Early Iron Age. *Natal Museum Journal of Humanities* 6: 1–64.

1995. Towards an Early Iron Age worldview: some ideas from KwaZulu-Natal. *Azania* 29/30: 37–50.

Wilding, R. 1980. The desert trade of eastern Ethiopia, pp. 379–80 in R. E. Leakey and B. A. Ogot (eds.) *Proceedings of the 8th Panafrican Congress of Prehistory*. Nairobi: Louis Leakey Memorial Institute.

Willcox, A. R. 1963. *The Rock Art of South Africa*. Johannesburg: Nelson.

Willett, F. 1962. The microlithic industry from Old Oyo, Western Nigeria, pp. 261–71 in G. Mortelmans (ed.) *Actes du 4e Congrès panafricain de préhistoire*. Tervuren: Musée Royal de l'Afrique Centrale.

1967. *Ife in the History of West African Sculpture*. London: Thames and Hudson.

Williams, M. A. J. and H. Faure (eds.) 1980. *The Sahara and the Nile*. Rotterdam: Balkema.

Williams, M. A. J. *et al.* 1993. *Quaternary Environments*. London: Arnold.

Willoughby, P. R. 1993. The Middle Stone Age in East Africa and modern human origins. *African Archaeological Review* 11: 3–21.

Wilson, M. 1969. The hunters and herders, pp. 40–74 in M. Wilson and L. Thompson (eds.) *The Oxford History of South Africa*, vol. 1. Oxford: Oxford University Press.

Wolpoff, M. H. 1989. Multiregional evolution: the fossil alternative to Eden, pp. 62–108 in P. Mellars and C. Stringer (eds.) *The Human Revolution: Behavioural and Biological Perspectives on the Origins of Modern Humans*. Edinburgh: Edinburgh University Press.

Wolpoff, M. H. *et al.* 1994. Multiregional evolution: a world-wide source for modern human populations, pp. 175–99 in M. H. and D. V. Nitecki (eds.) *Origins of Anatomically Modern Humans*. New York: Plenum.

Wood, B. A. 1985. Early *Homo* in Kenya and its systematic relationships, pp. 206–14 in E. Delson (ed.) *Ancestors: The Hard Evidence*. New York: Liss.

  1991. *Koobi Fora Research Project*, vol. 4: *Hominid Cranial Remains*. Oxford: Clarendon Press.

  1992. Origin and evolution of the genus *Homo*. *Nature* 355: 783–90.

Wood, B. A. and M. Collard 1999. The human genus. *Science* 284: 65–71.

Woodhouse, J. 1998. Iron in Africa: metal from nowhere, pp. 160–85 in G. Connah (ed.) *Transformations in Africa: Essays on Africa's Later Past*. London: Leicester University Press.

Wotzka, H.-P. 1995. *Studien zur Archäologie des zentralafrikanischen Regenwaldes*. Cologne: Heinrich-Barth-Institut.

Wright, H. T. 1993. Trade and politics on the eastern littoral of Africa, AD 800–1300, pp. 658–72 in T. Shaw *et al.* (eds.) *The Archaeology of Africa: Foods, Metals and Towns*. London: Routledge.

Wurz, S. 1999. The Howieson's Poort backed artefacts from Klasies River: an argument for symbolic behaviour. *South African Archaeological Bulletin* 64: 38–50.

Yellen, J. E. 1996. Behavioural and taphonomic patterning at Katanda 9: a Middle Stone Age site, Kivu Province, Zaïre. *Journal of Archaeological Science* 23: 915–32.

  1998. Barbed bone points: tradition and continuity in Saharan and sub-Saharan Africa. *African Archaeological Review* 15: 173–98.

Yohannes Haile-Selassie *et al.* 2001. Late Miocene hominids from the Middle Awash, Ethiopia. *Nature* 412: 178–81.

Yonas Beyene *et al.* 1996. Prehistoric research at Konso-Gardula, pp. 99–102 in G. Pwiti and R. Soper (eds.) *Aspects of African Archaeology*. Harare: University of Zimbabwe Publications.

  1997. The Acheulean at Konso-Gardula: results from locality KGA4-A2, pp. 376–8 in K. Fukui *et al.* (eds.) *Ethiopia in Broader Perspective*, vol. 1. Kyoto: Shukado Book Sellers.

Zangato, E. 1999. *Sociétés préhistoriques et mégalithes dans le nord-ouest de la République Centrafricaine*. Oxford: British Archaeological Reports.

Zohary, D. 1969. The progenitors of wheat and barley in relation to domestication and agricultural dispersal in the Old World, pp. 47–66 in P. J. Ucko and G. W. Dimbleby (eds.) *The Domestication and Exploitation of Plants and Animals*. London: Duckworth.

# Index

Note: Locators for illustrations appear in italics.